A Kayaker's Guide to
New York's Capital Region

Albany • Schenectady • Troy

Exploring the Hudson & Mohawk Rivers
From Catskill & Hudson to Mechanicville
Cohoes to Amsterdam

Russell Dunn

BLACK · DOME

www.blackdomepress.com

Published by

Black Dome Press Corp.
1011 Route 296, Hensonville, New York 12439
www.blackdomepress.com
Tel: (518) 734–6357

First Edition Paperback 2010
Copyright © 2010 by C. Russell Dunn

Library of Congress Cataloging-in-Publication Data
Dunn, Russell.
A kayaker's guide to New York's capital region: Albany, Schenectady, Troy; exploring the Hudson & Mohawk Rivers from Catskill & Hudson to Mechanicville, Cohoes to Amsterdam / Russell Dunn. — 1st pbk. ed.
    p. cm.
Includes bibliographical references and index.
ISBN-13: 978-1-883789-67-1 (trade pbk.)
ISBN-10: 1-883789-67-2
1. Kayaking—Hudson River (N.Y. and N.J.)—Guidebooks. 2. Kayaking—New York (State)—Mohawk River—Guidebooks. 3. Kayak touring—Hudson River (N.Y. and N.J.)—Guidebooks. 4. Kayak touring—New York (State)—Mohawk River—Guidebooks. 5. Hudson River (N.Y. and N.J.)—Guidebooks. 6. Mohawk River (N.Y.)—Guidebooks. I. Title.
GV776.N72H93 2010
797.122'4097473—dc22
                            2010020477

CAUTION: Outdoor recreational activities are by their very nature potentially hazardous and contain risk. See "Caution" beginning on page xxii.

Front cover: Photograph by Elizabeth Bovill, courtesy of the Albany County Convention and Vistors Bureau. "Bald Eagle in Flight" photograph by Larry Federman.

Back cover: Photograph by Dietrich Gehring, www.dietrichgehring.com.

Maps created with Delorme Topo USA 8 National, copyright 2008 Delorme (www.delorme.com)

Design: Toelke Associates, www.toelkeassociates.com

Printed in the USA

                            10 9 8 7 6 5 4 3 2 1

Dedication

To Joe Zoske, who has been as constant and true a friend
as the North Star

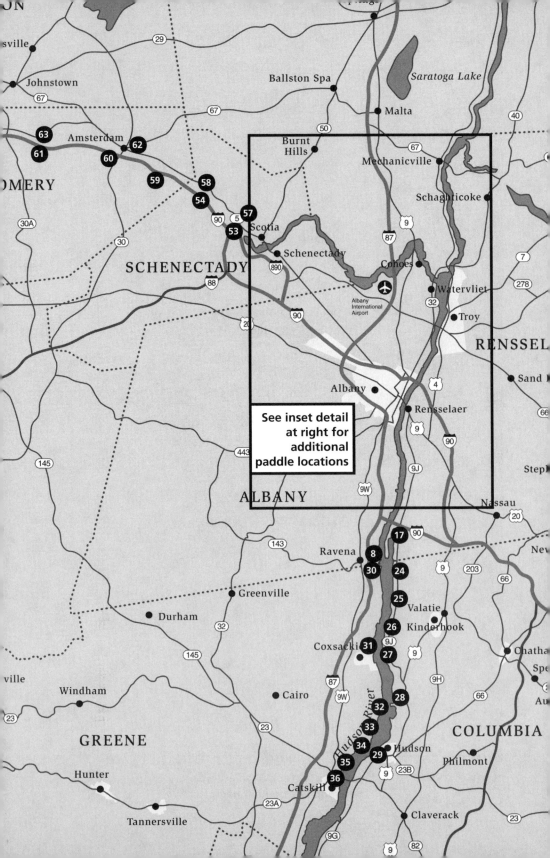

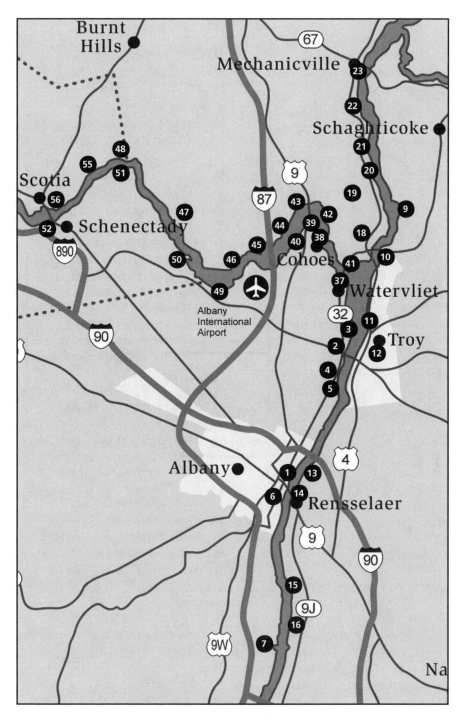

Inset from regional map at left.
See map key on next page.

MAP KEY

1. Corning Preserve (Albany)
2. Hudson Shores Park (Watervliet)
3. Green Island (Green Island)
4. The Little River (Watervliet)
5. Schuyler Flats (Watervliet)
6. Island Creek Park (Albany)
7. NYS Bethlehem Fishing Access Launch (Cedar Hill)
8. Coeymans Landing (Coeymans)
9. Lansing's Ferry (Pleasantdale)
10. Lansingburgh Boat Launch (Lansingburgh)
11. Ingalls Avenue Launch (North Troy)
12. Madison Street Launch (South Troy)
13. Rensselaer Boat Launch (Rensselaer)
14. Riverfront Park (Rensselaer)
15. Papscanee Island Nature Preserve (Stony Point)
16. Papscanee Creek (Stony Point)
17. Schodack Island (Castleton-on-Hudson)
18. Champlain Canal: Paddle #1 (South Waterford)
19. Champlain Canal: Paddle #2 (North Waterford)
20. Champlain Canal Lock C-1 (Waterford)
21. Halfmoon Hudson Riverfront Park (Halfmoon)
22. Champlain Canal Lock C-2 (Mechanicville)
23. Terminal Street Launch (Mechanicville)
24. Mill Creek: Lewis A. Swyer Preserve (Stuyvesant)
25. Stuyvesant Landing (Stuyvesant)
26. Nutten Hook Reserve (Nutten Hook)
27. Ferry Road Access (Nutten Hook)
28. Stockport Station (Columbiaville)
29. Hudson Waterfront Park (Hudson)
30. Cornell Park (New Baltimore)
31. Coxsackie Riverside Park (Coxsackie)
32. Four Mile Point Preserve (Coxsackie)
33. Athens State Boat Launch (Athens)
34. Athens Kayak Launch (Athens)
35. Cohotate Preserve (Athens/Catskill)
36. Dutchman's Landing (Catskill)
37. Cohoes Falls (Cohoes)
38. Crescent Plant (Crescent Station)
39. Freddie's Park (Crescent)
40. Colonie Mohawk River Park (Dunsbach Ferry)
41. Peebles Island (Waterford/Cohoes)
42. Paradise Island (Waterford)
43. Halfmoon Crescent Park (Crescent)
44. Vandenburgh-Dunsbach Ferry (Halfmoon Beach)
45. Wager's Pond (Vischer Ferry)
46. Vischer Ferry Nature & Historic Preserve (Vischer Ferry)
47. Mohawk Landing (Grooms Corner)
48. Alplaus Creek (Alplaus)
49. Railroad Station Park (Niskayuna)
50. Lock E-7 Boat Launch (Niskayuna)
51. Kiwanis Aqueduct Park Cartop Launch (Rexford)
52. Gateway Landing–Rotary Park (Schenectady)
53. Lock E-8 (Rotterdam)
54. Rotterdam Kiwanis Park (Rotterdam)
55. Freemans Bridge Boat Launch (Scotia)
56. Scotia Landing (Scotia)
57. Maalwyck Park (Scotia/Glenville)
58. Lock E-9 State Canal Park (Rotterdam Junction)
59. Lock E-10 (Pattersonville)
60. Port Jackson Boat Launch (South Amsterdam)
61. Schoharie Crossing (Fort Hunter)
62. Quist Road Boat Launch (Amsterdam)
63. Lock E-12 Dam (Tribes Hill)

Contents

Foreword

Daily, hundreds of thousands of travelers—long distance, local commuters, truck drivers and rail passengers—whiz through the great American crossroads between Buffalo and Boston, Montreal and Manhattan called New York's Capital Region.

Here is one of the oldest and busiest intersections in the country.

Since the rail lines and highways often hug the shores, commuters and train travelers especially have a chance to visually drink in the glory of the Hudson River, both the true river above the Federal Dam in Troy and the estuary from the dam to New York City. Understandably, many of these travelers over time feel they've come to know the river intimately by passing by so close, so often. They see its changing moods, the effects of tides and seasons along familiar stretches. It is a virtual intimacy, to be sure, since most high-speed travelers don't have occasion to actually touch or smell the river, or feel its pulsing strength.

Long before there was a New York State Thruway or Adirondack Northway, or even before Commodore Vanderbilt laid down along the eastern shore of the Hudson what were among the first rail tracks on the continent, the Hudson and the Mohawk rivers themselves were the highways that drew travelers and commerce. For hundreds of years after European settlers first trickled in, these were among the hardest worked and most important rivers in the country. That was true both on the water—with heavy boat traffic through the ages of sail and steam—and by dint of the continually evolving industries along the shores. New York's ascendency as the Empire State happened because the Hudson estuary was linked to the Erie and Champlain canals, opening up the west. Those canals in their various iterations, in the Capital Region at least, relied on the beds of the upper Hudson and Mohawk rivers for their existences. The shorelines close to the center of all that intersecting traffic have seen layer after layer of human activity over four centuries, sometimes leaving behind great, mysterious artifacts, sometimes leaving not a trace.

Russell Dunn has created a paddling guidebook like no other, a brilliant idea appropriately executed. And it is a paddling guide, no matter what the title says. Since the author emphasizes easily doable treks in half a day on generally placid waters, a tandem or even a solo canoe is as useful a craft as a kayak—and far easier to portage, I might add.

One of the many terrific features this guidebook offers is in doing all of the hard work in identifying access points for each one of these paddles, so portaging is rare. Most accesses are free and provide a short drop into the water. That's an advantage of having mazes of public roads and streets crisscrossing long-populated Capital Region shorelines, especially along the Mohawk and upper Hudson. Ironically, access to the Hudson estuary has been harder to come by in the past because of century-and-a-half-old railroad tracks between roads and the river acting as a barrier.

But through the diligence of the Department of Environmental Conservation and the development of the Hudson River Valley Greenway's water trail, there are now ninety launch sites between New York City and Waterford, and more coming all the time.

This guidebook comes to us at a terrific time, when there is undeniably a growing interest in reconnecting with the Hudson and Mohawk in actual, not virtual, ways. Kayaking is soaring in popularity, on the big Hudson particularly. Fran Dunwell, who clings as I do to a reverence for canoes and who manages the DEC's Hudson Estuary Program, has seen a dramatic increase in the number of kayaks and a shrinking number of canoes on the bigger waters of the Hudson in recent years.

As Dunn himself notes, with few exceptions the paddles in this guidebook are not on open or big water, and they are not marathons. For those inclined toward marathons, the Hudson River Greenway Water Trail annually for the last nine years sponsors an event in August from farther and farther up the upper Hudson down to the Battery in Manhattan. In 2009, thirty-seven seasoned kayakers putting in at Fort Edward took fifteen days to paddle 200 miles, camping along the water trail.

But as paddling enthusiast Scott Keller, who is trails and projects director for the Greenway and runs this paddling event points out, the drawback of a marathon is that rarely is there time or opportunity to meander and contemplate. Meandering into nooks and crannies, up big creeks and little creeks, along islands, into backwaters and against ruins and waterfalls, and contemplation of the layered past is exactly what this guidebook is about.

The most fun I had in a forty-three-year career as a newspaperman in the Capital Region was twice running the Hudson from its origins below Mt. Marcy, just to see what we could see. The first time, in 1998, a team of us went all the way down to Manhattan. In 2009, we came down as far as Albany. We traveled by raft, by powerboat and sailboat, and for much of the upper river, by canoe. My one regret as we swiftly descended with purpose and a deadline was not being able to go back to an intriguing rivulet, or rock or shoreline formation. Or pausing long enough to frame what historic nineteenth-century log drives must have been like at a particular spot.

This guide is a delicious history book, offering in nibbles an invitation to all the senses. It is one thing to be told such and such an icehouse was there, or a massive brickyard over here, and quite another to paddle in surprising solitude (on most occasions) right up to the remnants of both and pick up old bricks, smell the algal dank of a created backwater, or see the spindly ribs of a once-formidable dock sticking out from shore.

This guidebook assumes an intermediate level of competence as a paddler, which seems about right, although a beginner should never feel thwarted by a lack of experience. Even the mighty Hudson can be gentle on a first-timer, as long as your paddling partner more than makes up for your shortcomings and is patient, and you plan your adventures accordingly. Safety is everything on the water. Never paddle alone, unless you're with a group. I know that sounds contradictory, but you know what I mean. Always wear a personal flotation device.

Certainly what the Amtrak traveler gazing out at great blue herons by the score or watching a Turecamo tug pushing a giant barge can never feel is fear of the river. But you may, so be prepared for it. When the tide works against a rising wind and you find yourself in an unprotected place, when the chop laps higher and higher against the gunnels, it's a fool who doesn't feel growing apprehension. Any body of water can turn scary; the Hudson, as an arm of the sea, deserves special respect. Pay attention. When in doubt, get thee to shore, or better yet, hug it until you feel comfortable and confident enough to drift toward the channel.

Finally, Russell Dunn makes a persuasive case for why you should be a fair-weather paddler, and so does Scott Keller. Don't go out on the water until May, late May even, and get off by September. Always dress for the water, not the air temperature. Paddling is seductive and very satisfying, and I know I want to get on the water as early after ice out as I can. But sooner or later, if you haven't already, you *will* take a dunking. How you will remember that experience, whether laughing it off or scarred for life, is to a great degree in your hands.

And now, with all these shoulds and oughts in mind, get out there and begin to discover or rediscover what you thought you already knew firsthand. If your experience is anything like mine, you will be flat-out amazed how much there is to learn from Russell Dunn's gentle teaching.

Fred LeBrun
Times Union columnist
Albany, New York
May 2010

Acknowledgments

No book is a solo journey.

I am indebted to and specially honored by the gracious and stimulating foreword written by Fred LeBrun, *Times Union* columnist, Hudson River paddler, and all-around polymath.

I especially want to thank my wife, Barbara Delaney, who has accompanied me on many of the paddles described and who is my computer guru.

I send sincere thanks to Elizabeth Bovill and the Albany County Convention & Visitors Bureau for contributing the photograph for the cover of this book. Additional thanks are owed to Larry Federman for allowing us to use on the front cover of this book his photograph of a bald eagle in flight, and to Dietrich Gehring (dietrichgehring.com), one of our region's most talented professional photographers, for graciously permitting us to use his photograph on the back cover.

I am particularly fortunate to work with a publisher and editor whose diligence has turned Black Dome Press into the powerhouse publishing company that it is today. They are people whom I try to emulate, and their diligence has spurred me on to be a much better writer and more detail-oriented person. I am ceaselessly amazed at how Steve Hoare, my editor, can fine-tune a sentence or paragraph, often taking a lump of coal and turning it into a diamond, or sleuth out a mistake that would otherwise remain embedded to haunt me later. Debbie Allen, my publisher, is the ultimate networker who not only turns out great books, but knows all the right people to make things happen once the book is published. Her imprint is on every page of this book.

Ron Toelke and Barbara Kempler-Toelke of Toelke Associates brought the book to life with their graphic design and typesetting skills. They are the people who gave the book its unique look, which may have been what first intrigued you enough to pick it up.

What would I do without Bob Drew, postcard collector extraordinaire, who generously makes his collection of over 200,000 postcards available to me when my own comparatively miniscule collection of antique postcards proves woefully inadequate?

If errors are found in any of the chapters in this book, the fault lies entirely with the author and not with the reviewers who so generously gave of their time and expertise. I am extremely grateful to: Shari Aber, author of *A Kayaker's Guide to the Hudson River Valley*, for reviewing the entire manuscript and for her kind words for the back cover; Ann Aronson, photographer (Ann Aronson Photography) and avid kayaker, for reviewing the chapters on Gateway Landing–Rotary Park and Scotia Landing, and Katherine Chansky, Schenectady County Librarian, for helping us connect; Warren Broderick, Senior Archives and Records Management Specialist at New York State Archives, for reviewing major sections of the book, particularly those pertaining to Rensselaer County;

Clesson Bush for reviewing the chapters on Coxsackie Riverside Park, Cornell Park, and Coeymans Landing, and for providing valuable information about area history; Catherine Frank, coauthor of *A Kayaker's Guide to Lake Champlain*, for reviewing the entire manuscript and providing valuable commentary, and for her and coauthor Margaret Holden's supportive comments for the back cover; Scott Keller, Trails and Special Projects Director, Hudson River Valley Greenway, for reviewing the entire section on the Hudson River and making many valuable comments and suggestions, and for his generous comments for the back cover; Sharon Leighton, Director of Community Relations, New York State Canal Corporation, for reviewing canal-related access sites; Alan Mapes, instructor and guide for Atlantic Kayak Tours at Norrie Point Paddlesport Center and retired Chief of Bureau of Environmental Education (NYS DEC), for reviewing the chapters on Four Mile Point Preserve and Coxsackie Riverside Park, and for ongoing consultations; Susan McCuen and John Cannon for reviewing chapters on Coxsackie Riverside Park, Cornell Park, and Coeymans Landing; Natalie Mortensen for an excellent job as copyeditor; Jim Murphy for his comments on Scotia Landing and Reese Creek; Amelia O'Shea, author of *Canals of Albany County* and *The Erie Canal through Saratoga County*, for reviewing the introductory chapters to the Champlain Canal and the Erie Canal; proofreader Lauren Pacifico for exceptional work; Mark Peckham, National Register of Historic Places Coordinator, for providing significant practical and historical information on the chapters pertaining to Coxsackie Riverside Park, Cornell Park, and Coeymans Landing; Chuck Porter, retired Hudson Valley Community College geology professor, for reviewing major sections of the book; Nelson Ronsvalle, Grant Coordinator, Town of Halfmoon, for reviewing the chapter on the newly created Halfmoon Hudson Riverfront Park and for consultations on Halfmoon Crescent Park and Vandenburgh-Dunsbach Ferry; John Scherer, Clifton Park historian and author of three history books on Clifton Park, for reviewing the chapters on Rexford, Wager's Pond, Vischer Ferry Nature & Historic Preserve, and Alplaus Creek; Heidi Carl-Seebode, Administrative Assistant at the County Office Building, Cairo, for reviewing the chapter on the Cohotate Preserve; Tricia Shaw, Education Coordinator, Schoharie Crossing State Historic Site, for reviewing the chapter on Schoharie Crossing; Ned Sullivan, president of Scenic Hudson, for reviewing the introductory chapter to the Hudson River; Rob Taylor, Park Manager with the New York State Office of Parks, Recreation and Historic Preservation, for reviewing the chapters on Schodack Island, Stockport Station, Nutten Hook Reserve, Stuyvesant Landing, Athens State Boat Launch, Four Mile Point Preserve, and Coxsackie Riverside Park; Richard Tuers, author of *Lighthouses of the Hudson River*, for reviewing material on the Stuyvesant, Hudson-Athens, Four Mile Point, and Rattlesnake Island lighthouses; Brad L. Utter, Director of the Waterford Historical Museum & Cultural Center, for reviewing the chapters Champlain Canal Paddle #1 & #2.

    Special thanks are due: Rich Macha, owner-operator of Adirondack
Paddle'n'Pole; Rita D. Shaheen, ASLA, Director of Parks, Scenic Hudson; Mike
Oliviere, Hudson River Lighthouse Historian; Alan Lasker; Michael Kalin and
Julie Elson; Ed Tremblay, Director, Community & Economic Development,
City of Cohoes; Andrew Kreshik, Assistant Planner, City of Troy; Prudence
Pechenik, Secretary to the Mayor of Troy, Bill Quick (www.KayakGuy.com);
and the NYS Library in Albany.
    A further debt of gratitude is owed to Jeff Anzevino, Vincent Bilotta, Jim
Clayton, Michael Fischer, James Gold, Ed Lamon III, Mike Prescott, and Jeanne
Williams.

Preface

From the time when the first nomadic hunter-gatherers set foot in the New World until two centuries ago, streams and waterways were the main transportation routes in what is now eastern New York State, threading through a forested wilderness that was otherwise often impenetrable. Native Americans initially exploited these interconnecting waterways by hollowing out logs to fashion primitive dugout canoes; later, beginning in the northern boreal forests, they used birch bark to construct lighter-weight canoes. Despite being rudimentary, these forerunners to today's high-tech canoes and kayaks were sleek and elegant. Powered by a war party or crew of determined hunters pursuing game, they could glide through the water with incredible speed and economy of motion.

Native Americans found the region's streams to be of varying suitability for their purposes. They were not particularly keen on running rapids or negotiating small cascades, for the presence of these obstacles meant that water travel could only be in one direction—downstream. They were most drawn to waters that were deep and relatively slow-moving, for it was on these rivers and streams that two-way travel was possible.

The Hudson River is the largest two-way river in New York State and can be readily paddled or sailed upriver from the Atlantic Ocean to Albany and back. In 1609, not only did Henry Hudson sail up the river to near Albany, but a smaller craft (a gig) launched from Hudson's ship the *Half Moon* managed to make it even farther upriver, possibly to or slightly beyond Waterford. Farther north, unknown to Hudson's crew at the time, were a series of waterfalls that presented serious obstacles to navigation, beginning with Baker's Falls at Hudson Falls, and continuing with Glens Falls at Glens Falls, Palmer Falls and Curtis Falls at Corinth, and Rockwell Falls at Hadley-Lake Luzerne. Any one of these falls was sufficient to block further advancement by boat, which means that north of Troy the Hudson River is and has always been a one-way river.

Sections of the Mohawk River also offered two-way navigation to early paddlers. Once seventy-foot-high Cohoes Falls had been bypassed via a difficult portage during the seventeenth, eighteenth, and nineteenth centuries, paddlers encountered a river of varying depth, often no deeper than up to a man's thigh, but free of major cascades and waterfalls until Little Falls. Although shallow in many places, the Mohawk River was mostly canoeable. The Mohawk River that we see today, of course, is radically different from the one earlier traversed by Native Americans and European settlers. Its waters have been artificially deepened through dredging and by the establishment of a series of locks and dams.

The wide valleys cut by these two enormous rivers were natural corridors for providing uninterrupted travel from the Atlantic Ocean to Lake Champlain and from the Capital Region to Lake Erie. To accomplish this, engineers needed to build canals paralleling the Mohawk River and the upper Hudson River and to establish an occasional aqueduct so that boats could cross over to the opposite side of the river when an impasse was encountered.

This was accomplished on the Hudson River in 1823, when the Champlain Canal was opened linking Albany with Lake Champlain and areas farther north, and in 1825 on the Mohawk River, when the Erie Canal was inaugurated linking Albany with northwestern New York State at Buffalo. As a result, we not only have the Hudson and Mohawk rivers as waterways today, but significant portions of the Erie and Champlain canals that have survived into the twenty-first century. Sections of these canals are explored in the chapters on the Champlain Canal paddles at Waterford and in the chapters on Wager's Pond, Schoharie Crossing, and the Vischer Ferry Nature & Historic Preserve.

But there is yet more to this region's wealth of waterways. The Hudson and Mohawk rivers have dozens of significant tributaries. Some are of respectable and navigable size; others along the tidal Hudson River are periodically deepened and made temporarily canoeable by tidal swells. Of these, a number can be paddled on for short distances and therefore have been included in the book.

The Albany region also contains numerous lakes and ponds that came into existence at the end of the last ice age. Other, artificial lakes and ponds were created when streams were dammed by industrialists. These bodies of water will be presented in a later book in this series.

The Albany region is surrounded by mountains: to the north are the Adirondacks (New York State's highest peaks); to the south are the Catskills (New York State's second-highest peaks); to the east can be found the Rensselaer Plateau and, farther east yet, the Taconics; to the southwest are the Helderbergs; and to the west are many hills that rise up on each side of the Mohawk River, with the northern hills constituting the foothills of the southern Adirondacks. These mountain ranges collect snow during the winter and then release it as snowmelt during the warming days of spring and early summer. These naturally timed discharges of water keep the region's waterways animated until summer's desiccation sets in.

Typically the paddles described in this book are located along sections of the Hudson River and Mohawk River where the waters are fast-moving in the early spring, but moderate-to-slow-moving in the summer, allowing kayakers/canoeists to choose the conditions that best match their abilities. Paddles across lakes and ponds or along their perimeters, where the water is essentially motionless, will be presented in a subsequent book in this series.

When heading out to explore a number of the Hudson's tributaries, such as Mill Creek, the Vloman Kill, or Papscanee Creek, it is important to first consult local tide tables. Failure to do so could result in reaching your destination at low tide and finding the tributary too shallow to paddle or, worse yet, setting out on your trip and then discovering that the water is running out of the creek around you as though down the drain of a bathtub. Ending up grounded on a mudflat is not a satisfying way to bring your adventure to a conclusion. (See tide-related Web sites in "Caution.")

To be sure, it is important to consult tide tables any time you are out on the Hudson River. Paddling downstream against a flood tide or upstream against an ebb tide can further add to your trials and tribulations. Far better to paddle downstream with an ebb tide and back upstream with a flood tide, if such a trip can be arranged conveniently.

Irrespective of tides, other factors can cause variable water levels. Several Hudson River tributaries draw upon limited watersheds and therefore may contain an insufficient volume of water for paddling during the summer months. To explore these streams it is best to venture out in the late spring or following particularly heavy rainfall when the stream is engorged. As summer arrives, billions of trees are literally sucking up trillions of gallons of water each day for wood production, leaving little left to run off into streams.

One should also be prepared to make unexpected portages when paddling on streams. A creek can be clear of blowdown and debris one year, only to become blocked the next year by a fallen tree or beaver dam. Always be ready for the unexpected and be willing to turn around and go back if the way ahead is too difficult.

When traveling on streams noted for good fishing, one should be considerate of other users of the water and only paddle between the hours of 9:30 AM to 5:30 PM, when anglers are least likely to be out fishing.

Many of the paddles along the Hudson River and Mohawk River are in areas where the region's historical heritage abounds. For this reason most of the chapters contain fairly expansive sections on history—material that can further enrich your experience while on the water.

No two paddles in this book are alike; they were selected for their variety. Some lead to natural islands, others to artificial islands. Some lead to waterfalls, others to dams and canal locks. Some take you to gorges and chasms, others past caves and grottos. Some pass through areas of fascinating history, others through areas of surpassing beauty. Some cruise along natural waterways, others through artificial channels. The adventure begins when you push out onto the water.

As an explorer's guide to kayaking the Capital Region, this book is intended to help paddlers find numerous access points along the Hudson River and Mohawk River, all within the context of the multilayered history of the region. This is not a guidebook for hard-core kayakers whose concept of an adventure is to paddle twenty miles through formidable terrain, traverse across a series of lakes interspersed by mile-long portages, or shoot down Class IV and V waters.

Paddles involving long portages are excluded. The goal of this book is to get the reader out onto the water as quickly as possible, not to lead the reader across endless terrain. The treks described are generally two to ten miles in length (round-trip)—the right length for a half-day outing. Once you are out on the Hudson or Mohawk rivers, many miles of river stretch in both directions offering outings of virtually any duration.

Locks can be readily negotiated by waiting for a boat to arrive and then accompanying it through the lock, holding onto ropes along the sidewalls as the water level rises or falls. It's a good idea to notify the lockkeeper in advance if you plan to do this. This can be done by tuning in to channel 13 on a marine radio or using your cell phone to call the following numbers:

Lock C-1 (518) 237-8566   Lock E-9 (518) 887-2401
Lock C-2 (518) 664-4961   Lock E-10 (518) 887-5450
Lock C-3 (518) 664-5171   Lock E-11 (518) 843-2120
Lock E-7 (518) 374-7912   Lock E-12 (518) 829-7331
Lock E-8 (518) 346-3382

Sometimes a kayak or canoe can go through the lock solo if no other boats are around.

Despite the Capital Region being heavily populated, with major cities, large villages, and sprawling suburbs crisscrossed by highways, once you set out on a stream or lake and begin to paddle, the sights and sounds of civilization begin to melt into the background and sometimes vanish completely. This is the beauty of exploring the Capital Region by water.

A Guide to the Paddles

Launch Sites: Most of the launch sites demand little if any effort to reach and, once there, only the slightest nudge to set a watercraft afloat. In the several instances where these generalities don't apply, a canoe/kayak carrier can prove to be very helpful. At a few locations, access may prove challenging because of a steep riverbank or large rocks along the shoreline.

In most instances, the launch site may be accessed from sunrise to sunset. Exceptions are noted. Most of the access sites are free. Admission is charged at New York State boat launch sites and parks (but usually only on a seasonal basis) and at private marinas. Fees are noted where applicable.

Delorme: Delorme's New York State Atlas & Gazetteer, fifth edition, is an invaluable tool for plotting out driving routes, particularly if you are going from one launch site to the next. The coordinates listed in each chapter start with the page number, followed by the row, and end with the column. Thus, "p. 10, C6" tells you to turn to "page 10," look across row "C" (horizontal axis), and then down column "6" (vertical axis) to find the intersection of these coordinates.

GPS Coordinates: The coordinates given are reasonably accurate, but some were generated by computer software rather than an on-site read. There may be minor discrepancies.

Destinations: This section enumerates the areas you will be paddling.

Mileage: Mileages are given either as "one-way," "round-trip," or "around" (as when circumnavigating an island). Because the Hudson River is tidal, the amount of exposed land fluctuates with the tides. This can affect mileage.

Comments: Different waters contain different hazards, and these are addressed in the "Comments" section of each paddle, in addition to other pertinent information that may apply. This supports but in no way supplants the "Caution" section near the beginning of this book and the Hudson River and Mohawk River cautions that introduce Part I and Part II, with which readers are strongly advised to thoroughly acquaint themselves before setting out.

Directions: Knowing where to go and how to get there is the most crucial element of any guidebook. If you can't get to the water, then the value of the rest of the book becomes academic. For this reason every effort has been made to ensure that the directions are clear and free of ambiguity.

The Paddles: The "bare bones" of the paddle are described here, the focus being on mileage and points of interest. Some paddles can be extended by using the New York State Barge Canal system of locks to go from one section of the river to the next.

The Hike: Several chapters contain a short, supplemental hike or walk.

History: A significant part of the text is devoted to history. The paddles typically travel along a riverbank where important physical structures—factories, hotels, houses, and mills—once stood, or where momentous historical events took place. Enjoy the region's incredibly rich history and incorporate it into your adventure while paddling.

CAUTION

Outdoor recreational activities are by their very nature potentially hazardous and contain risk. All participants in such activities must assume responsibility for their own actions and safety. No book can be a substitute for good judgment. The outdoors is forever changing. The author and the publisher cannot be held responsible for inaccuracies, errors, or omissions, or for any changes in the details of this publication, or for the consequences of any reliance on the information contained herein, or for the safety of people in the outdoors.

This book is intended for experienced paddlers who are comfortable being on the water, are well-versed in self-rescue procedures, and can handle sudden changes in weather, strong tides and currents, and heavy boat traffic.

Wind, current, and waves on the Hudson and Mohawk rivers can change abruptly, often with little warning and in spite of the weather forecast. Always check the forecast and weather before setting out. Do not leave shore if storms and/or high winds are predicted or if the weather forecast is at all questionable.

The Hudson River is tidal as far north as the Federal Dam in Troy, and these tides exert a strong pull on watercraft. Thoroughly familiarize yourself with tides and tide tables before putting in on the Hudson.

The Hudson and Mohawk rivers experience heavy boat traffic. Operators of small watercraft like kayaks and canoes must be ever-vigilant on these waters. Don't assume boats can see you. Wear bright colors. Know where the boat channels are and avoid those waters. If you must cross a boat channel, cross in a group and keep the group together. If you see a boat in the distance, let it pass before you set out. Some large boats move surprisingly fast, and distance can be hard to judge.

Users of this guidebook should acquaint themselves with all of the advice and cautions that follow.

Before You Take the Plunge

Take a water safety course and learn self-rescue techniques. (See appendices A and C on pages 257 and 259.) Study navigational charts for the section of the river you intend to paddle, familiarizing yourself with shipping lanes and underwater hazards.

Hudson River Tides: The Hudson River is tidal from the Atlantic Ocean to the Federal Dam at Troy, which means that the river changes direction several times a day. It is said that for every eight miles a floating object travels downstream, the backwash typically returns it upstream by as much as seven and a half miles.

For this reason, tides can create currents that are different from the normal river currents to which you may be accustomed. The shoreline can also change dramatically with the ebb and flow of the river, exposing rocks and shoals that were previously submerged, or creating claustrophobic channels on its tributaries. If you are planning to go downriver and to return later on the same route, make sure to first check that you can paddle against the current before embarking on your trip. It would be unfortunate to complete half your trip only to discover that the river is too strong for you to make your way back upstream without being overpowered. You may want to abort your trip or place a second car farther downstream at a lower access site, thereby turning the paddle into a manageable one-way trip.

High and low tides must be reckoned with every twelve hours as the moon and, to a lesser extent, the sun pull on the Earth, causing it to bulge slightly on opposite sides as the planet rotates. The average tide varies from 3.7 to 4.6 feet.[1] But the ebb and flow of tides are subject to lunar variations. With the arrival of a full or new moon, when the sun and moon are in alignment, **spring tides** are produced. These are much stronger than regular tides and can change the height of the river by over six feet.[2] When the moon and sun are at right angles to each other, they partially cancel out each other's gravitational pull and a **neap** (or weak) **tide** is produced, with water levels lower than normal.[3]

A **peak tide** occurs when three inches or more of rain fall during a spring tide. This can produce unusually high water levels and the potential for rampant flooding in low-lying areas. There is also a rare phenomenon called a **blowout tide**, which happens when a combination of factors such as low tide, high winds, and drought cause the river level to plummet dramatically, temporarily exposing large areas of the riverbed near shallows, marshes, and tributaries.[4]

It takes one and one-half hours for the full volume of the Hudson River to reverse itself once the tide has changed. This is the result of the river being reluctant to give up its momentum—a reluctance that increases the closer one gets to the middle of the river.[5]

The northbound tidal current is called the **flood**, and the southbound current the **ebb**. In between is the **slack**, where the water has minimal velocity, if any. Obviously, if you are consulting tide tables, the optimal paddle is to head north during flood or slack periods, and south during the ebb or slack, so as to maximize the benefit of tidal currents.

It is important to recognize, however, that it is impossible to achieve 100 percent accuracy when making tidal predictions. In addition to the relative positions of the moon and sun, a multitude of other factors contribute to tidal variations—the river's starting height on any given day, barometric pressure, the arrival or departure of stormy weather, wind speed, and so on.

For that matter, tides do not occur simultaneously along the Hudson River. The tides are derivative, meaning that they occur because of the Hudson River's intimate connection with the Atlantic Ocean. It typically takes 4.5 hours for the incoming tide to reach Poughkeepsie from New York City, 6.7 hours to reach Catskill, and 9 hours to arrive at Albany. One must always be ready to extrapolate when venturing out onto a section of the Hudson where tide times aren't listed.

With these factors in mind, the following sources can be consulted:

- tidesandcurrents.noaa.gov
- xtide.ldeo.columbia.edu/hudson/tides/predictions.html
- hudsonriver.com/tides.htm
- hrfanj.org/river_conditions.htm (Use the Hudson River tide calculator on this Web site for the section of the river in which you are interested.)
- castletonboatclub.com/ (Go to "Resource" and open up "Tides at CBC.")
- mobilegeographics.com:81/locations/1087.html
- *Times Union*, meteorology section, A2

Choosing the Right Craft for River Paddling: There is a dizzying array of types of canoes and kayaks to choose from. A craft that is perfect for white-water kayaking may not be suited for paddling on a quiet pond or riding in the wake of a supertanker on a tidal river. Your local canoe/kayak dealer can help you select a craft that will best meet your particular needs. See Appendix C for dealers in the greater Capital Region.

Wind and Waves: Turn back and return on another day if the current looks too strong or the water too choppy. This applies especially following episodes of prolonged, intensive rainfall, or in the early spring, when the rivers' currents, fed by winter's snowmelt, are unusually strong. Fast-moving currents increase the potential for trouble. Strainers (downed trees with branches raking the water) can become more than obstacles if the current pushes you against one. Your canoe or kayak could capsize, exposing you to the possibility of getting caught underwater and pinned. Remember that water in motion can exert tremendous force—thousands of pounds of pressure per square inch—that can easily snap a canoe or kayak in half. Violently moving waters can even roll large boulders along a riverbed.

Always be mindful of wind when you are out on the water. Long, finger-like lakes and wide rivers unbroken by islands can produce significant waves, even on days with mild to moderate winds. Wind speed over water can be as much as 50 percent greater than it is over land.[6]

The Hudson River plays by its own set of rules. Because of its north-south orientation, the valley walls catch a fair amount of breeze and funnel it down to the river. This can quickly set up choppy waters and strong headwinds. Contrary to expectations, these strong winds often come up from the south, at times making a downriver paddle more demanding than an upstream one.

Hypothermia: Most paddlers should restrict their excursions to the summer season. True, there is more boat traffic in the summer, but should you capsize—and sooner or later you will—summer water is infinitely more comfortable than spring or fall water, as the following illustrates:

Mean Monthly Water Temperature of the Hudson River

January—34°F	February—34°F	March—37°F
April—46°F	May—59°F	June—70°F
July—75°F	August—76°F	September—72°F
October—61°F	November—48°F	December—37°F

If you unexpectedly become immersed and feel chilled, abort the rest of your planned adventure and return to your car at once. Hypothermia (a lowering of one's core body temperature) can kill, and the water and air temperatures don't have to be below 32 degrees Fahrenheit for hypothermia to occur. Immersion in water drains heat from the body 30 times faster than air.[7] As a general rule of thumb, paddlers should never head out onto the water without a wetsuit if the combined air and water temperature totals less than 100 degrees Fahrenheit. For kayakers, a spray skirt would be desirable under these conditions. Some paddlers, more zealous than most, even wear drysuits for going out when the water is numbingly cold. For more information regarding hypothermia, visit www.hypothermia.org.

Water Temperature (°F)	Exhaustion or Unconsciousness	Expected time of survival
32.5	Under 15 min.	Under 15–45 min.
32.5–40	15–30 min.	30–90 min.
40–50	30–60 min.	1–3 hrs.
50–60	1–2 hrs.	1–6 hrs.
60–70	2–7 hrs.	2–40 hrs.
70–80	2–12 hrs.	3 hrs–indefinite
Lake Champlain Paddlers' Trail, 2008 Guidebook & Stewardship Manual, 10th edition (Lake Champlain Committee), p.16.		

Other Boats: Scan the river up and down before setting out to cross it. Don't assume that boats can see you. Wear bright colors. You will not be the winner if you and a fast-moving boat cross paths. Know where the boat channels are and avoid those waters. When it is necessary to cross shipping lanes to reach your objective, cross as quickly as possible and continually check for traffic in both directions. Cross in a group and keep the group together. If you see a boat in the distance, let it pass before you set out. Some large boats move surprisingly fast, and distance can be hard to judge.

Watch out for incoming waves that have the potential to flip your watercraft over; turn into heavy waves to meet them head-on. Waves are produced by winds and boats. The size of the wave is affected by the force produced by the wind or boat, the water depth, and the fetch (the uninterrupted distance over water that the wind has blown). The longer the fetch, the greater the power of the wave. Watch out for rebounding waves that come at you for a second time after bouncing off the opposite shore. Remember that boat traffic on both the Hudson and Mohawk increases significantly during the summer season. You can't always rely on boaters to remember to slow down when they pass by a paddler. Don't stay too close to the shore when a huge tanker or cargo barge passes by. The ship's large hull displacement causes water to rush in quickly behind it, pulling water momentarily away from the shoreline and then slamming it back.

Boat Channels (Shipping Lanes): Boats heading upriver on the Hudson and Mohawk keep the red buoys to their right (starboard) and the green buoys to their left (port), and the reverse when going downriver. This information could prove helpful if you need to know on which side of a buoy a speeding boat heading toward you will pass. In most instances, it will be on the side farthest from the shoreline.

Now, Where Did I Put In? When leaving the launch site, take a moment to look back at the shoreline to familiarize yourself with the surroundings as seen from the water. This will save you time and aggravation later, on your return trip, when an otherwise featureless shoreline could make finding your starting point difficult. As an added precaution, locate alternate take-out points above and below your launch site in the event you cannot locate that site or strong currents prevent you from returning to it.

So Obvious We Shouldn't Need To Mention, But ... If you don't know how to swim, now is the time to learn, before you get into a canoe or kayak. Do not consume alcohol before embarking or while on the water. Most water-based accidents involve alcohol, so be advised—alcohol and water, like oil and water, don't mix.

Safety Practices: When exploring the Hudson River and its tributaries (and, to a lesser extent, the Mohawk River), exercise caution while walking along mud-flats that extend out from the shoreline or surround islands. At the first sign of sinking into the ground for more than a few inches, return to your watercraft or to more solid ground along the riverbank without further hesitation. There are places where you can sink in right up to your thighs if you are not careful, leaving you virtually immobilized in the muck.

- Portages may be necessary on some tidally dependent Hudson River tributaries where the stream lacks sufficient current to clear out blowdown and other debris.
- Always tell someone where you are going and when you expect to return—and what to do if you are not back by the designated time.
- The "buddy system" applies to paddling as much as it does to swimming (which, of course, is always a possible though unintended outcome of paddling). Always paddle with a friend.
- If you fall out of your watercraft in moving water, particularly white water, always point your feet downstream to absorb the impact should you collide with an obstacle. If you are in fast-moving water, don't try to stand up in the stream; should your foot become caught on an obstacle below, the force of the current could bend you over like a bow despite your struggles, possibly drowning you in waters that are only chest-deep.
- Keep a safe distance from dams, whether above or below them. Treacherous hydraulics can wreak havoc on even experienced paddlers.
- If caught in a fast-approaching thunderstorm, head promptly to shore. Then, if there is no shelter, sit on your PFD (personal flotation device) to help keep yourself insulated from a possible lightning strike.
- Be on the lookout for deer ticks and be aware of contracting Lyme disease, a threat that has grown more severe with each passing year.
- Always make it a point to visually inspect your body after every paddle to make sure no ticks are attached, especially if you have been near brush or pushed your way through areas of overhanging trees and weeds.

Ready for the river. Photograph 2009.

What To Pack, What To Wear: Always—repeat, ALWAYS—wear a brightly colored personal flotation device (PFD) with reflective tape when you are on the water. Most paddlers wear a Coast Guard-approved Type 3 vest. Insist that anyone with you do the same. This applies even if you are an expert swimmer.

- Take along a whistle or signaling device in case you need assistance or need to alert an oncoming, inattentive motorboat. To maximize your readiness, attach the whistle to your personal flotation device.
- Take a flashlight with you, just in case. If your trip lasts longer than you expected and dusk is falling, you'll be glad to have a spare light—particularly if you need to signal large boats of your presence.
- Pack a waterproof dry bag with all the small items that may be needed during the trip. These include, but are not limited to: sunblock, SPF-rated lip balm, bug repellent, compass, sunglasses, gloves (in case blisters developed on your hands), car keys, money, first-aid kit, cell phone, waterproof matches, extra clothing layers to keep warm, a Swiss army or Leatherman knife, and duct tape. While you're at it, also pack toilet paper, a trowel, and a plastic bag (just in case …). It is also advisable to stash a towrope and bilge pump in the kayak. A waterproof waist pouch is particularly handy for storing items you may want to access quickly, such as a camera or binoculars.
- Be sure to have an extra change of clothing in your car. You may return from the paddle soaking wet. For long paddles, wear gloves to minimize blisters.

Views of the Mohawk River from Mohawk Landing. Photograph 2009.

- Always take along three to four liters of water per person to ward off dehydration and hyperthermia. If the weather is hot, increase it to five to six liters per person. Also pack some food and snacks to maintain proper energy levels. Keep them stored in a waterproof container when you're not munching.
- Take along an extra paddle in case the one you're using becomes lost or broken. A paddle leash will help prevent you from losing your paddle.
- Wear a spray skirt, even if not attached to the kayak, in case the river suddenly gets rough and you need to keep water from entering the kayak.
- Be sure to apply liberal portions of sunscreen and wear sunglasses if you are paddling under a hot, glaring sun. Wear a wide-brimmed hat as well. Remember that water reflects light and heat, intensifying both.
- Always take along personal identification, including emergency contacts and relevant medical information should you become unconscious and require emergency treatment.
- Do not wear bulky clothing. Should you capsize, soaked-through bulky clothing could interfere with swimming.

For more information concerning safety and safety equipment, contact uscgboating.org or nysparks.com/boats.

Your Responsibilities as a Paddler

1. Life is hard enough for birds and other wildlife without additional pressures being caused by thoughtless humans. Keep at a respectable distance, particularly during nesting season.
2. Maintain a considerate distance from shore when paddling past private residences and properties. Never trespass on private property unless there is an emergency.
3. Be considerate of others on the water, whether they be anglers, boaters, swimmers, or fellow paddlers. Steer clear of duck blinds and familiarize yourself with hunting seasons.
4. Cart out whatever you bring along with you on your trip. If you see a stray piece of litter lying about or in the water, pick it up and haul it out. Nature has been good to you; it doesn't hurt to reciprocate.
5. Be sure to properly clean your watercraft and gear each time after entering a different body of water to avoid inadvertently transporting invasive aquatic species.
6. Know the "rules of the road." As "captain" of your kayak or canoe, you are under the same obligations as commercial tugboat and ship captains. Generally, paddlers do not have the right of way in shipping channels.

Paddles for Beginners—Learning Your Craft

Beginners to the sports of kayaking and canoeing are strongly advised to hone their skills on lesser streams before tackling the Hudson or Mohawk rivers. With this in mind, the following paddles are suggested as places to "learn your craft." Each paddle is described in greater detail in the main section of the book.

Schodack Island: Schodack Creek (Castleton-on-Hudson, Rensselaer County)—This is an ideal paddle for beginners. Head downstream on Schodack Creek, which is easily navigable even at low tide and is also fairly removed from the heavy winds and waves that can beset the Hudson River.

Stockport Station (Columbiaville, Columbia County)—Put in at the confluence of Stockport Creek and the Hudson River, and paddle upstream on Stockport Creek for 0.9 mile to the Rt. 9L bridge and then back, a round-trip of 1.8 miles.

Papscanee Creek (Stony Point, Rensselaer County)—Although access to Papscanee Creek is challenging, once you are on the water you can easily paddle downstream to its confluence with the Hudson River and then back. You can also paddle upstream beyond the access point for a short distance farther, tides permitting.

Wager's Pond (Vischer Ferry, Saratoga County)—As long as you head out in the early spring, before invasive plants have carpeted the water's surface, you can easily paddle around the pond or, before reaching the Mohawk River, veer right onto the old Erie Canal and explore its length for a significant distance.

Vischer Ferry Nature & Historic Preserve (Vischer Ferry, Saratoga County)—The old Erie Canal is easily accessed from Clute's Dry Dock. From the put-in, you can travel for a distance either east or west on water without current or waves.

Alplaus Creek (Alplaus, Saratoga County)—This requires paddling on the Mohawk River for a very short distance (0.1 mile) and then turning left onto Alplaus Creek, which you can paddle upstream for over 1.0 mile.

PART I

The Hudson River: From Catskill & Hudson to Mechanicville

Do not venture out onto the Hudson River unless you are at least an intermediate-level paddler, capable of handling a variety of water and weather conditions and able to self-rescue.

Caution

When heading out onto the river, choose a calm day and watch the weather. Tide, current, and winds can be severe at times. The wind tends to be quietest in the early morning and early evening. Always check the forecast and weather before setting out. Do not leave shore if storms and/or high winds are predicted or if the weather forecast is at all questionable. Be aware that the weather can change abruptly, often with little warning and in spite of the forecast. Wind and current increase as you move away from the shoreline.

The Hudson River is tidal as far north as the Federal Dam at Troy, and these tides exert a strong pull on watercraft. Thoroughly familiarize yourself with tides and tide tables before putting in on the Hudson. Check tides at: tidesandcurrents.noaa. gov. Generally the current is strongest when the tide is going out.

Watch out for boat traffic, particularly large ships and barges whose wakes can capsize a small watercraft. When close to a rocky or diked section of shoreline, stay alert for rebounding waves as well as incoming ones. The Hudson River experiences heavy boat traffic. Operators of small watercraft like kayaks and canoes must be ever-vigilant. Don't assume boats can see you. Wear bright colors. Know where the boat channels are and avoid those waters. If you must cross a boat channel, cross in a group and keep the group together. If you see a boat in the distance, let it pass before you set out. Some large boats move surprisingly fast, and distance can be hard to judge. Take into account tide, current, and wind when planning your trajectory across the river.

Be prepared for an increase in boat traffic as you pass by harbors, marinas, docks, or wharves. Memorize the shoreline as you leave so that you can return to the same starting point.

Introduction

The Hudson River is New York State's largest and most regal river, the "Rhine of America," with a basin encompassing an area of 13,370 square miles.[1] Its enormity becomes all the more apparent when you stop to consider that the Mohawk, the state's second-largest river, is but one of the Hudson's many tributaries.

The Hudson River begins as a mere trickle, rising from the High Peaks Region of the Adirondack Mountains. It grows in strength as tributaries feed into it, flowing south until it becomes full-grown and races into the Atlantic Ocean, approximately 315 miles distant. Even as it leaves the continent behind, however, the Hudson's course is not completely run. It pushes out into the Atlantic Ocean as a freshwater stream for more than another 90 miles before eventually dissipating entirely.[2]

The Hudson River is a long arm of the Atlantic Ocean, rising and falling approximately every six hours in lockstep with the ocean's tides. These tidal impulses are so powerful that they push upriver to as far as the Federal Dam in Troy, at which point the ocean's spell on the Hudson is finally broken. It is said that if you were to drop a twig into the river at Troy, it would take 126 days for it to reach the Atlantic Ocean 150 miles away because of the back-and-forth actions of the tides as the water makes its way downstream. For this reason Native Americans called the river *Muhheakantuck*, or "the river that flows two ways."

Because it is a two-way river from Manhattan to Troy, unencumbered by waterfalls or dams, large ships and barges are able to make their way safely upriver to the Port of Albany, 145 miles from the Atlantic Ocean. This is partly due to human intervention. The section of the Hudson between Catskill and Troy has been repeatedly dredged and deepened over the last two centuries to ensure a median low-water depth of thirty-two feet up to Albany. The mud, gravel, and rocks brought up from the riverbed during the dredging have been added to the shoreline, piled high on mudflats to create artificial islands, or used to connect islands to the mainland, turning the islands into peninsulas. You will see much evidence of past dredging along the shoreline and islands as you paddle along the Hudson River between Catskill and Troy where shoals, islands, and channels have been modified, consolidated, or eliminated, and where dikes have been set into place to buttress up parts of the riverbanks. Despite all of these changes, however, the Hudson River between Catskill and Stillwater remains a river of islands, making that section uniquely different from the other parts of the river above and below it.

Although the Hudson River is powerful enough to push its way out into the Atlantic Ocean, the Atlantic Ocean pushes back with even greater force. For this reason the Hudson can be brackish for as far inland as sixty miles. At times the ocean's salt line even advances as far upriver as Poughkeepsie and Hyde Park. When this happens, local sources of drinking water are at risk of contamination and the Great Sacandaga Lake (a twenty-nine-mile-long reservoir in the southern Adirondacks) must be called upon to release some of its stored waters to help the Hudson River push back the invading salt line.

So great is the connection between the Hudson River and the open sea that in 1647 colonists at Fort Orange (Albany) reported sighting a white-colored, 40-foot-long whale that surfaced for a while, continued upstream to Troy, and then made its way back downriver toward the sea. It is possible that this story, passed down through the years, may have contributed to Albany native Herman Melville's tale of an albino whale and a captain whose obsession with it led to his ultimate destruction.[3]

The Hudson has been known by a variety of names. To the Mohawks it was "the river beyond the pines"; to the Algonquins it was the "river that comes from the mountains beyond Cohoes Falls."[4] Henry Hudson called it Manhatees. The early Dutch called it the Mauritius, after the Stadtholder Prince Maurice,[5] and the Nassau after the reigning family in Holland.[6] In 1664 Great Britain christened it the Hudson River, after explorer Henry Hudson who, although he sailed for the Dutch, was an Englishman. It has been known as the Hudson ever since, except for during the heyday of the Erie and Champlain canals when canal boatmen often called it the North River.

The Hudson River is an extraordinarily unique and special river with numerous islands, bays, and tributaries, all layered with human history that has accrued over the course of many centuries like deepening deposits of sedimentation. The valley containing the Hudson River is recognized as a 154-mile estuary, a semi-

"Henry Hudson's "Half Moon." Discovery of the Hudson River 1609."

Henry Hudson will always be remembered for the river that bears his name. Postcard ca. 1900.

Major sections of the Hudson River are walled by dikes to slow down the inevitable erosion of the shoreline. Photograph 2006.

enclosed, coastal body of water freely connected to the open sea, where fresh-water and seawater intermix. This estuary provides the spawning grounds and nursery for 207 different species of fish and is designated by the federal government as a National Heritage Area and an American Heritage River.

In 2001 the Hudson River Greenway Water Trail (www.hudsongreenway. state.ny.us) was established as a 156-mile water trail connecting Battery Park in Manhattan with Battery Park in Waterford. The water trail promises to ensure at least one access point for every ten miles of shoreline on both sides of the Hudson River, and at least one campsite, hotel, motel, guesthouse, inn, or B&B for overnight lodging every fifteen miles. Currently there are ninety designated access sites and most sites are less than five miles apart.

It is fortunate that we are living in a time of environmental consciousness. Up until more recent times the river was a sewer, polluted and reeking from industrial waste and municipal discharges. The "Albany pool" of pollution between Troy and the south tip of Houghtaling Island was particularly noxious. Much of the river has been brought back to life, thanks to the efforts of conservationists, environmentalists, the New York State Department of Environmental Conservation (DEC), future-oriented organizations like Scenic Hudson (scenichudson.org), Clearwater, and the Open Space Institute (osiny.org), and socially responsible individuals and groups. The river's cleanup was accelerated by the Clean Water Act of 1972.

At the same time, efforts are being made to preserve the land adjacent to the river. It is a story that began in 1963 when Scenic Hudson successfully fought to save Storm King Mountain (the northern gateway to the Hudson Highlands) from falling victim to development. Today, paddlers on the Hudson can enjoy a river that has much to offer in terms of both scenery and history. It also offers challenges and dangers for paddlers. The Hudson is a dynamic river, possessing strong currents and a shoreline that can alter dramatically with the ebb and flow of its tides.

The year preceding this book's publication, 2009, proved to be a celebrative one for the Hudson River, its people, and its communities, for it marked the 400th anniversary of Henry Hudson's epic voyage up the Hudson River. Just two years earlier, 2007 marked the 200th Anniversary of Robert Fulton's triumphant trip up the Hudson River by steamboat (the *North River*) from New York City to Albany. Today there is much to continue celebrating, for the Hudson is truly one of the world's great historic rivers, different every time you go out to enjoy it, affected by the seasons, the weather, and the tides. It is a river that commands respect and must receive it in order to be safely paddled. Treat it with reverence and appreciation, and the river will be your friend for life.

1

Corning Preserve (Albany)
Accessing the Hudson River at Albany

- **Launch Site:** Albany Municipal Launching Ramp at Corning Preserve Riverfront Park under I-787 overpass in Albany (Albany County); concrete ramp. Designated Greenway Water Trail Site with lockable kayak storage racks (four-boat capacity), port-a-sans (chemical toilets), picnicking facilities, and access to restaurants, lodging, and retail/supplies. During the months of June, July, and August, the area is closed to all but concert-goers every Thursday evening between the hours of 6 PM–10 PM for the "Alive at Five"concert series. For more information: albany.org/pages/listings/show_listingDetail. asp?ent_id=422&mem_id=Yes&sort=Attractions&hd.
- **Delorme NYS Atlas & Gazetteer:** p. 66, CD3–4; **Estimated GPS:** 42°39.35′N; 73°44.55′W
- **Destinations:** Patroon Island Bridge, Troy-Menands Bridge, Dunn Memorial Bridge
- **Mileage:** To Patroon Island Bridge—0.9 mile (one-way); to Troy-Menands Bridge—3.9 miles (one-way); to Dunn Memorial Bridge—0.9 mile (one-way)
- **Comments:** Read "Caution" beginning on page xxii and "The Hudson River: Caution" on page 1. Be prepared for an increase in boat traffic near the Albany Yacht Club.
- **Directions:** Proceeding north on I-787, get off at Exit 4 for "Downtown Albany, Rt. 9 & Rt. 20," setting your odometer to 0.0 as you head down the ramp. Stay to the right at street level and begin driving north on Rt. 9 North (a one-way street that parallels I-787 and the Hudson River). At 0.7 mile veer to your right, following signs for Colonie Street and the Corning Preserve. When you have gone 1.0 mile, you will pass by the Erastus Corning 2nd Riverfront Preserve entrance. Keep going for another 0.1 mile, following signs for "Event Parking," and then turn right into a large parking area underneath the I-787 overpass. Park at the north end, closest to the boat launch, which is called the Albany Municipal Launching Ramp. Approaching Albany heading south on I-787, get off at Exit 4A (Colonie St. & Columbia St.). As you start down the ramp, clock off 0.3 mile and then turn left into the large parking area beneath the I-787 overpass. Park near the north end of the lot where the Albany Municipal Launching Ramp is located.

The Paddle:

North—The Patroon Island Bridge was built in 1969 to carry I-90 over the Hudson River. The west end of the bridge extends over what was once Lower Patroon Island. Along the way to the bridge, you will pass by a tiny cove at 0.3 mile, likely created by Patroon Creek (sections of which run under the city). Less than 0.2 mile farther north you will pass by a channel to your left that dead-ends after several hundred feet. At 0.9 mile you will reach the Patroon Island Bridge. A long beach just south of the bridge on the east shore provides a chance to stretch your legs if you wish.

 Corning Preserve

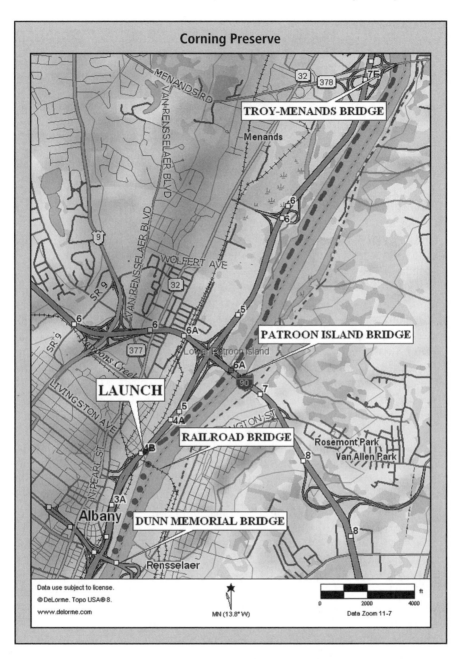

Continuing farther upriver from the Patroon Island Bridge will take you to the Troy-Menands Bridge (Route 378), in 3.9 miles. Piers rising up from Breaker Island (an island now in name only) support the west end of the bridge. Breaker

Albany Skyline, at Night, Albany, N. Y.

The Albany sky-line prior to the creation of the Empire State Plaza in the 1960s. Post-card ca. 1940.

Island (also known as Cuyler's Island) was joined with Hillhouse Island and Mix Island and wedded to the mainland many years ago. A foundry once operated on Hillhouse Island.[1]

Roughly halfway between the Patroon Island and the Troy-Menands bridges, you will see a culvert along the west bank, at 2.4 miles, with a wooden rail fence above it. A lower section of the Little River passes through this culvert to mingle with the Hudson River. Midway between high and low tide, it is easy to paddle through this culvert, proceeding under the Mohawk-Hudson Bikeway, and to follow the Little River north for 0.1 mile. The stream continues north on the other side of I-787, but it is marshy most of the way. Several hundred yards downstream from the junction of the Little River with the Hudson is the site of a former amusement park called Al-Tro Park. Nothing remains of the park today.

Al-Tro Park was a twentieth-century amusement park established in 1906 by the Albany & Troy Steamboat Company on Patroon Island near the confluence of the Hudson and the Little River. The name was a portmanteau word combining *Al*bany and *Tro*y. The park offered a wide variety of diversions including a dance hall, a 4,000-seat amphitheater, a 900-foot-long boardwalk, a concert hall, vaudeville shows, performing acrobats, band concerts, and a roller skating rink. It only lasted until 1909.[2]

Al-Tro Park was not the first amusement center at this site, however, nor was it the last. Pleasure Island operated there in the late 1800s. Then, in 1910, after Al-Tro Park's demise, Maple Beach Park took over, but only managed to keep the business going for a couple of seasons before shutting down in 1913, possibly because of serious damage inflicted by heavy floodwaters that year. In 1915 a new park opened, lasting until 1921. Called Midway Beach Park, it offered a bathhouse, roller skating rink, dance hall, and an assortment of rides. Its demise in 1921 was undoubtedly accelerated by the opening that year of Mid-City Park in Menands, merely half a mile away.[3]

South—Paddle downstream to reach the Dunn Memorial Bridge in 0.9 mile. At the very beginning of the paddle, you will pass under the old New York Cen-

▶ **Corning Preserve**

tral Railroad Bridge (now called the Livingston Avenue Rail Bridge) at 0.05 mile. When tall boats need to pass under it, the middle section of the bridge rotates as though on a turntable, moving out of the way. The Livingston Avenue Rail Bridge was at one time also called the North Bridge, to distinguish it from the Maiden Lane Rail Bridge, farther south, which was called the South Bridge. Unlike the Maiden Lane Rail Bridge, which carried passengers to Union Station, the Livingston Avenue Rail Bridge carried mostly freight.[4] Just south of the bridge, on the west bank, is a floating restaurant that is open seasonally. Access to the restaurant is by dock or at the Erastus Corning 2nd Riverfront Preserve entrance.

Shortly after leaving the railroad bridge behind, you will see culverts that go between the river and two small ponds on the west side of the bikeway. The ponds are vestiges of the Albany Basin, constructed in 1825 to accommodate the vast rise in shipping as a result of the opening of the Erie Canal. The ponds rise and fall with the tides, just like the Hudson River.

In less than 0.3 mile you will come to the main section of the river promenade, on your right, where concerts are held in the summer at an outdoor amphitheater. A newly created Hudson River Way Pedestrian Bridge crosses over I-787 at this point. The footbridge was installed in 2003 and is lined with thirty lampposts containing murals of Albany's past painted by local trompe l'oeil artist Jan Marie Spanard.

In another 0.1 mile you will pass by the Riverfront Pumping Station (part of the New York State Office of General Services), which is constructed of stone but was designed to give the appearance of a wooden fort. The distinctive building farther inland behind the Pumping Station is the old D & H (Delaware & Hudson Railroad) Building, which currently houses the State University System of New York. Look for the weathervane of Henry Hudson's *Half Moon* atop the highest steeple on the building. The D & H Building was constructed in 1918 by the architect Marcus T. Reynolds, who modeled it after thirteenth- and fourteenth-century Belgium edifices. With its abundance of turrets and pinnacles, it is one of Albany's most distinctive buildings.[5]

It is only another 0.3 mile from here to the Dunn Memorial Bridge.

During the entire paddle you will have constant views of the Albany riverfront, I-787, and the Albany skyline. In the early 1800s a much different view was offered. James L. Buckingham, a British member of parliament, wrote of seeing Albany from the river during an 1838 voyage on the Hudson: "The slope of the western bank, on which it stands, represents a city rising upward from the shore of the river to an elevated ridge of land, and the number of towers and domes scattered among the general mass of dwellings, one of them, that of the City Hall, having its surface gilded, and several others of a burnished and dazzling white, being overlaid with plating of zinc and tin, gave us the whole a very brilliant aspect."[6]

The east side of the river is lined by trees for the most part, but behind them are the residences and commercial buildings of Rensselaer.

The 1989 replica of the *Half Moon*. An earlier version was shipped over from the Netherlands in 1909 to help the United States celebrate the tercentennial. Photograph 2005.

History: The Corning Preserve Riverfront Park, named after Erastus Corning III, mayor of Albany for forty-one years, is a linear park that follows the Hudson River north for about five miles. It is part of the Mohawk-Hudson Bikeway and the Hudson River Greenway Trail System, and the culmination of many years of planning.[7] Along this section of the river, the Hudson has cut out a channel through the bed of former Lake Albany, which is why the banks of the river, composed of soft clay and gravel, have been so easily eroded[8] and why cement dikes are so prevalent along the shoreline.

The general area by the boat launch marks the terminus of the old Erie Canal.[9] As a nearby sign points out, the site is 145 miles from New York City and 360 miles from Buffalo by water.

A section of Riverfront Park was once open water. Back then it was part of the Albany Basin,[10] where large ships and boats could dock along a 4,323-foot-long pier that was 126 feet wide. The basin was so large that it could hold up to 1,000 canal boats and 50 larger vessels. All that remains today of what was previously open water are two small ponds near the Hudson River Way Pedestrian Bridge; the rest has been filled in.[11]

A replica of Henry Hudson's *Half Moon* is periodically moored at the preserve's waterfront. The original *Half Moon* (which the Dutch called *Halve Maen*) was built by the Dutch East India Company in 1609 and was captained by Henry

▶ **Corning Preserve**

Hudson, an Englishman. Although Hudson failed in his goal to find a direct route to the Orient, he did explore a grand waterway leading up into the interior of New York State, and it was this corridor that ultimately led to the expansion of New York and its rise to commercial preeminence as "the Empire State."

The present replica of the *Half Moon* was built in Albany in 1989. It was designed and built by Nicholas Benton, a thirty-five-year-old man who met an untimely death later in 1989 when the mast of a schooner he was working on in Rensselaer snapped, causing Benton to fall seventy-five feet. The *Half Moon* is eighty-five feet long, with six sails set on three masts each seventy-eight feet high, and carries a compliment of six cannons. When under sail, it is manned by twelve volunteers (the original had a crew of fifteen to twenty sailors).[12]

The first replica of Hudson's *Half Moon*[13] was built by the Dutch in 1909 and given to the United States in celebration of the tercentennial of Hudson's heroic voyage.[14] That replica ended up being grossly neglected in the decades that followed. Finally, in disrepair and no longer seaworthy, it was donated to the City of Cohoes in 1924. The city wisely moved the ship inland to East Side Park on Van Schaick Island, where the *Half Moon* was fenced in and exhibited, but neglected even further—and vandalized as well. After numerous small fires of suspicious origin, the ship was finally lost when it was consumed by fire in 1934.[15]

Albany at one time was the largest lumber market in the eastern United States, particularly of white pine. Lumber was brought down from the Adirondacks by canal boats and stored along the Hudson's west bank just south of the present-day Patroon Island Bridge in piles often as high as sixty feet. From here the lumber would be shipped out on larger boats heading downstate, or loaded on freight cars and shipped by rail.[16]

Patroon Creek may earlier have been called Mill Creek. Historian Benson Lossing described it in the mid-1800s as coming down the hills from the west side of Albany, through the Vale of Tivoli (perhaps near the area where Tivoli Park is located today), and then over a cascade, which he called "the falls of Tivoli."[17] All or most of this—as with much of Albany's original landscape—has been buried beneath the modern city.

Although the city of Albany is devoid of creeks today, with the exception of the Normans Kill, at one time four other streams flowed down the hill through the city and into the Hudson River—the Beaver Kill (Buttermilk Creek), the Foxen Kill, Patroon Creek, and the Rutten Kill. None exist today for any extent as surface features, having been integrated into Albany's underground sewerage/sanitation system. Several of these streams were of respectable size. The Beaver Kill, rising up west of the city, was energetic enough to power several industries. The Foxen Kill, which the North Pearl Street bridge crossed over, attracted fishing enthusiasts. The Rutten Kill, starting just above Lark Street and appreciably shorter than the other streams, was still powerful enough to erode a 350-foot-wide ravine 50 feet deep.[18]

2 | Hudson Shores Park (Watervliet)
Accessing the Hudson River near Troy

- ■ **Launch Site:** Hudson Shores Park off of 23rd Street in Watervliet (Albany County); 100-foot carry to water's edge, followed by 50-foot carry on ramp leading out to floating dock. Designated Greenway Water Trail Site with restrooms and port-a-sans, picnicking facilities, and a trail system within the park. During the summer, a floating restaurant called the Rusty Anchor is moored at the park.
- ■ **Delorme NYS Atlas & Gazetteer:** p. 66, BC4; **GPS:** 42°43.70'N; 73°41.93'W
- ■ **Destinations:** Center Island, Federal Lock & Dam, Congress Street Bridge, Poesten Kill, Wynants Kill, Troy-Menands Bridge
- ■ **Mileage:** To Center Island—0.3 mile (one-way); around Center Island—1.7 miles; to Federal Lock & Dam—1.5 miles (one-way); to Poesten Kill—0.5 mile (one-way); to Wynants Kill—1.6 miles (one-way); to Troy-Menands Bridge—1.8 miles (one-way)
- ■ **Comments:** Read "Caution" beginning on page xxii and "The Hudson River: Caution" on page 1. Stay a safe distance back from the Federal Dam. Be prepared for an increase in boat traffic from the marina at the south end of Center Island and the riverfront wharf in Troy.
- ■ **Directions:** From 1-787, get off at Exit 8 for Green Island and 23rd Street. From underneath the I-787 overpass, drive east on 23rd Street toward the Hudson River for over 100 feet and turn right into the entrance to the Hudson Shores Park. Proceed south for 0.3 mile to the last parking area, which you will reach soon after passing under the Congress Street Bridge. From here, carry your canoe or kayak 100 feet south to a 50-foot-long aluminum ramp that leads out to a floating dock. The dock was created with funding from the Hudson River Greenway Water Trail Grant Program.

The Paddle:

North—Head upstream for 0.3 mile to the south end of Center Island (also known as Starbuck Island). From here, you can either paddle around the island, circumnavigating it in 1.7 miles while passing under the Green Island Bridge and the Collar City Bridge twice, or you can continue paddling north for 1.7 miles until you reach the Federal Lock & Dam. Bear left at the south end of Center Island to proceed clockwise around the island and you will enter a fairly calm stretch of water until you reach the island's north end. Take note that at low tide this section can become impassable to paddlers. Along the way you will pass by a couple of tiny islands near the Green Island and Collar City bridges. Rounding the north end of Center Island, you will come out to excellent views of Stony Island (straight ahead), the Federal Dam (0.5 mile beyond Stony Island), and Adams Island (to the right). Adams Island may look at first as though it is the east bank of the Hudson River.

▶ **Hudson Shores Park**

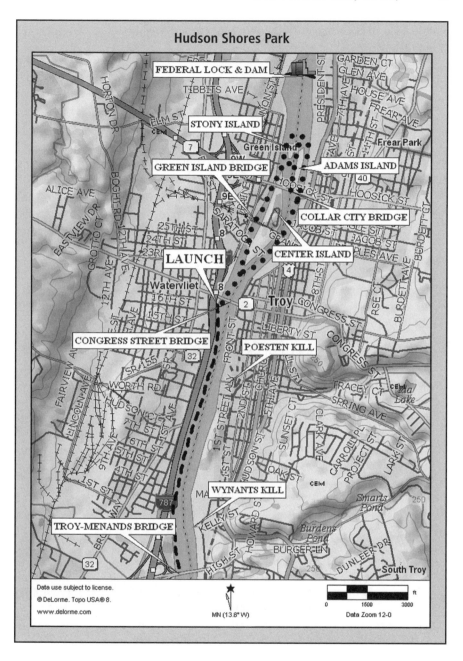

Round the stony tip of Center Island, heading south, and you will approach the Collar City Bridge within 0.3 mile. Just before you reach the bridge, you will see a stone-block dock and obvious landing point to your right on the island, but it ultimately leads nowhere and there is little to see if you debark.

Center Island is interesting in that the south portion of the island is occupied by homeowners, while the north half (bisected by the Collar City Bridge) is essentially uninhabited.

South—Proceed downstream for 1.8 miles until you reach the Troy-Menands Bridge (Route 378), which serves as a good turnaround point. Along the way you will pass by the Poesten Kill at 0.5 mile (look for it just south of an enormous earthen mound along the shore) and the Wynants Kill at 1.6 miles, both coming in along the east bank. The last part of the Poesten Kill has been turned into a canal as it passes west through Troy into the Hudson River. At high tide it can be paddled upstream for several hundred feet.

At 0.7 mile, you will pass by the Watervliet Arsenal along the west bank.

Scrap yards, continuous piers, and bulk-storage units are visible along the east bank riverfront for much of the distance.

History: The Green Island Bridge with its rounded towers and light-green color is one of the most distinctive bridges along the Hudson River.[1] There have been a number of earlier bridges at this site. The first, a railroad bridge for the Rensselaer & Saratoga Railroad, was erected in 1835 and burned down in 1862. Called the Troy Bridge (and also the Long Bridge), it was 1,600 feet long and had an opening near its center so that employees could descend to the Starbuck Machine Shop on Center Island.[2] The second bridge was built by the Delaware & Hudson Railroad in 1884, rebuilt in 1925, and then conveyed to the counties of Albany and Rensselaer in 1963, which converted it for automobile traffic. This bridge collapsed in 1977 and was replaced by the current bridge.[3]

The Watervliet Arsenal (wva.army.mil or dmna.state.ny.us/historic) is the oldest continuously operating manufacturing arsenal in the United States. It was founded in 1813 to support the War of 1812, and by 1887 had become the cannon factory for America. Contained in the arsenal's museum is "George the 2nd," a 24-pounder cannon that was surrendered by the British at the Battle of Saratoga.

The Erie Canal originally passed through the arsenal until 1923, when the canal was relocated to Waterford.[4]

The Poesten Kill was named after Jan Barentsen Wemp (he was also known as "Poest"), who settled in Troy in 1657.[5] The Wynants Kill was named after Wynant Gerritse van de Poel, who operated a mill on the stream in 1658.[6]

Hudson Shores Park is dedicated to James F. Cavanaugh (1910–1973), who was mayor of Watervliet from 1967 until his death in 1973.

▶ **Hudson Shores Park**

Green Island (Green Island)
Islands, Bridges, and the Federal Lock & Dam

■ **Launch Sites:** Informal accesses off of Tibbits Avenue along west bank of Hudson River at Green Island (Albany County). One access is next to the Green Island Gazebo via an access gate at the end of Tibbits Avenue, and the other one is provided by the Green Island Power Authority at the northeast end of the parking area. Both accesses involve a challenging 100-foot carry down a steep, gravelly slope. The footing can be slippery from loose rocks.

■ **Delorme NYS Atlas & Gazetteer:** p. 66, BC4; **Estimated GPS:** 42°44.89'N; 73°41.35'W

■ **Destinations:** Federal Lock & Dam, Center Island, Adams Island, Stony Island, Poesten Kill, Troy-Menands Bridge

■ **Mileage:** To Federal Lock & Dam—0.2 mile (one-way); to Stony Island—0.2 mile (one-way); around Center, Stony, and Adams islands—2.2 miles; to Poesten Kill—1.9 miles (one-way); to Troy-Menands Bridge—3.4 miles (one-way)

■ **Comments:** Read "Caution" beginning on page xxii and "The Hudson River: Caution" on page 1. Stay a safe distance back from the Federal Dam. Be prepared for an increase in boat traffic as you pass by the marina at the south end of Center Island and riverfront wharf in Troy.

■ **Directions:** From I-787, turn east onto Tibbits Avenue, approximately 1.8 miles south of I-787's terminus at Cohoes. Follow Tibbits Avenue east for less than 0.5 mile until you reach a "Do Not Enter" sign where the street becomes one-way. Turn right onto George Street and proceed south for less than 0.1 mile. When you come to Bleecker Street, turn left and head east for 100 feet. Then turn left on Hudson Avenue (a one-way street) and drive north for less than 0.1 mile, passing by the Green Island Gazebo (GIG) Park in the process. At the end of the street (junction of Tibbits Avenue & Hudson Avenue), continue straight into a large parking area.

You are now straddling two access points to the Hudson River—one next to Green Island Gazebo via an access gate at the end of Tibbits Avenue, and one provided by the Green Island Power Authority at the northeast end of the parking area. Both are intended only for fishing access or cartop watercraft. Of the two sites, the Green Island Power Authority shoreline access is probably the easier one, simply because of the better footing (although the descent is still steep and gravelly).

The Paddle:

The paddle essentially covers the same destinations as described in the chapters "Hudson Shores Park" and "Ingalls Avenue Approach."

When you set out onto the Hudson River, you are 0.2 mile from Stony Island, the smallest of the three islands that cluster together in the distance downstream from the Federal Lock & Dam. Take note that the passage

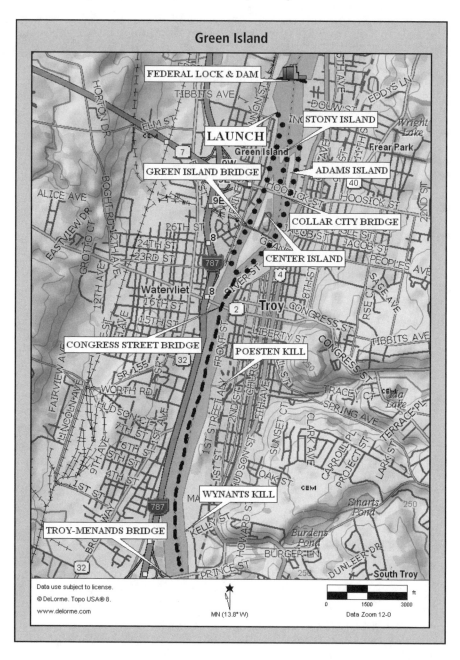

between Center Island and the mainland can become obstructed by mudflats during low tide, so pay attention to water depth while paddling along the west bank.

► **Green Island**

Although the Federal Dam is close by, stay a safe distance back from its powerful hydraulics.

History: Green Island is undoubtedly best known for its association with Henry Ford. In 1923 the Ford Motor Company established a plant at Green Island and began manufacturing radiators and springs. The plant thrived for most of the twentieth century, but then closed in 1988. In 2004 the factory portion was demolished, which explains the vacant land that now exists north of Tibbits Avenue.

Several centuries ago Green Island, Jan Gownsen Island, Center Island, and another tiny island were part of the Bower Turkee (*bower* is Dutch for "farm") of Green Island that was transferred by Kiliaen Van Rensselaer to Pieter Schuyler.[1] Green Island was a genuine island until the 1960s, when I-787 was built and the channels separating the island from the mainland were filled in.[2]

The Green Island Power Authority (GIPA) is one of three public power authorities in New York State. The other two are the New York Power Authority and the Long Island Power Authority. The Green Island Hydroelectric Station is run by GIPA, which acquired the eight-megawatt power plant from the Ford Motor Company in 2000. Earlier the plant was known as the Green Island Electric Company. It was founded in 1895.[3]

4 The Little River (Watervliet)
An Oft-Forgotten Offshoot of the Hudson River

■ **Launch Site:** Informal access at the end of Fourth Street in Watervliet (Albany County); put-in can be challenging because of rocky shoreline.
■ **Delorme NYS Atlas & Gazetteer:** p. 66, C4; **Estimated GPS:** 42°42.56'N; 73°42.29'W
■ **Destination:** Along Little River
■ **Mileage:** 0.4–0.6 mile (round-trip)
■ **Comments:** Read "Caution" beginning on page xxii. The level of the stream varies markedly with the tides. For this reason the paddle is best taken around high tide. Check tides at: tidesandcurrents.noaa.gov.
■ **Directions:** From I-787, get off at Exit 6 for Menands and drive west for approximately 0.7 mile until you reach Rt. 32. Turn right onto Rt. 32 and drive north for 2.0 miles. Turn right onto Fourth Street and follow it east as it zigzags, crossing Second Avenue and First Avenue. When you come to I-787, drive through a tunnel underpass to reach a medium-sized paved parking area at the end of the road used by the Mohawk-Hudson Bikeway.

Put in along the rocky shoreline of the Hudson. Immediately to your right is a culvert that leads under the Mohawk Hudson Bikeway. This is the north end of the Little River. If you are there midway between high and low tide, you should be able to paddle through the culvert without difficulty and then follow the Little River upstream for a short distance.

The Paddle:

The Little River runs between I-787 and the main bikeway (to the east), and the Schuyler Flats Bikeway offshoot (to the west), paralleling the two. The stream starts at two drainpipes that extend under I-787, connecting the creek with the Hudson River next to the Mohawk-Hudson Bikeway's parking area. The Little River is fairly shallow, with a depth of three to ten feet,[1] the depth decreasing as you progress south.

Within 0.2 mile you will see off to the right through the trees a side trail leading up from the bike path to the Schuyler Flats Cultural Center. From there continue south for as far as you can. The length of the paddle will depend upon the water level and any blow-down that has fallen across the creek. Because the stream is connected to the Hudson River, it is markedly affected by tidal fluctuations. But regardless of tidal factors, by 0.3 mile the stream is pretty much marshland and is impassable.

What makes this little journey unique and worth undertaking is the fact that very few paddlers even know about it.

 Little River

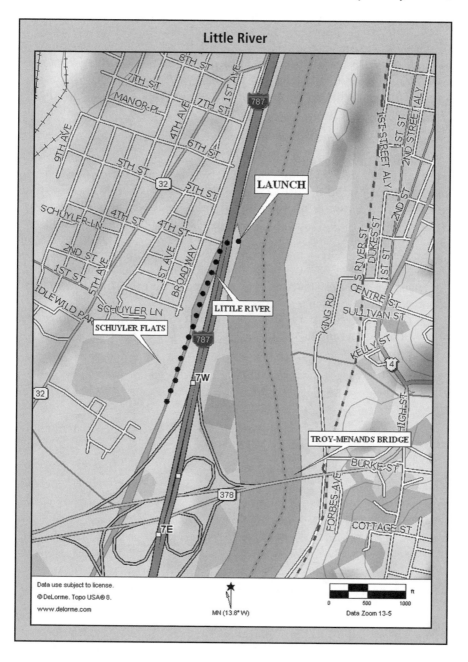

Little River

LAUNCH

LITTLE RIVER

SCHUYLER FLATS

TROY-MENANDS BRIDGE

Data use subject to license.
© DeLorme. Topo USA® 8.
www.delorme.com

MN (13.8° W)

0   500   1000   ft

Data Zoom 13-5

History: The Little River is a tiny stream that at one time helped to delineate a number of small islands. These islands are now joined to the mainland, and the Little River has become very little indeed.

Schuyler Flats (known by the Dutch as *Groote Vlachte*)[2] is a historically significant area with multiple layers of history. Like other nearby sections of the Hudson Valley, it was crisscrossed by nomadic hunter-gatherers who foraged for nuts and other edibles and hunted game and fish. By the year 1200 a semipermanent village had been established on the flats. Land was cleared for farming, and corn was grown and stored in pits. In the early 1600s, with the arrival of the Dutch, Native Americans began trading fur in exchange for European goods.[3]

The first European house on the flats was built prior to 1660. It was subsequently purchased from the Van Rensselaers by Philip Pieterse Schuyler in 1672, and was owned by succeeding generations of his family for more than two and a half centuries. During this time the estate was a well-known center of social and military life, and also served as the home of Pieter Schuyler, the first mayor of Albany. The house burned down in 1962,[4] but parts of the foundation remain. An eighteenth-century book called *Memoirs of an American Lady* by Anne Grant gives an account of life at Schuyler Flats in the late 1700s.[5] Schuyler Flats was designated as a National Historic Landmark in 1993 and became a town park in 2002.

At the southwest corner of the property (next to Route 32) is a section of the original Erie Canal built in 1823.

 Little River

Schuyler Flats (Watervliet)
Along a Historic Section of the Hudson River

5

■ **Launch Site:** Informal access at the end of Fourth Street in Watervliet (Albany County); put-in can be challenging because of rocky shoreline.
■ **Delorme NYS Atlas & Gazetteer:** p. 66, C4; **Estimated GPS:** 42°42.56′N; 73°42.29′W
■ **Destinations:** Congress Street Bridge, Troy-Menands Bridge
■ **Mileage:** To Congress Street Bridge—1.4 miles (one-way); to Troy-Menands Bridge—0.6 mile (one-way)
■ **Comments:** Read "Caution" beginning on page xxii and "The Hudson River: Caution" on page 1.
■ **Directions:** From I-787, get off at Exit 6 for Menands & Rt. 32 and drive west for approximately 0.7 mile until the road ends. Turn right onto Rt. 32 and drive north for 2.0 miles. Turn right onto Fourth Street and follow it east for nearly 0.3 mile as it zigzags across Second Avenue and First Avenue. When you come to I-787, drive through a tunnel underpass to reach a medium-sized paved parking area at the end of the road, used for the Mohawk-Hudson Bikeway.

The Paddle:

North—Head upstream following the west bank of the Hudson River. Look across the river and you will see continuous signs of industrialization along the South Troy riverbank. At 0.8 miles you will pass by the Poesten Kill coming in on the opposite (east) bank of the river. At 1.4 miles you will reach the Congress Street Bridge (Route 2), connecting Watervliet and Troy.

South—Proceeding downstream, you will immediately pass by two large drainpipes next to the parking area. The pipes provide a connection between the Hudson and the Little River, a small creek that runs along the west side of I-787, paralleling the Hudson River. (See chapter "The Little River.")

After paddling 0.3 mile, look across the river and you will see the Wynants Kill rushing out of a culvert and into the Hudson River. A number of industries were once located along this section of the river, including part of the Burden Iron Works.

At around 0.4 mile you will encounter a tiny canal on your right. You may enter the canal when the tide is right, but only for several hundred feet before it dead-ends at the foot of the Mohawk-Hudson Bikeway.

At 0.5 mile you will pass by a site just slightly inland where the Troy Steel & Iron Company once operated. All traces of it have fortunately vanished. Were it still in existence, its three 80-foot-high blast furnaces would be visible from the water.

At 0.6 mile you will reach the Troy-Menands Bridge (Route 378). At one time the Molten Iron Ferry made regular trips across the river just upstream from the bridge.

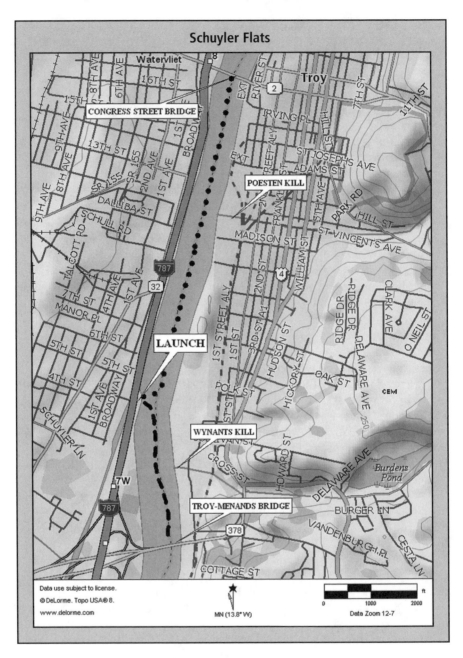

Schuyler Flats

History: The paddle starts off near historic Schuyler Flats, an area of low-lying land named after Philip Pieterse Schuyler, who bought the property in 1672. The area was initially settled by Arent Van Curler, an enterprising man whom Kiliaen

▶ **Schuyler Flats**

Van Rensselaer appointed as secretary and overseer of the colonists on Rensse-laerswyck Manor in 1640.[1]

The Troy Steel & Iron Company dates back to the nineteenth century. In 1875 the Albany Iron Works and the Rensselaer Irons Works merged to form the Albany and Rensselaer Iron & Steel Company. In 1885 the name changed to the Troy Steel & Iron Company, and a new factory was established on Breaker Island to supplement the Troy-based facilities. It is this site, located approximately 0.1 mile north of the Troy-Menands Bridge on the west side of the Hudson River, that is historically remembered today along the Mohawk-Hudson Bikeway. The Breaker Island works consisted of three 80-foot-high blast furnaces along with a 150-foot-long casting house, 500 feet of dock, and a number of other structures. In 1898 the company ceased operations and was sold to the U.S. Steel Corporation in 1903. Fourteen years later the structures were dismantled.[2] If any ruins were still left behind, they were permanently obliterated during the construction of I-787.

As for Breaker Island, it doesn't exist anymore either. The channels around it and Hillhouse Island were filled in during the 1960s when I-787 was constructed. All that remains of the waterways is a short section of the Little River.

| 6 | **Island Creek Park (Albany)**
Near the Port of Albany |

■ **Launch Site:** Island Creek Park off of Church Street in Albany (Albany County); slip-in can be challenging at low tide because of muddy shoreline.

■ **Delorme NYS Atlas & Gazetteer:** p. 66, CD4; **Estimated GPS:** 42°38.17′N; 73°45.24′W

■ **Destinations:** Dunn Memorial Bridge, Corning Preserve, Normans Kill

■ **Mileage:** To Dunn Memorial Bridge—0.6 mile (one-way); to Corning Preserve —1.0 mile (one-way); to Normans Kill—2.0 miles (one-way); up Normans Kill— 2.6 miles (round-trip)

■ **Comments:** Read "Caution" beginning on page xxii and "The Hudson River: Caution" on page 1. Be prepared for heavy boat traffic as you approach the Port of Albany. Watch out for large vessels and barges, particularly as they turn in the river to head downstream. Be alert for an increase in boat traffic around the Albany Yacht Club and Corning Preserve Riverfront Boat Launch.

■ **Directions:** Near the center of Albany (junction of Broadway & Madison Avenue), drive south on Broadway. At 0.2 mile you will pass under I-787. Directly ahead will be the waterfront USS Slater exhibit (ussslater.org). Turn immediately right, continuing on Broadway, and follow signs to the "Port of Albany." At 0.7 mile you will reach a stop sign at the junction of Broadway and Church Street. Turn left onto Church Street and then, in less than 100 feet, left into Island Creek Park (note: pay close attention—the entrance is easy to miss).

Approaching from Kenwood (junction of Rtes. 9W & 32 North), head down-hill east on Rt. 32 for 0.6 mile. At the bottom of the hill, turn left, following Rt. 32 as it heads north away from Rt. 144. In another 0.9 mile bear right, continu-ing to follow Rt. 32 until you reach a traffic light at 1.5 miles. Turn right and, in 0.1 mile, immediately left into Island Creek Park (note: pay close attention—the entrance is easy to miss).

From the parking lot, a paved walkway leads down to the water's edge within a couple of hundred feet.

The Paddle:

North—Head upriver for 0.6 mile to the Dunn Memorial Bridge, whose west end approaches the site of seventeenth-century Fort Orange. The marina vis-ible along the way across the river at 0.2–03 mile is the Albany Yacht Club (albanyyachtclub.com). At roughly 0.4 mile you will pass by two large con-duits to your left, where streams that channeled underground beneath Albany issue into the Hudson.

At 0.5 mile you will pass by Dutch Apple Cruises (dutchapplecruises. com) and, immediately after that, the *USS Slater*, which has become a major Albany tourist attraction (see chapter "Rensselaer Riverfront Park" for further details).

▶ **Island Creek Park**

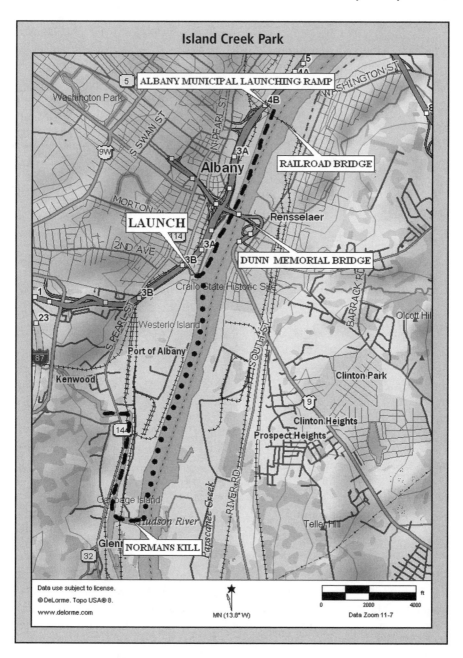

Island Creek Park

If you look across the river just before reaching the Dunn Memorial Bridge, you can see the mouth of Mill Creek, entering the Hudson from the east.

Continue paddling north to reach the Albany Municipal Launching Ramp at the Corning Preserve in roughly 1.0 mile. This is a good turnaround point.

South—Paddle downstream, paralleling the Port of Albany. Along the way you will pass by enormous piers, docks, refineries, moored ships and barges, and piles of slag on both sides of the river. At roughly 0.9 mile you will see an inlet to your left (looking east)—the "Turning Basin"—where large ships backing out from the Port of Albany can turn around to head downstream. A second turning basin is seen a little farther downriver along the east shore. At 2.0 miles you will reach the mouth of the Normans Kill.

As you get closer to the Normans Kill, Teller Hill (elevation 407 feet) is off to the east, followed by Granview Hill (elevation 420 feet) 0.5 mile farther south. Both hills are inland from the river. Granview Hill is of particular interest, for it was here, at *Schotiack*, where the Mohicans maintained an ever-burning council fire.[1]

For almost the entire distance you will be paralleling the Port of Albany, a heavily industrialized section of Albany. If you are looking for a quiet, pristine, and natural scene to enjoy, this is not the paddle to take, but its very "unnaturalness" makes for an interesting and different kind of paddle, serving up a part of Albany that is rarely seen by local residents.

Up the Normans Kill—Turn right onto the Normans Kill by Scarano Boat Builders and begin heading west. In 0.2 mile you will pass under an old iron bridge. In another 0.1 mile the creek turns right and heads north. Continue paddling upstream, with the Port of Authority to your right and Rt. 144 paralleling the creek to your left. After you have paddled another 1.0 mile you will once again turn sharply as the creek veers from north back to west. You will immediately pass under a railroad bridge and then under the Route 32 bridge.

From here it may be possible, depending upon tides, to head upstream for another 0.1 mile before encountering impassable rapids. The lack of navigable waters farther upstream is unfortunate, for in another 0.5 mile the Normans Kill has carved out a deep gorge, parts of which can be glimpsed if you look down while driving across the Route 9W bridge or the NYS Thruway bridge spanning the Normans Kill. The gorge is associated with the great Native American chief Hiawatha and the Vale of Tawasentha.

History: Island Creek Park is a tiny waterfront park named for Island Creek, a channel/stream that once separated Westerlo Island/Castle Island from the mainland. The stream is no longer recognizable as such, however, and hasn't been for years. All that remains is the tiny inlet at Island Creek Park and, farther south, the lowermost portion of what was channelized to form the terminus of the Normans Kill.[2] The park's southern boundary lies next to the Riverside Travel Plaza, followed by over a mile of port facilities.

The Port of Albany was established in 1932 as an inland destination for commercial freighters and ocean-faring ships. It consists of 200 acres of land

▶ **Island Creek Park**

on the west side of the Hudson River and 35 acres of land along the river's east side.[3] Some claim that it is the largest inland seaport in the United States.[4] Although a natural channel existed up to Albany that allowed smaller boats (like Henry Hudson's *Half Moon*) to sail the river, mudflats—particularly around Castleton-on-Hudson—made the journey perilous and often impossible during low tide. To alleviate this problem, extensive dredging and dike-building operations began in 1868 and continued into the next century. Mudflats and obstacles were removed or piled high with fill so as to be identifiable during high tide, and the channel was deepened to a low-water depth of twelve feet. These efforts, however, eventually proved insufficient. As a result, in 1930 additional dredging began and the depth of the main channel was increased to twenty-seven feet, more than enough clearance for large ships. This also meant that the river, which until then had been allowed to freeze over during the winter, could now be kept open year-round.

The Port of Albany is actually made up of several islands connected together through dredge fill. These former islands were Westerlo/Castle Island, Marsh Island, and Bogart Island.[5]

The Normans Kill is named after Albert Andriessen Bradt, an early settler who was nicknamed "de Noorman"[6] by the Dutch to indicate that he came from Norway, not the Netherlands.[7] The creek has also been known by other names. In 1632 Van Rensselaer recorded it as the Godyns Kil. At another time it was called Mill Creek after an early mill that was established along its bank.[8]

The Port of Albany is reputedly the largest inland seaport in the United States. Postcard ca. 1940.

The Normans Kill is a good-sized stream that rises from the Watervliet Reservoir and is, in effect, a continuation of the Bozen Kill, the reservoir's inlet stream. The stream drains a watershed of roughly 170 square miles and is the northern-most major tributary of the upper Hudson River estuary.[9]

At one time authorities considered turning the Normans Kill into the All-American Ship Canal, which would have linked the Hudson River with the Mohawk River south of Schenectady.[10] No concrete action was ever taken on this proposal, however.

The Vale of Tawasentha, alternately translated as the "place of many dead" or the "place of many waterfalls," is today known as the Normans Kill Gorge. According to Native American legend, the Vale of Tawasentha was one of the main dwelling places of the famous chief Hiawatha,[11] immortalized by Henry Wadsworth Longfellow's poem with the same name. The Vale was part of a main Indian trail used by the Mohawks when coming east to trade with the Dutch at Fort Orange.[12] In 1618 a treaty was established between the Dutch and Native Americans at the Normans Kill. Unfortunately, the treaty unraveled when the English, having taken New Amsterdam from the Dutch, broke it in 1674.[13]

The first mile of the Normans Kill is what remains of Island Creek, channelized as the Port of Albany expanded.[14] It is an area of river frontage that has changed markedly and beyond recognition. At one time Island Creek flowed past a body of land called Castle Island. The island no longer exists, having been integrated into the mainland following extensive dredging and reshaping of the shoreline. Castle Island, however, played a prominent role in the early history of the Hudson Valley's colonization. In 1614 (just five years after Hudson's voyage) the Dutch, under the leadership of a sea captain named Hendrick Christaensen,[15] built a trading post called Fort Nassau on the island.[16] The fort, however, was erected with little foresight and was destroyed by floodwaters in 1617. No efforts were made to rebuild it, and trade with Native Americans for pelts and fur was later established farther north at Fort Orange (present-day Albany).

Prior to the creation of the Port of Albany, Castle Island served as an airfield from 1909 to 1927, allowing planes to land and take off close to the city of Albany. The airfield was named Quentin Roosevelt Field after the son of President Theodore Roosevelt.[17] A pilot named Glenn Curtiss flew from there to New York City in 1910—one of the first long-distance flights in America. Curtiss won a $10,000 prize for his historic flight.[18]

▶ **Island Creek Park**

NYS Bethlehem Fishing Access Launch (Cedar Hill)
A Tributary with a Cascade

7

■ **Launch Site:** NYS Bethlehem Fishing Access Launch off of Lyons Road (Albany County); cement ramp. Designated Greenway Water Trail Site with port-a-sans, potable water and a hose, and a water trail kiosk. The site is operated by the Town of Bethlehem in cooperation with the NYS Department of Environmental Conservation (DEC).

■ **Delorme NYS Atlas & Gazetteer:** p. 66, D3-4; **Estimated GPS:** 42°32.86'N; 73°45.52'W

■ **Destinations:** Cascade on Vloman Kill, Paarda Hook, Papscanee Creek & Moordener Kill, Castleton-on-Hudson

■ **Mileage:** To Vloman Kill—0.3 mile (one-way); up Vloman Kill to cascade—0.7 mile (one-way); to Paarda Hook—0.7 mile (one-way); across Hudson River to Papscanee Creek and Moordener Kill—0.2 mile (one-way); up Papscanee Creek—up to 2.1 miles (one-way); up Moordener Kill—0.3 mile (one-way); to Castleton-on-Hudson—1.0 mile (one-way)

■ **Comments:** Read "Caution" beginning on page xxii and "The Hudson River: Caution" on page 1. Wait for high tide to paddle up the Vloman Kill. Check tides at: tidesandcurrents.noaa.gov. Current is generally mild to moderate. Look both ways for oncoming boats and paddle quickly across the Hudson River to reach the tiny bay formed by Papscanee Creek and the Moordener Kill. Take into account tide, current, and wind when planning your trajectory. Watch out for a wooden bulkhead with upthrusting steel rebars by the mouth of Papscanee Creek. The upper section of Papscanee Creek, above the abandoned bridge, may become impassable at low tide. Expect an increase in boat traffic near the Castleton Boat Club.

■ **Directions:** From the junction of I-787 & Rt. 9W (southeast of Albany), drive south on Rt. 9W for 1.1 miles. Turn left onto Rt. 32 North and drive east, going steadily downhill, for over 0.6 mile. At the bottom of the hill (junction of Rtes. 32 & 144), turn right and drive south on Rt. 144 for 4.8 miles. Just before you cross over the Vloman Kill, turn left onto Barent Winnie Road and proceed southeast. At 0.4 mile you will come to a fork in the road. Bear right onto Lyons Road. At 0.2 mile you will come to the Bethlehem Fishing Access Site where you can put in your watercraft. The access site adjoins Henry Hudson Park and 1,200 feet of public waterfront.[1]

From Coeymans (junction of Rtes. 144 & 143), drive north on Rt. 144 for 5.8 miles. Turn right onto Barent Winnie Road as soon as you cross over the Vloman Kill, and head southeast for 0.4 mile. Bear right and follow Lyons Road 0.2 mile to the Bethlehem Fishing Access Site.

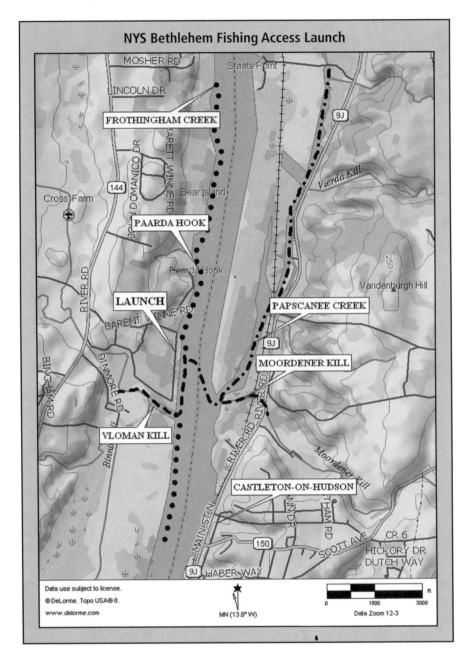

The Paddle:

West—This is a fairly simple but rewarding outing. Paddle downriver for 0.3 mile and then turn right into the mouth of the Vloman Kill. Although not immedi-

▶ **NYS Bethlehem Fishing Access Launch**

ately visible, a New York State Permitted Discharge Site is situated near the south bank. Proceed upstream, heading northwest, for 0.7 mile, following a stream that is generally 40–50 feet wide. The setting is fairly bucolic, with an old house visible on the left at one point, but otherwise reasonably free of civilization. Lyons Road, off to the right, is not visible.

You will eventually come to a point where the stream steadily veers left and then suddenly emerges into a large circular glen, over 100 feet in diameter, where a 12-foot-high, broad cascade can be seen and paddled to. The scene is marred only by the presence of a private home next to the top of the waterfall. A breached cement dam is located just upstream from the top of the cascade.

North—Head upstream for 0.7 mile to reach an inlet along the west bank called Paarda Hook. It will be marked by a green buoy and light #209. At 1.6 miles you will reach tiny Frothingham Creek coming in along the west bank as it drains Frothingham Lake, 0.2 mile to the west.

East—Paddle straight across the Hudson River for 0.2 mile to reach the mouths of Papscanee Creek and the Moordener Kill. This should only be attempted, however, if the weather is calm, no boats are coming from either direction, and you are confident in your abilities to paddle across open water.

A scenic waterfall is the big payoff for this paddle. Photograph 2004.

Papscanee Creek can be explored upstream for up to 2.1 miles, conditions permitting, and the Moordener Kill for 0.3 mile (see chapter "Papscanee Creek" for further details). Watch out for a wooden bulkhead with upthrusting steel rebars that spans the mouth of Papscanee Creek. Except at high tide, you will need to carefully negotiate your way through a short open section.

South—Paddle downstream for 1.4 miles until you come to Castleton-on-Hudson, visible across the river along the east bank. The village was named for a Mohican castle (a palisaded village) that once occupied the general area.[2] The Castleton Boat Club is the most prominent feature along the waterfront.

The section of flat land between the Moordener Kill and the village of Castleton-on-Hudson was at one time separated from the mainland and called Cow Island.

The tiny creek coming into the Hudson just south of Castleton-on-Hudson is the Vlockie Kill.

History: The Vloman Kill rises south of Voorheesville and passes through the Five Rivers Environmental Education Center west of Delmar. The name Vloman Kill is a corruption of Vlaaman's, or Vlaumans, Kil.[3]

Pieter the Fleming, an early settler, leased a sawmill from Nicholas Van Rensselaer near the mouth of the Vloman Kill in 1652. By 1677 he had saved enough money to buy the property.[4]

Paarda Hook is from the Dutch word *paard*, meaning "horse." When winters were severe in centuries past, the Hudson River froze sufficiently for both ice-boat racing and horse racing. Reputedly, a horse broke through the ice at Paarda Hook during a race and drowned[5]—hence the name.

▶ **NYS Bethlehem Fishing Access Launch**

Coeymans Landing (Coeymans)
Coeymans Creek & Hannacroix Creek

8

- **Launch Site:** Coeymans Landing at end of Westerlo Street in Coeymans (Albany County); two-lane cement boat ramp with sufficient parking for fifty cars/trailers. Designated Greenway Water Trail Site with port-a-sans, access to restaurants, fishing, and lockable kayak storage racks.
- **Delorme NYS Atlas & Gazetteer:** p. 52, A3; **GPS:** 42°28.40'N; 73°47.39'W
- **Destinations:** Coeymans Creek, Binne Kill, Hannacroix Creek
- **Mileage:** To Coeymans Creek—0.1 mile (one-way); up Coeymans Creek— 0.1 mile (one-way); to Binne Kill—2.4 miles (one-way); up Binne Kill—0.2 mile or more (one-way); to Hannacroix Creek—1.0 mile (one-way); up Hannacroix Creek—0.2 mile (one-way); to Hudson River Interpretive Trail from Hannacroix Creek—0.1 mile (one-way)
- **Comments:** Read "Caution" beginning on page xxii and "The Hudson River: Caution" on page 1. Take note that a long dike between two skeletal green-marked towers, 0.05 mile offshore, parallels the shoreline on both sides of Coeymans Landing, creating a safe harbor for moored boats. The stone breakwater is submerged at high tide and can damage or capsize a kayak. Current on Coeymans Creek to the gorge and falls is generally mild to moderate except during early spring's rush of snowmelt. Watch out for the dike at the south end of Hannacroix Bay that is revealed at low tide. Current on Hannacroix Creek is generally mild to moderate. Plan the trip upstream during high tide. There are reliable reports of six-foot-wide whirlpools in front of the harbor in the main stem of the river during high tide and high wind conditions. Expect an increase in boat traffic near Ravena Coeymans Yacht Club and Coeymans Landing Marina.
- **Directions:** From the traffic light on the west side of Ravena (junction of Rtes. 9W & 143 East), turn onto Rt. 143 and drive east for 1.4 miles. When you arrive at Rt. 144, turn right and go south on Rt. 144 for 0.1 mile. Turn left onto Westerlo Street and drive downhill for 0.1 mile. Park next to the Fishing Access Site.

The Paddle:

North—Head north, quickly passing by the Coeymans Landing Marina. As soon as you clear the marina, bear left into the outflow of Coeymans Creek. If you end up at the Ravena Coeymans Yacht Club, then you have gone too far north.

Paddle Coeymans Creek upstream for 0.1 mile until you reach the mouth of a gorge. This is a grotto-like area, with a high rock wall to your left and long strands of vegetation hanging down the rock face. Be advised that, following periods of torrential rainfall or spring's release of snowmelt, the flow of water through the gorge can be quite turbulent.

Paddle over to the base of the first of a series of cascades, each larger than the next. The waterfalls extend upstream to the Rt. 144 bridge.

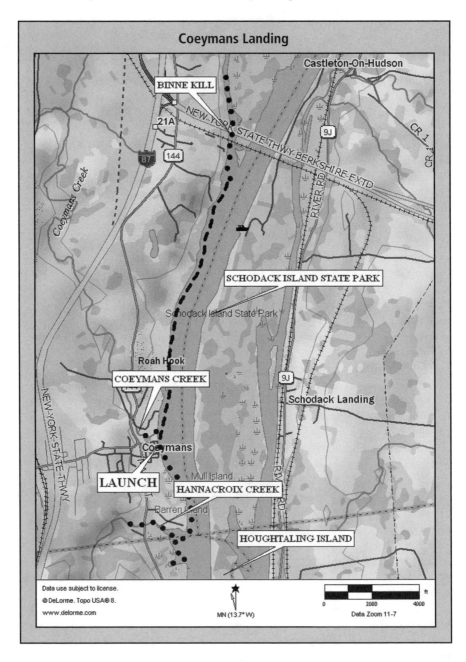

Although not visible from below, the historic Ariantje Coeymans House stands on top of the north bank in close proximity to the falls. The house is one of the largest and most imposing Dutch structures in the Hudson Valley. The main part of the house was built circa 1716 and then was modified during the mid-eighteenth century, giving it a more Georgian style. It is now listed on the National Register.[1]

Returning to the Hudson River, continue north for 2.4 miles farther until you come to the Binne Kill and two, high, mile-long bridges that span the Hudson River. This is a good point to turn around.

Very shortly thereafter you will pass by the rocky bluffs of Barren Island, which is no longer an island.

When you have gone 1.0 mile, turn right into a bay formed by the outflow from Hannacroix Creek. Beware of pilings just below the water's surface, which are evident during low tide. As you paddle west, the bay gradually narrows and becomes more stream-like. In 0.2 mile you will pass under the Route 9W bridge. The old bridge abutments still standing are from the Albany and Greene Turnpike, which was built circa 1806 during the height of the turnpike era.[3] The stone house on the bank overlooking the mouth of Hannacroix Creek just before the bridge is the National Register-listed circa 1765 Coeymans-Bronck House.[4]

Continue up Hannacroix Creek, passing by the site of a nineteenth-century mill. Note the gigantic stone-slab stairway that leads down to the creek, a relic from earlier days when boats would sail in from the river. Near the private residence that now occupies the site is a towering factory chimney that has survived from the past. The bank of the stream is littered with thousands of bricks and pieces of stones.

Proceed upstream for another 0.05 mile before the shallow rapids become impassable. When you come to a pretty glen at the bottom of rapids, you will know that you have reached your turnaround point. Roughly 0.3 mile farther upstream is a twelve-foot-high falls where a paper mill once operated.

Returning to the mouth of Hannacroix Creek, continue paddling to your right until you reach the southwest corner of the bay. Look for the mouth of a tiny stream (which may be hard to find) and then follow it southwest. Depending upon the tides and prevailing blowdown, you may or may not be able to paddle far enough upstream to glimpse the Plastic Bridge. The Plastic Bridge is reputed to be the first of its kind in the world and is made out of high-strength recycled plastic lumber. It took 68,000 one-gallon milk cartons to make the structure, which has a load-bearing capacity of fifteen tons.[5] The bridge is eleven feet wide and thirty feet long, and has a life expectancy of seventy to one hundred years, which is over twice as long as the normal lifespan of a bridge.[6] It was designed by the McLaren Engineering Group and built in 2000.

If you are unable to reach the Plastic Bridge, paddle back into the bay and then head east, following the contour of the south shoreline for several hundred feet. Look for an obvious landing site next to a sign for the Hudson River Interpretive Trail, which leads hikers through a forty-acre preserve and is a component of the Hudson River Greenway Trail System. Leave your watercraft there and follow the trail west on foot for 0.05 mile until you arrive at the Plastic Bridge. Before you leave your canoe or kayak, be sure to pull it up past the waterline to avoid the tide claiming your watercraft and you facing a long walk to your car.

If you continue up the Interpretive Trail for a short distance farther, you will come to an observation deck that overlooks a tidal pond (which may have been used by ice-harvesters when the Hudson River failed to ice over sufficiently). You will also see a tall chimney from a former icehouse less than 0.1 mile up the trail (this structure, however, is on private land and cannot be accessed). Although a hot chimney in a cold icehouse may seem paradoxical, the smokestack was used to vent heat produced by oil- or coal-powered machinery.

Back on the water take note of the dike, which is often submerged, along the south end of the bay.

History: The village of Coeymans (pronounced *kwee-mans*) was settled in 1673 by Barent Pieterse Koijemans (Coeymans). He came to the New World from the Netherlands in 1639 and ended up obtaining the Coeyman Patent in 1673.[7]

During the nineteenth century, ice harvesting was the town's major industry.[8] The Hudson River at that time would generally freeze over completely and deeply every winter. One source states that on a pleasant Sunday afternoon it was commonplace for people to skate from Troy to Coeymans and back again.[9]

Coeymans Creek rises near New Salem, draining a watershed of roughly fifty square miles. It provides a spawning habitat for both freshwater and anadromous (migrating upriver from the sea) species of fish including alewife, blueback herring, white perch, and American shad.[10]

Coeymans Landing was established in cooperation with the Town of Coeymans and the State of New York to provide river access to the community.

Hannacroix Creek (also spelled Hannacrois) drains a watershed of approximately sixty square miles. The lower, bay-like section of the creek is a favorite resting and feeding ground for migratory waterfowl and a natural spawning habitat for American shad, alewife, blueback herring, and white perch.[11] The stream has a number of distinctive waterfalls on its upper reaches, possibly more than any other Hudson River tributary. In descending order they are: falls along Tan Hollow Road, falls at the Hannacroix Preserve, Dickinson Falls, falls at Alcove, Deans Mills Falls, and Hannacroix Falls. The name Hannacroix means "crowing cock," a reference to an incident in which a cock was seen crowing defiantly on a barn door as it was being swept along by floodwaters.[12]

Barren Island was once known as Bear Island. Apparently at that time it was a separate body of land and not joined to the mainland. O'Neil describes it as being 567 yards long and 160 yards wide.[13] The fact that Bear and Barren are somewhat similar in sound suggests that one name may have given rise to the other. Some scholars hypothesize that Barren Island may be a corruption of a Dutch name, *Beam* Island.[14] During the seventeenth century, attempts were made to cultivate indigo on the island, but they were unsuccessful.

▶ **Coeymans Landing**

Barren Island is the site of Rensellaerstein (Castle Rensselaer), which was described by Washington Irving in his somewhat fanciful book *Knickerbocker's History of New York*.[15] As the overseer for Patroon Kiliaen Van Rensselaer's holdings in the New World (and at Rensellaerstein), Nicholas Kroon was instructed to demand tribute from passing ships, with the exception of those operated by the West India Company. All others who hesitated were threatened by cannon fire. The reason why ships were put into a compromising position here to begin

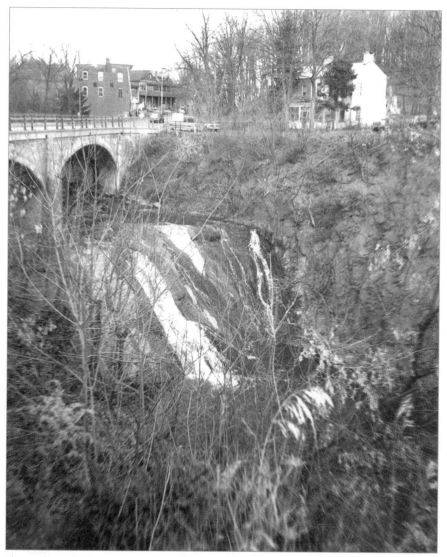

The main cascade on Coeymans Creek. Photograph 1994.

with was because of Houghtaling Island, which rises in the middle of the Hudson River, forcing vessels to move into a more constricted channel along the west bank where extortions could be made for guarantees of safe passage. As late as the nineteenth century, treasure hunters were still looking for buried treasure on the island supposedly hidden away by the notorious Captain Kidd.

In years past, before dredging changed the topography of the river, Coeymans villagers would go across the river to Pulver Beach to swim and enjoy the exceptionally fine sand.[16]

 **Coeymans Landing**

Lansing's Ferry (Pleasantdale—Troy/Schaghticoke)
A Historic River Crossing

9

- **Launch Site:** Boat Launch at end of Marion Avenue (Rensselaer County); slip-in from gravel sandbar.
- **Delorme NYS Atlas & Gazetteer:** p. 67, B4–5; **Estimated GPS:** 42°47.97'N; 73°39.96'W
- **Destinations:** Campbell Island, 126th Street Bridge, dam at Champlain Canal Lock C-1
- **Mileage:** To Campbell Island—1.1 miles to south end (one-way); around Campbell Island & its satellite islands—1.6 miles; to dam at Champlain Canal Lock C-1—1.8 miles (one-way); to 126th Street Bridge—1.0 mile (one-way)
- **Comments:** Read "Caution" beginning on page xxii and "The Hudson River: Caution" on page 1. Stay a safe distance back from the Lock C-1 dam.
- **Directions:** From Waterford (junction of Rtes. 4 & 32), drive east on Rt. 4 for 0.4 mile, crossing over the Hudson River into Lansingburgh. When you come to the stoplight at the end of the 126th Street Bridge (linking Waterford and Lansingburgh), turn left onto Second Avenue, which becomes River Road, and drive north for 0.7 mile. At the junction of Tampa Avenue (left), Marion Avenue (straight ahead), and the main road (right), proceed straight onto Marion Avenue, now paralleling a stream to your right known as the Paensic Kill. In less than 0.2 mile you will come to the junction of Marion Avenue and River Bend Road. Continue straight on Marion as River Bend Road goes right and you will come to the river's edge within 100 feet. This area, partly in Troy and partly in Schaghticoke, is known as Pleasantdale.

The Paddle:

The launch site lies between a prominent shale outcropping and the Paensic Kill. Take note that you are at a point where the river bends appreciably, veering west momentarily. It was on the twenty-foot-high bluffs next to this site that a young man died in 2008 while jumping into the river. The river can be cruel and unforgiving, even for those engaged in what seems like innocent fun.

North—Head upstream for 1.1 miles to the south tip of Campbell Island. Near the beginning of your paddle you will pass by a series of camps along the west bank, ending at a tiny cove that can be paddled into for several hundred feet. From this point on, the river has a much wilder feel to it. Once you reach Campbell Island, you can continue north for another 0.5 mile, exploring the west side of the island and then paddling around several of the smaller islands that have formed where the river bulges to the east. The area is quiet and peaceful, marred only by huge power lines that span the Hudson over the middle section of Campbell Island, the Momentive Filtration plant (Momentive Performance Materials is the world's second-largest producer of silicones and silicone derivatives) along the river's west shore just below the exit channel from Champlain

Eastern Shore: Rensselaer County

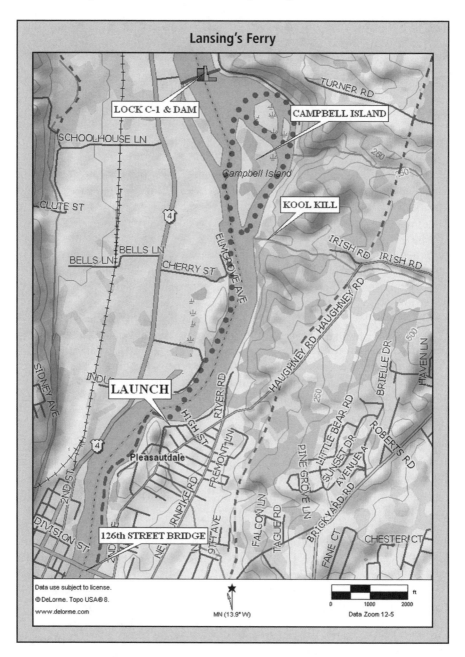

Canal Lock C-1 (where you will see a violent stream of water discharge from a large pipe), and a smattering of houses on River Road before the road dead-ends northeast of Campbell Island. Most noticeable is an eighty-foot-high eroded

► **Lansing's Ferry**

earthen bank above River Road (with a house resting near its top) just southeast of the dam.

Campbell Island is presently leased by the Canal Corporation to the Troy Motor Boat and Canoe Club,[1] which has a dock at the southeast end of the island. Long ago the island was deforested and its fertile lands used for agriculture. Since then Campbell Island has been reclaimed by a forest of fast-growing trees. Campbell Island's highest point, twenty-five feet above the water, is toward the island's northwest end. Campbell Island and its satellite islands can be circumnavigated in 1.6 miles.

Although this pretty area may feel remote today, it wasn't always so. At one time a section of River Road followed along the east bank, but it was abandoned years ago. Now mudslides and blowdown have rendered the road impassable even for 4-wheel-drive vehicles.

As you head south from the tip of Campbell Island, you will immediately pass by the Kool Kill, to your left, which comes down through Thieves Hollow into the Hudson River. It was named after highwaymen who once occupied the hollow.[2] In times past an old roadhouse, earlier known as Camp Coolkill, stood near the river.[3]

In another 0.2 mile you will arrive at a second tributary flowing into the Hudson River from its east bank. One of the largest cottonwood trees in New York State can be found here.

It is another 0.9 mile back to the launch site from this point.

South—Proceed downstream for 1.0 mile to the 126th Street Bridge. As you head downriver, take note of the high bluff along the east bank virtually at the confluence of the Hudson River and the Paensic Kill.

History: This site has a long history, going back to Native Americans who used it as a river ford. The area between 126th Street and Lansing's Ferry contains Native American quarries as well as a former burial site.[4]

This is commonly known as Lansing's Ferry after Jacob Abraham Lansing, who operated a ferry between Half Moon and Pleasantdale until 1804.[5] It has also been called Halfmoon Ferry.[6] During the time that Lansing's ferry was in operation, inns were established on both sides of the river to provide food and lodging to travelers.[7] Later a picnic area known as Lansing's Grove was established nearby.[8]

The village of Lansingburgh is named after Jacob Abraham Lansing, who had the land surveyed and divided into town lots in 1770.[9]

During colonial times, Lansing's Ferry was one of the few places where it was possible to ford the Hudson River. This was because of the river's comparatively shallow depth here, thanks to its location upstream from where the Mohawk River empties into the Hudson. The Mohawk's waters made the Hudson too deep to cross by foot from that point downriver. During the 1690s the area was guarded by the Halfmoon Fort,[10] an outpost established by the British during the

French and Indian War. The fort overlooked the Hudson River roughly one mile above the ford and served as an encampment for 5,000 soldiers. It was from the Halfmoon Fort that General Winslow led his men to secure Fort William Henry while General Amherst captured Fort Ticonderoga.[11]

In January 1776, Henry Knox attempted to make a crossing here with fifty-nine artillery pieces captured from forts along Lake Champlain. The cannons were being dispatched to General George Washington so that Boston, occupied by the British since the Battle of Bunker Hill, could be recaptured. Thin ice at the time made the crossing treacherous.[12]

 **Lansing's Ferry**

Lansingburgh Boat Launch (Lansingburgh)
Across from the Confluence of the Hudson and Mohawk Rivers   **10**

■ **Launch Site:** Lansingburgh Boat Launch in Lansingburgh (Rensselaer County); cement ramp plus 200 feet of dock. Designated Greenway Water Trail Site with port-a-sans, picnicking, fishing, and retail/supplies.

■ **Delorme NYS Atlas & Gazetteer:** p. 67, B4; **Estimated GPS:** 42°47.07'N; 73°40.47'W

■ **Destinations:** Campbell Island, Lock C-1 of Champlain Canal, Peebles Island, 112th Street Bridge, south sprout of Mohawk River, Federal Lock & Dam

■ **Mileage:** To Campbell Island—2.2 miles (one-way); to Lock C-1 of Champlain Canal—3.0 miles (one-way); to Peebles Island—0.2 mile to east side of island (one-way); from middle sprout of Mohawk River to 112th Street Bridge—0.8 mile (one-way); from middle sprout of Mohawk River to south sprout of Mohawk River—1.6 miles (one-way); from middle sprout of Mohawk River to Federal Lock & Dam—2.2 miles (one-way)

■ **Comments:** Read "Caution" beginning on page xxii and "The Hudson River: Caution" on page 1. Stay a safe distance back from the Lock C-1 dam and the Federal Lock & Dam.

■ **Directions:** Approaching Cohoes near the northern terminus of I-787, turn right onto Ontario Street (Rt. 470) and drive east for 0.9 miles, in the process crossing over two sprouts of the Mohawk River and then the Hudson River. When you come to Second Avenue (Rt. 4) at the traffic light, turn left and drive north for 1.0 mile. Turn left onto 123rd Street (look for the green-colored boat launch sign) and drive west for less than 0.1 mile. Turn right into a parking area opposite the end of 1st Street. A cement ramp at the terminus of 123rd Street allows for easy access to the Hudson River.

The Paddle:

North—Head upstream, immediately passing by an old bridge pier to your left that once served as a water supply intake. In 0.2 mile you will pass under the 126th Street Bridge between Waterford and Lansingburgh. In 2.2 miles you will reach the south end of 0.5-mile-long Campbell Island. 3.0 miles represents the turnaround point below Lock C-1 of the Champlain Canal.

West to Peebles Island—Paddle straight across the river for 0.2 mile to the confluence of the Hudson and Mohawk rivers. Do not attempt this unless the weather is calm, no boats are coming from either direction, and you are confident in your abilities to paddle across open water. Waterford will be to your right, Peebles Island slightly to the left, and Van Schaick Island to your far left. From here, the north and middle sprouts of the Mohawk River along Peebles Island can be explored for short distances (see chapter "Peebles Island").

South—Paddle straight across the river for 0.2 mile to the confluence of the Hudson and Mohawk rivers. Do not attempt this unless the weather is calm, no

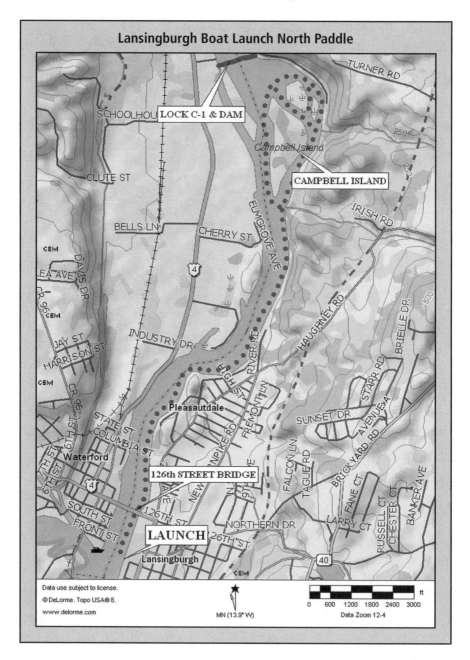

boats are coming from either direction, and you are confident in your abilities to paddle across open water. Head downriver on the Hudson, paralleling the east shore of Van Schaick Island until you reach the 112th Street Bridge in 0.8 mile.

► Lansingburgh Boat Launch

Be sure to look for the historic Matton Shipyard on your right, 0.2 mile after you start down the Hudson River. Watch for the solid pier that extends out into the river and the "way," just before the shipyard, where finished boats would be slid down into the river along metal guide beams.

From the 112th Street Bridge, continue paddling south for another 0.8 mile until you reach the south end of Van Schaick Island, formed by the south sprout of the Mohawk River (see chapter "Peebles Island" for description of paddle up the south sprout of the Mohawk River).

From here it is another 0.6 mile south to the Federal Lock & Dam. Along the way you will pass by tiny Jan Gowson Island (a narrow strip of land)[1] to your right, immediately offshore from Green Island (which is now part of the mainland). Jan Gowson Island can be circumnavigated in 0.4 mile. The island is separated from the mainland by a tiny channel.

The Federal Lock & Dam is the turnaround point.

History: Lansingburgh was alternately called New City and Stone Arabia at the time of the Revolutionary War.[2] It was called New City to differentiate it from Albany, the "old city." The New City of today is a hamlet in Rockland County, and Stone Arabia a village in Montgomery County. Prior to European settlement the area was known by Native Americans as *Tascamcatick*.[3]

The very first bridge across the Hudson River was erected between Waterford and Lansingburgh in 1804. It was called the Union Bridge and measured 797 feet long, 34 feet wide, and contained 4 spans.[4] In 1814 the bridge was covered, a common practice in those days when the wooden structures were vulnerable to the elements. Then, in 1889, an electric trolley line was established across the bridge. This was undoubtedly what ultimately led to the bridge's destruction. In 1909 a fire, likely caused by faulty wire insulation, broke out and consumed the bridge.[5] The stone piers from the 1804 wooden bridge remain in use today.

Herman Melville, author of *Moby Dick* and *Billy Budd*, was a resident of Lansingburgh for part of his life.[6]

Van Schaick Island is named after the Van Schaick family. In the early 1700s Goosen Gerritse Van Schaick built a wooden house just south of the present Van Schaick Mansion. It lasted for only a short length of time. In 1755, Anthony Van Schaick, one of Goosen Gerritse's sons, built the present mansion. By the circumstance of its location, the house became a military headquarters during the French and Indian War, the Revolutionary War, and the War of 1812.[7] Today only the roof of the Van Schaick home can be seen from the Hudson River. It can be visited by driving onto Van Schaick Island and turning south onto Continental Avenue from Route 470. For further information consult vanschaickmansion.org.

The island has been known by a variety of other names as well. Native Americans called it *Quahemesicos*; the Dutch named it Long Island. When Anthony

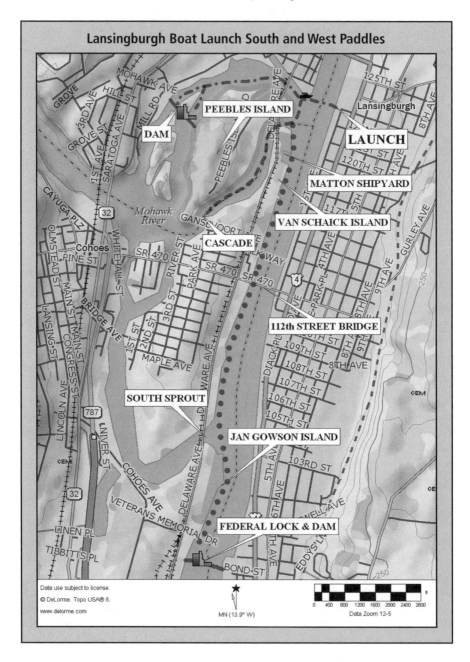

Lansingburgh Boat Launch South and West Paddles

Van Schaick took possession of his father's estate, the island became known as Anthony's Island. Other names include the Isle of Cohoes, Cohoes Island, and Adams' Island.[8]

▶ **Lansingburgh Boat Launch**

The old D & H Railroad Bridge with the Cluett Peabody Factory visible along the east bank of the river. Postcard ca. 1930.

In 1795 the island was the site of an unsuccessful attempt by the Northern Inland Lock Navigation Company to establish a northern canal.[9]

Matton's Shipyard, located near the northeast end of Van Schaick Island, is the remains of a once-thriving boat-building and repair shop run by John E. Matton. Originally the shipyard was located on the old Champlain Canal next to Lock 6 (see chapter "Champlain Canal Paddle #2"), but Matton, seeing new opportunities opening up with the creation of the New York State Barge Canal, relocated to Van Schaick Island to take advantage of its ideal location on the Hudson River by the Mohawk River and the Barge Canal.

Later, when Matton's son Ralph took over the company, the shipyard began building steel tugboats and even ran a towing business. In 1964, a year after Ralph's death, the company was sold to Bart Turecamo, who operated the yard until 1983. In October of 1982, the *Mary Turecamo* was launched, the 345th vessel to be built at the shipyard and the last one to be launched before the shipyard closed.

In 1987 the property was bought by New York State, at which time the shipyard became part of Peebles Island State Park.[10] Today a number of historic buildings can be seen around the shipyard, but many are deteriorating rapidly and only limited time remains for their preservation before they collapse into piles of decaying wood.

The 112th Street Bridge is an attractive, fixed-arch bridge that opened in 1996. It replaced an arched double-draw bascule bridge that was constructed in 1921–1922 by the Joseph Strauss Bridge Company, best known as builders of the Golden Gate Bridge.[11]

111th Street Boat Launch—An unimproved launch site, part of the Greenway Water Trail, can be found at the end of 111th Street in Lansingburgh. From the junction of Rtes. 470 & 4, proceed south for less than 0.1 mile and turn right onto 111th Street. Head west for 0.05 mile to the end of the street, where a small parking area overlooks the river. A short but challenging 50-foot carry down a small embankment brings you to the river's edge, almost directly across from the confluence of the Hudson and Mohawk rivers.

11 Ingalls Avenue Launch (North Troy)
At the End of the Tidal Hudson River

- **Launch Site:** Boat launch at end of Ingalls Avenue in Troy (Rensselaer County); dirt ramp.
- **Delorme NYS Atlas & Gazetteer:** p. 67, BC4; **Estimated GPS:** 42°44.94'N; 73°41.11'W
- **Destinations:** Adams Island, Stony Island, Center Island, Congress Street Bridge, Poesten Kill, Troy-Menands Bridge (Rt. 378)
- **Mileage:** To Adams Island—0.3 mile (one-way); to Stony Island—0.3 mile (one-way); to Center Island—0.4 mile (one-way); around Center Island—1.6 miles; to Congress Street Bridge—1.5 miles (one-way); to Poesten Kill—2.1 miles (one-way); to Troy-Menands Bridge—3.5 miles (one-way)
- **Comments:** Read "Caution" beginning on page xxii and "The Hudson River: Caution" on page 1. Stay a safe distance back from the Federal Dam. The first 0.1 mile of the downstream paddle can be choppy because of the proximity of the Federal Dam 0.2 mile upstream. Look for increased boat traffic near the Troy Town Dock. After early spring's high waters, the river typically leaves behind a considerable amount of debris along the shoreline access as it recedes. Efforts are usually made to clean up the launch site before June.
- **Directions:** From I-787, get off at Exit 9E for Troy, Bennington, and Rt. 7 and cross over the Hudson River, going east on Rt. 7. From the stoplight at the end of the bridge, go uphill for less than 0.1 mile and turn left onto 10th Street (Rt. 40). Drive north for 0.4 mile. At a traffic light turn left onto Middleburgh Street and drive west for 0.4 mile. At River Street (Rt. 4) turn right, drive north for 0.1 mile, and then turn left onto Ingalls Avenue.

  Approaching from Lansingburgh (junction of Rtes. 470 & 4), drive south on Rt. 4 for 1.7 miles and turn right onto Ingalls Avenue.

  From either approach, follow Ingalls Avenue west for less than 0.1 mile, parking off to the side where the road begins going downhill to the river's edge.

The Paddle:

Look upstream for an inspiring view of the Federal Lock & Dam (also called the Troy Lock), 0.2 mile away. It is called the Federal Lock & Dam because federal jurisdiction over the river ends here.[1] The lock is administered by the U. S. Army Corps of Engineers. An abandoned 0.05-mile-long wharf can be seen directly upstream next to the east bank.

The present lock and dam were built in 1916[2] at the time of the New York State Barge Canal's creation. An earlier version, called the Federal Dam and Stoop Lock, was constructed in 1823, approximately one block south of the present site. That dam was 1,100 feet long and 9 feet high.[3]

From the launch site proceed south, downstream. At 0.3 mile you will encounter Adams Island (formerly Big Stony Island) near the east side of the

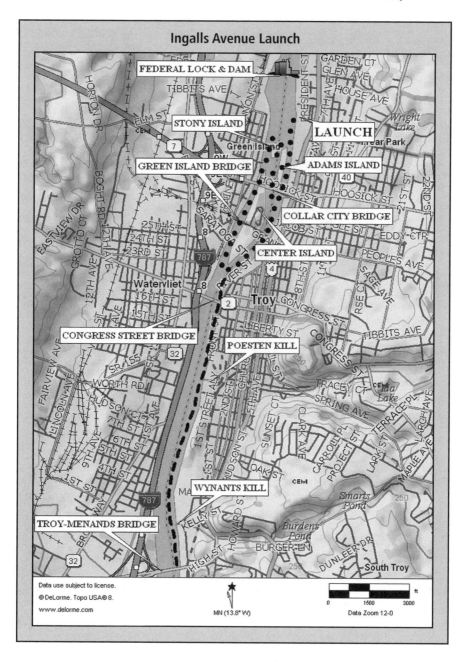

Ingalls Avenue Launch

river, and Stony Island near the west side. Of the two islands, Adams (0.3 mile long) is by far the larger. Downstream from Stony Island and adjacent to the lower section of Adams Island is 0.7-mile-long Center Island (also called

The historic Ford Motor Company plant near the Federal Dam. Postcard ca. 1940.

Starbuck Island and Fish Island in the past), which the Collar City Bridge (Route 7) and Green Island Bridge cross over. The southern half of the island has been built up with new homes and apartments. The west side of Center Island is perfect for paddling, since its shallow waters are sufficient to discourage most motorboats from entering. At low tide, however, the shallows can turn into mudflats and become impassable even for paddlers.

Across the river, downstream from the Green Island Bridge, is the Troy Town Dock, whose 1,400-foot-long floating face dock is intended for the mooring of boats larger than a canoe or kayak.

Continue paddling down to and around the southern tip of Center Island and back to the launch site, a trip of roughly 2.5 miles. Or, if you wish, you can continue south from the south end of Center Island. In 0.3 mile from Center Island, you will pass under the Congress Street Bridge, which connects Troy with Watervliet. In 0.8 mile you will pass by the Poesten Kill, coming in from the east bank (at high tide it is possible to paddle up the stream for several hundred feet). In 2.7 miles you will arrive at the Troy-Menands Bridge. As you paddle this stretch of the river, bear in mind that the flatlands occupied by lower Troy were once called *Paanpaak* by the Mohicans, meaning "field of standing corn." The Mohicans had a stockaded village near the current south end of Lansingburgh.[4]

▶ **Ingalls Avenue Launch**

History: The Federal Lock & Dam marks the head of tidewater navigation, the point 158 miles from the Atlantic Ocean where Hudson River tides cease. The Troy Government Lock is the largest lock in the canal system, measuring 492 feet long and 44 feet wide (compared to the average-sized lock, which is 300 feet long and 43 feet wide).[5]

The building on the west bank next to the Federal Dam is a still-operating hydroelectric plant built by Thomas Edison over 100 years ago. There are plans to revamp it in the future. The site was chosen by Henry Ford after visiting Green Island in 1922.[6] The Ford Motor Company automobile assembly plant, which once operated nearby, was taken down several years ago.

The Route 7 Collar City Bridge (also called the Hoosick Street Bridge) was erected in 1981 to carry traffic from I-787 over to Troy.

The present Green Island Bridge is the latest incarnation of several that crossed over the Hudson River between Troy and Watervliet. The first bridge was built by the Rensselaer & Saratoga Railroad in 1835. In 1862, sparks from a passing locomotive ignited the covered bridge's shingled roof. High winds then swept the flaming tinder into the city, causing the Great Troy Fire of 1862 in which more than 507 buildings were consumed. The second bridge was erected by the Delaware & Hudson Railroad in 1884, and rebuilt in 1925. When rail operations ceased in 1963, the bridge was converted to automobile traffic. After floodwaters caused that bridge to collapse in 1977,[7] the present Green Island Bridge was erected in 1981 at a cost of $22.1 million (which included the cost of removing the old structure).[8]

There have been three Congress Street Bridges over the last two centuries. The first bridge opened in 1874 and the second in 1917. The current bridge was opened to the public in 1971.[9]

According to John Klein's 1818 map of Troy, Center Island was originally called Fish Island. The name changed temporarily to Starbuck Island when a number of buildings were erected on the island in 1853–1854[10] by George H. Starbuck. The area of open space at the north end of the island served as a baseball field during the late 1800s.

During a huge freshet in 1647, whose rising waters flooded and nearly washed away Fort Orange (Albany), several whales made their way up the Hudson River to as far as Troy. It was reported that a white whale ended up beached on an island that became known as Walvisch (Whale Fish) Island. That island no longer exists; it was destroyed when the Federal Lock and Dam were created.[11] The story may later have inspired Herman Melville, who grew up in the Capital Region, when he wrote *Moby Dick*.

Atop the east bank and overlooking the river and Troy is the Rensselaer Polytechnic Institute (RPI), the oldest technological university in the nation. It was founded in 1829 by Stephen Van Rensselaer.[12]

12

Madison Street Launch (South Troy)
Near the Poesten Kill   (to open in late 2010)

■ **Launch Site:** West end of Madison Street in South Troy (Rensselaer County); launch to be established next to fishing pier in 2010

■ **Delorme NYS Atlas & Gazetteer:** p. 66, C4; **Estimated GPS:** 42°43.17'N; 73°41.93'W

■ **Destinations:** Congress Street Bridge, Center Island, Troy-Menands Bridge

■ **Mileage:** To Congress Street Bridge—0.7 mile (one-way); to Center Island—1.0 mile (one-way); to Troy-Menands Bridge—1.3 miles (one-way)

■ **Comments:** Read "Caution" beginning on page xxii and "The Hudson River: Caution" on page 1. Be prepared for an increase in boat traffic from the marina at the south end of Center Island and from the riverfront wharf in Troy.

■ **Directions:** Driving north on I-787 from Albany, take Exit 7E-W (South Troy, Watervliet, & Rt. 378). Cross over the Hudson River and continue on Rt. 378 until you come to the second traffic light, at Rt. 4. Proceed straight, following Rt. 4 north for over 0.2 mile. At a fork in the road, veer left onto 1st Street. In less than 0.1 mile bear right onto 2nd Street (now a one-way street) and proceed north for 0.7 mile. When you come to Madison Street, turn left and drive west for 0.2 mile. Park to your left at the end of the road.

From Troy (junction of Rt. 2 & 1st Street), drive south on 1st Street for 0.7 mile. When you come to Madison Street, turn right and head west for 0.1 mile. Park to your left at the end of the road.

From either direction, the kayak launch will be to the left of the fishing pier at the end of the road.

The Paddle:

North—Heading upriver, you will pass by the Poesten Kill on your right at 0.1 mile. At high tide the Poesten Kill can be navigated upstream for several hundred feet. Continuing on the river past the Poesten Kill, at 0.7 mile, you will pass under the Congress Street Bridge. Hudson Shores Park is to your left. You will reach the south end of Center Island at 1.0 mile. Center Island, along with its satellite islands, can be explored further if you wish (see "Hudson Shores Park" chapter).

South—Proceeding downriver, you will pass by the Wynants Kill coming in on your left at 1.0 mile. The stream was the site of the famous Burden Iron Works. The Troy-Menands Bridge is reached at 1.3 miles.

History: The fishing pier at the terminus of Madison Street was just recently erected. In 2010 an eco-dock for non-motorized craft will be constructed to the left (south) of the pier.

The building just north of the parking area is a former foundry that produced horseshoes. In the future it will be razed or refurbished, and the site will then be occupied by the Beacon Institute for Rivers and Estuaries.[1] The abandoned

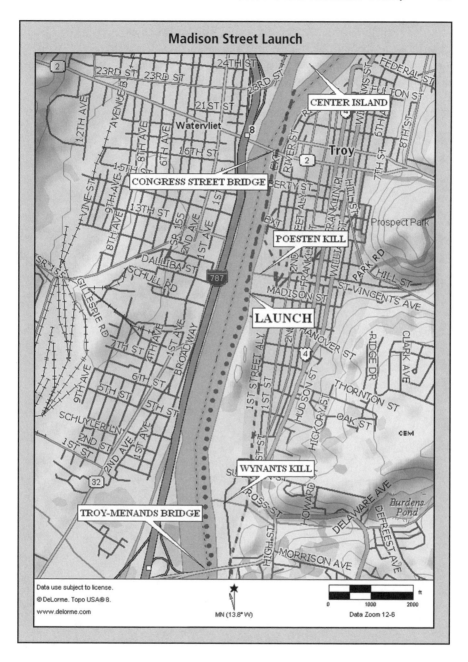

Madison Street Launch

building just south of the parking lot formerly belonged to Bruno Machinery Corporation, manufacturers of heavy machinery. They have since relocated to Albany near the Albany Pine Bush area.

The Burden Iron Works Museum (hudsonrivervalley.com/SiteDetail. aspx?ID=83), located nearby on One East Industrial Parkway, is well worth a visit while exploring the river so that you can gain a greater appreciation of Troy's industrial history and, in particular, how the Wynants Kill was used to power the Burden Iron Works. Appointments can be scheduled by calling (518) 274-5267. A modest admission fee is charged.

Steamboats were once a common sight along the Hudson River. Postcard ca. 1900.

▶ **Madison Street Launch**

Rensselaer Boat Launch (Rensselaer)
Access to the Hudson River

13

- **Launch Site:** Rensselaer Boat Launch off of Forbes Avenue in Rensselaer (Rensselaer County); wide cement ramp, short floating walkway leading to dock. Designated Greenway Water Trail Site with lockable kayak storage racks, picnicking, and train service nearby.
- **Delorme NYS Atlas & Gazetteer:** p. 66, CD3–4; **GPS:** 42°39.52′N; 73°44.07′W
- **Destinations:** Patroon Island Bridge (I-90), Troy-Menands Bridge (Rt. 387), west bank and cove, Dunn Memorial Bridge (Rt. 20)
- **Mileage:** To Patroon Island Bridge—0.5 mile (one-way); to Troy-Menands Bridge—3.3 miles (one-way); to west bank and cove—0.6 mile (one-way); to Dunn Memorial Bridge—1.2 miles (one-way)
- **Comments:** Read "Caution" beginning on page xxii and "The Hudson River: Caution" on page 1. Be prepared for an increase in boat traffic near the Albany Municipal Launching Ramp at the Corning Preserve Riverfront Park.
- **Directions:** From I-787 take Exit 3 for Rensselaer/Empire State Plaza. Head east toward Rensselaer, exiting at the sign for "Rail Station & Broadway." When you come to the traffic light at Broadway, turn left and drive north for over 1.0 mile. At Tracy Street turn left and drive west for 0.05 mile. Turn right onto Forbes Avenue and proceed north for over 0.05 mile, bearing left into the Hilton Industrial Park where a green-colored boat launch sign points the way. Turn left and cross over railroad tracks to reach the Rensselaer Boat Launch. Park in the large area to the right of the launch.

    From I-90 take Exit 7. Turn southwest onto Washington Avenue and drive over 0.2 mile until you reach Forbes Avenue. Turn right and go downhill for 0.5 mile, then turn sharply right, drive past the Hilton Center, cross over the railroad tracks, and you will be at the Rensselaer Boat Launch. Park in the large area to the right of the launch.

The Paddle:

Before pushing off, take a moment to appreciate the spectacle of the Albany skyline across the river to your southwest and the towering Patroon Island Bridge, upriver to the northeast. Be prepared for the constant drone of cars traveling along I-787 while undertaking this paddle. You will observe many walkers and bicyclists along the Mohawk-Hudson Bikeway, which parallels the west shore.

From Albany to Troy, a mean water depth of fifteen feet is maintained to ensure that the river is commercially navigable for large boats (but not ocean liners) as far upstream as Troy.

North—Follow the east shoreline upriver. You will reach the Patroon Island Bridge—an imposing structure—in 0.5 mile. Continuing north you will come to a red-colored navigational tower (#224) to your right at 1.0 mile. Less than 0.1 mile beyond is a tiny cove that goes east for over 100 feet. Old

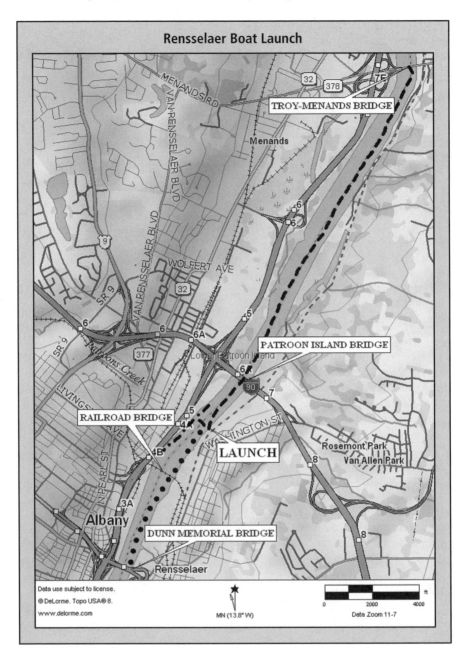

maps show that this tiny inlet of water once extended northeast for nearly 0.4 mile. Just past the cove, huge cement slabs line the shoreline, creating an effective dike.

▶ Rensselaer Boat Launch

The Patroon Island Bridge looms high above the Hudson River. Photograph 2009.

If you continue farther upriver, you will pass under high-tension lines at 1.8 miles, with a water treatment plant along the east bank coming into view within another 0.1 mile. You will reach the Troy-Menands Bridge in 3.3 miles.

West—Paddle rapidly across the river to reach the opposite shore. Do not attempt this unless the weather is calm, no boats are coming from either direction, and you are confident in your abilities to paddle across open waters. If you head 0.2 mile upriver, you will come to a man-made channel that can be followed west for 100 feet. Likely this channel was used at one time as a tiny port for unloading boats.

Head downriver for less than 0.4 mile and you will come to a green navigational tower (#223) at the south tip of a tiny cove. Paddle into this cove to go north for several hundred feet.

South—Paddle downstream for 1.2 miles until you reach the Dunn Memorial Bridge. Along the way you will pass under a railroad bridge at 0.4 mile. (See chapter "Corning Preserve" for more details on this paddle.)

History: The launch site is located in the former village of Bath-on-Hudson, now part of the City of Rensselaer. This community was the terminus of a 1773 colonial road from Deerfield, Massachusetts. From here a ferry then crossed the Hudson River to Albany. In 1802 the colonial road became the Eastern Turnpike.[1]

Several of the piers supporting the Patroon Island Bridge rest on Lower Patroon Island (now part of the mainland), which is how the bridge came to be named. The bridge opened in 1970 at a cost of $12 million, replacing an earlier version built in 1932.[2]

The Troy-Menands Bridge was built in 1933.[3] There is talk now about replacing it in the near future.

14 **Riverfront Park (Rensselaer)**
Accessing a Section of the Hudson River between Two Cities

■ **Launch Site:** Riverfront Park in Rensselaer (Rensselaer County); 200-foot carry to riverside dock. Designated Greenway Water Trail Site with port-a-sans and nearby train service.

■ **Delorme NYS Atlas & Gazetteer:** p. 66, CD3–4; **Estimated GPS:** 42°38.55'N; 73°44.78'W

■ **Destinations:** Patroon Island Bridge, Mill Creek, Normans Kill

■ **Mileage:** To Patroon Island Bridge—1.8 miles (one-way); up Mill Creek—0.2 mile (round-trip); to Normans Kill—2.6 miles (one-way)

■ **Comments:** Read "Caution" beginning on page xxii and "The Hudson River: Caution" on page 1. Be prepared for heavy boat traffic as you approach the Port of Albany. Watch out for large vessels and barges, particularly as they turn in the river to head downstream. Expect an increase in boat traffic near the Albany Yacht Club, Rensselaer Boat Launch, and Albany Municipal Launching Ramp at the Corning Preserve Riverfront Park.

■ **Directions:** From I-787 take Exit 3 for Rensselaer/Empire State Plaza. Crossing east over the river, head toward Rensselaer, exiting at the sign for "Rail Station & Broadway." When you come to the traffic light at Broadway, turn left and drive north for less than 100 feet.

From the east, driving northwest on Rtes. 20/9 through Rensselaer toward Albany, turn right onto Broadway just before reaching the Hudson River. Drive north for 0.4 mile.

From either approach, turn left off Broadway onto 5th Avenue and drive west for less than 0.2 mile to a secondary parking area located directly under the Dunn Memorial Bridge. Put in at the dock 200 feet south of the bridge (accessible by a paved walkway).

The Paddle:

Look across the river during tourist season and you will see the *USS Slater* moored next to the west bank; above it looms the majestic Albany skyline. The large monastery-like building just north of the bridge is the headquarters of the State University of New York (SUNY). Modeled after the guild halls in Belgium, the building was designed to conceal the State Capitol, farther up the hill.[1]

North—Head upriver for 1.8 miles until you reach the Patroon Island Bridge. Along the way are views of Albany to the left and Rensselaer to the right. Until it was incorporated as a city in 1897, Rensselaer was known as Greenbush, from the Dutch word *Greenbosch*, meaning "green woods."[2]

Southeast—Paddle downriver for 0.1 mile and then turn left up Mill Creek, following the creek east for 0.1 mile through Riverfront Park. Further progress is abruptly halted at the Broadway bridge, where a five-foot-high dam is

▶ **Riverfront Park**

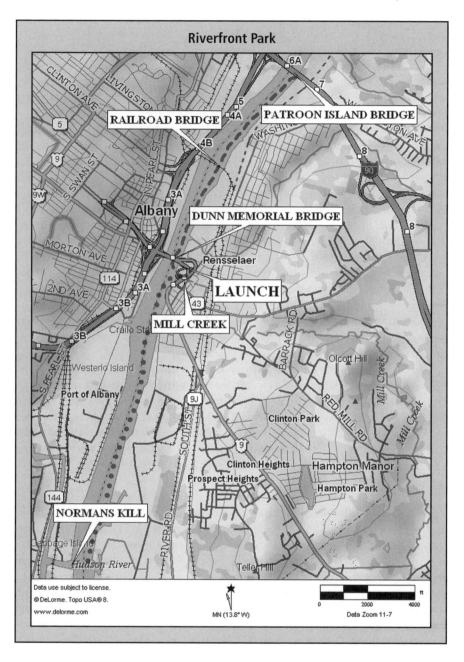

Riverfront Park

encountered. At the Capital View Office Park Buildings along Washington Street, 0.05 mile farther upstream, the stream goes temporarily out of sight beneath several of the buildings. Mill Creek rises from west of Snyder's Lake and produces

Mannix Falls (a tiny cascade) and Red Mill Falls (an impressive, much larger cascade). Both falls are on private property and therefore inaccessible, however.

Just farther downriver, 0.4 mile south of the Dunn Memorial Bridge, is the Albany Yacht Club, which relocated from Albany to the east side of the river around 1955.[3] At 0.6 mile you will pass by Fort Crailo (an eighteenth-century house) to your left, which faces the river from Riverside Avenue.

If you wish, you can continue paddling downstream south for 2.6 miles until you see, looking across the river, the mouth of the Normans Kill along the west bank.

History: The Dunn Memorial Bridge, connecting Rensselaer with Albany, is one of eight bridges spanning the Hudson between Albany and the Federal Lock & Dam at Troy. The bridge was named after Private Parker F. Dunn, an Albany native and WWI war hero. There have been previous bridges at this spot. The present bridge opened for traffic in 1969[4] and replaced one known as "lower bridge." During the winter people would skate on makeshift ice rinks near that bridge while band concerts held on the ice provided melodious accompaniment.[5]

In July 2005 the Dunn Memorial Bridge achieved momentary notoriety when an underlying support failed, causing a section of the ramp near I-787 to drop a foot. Miraculously, no one was killed.

In recent times the Dunn Memorial Bridge's undercarriage has become the home of a pair of nesting peregrine falcons. Peregrine falcons are noted for their extensive range of territory, having been found everywhere in the world except Antarctica. Falcons move incredibly fast and have been clocked diving at speeds of close to 200 MPH to seize prey. A video of the nesting falcons is available in the spring at the Empire State Plaza and on the NYS Department of Environmental Conservation's Web site. A history of the project is available at dec.ny.gov/animals/7695.html.

The *USS Slater* is a WWII cannon-class destroyer commissioned to escort ships across the Atlantic and Pacific oceans to defend against enemy submarines and airplanes. Out of 563 destroyer escorts built during WWII, the *USS Slater* is the only one that has survived into the twenty-first century.

In 1951 the *USS Slater* was retired by the U.S. Navy and, under the Mutual Defense Pact, given to the Greek Navy. Forty years later the vessel was decommissioned by the Greeks and, in 1993, returned to the United States, where it remained in New York City as part of the Intrepid Sea-Air Space Ship Museum until 1999, when a spot for it at the Port of Albany was secured. The vessel was named after Frank O. Slater, a sailor killed during the 1942 Battle of Guadalcanal while aboard the *USS San Francisco*.[6]

The destroyer played a cameo role in the film *The Guns of Navarone*, has been featured in a number of History Channel documentaries, and was cast in a Japanese World War II film produced in 2008 originally called *Orion in the*

▶ **Riverfront Park**

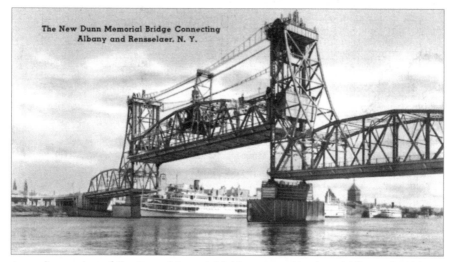

The New Dunn Memorial Bridge Connecting
Albany and Rensselaer. N. Y.

An earlier version of the Dunn Memorial Bridge opened in the middle to allow the passage of large boats. Postcard ca. 1940.

Midsummer[7] and since retitled *Battle under Orion*. For more information about the *USS Slater*, go to ussslater.org. Tours are offered from April–November, 10 AM–4 PM, Wednesday–Sunday and major holidays. Access to the ship is from the end of Madison Avenue, at 141 Broadway in Albany.

Fort Crailo is an imposing three-story house built in the early eighteenth century by Hendrick Van Rensselaer, grandson of the first Van Rensselaer patroon. Crailo, spelled Crayloo and Cralo in the seventeenth century, is Dutch for "crows' wood."[8] The house and grounds were used intermittently to quarter troops during both the French and Indian War and the Revolutionary War. It was at Fort Crailo that British surgeon Richard Shuckburgh reputedly wrote the lyrics to "Yankee Doodle,"[9] a song meant to poke fun at the "bumbling" colonials, but which, in an ironic turnabout, was embraced by the Americans and became one of their rousing fighting songs.

By the 1840s the house was being used as a boys' boarding school. Later it served as a church rectory. In 1924 the house was donated to New York State and has become the Crailo State Historic Site (nysparks.state.ny.us/sites/info.asp?siteID=7)—a museum for preserving colonial New Netherlands history in the upper Hudson Valley. The fort is one of about 100 sites in the Hudson River Valley National Heritage Area (hudsonrivervalley.com).

<table>
<tr><td>**15**</td><td>**Papscanee Island Nature Preserve (Stony Point)**
From a Quiet Nature Preserve into the Busy River</td></tr>
</table>

■ **Launch Site:** Papscanee Island Nature Preserve, south entrance (Rensselaer County); 0.3-mile carry to Hudson River, informal slip-in at shoreline. Open April 1–October 30. Designated Greenway Water Trail Site with picnicking, trails, swimming, and fishing.

■ **Delorme NYS Atlas & Gazetteer:** p. 66, D3–4; **Estimated GPS:** 42°34.34'N; 73°44.98'W

■ **Destinations:** Normans Kill, Papscanee Creek

■ **Mileage:** To Normans Kill—2.4 miles (one-way); to Papscanee Creek—2.2 miles (one-way)

■ **Comments:** Read "Caution" beginning on page xxii and "The Hudson River: Caution" on page 1. Be prepared for heavy boat traffic as you approach the Port of Albany. Watch out for large vessels and barges, particularly as they turn in the river to head downstream. When venturing up Papscanee Creek, be prepared for mild to moderate current. If the tide is going out, turn around at the derelict bridge, roughly 1.0 mile upstream, to avoid the upper section of Papscanee Creek, which can become impassable at low tide. Be mindful that a wooden bulkhead with upthrusting steel rebars spans the bay at the mouth of Papscanee Creek. Except at high tide, you will need to carefully negotiate your way through a short open section to venture up Papscanee Creek. A canoe/kayak carrier would be helpful to reach the put-in.

■ **Directions:** From Castleton-on-Hudson (junction of Rtes. 9J & 150), drive north on Rt. 9J for 3.0 miles. Turn left onto Staats Island Road.

From Rensselaer (junction of Rtes. 9/20 & 9J), drive south on Rt. 9J for roughly 4.2 miles and turn right onto Staats Island Road.

From either direction, drive west on Staats Road for 0.5 mile. As soon as you cross over railroad tracks (look carefully for high-speed Amtrak trains,) turn right into the entrance of the small parking area for the preserve. From the parking area, follow the red-blazed trail northwest to reach the Hudson River in less than 0.3 mile.

The Paddle:

There are continuous views of private residences across the river as you make your way along the Hudson's east shoreline. Many of these homes are quite palatial. Some are set back from the river with long sloping lawns extending down to the waterfront.

North—Proceeding upstream, you will pass by Van Wies Point—identified by a bluff of rock along the west bank—in 0.5 mile. At 1.6 miles you will go past the Bethlehem Energy Center (BEC) to your left. Look for the imposing red-brick structure, the three smoke stacks, and the high-tension power lines crossing the river just to the north. The BEC began energy production in 2005, replacing the Albany Steam Station, which had operated from 1952 to 2002.[1]

▶ **Papscanee Island Nature Preserve**

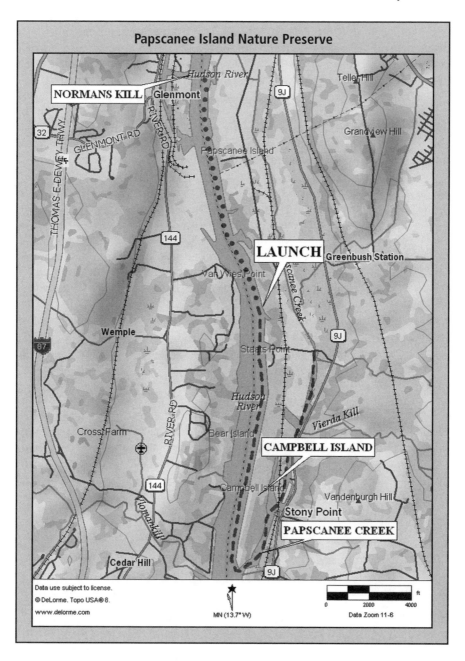

Papscanee Island Nature Preserve

At roughly 2.0 miles you will float over what was once the Overslaugh Bar. At 2.4 miles you will reach the mouth of the Normans Kill, coming in on the west side of the Hudson.

If you were to continue farther north, you would soon approach the ports of Albany and Rensselaer. Both sides of the Hudson River are heavily industrialized along this stretch, loaded with refineries and warehouses. Great care must be taken to avoid large commercial vessels if you venture into this area.

South—Heading downstream, you will pass by Staats Point in less than 0.1 mile, where a tiny cove can be seen. Look for the imposing eight-foot-high pile of rocks a hundred feet from the shore, with light #212 set on top. In 2.2 miles you will come to the mouth of Papscanee Creek, which can be explored upstream for up to 2.5 miles, conditions permitting (see "Papscanee Creek" chapter).

History: To ensure the protection of this unique area of riverfront land from future development, a number of interlocking parcels of land were purchased by the Open Space Institute between 1993 and 1995. The 156-acre Papscanee Island Nature Preserve now contains six miles of trails and approximately two miles of Hudson River shoreline. In 1996 a small parking lot was established off of Staats Island Road to provide ready access to the preserve. Initial funding for the preserve was made possible through the Lila Wallace–Reader's Digest Fund, set up by the founders of Reader's Digest.[2] In 1997 the Rensselaer County Environmental Management Council (RCEMC), under the auspices of the county legislature, joined with the Open Space Institute and now oversees and manages the preserve.[3] The trails are dedicated to the memory of Martin G. "Mickey" Mahar (1950–2003), who was director of the country's Environmental Management Council and a staunch supporter of the preserve.

The Mahicans were the first to farm the rich floodplain, occupying the area until 1637, at which time they sold the land to Kiliaen Van Rensselaer. Europeans have farmed the land ever since, and continue to do so at the island's northern end,[4] making it one of the oldest tracts of continuously farmed lands in the United States.[5] Papscanee Island was once favored for producing wheat.[6] The word "Papscanee" comes from a Native American named Papsichene, a dominant sachem in the region.[7]

Staat Point is named after the Staat family, who occupied the land in 1688. The Staat home, visible from the river, is one of the oldest homes on the Hudson River.[8]

Van Wies Point is named after Hendrick Gerritse Van Wie, a Dutch colonist who came to Fort Orange in 1664 and built a house in 1679 at what is now Van Wies Point.[9] Prior to the twentieth century and further dredging of the Hudson River, the point was a popular docking area for passengers on medium-sized boats endeavoring to reach Albany.[10] Back then, ice would tend to lodge at this point, forming a temporary dam in the river until spring.[11]

The Overslaugh Bar (also called the Castleton Bar) was a major low-tide impediment to early navigation.[12] One source claims it wasn't unusual to see as many as fifty boats caught up on the hidden sandbar at one time.[13] Today you will float right over this site, thanks to the area having been repeatedly dredged and deepened.

▶ **Papscanee Island Nature Preserve**

Papscanee Creek (Stony Point)
The Hudson River's Northernmost Wetland

16

■ **Launch Site:** Informal access to Papscanee Creek off of Rt. 9J between Rensselaer and Castleton-on-Hudson (Rensselaer County); the steep, weedy bank on both sides of the derelict bridge makes for a challenging put-in. Beware of poison ivy. Be sure to park along the side of the road to leave sufficient room for firefighters, who access the river here to refill their water tanks.

■ **Delorme NYS Atlas & Gazetteer:** p. 66, D4; **Estimated GPS:** 42°33.35'N 73°44.77'W

■ **Destinations:** Papscanee Creek, Moordener Kill

■ **Mileage:** Down Papscanee Creek—0.9 mile to Hudson River (one-way); up Papscanee Creek—1.3 miles, depending upon tidal conditions (one-way); up Moordener Kill from Hudson River—0.3 mile (one-way)

■ **Comments:** Read "Caution" beginning on page xxii. When heading out onto the creek, choose a calm day and watch the weather. The current is generally mild to moderate. The wind tends to be quietest in the early morning and evening. Heading downstream, watch out for the wooden bulkhead with upthrusting steel rebars that spans the bay away from the mouth of Papscanee Creek. You will need to carefully negotiate your way through a short open section (except at high tide) if you plan to go out onto the Hudson River. If you do enter the Hudson, see "The Hudson River: Caution" on page 1. Head upstream to explore the northern section of Papscanee Creek with the approach of high tide. Check tides at: tidesandcurrents.noaa.gov. At low tide the northern reach can turn into mudflats. While planning your trek, take note that there may be insufficient clearance under the abandoned steel I-beam bridge at high tide. Like Papscanee Creek, the Moordener Kill is also affected by the tides and is best paddled at high tide.

■ **Directions:** From Castleton-on-Hudson (junction of Rtes. 9J & 150), drive north for 1.8 miles (or 0.3 mile north past Stony Point Road) and turn left.

From Rensselaer (junction of Rtes. 20/9 & 9J), drive south on Rt. 9J for 5.3 mile and turn right.

From either direction, follow a short, abandoned road west. The road ends within 100 feet at an old bridge that has been reduced to girders.

The Paddle:

Although Papscanee Creek runs both north and south from the bridge, the easier paddle by far is to head south, following a creek that can be surprisingly wide during high tide.

South—Paddle downstream for 0.3 mile, then bear right and go under the Amtrak railroad bridge. You are now at the south end of Papscanee Island (once called Staat's Island), where Campbell Island, up ahead, was once separated from Papscanee Island but is now attached. A tiny stream named Campbell

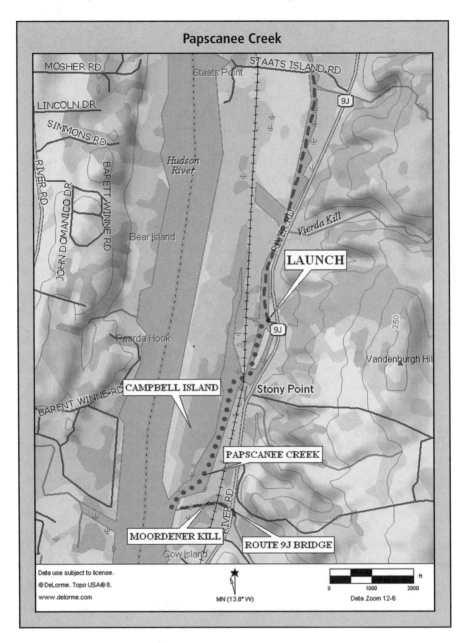

Creek inserts itself between the two islands for a short distance and invites brief exploration, possibly for as far north as 0.3 mile.

Here, lower Papscanee Creek becomes enormously wide, easily several hundreds of feet across, and feels more like a part of the Hudson River (which it now

▶ **Papscanee Creek**

is) than the unassuming creek from which it came. If you continue south along Papscanee Creek from the Amtrak bridge for 0.6 mile, you will come to the Hudson River. Take note along the way of the numerous duck blinds that are partially concealed in the thickets along the east bank to your left.

When you come out to the Hudson River, the Henry Hudson Town Park and the New York State Bethlehem Fishing Access Launch (see chapter "NYS Bethlehem Fishing Access Launch") will be visible across the river along the west bank. The Bethlehem Fishing Access Launch provides an alternate way of reaching the mouth of Papscanee Creek, but requires crossing the Hudson River to do so. Be aware that the wooden bulkhead with protruding steel rebar of the old Cow Island dike can present an obstacle except at high tide, when you can float over it.

Just barely visible 2.5 miles downriver are the distant outlines of the mile-long Castleton-on-Hudson and Alfred H. Smith bridges.

To explore further, follow the Hudson downriver from Papscanee Creek for a couple of hundred feet until you come to the outflow from the Moordener Kill, on your left. Like Papscanee Creek, the Moordener Kill is tidal and can be explored for 0.3 mile of its length. Turn left and follow the Moordener Kill east upstream, staying close to the north bank at the beginning of the paddle to avoid meandering into a dead end on your right. In less than 0.2 mile you will pass under another Amtrak bridge and then, farther upstream, under Route 9J. As soon as you clear the Route 9J bridge take note of the remnants of a former bridge abutment to your right. From here the paddle quickly comes to an end as you encounter shallow water and driftwood.

North—Paddle upstream from the put-in for up to 1.3 miles, at which time Papscanee Creek dead-ends at Staats Island Road. Be prepared to encounter increasing thickets of aquatic weeds the farther north you go. This section of Papscanee Creek has a more claustrophobic feel to it than its southern component and should only be explored during high tide.

History: Papscanee Creek is a fairly unobtrusive stream, rising to prominence principally through its close association with the Hudson River. The stream parallels Route 9J to the east and the Hudson River to the west, flowing south from Prospect Heights to north of Castleton-on-Hudson. It is fed by two small creeks. Papscanee Creek currently separates Campbell, Pixtaway, and Papscanee islands from the mainland. The creek has also been called Dead Creek,[1] presumably because of its stagnant, seemingly motionless waters.

The creek is the northeasternmost navigable wetland in the Hudson River estuary—an ideal resting place for migratory waterfowl such as mallards, black ducks, teals, wood ducks, and pintails, and for nesting during mating season. It is also a spawning ground for anadromous fish such as herring, white perch, American shad, and blueback herring.[2]

The Moordener Kill is a medium-sized stream that rises near Sand Lake and passes by the former Fort Orange Paper Company at the edge of Castleton-on-Hudson. The stream acquired its name from a colonial murder, when a young girl was supposedly dragged to her death by Indians on horseback.[3] The Moordener Kill possesses a number of waterfalls farther upstream. The Fort Orange Paper Company, which made postcards in its early days, was founded in 1881.[4]

Prior to the dredging of the Hudson, the worst gravel bars in the river were found just below Castleton.[5]

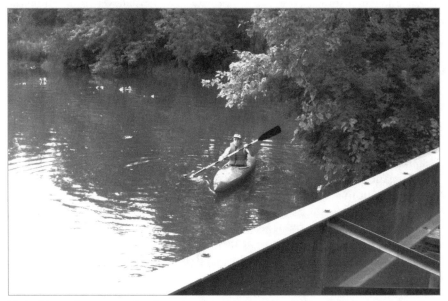

High tide on Papscanee Creek at the abandoned bridge access. Photograph 2008.

▶ **Papscanee Creek**

Schodack Island (Castleton-on-Hudson)
Access to Hudson River & Schodack Creek

17

■ **Launch Site:** Schodack Island State Park near Castleton-on-Hudson (Rensselaer County). Schodack Creek access—parking for up to five cars, 0.1-mile carry to floating dock. Hudson River access—parking for up to sixty-five cars & trailers, wide cement ramp with walkways on both sides. Designated Greenway Water Trail Site with lockable kayak storage racks, restrooms, picnicking, trails, fishing, hunting, bird watching, and a water trail kiosk.

Modest daily fees are charged from Memorial Day through Labor Day; fees are charged on weekends only from May to Memorial Day and from Labor Day to Columbus Day. No entrance fees from Columbus Day to May. For more information: Schodack Island State Park, (518) 732-0187, nysparks.com.

■ **Delorme NYS Atlas & Gazetteer:** p. 52, A3; **Estimated GPS:** Schodack Creek—42°30.21'N; 73°46.14'W; GPS: Boat Launch—42°30.01'N; 73°46.56'W

■ **Destinations:** Hudson River, Schodack Creek, Binnen Kill

■ **Mileage:** Down Schodack Creek to south tip of Houghtaling Island—5.0 miles (one-way); up Schodack Creek to beyond Rt. 9J bridge—1.3 miles (one-way); down Hudson River to south tip of Houghtaling Island—5.0 miles (one-way); up Hudson River to Moordener Kill and Papscanee Creek—3.0 miles (one-way); across Hudson River to Binnen Kill—0.2 mile (one-way); up Binnen Kill—0.2–0.8 mile (one-way), depending upon water level

■ **Comments:** Read "Caution" beginning on page xxii and "The Hudson River: Caution" on page 1. *Schodack Creek*—The current is generally mild. Short portages may be required if blowdown is encountered farther upstream where Schodack Creek turns into the Muitzes Kill. Schodack Creek is passable on most of its length even at low tide, but to be sure check tides at: tidesandcurrents. noaa.gov. *Hudson River*—Be prepared for possible boat traffic from the little marina across the river.

■ **Directions:** From the blinking light at Stuyvesant, drive north on Rt. 9J for 9.3 miles. Before entering the village of Castleton-on-Hudson, turn left onto Schodack Island Way.

From Castleton-on-Hudson (junction of Rtes. 9J & 150), drive south on Rt. 9J for 1.0 mile and turn right onto Schodack Island Way.

Drive south on Schodack Island Way for 1.2 miles until you come to the contact station. In doing so you will pass under the Alfred H. Smith Railroad Bridge (named after a former president of the New York Central Railroad)[1] and the 5,330-foot-long Castleton-on-Hudson Bridge (which carries the eastbound section of the NYS Thruway toward the Berkshires and the Massachusetts Turnpike) approximately 0.1 mile before reaching the contact station. The Castleton-on-Hudson Bridge rises to a height of 144 feet above the river. It was opened in 1959 at a cost of $17 million.[2] The concrete and steel Alfred H. Smith Bridge[3] was built between 1926 and 1928 at a cost of $20 million. Like

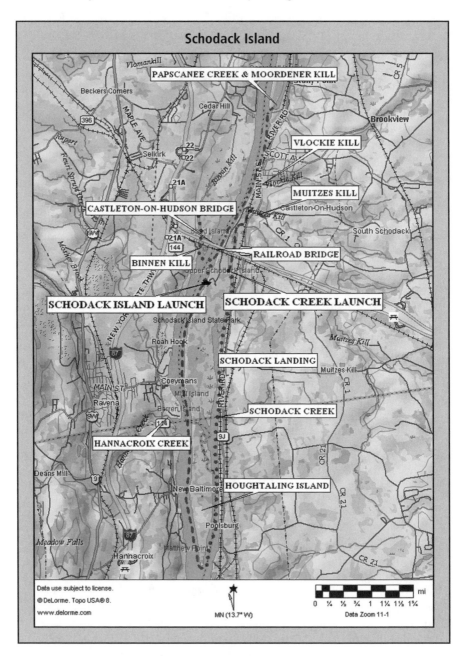

the Castleton-on-Hudson Bridge, it is over a mile long[4] and crosses over not only the Hudson River, but Shad Island, the Binnen Kill, and Schodack Creek as well.

▶ Schodack Island

To access launch site on Schodack Creek—From the contact station, proceed south on Schodack Island Way for 0.2 mile and park to your left in a well-groomed pull-off by a kiosk. Follow a wide, yellow-blazed trail east for 0.1 mile. When you come to an open area, bear left. At a second kiosk either slide your canoe/kayak down to the bottom of a small hill via a specially constructed slide, or continue left down the road for another couple of hundred feet to the edge of the creek. At the bottom, a metal walkway and floating dock provide ready access to Schodack Creek.

To access launch site on Hudson River—From the contact station, continue south on Schodack Island Way for 0.6 mile to the main parking area. Follow the one-way road, which leads to the launch ramp at 0.7 mile. Drop off your canoe or kayak here and return to the main area to park your vehicle.

The Paddles:
Schodack Creek Launch

South down Schodack Creek—Schodack Creek is an inlet fed by the Muitzes Kill, a little stream that rises in the hills just northwest of Kinderhook Lake and produces a series of small falls just east of Route 9J before reaching the water level of the inlet. Jacob Gardenier established a mill at the falls as early as 1649.[5] For most of its final length, Schodack Creek is but an arm of the Hudson River.

Head downstream on Schodack Creek, keeping in mind that at low tide parts of the stream can narrow to a width of less than ten feet and a depth of only five inches, or less at severe low tides. At high tide the stream expands considerably, turning mudflats into waterways.

At 1.2 miles you will reach a wide expanse on your right called Hell's Gate, which leads northwest to a small stream that can be followed northward for up to 1.0 mile—but only at high tide. Opposite Hell's Gate is 0.3-mile-long Little Schodack Island. Roughly 0.1 mile downstream from the south end of Little Schodack Island, along the Hudson's east bank to your left, is the tiny village of Schodack Landing. As you paddle between Little Schodack Island and Schodack Island, you will pass by Observation Point to your right, accessible inland via the state park's trails. You will only know that you've passed this point, however, if there are people standing slightly above the west bank.

Continuing south past Schodack Landing, Schodack Creek becomes deeper, increasing to a minimum depth of seven feet.[6] In roughly 1.2 miles from Schodack Landing, you will pass by the wide mouth of the Moesman's Kill to your right. The creek can be explored upstream for up to 0.7 mile, but that is dependent on high tide rolling in and a lack of blowdown.

You will reach the south end of Houghtaling Island, with its jetty and warning light, at roughly 5.5 miles. Just before that, you will pass by the Hook Boat Club to your right.

North up Schodack Creek—Schodack Creek can be explored upstream for some distance if you time the paddle to coincide with the approach of high tide.

At 1.2 miles you will pass under the Amtrak railroad bridge, and in 1.3 miles under the Rt. 9J bridge, where three large drainpipes conduct the stream under the road. Each of the pipes measures about eight feet in diameter. Although such distinctions are arbitrary, some consider this to be where Schodack Creek ends and the Muitzes Kill begins. Just upstream from the Rt. 9J bridge is a still-intact abandoned bridge that presents no barrier to navigation. Even at high tide, there is sufficient clearance for you to make your way upstream under the two bridges and through the large drainpipe.

The best is yet to come. In less than another 0.1 mile from the Rt. 9J bridge, you will reach the base of a series of pretty waterfalls formed on the Muitzes Kill where the stream drops forty feet. This alone is worth the paddle.

Just be sure to time your trip up Schodack Creek to coincide with the approach of high tide. If you attempt this paddle at low tide, you will not be able to complete the trek because of insufficient waters. In addition, be prepared for the possibility of having to portage around blowdown. Schodack Creek lacks sufficient current to push away any trees or obstacles that may have fallen across its path.

Schodack Island Launch

South down Hudson River—Head downstream from the boat launch for 5.0 miles until you reach the south tip of Houghtaling Island. Along the way you will pass by the Ravena Dock at 0.8 mile and the mouth of Hannacroix Creek at 2.5 miles, both of which are on the opposite side of the river. The Ravena Dock is a cement-loading dock. Materials are transported between the dock and the main plant (located over a mile to the west) via a covered conveyer system. The plant is owned by a French-based global industry named Lafarge, believed to be the largest construction materials company in the world.[7]

North up Hudson River—From the boat launch head north. You will pass under the Alfred H. Smith Railroad Bridge and the Castleton-on-Hudson Bridge (which span the Hudson River side by side) at 0.3 mile. At 1.8 mile you will come to the Vlockie Kill, which enters the Hudson from the east bank. It is possible to paddle up this tiny creek for 0.1 mile, but only at high tide. The Vlockie Kill is a small stream that rises in the hills west of Nassau and flows into the Hudson River near Castleton-on-Hudson. Farther upstream, near South Schodack, several small cascades have formed in an area that is inaccessible to hikers.

At 1.9 mile the village of Castleton-on-Hudson comes into view, a village that lies tantalizingly close to the Hudson River, but cut off from it—except for the Castleton Boat Club—by the Amtrak railroad tracks. The village remains in view for 0.4 mile.

If you continue farther north, you will eventually reach the mouth of the Moordener Kill and Papscanee Creek, at 3.0 miles. Across the river on the opposite shore is Henry Hudson Park and, just downriver from that, the Vloman Kill.

West across the Hudson River—Head upriver from the boat launch for over 0.1 mile, staying close to the Hudson's east bank. Before reaching the two

▶ **Schodack Island**

bridges, turn sharply left and paddle straight across the river for 0.2 mile to the west side of the Hudson, where a private yacht club is located at the mouth of the Binnen Kill. Do not attempt this unless the weather is calm, no boats are coming from either direction, and you are confident in your abilities to paddle across open waters.

Take note of the jetty in front of the yacht club where rocks have been pushed together to provide a safe harbor. If the tide is high, you can paddle right over the top of this jetty; otherwise stay close to the yacht club, where the water is deepest, and go around the rocks.

The Binnen Kill rises north from Cedar Hill (named for the cedar trees that once populated the area), paralleling the Hudson River along most of its length. "Binnen" is Dutch for "inland." In 2006, Scenic Hudson bought 123 acres of land along 0.5 mile of the creek's shoreline to preserve the land for its natural beauty.[8]

Proceed up the Binnen Kill, following along its steeply rising west bank. To your right you will see Shad Island, where pillars were sunk into the ground to support the Castleton-on-Hudson and Alfred H. Smith bridges. Dredging on the Hudson River during the late 1800s left Shad Island connected to the mainland.

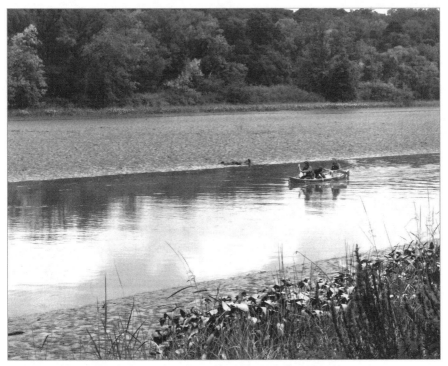

Paddling along Schodack Creek at low tide. Photograph 2009.

Before you reach the bridges, you will pass by old ruins on the left, followed by a large cement building that is a NYS Permitted Discharge Site. Don't be surprised if during low tide you notice a number of spots in front of this building where water is bubbling up to the surface of the Binnen Kill with jet-like force from underwater pipes.

Continue under the two bridges and then proceed upstream until the creek finally becomes impassable—a distance that will vary because of tidal influences. Depending upon the time of year, you may see peregrine falcons, which nest nearly every year under the Alfred H. Smith Railroad Bridge.

History: Schodack Island State Park consists of 1,470 acres of land and 8 miles of hiking trails set apart by Schodack Creek to the east and the Hudson River to the west. The park occupies roughly the middle 5 miles of a 7-mile-long, 0.5-mile-wide peninsula created by Upper and Lower Schodack islands and Houghtaling Island.[9] The northern part of Upper Schodack is privately owned, and the lower half of Houghtaling Island belongs to the Army Corps of Engineers. The park was formerly called Castleton Island State Park because of its proximity to Castleton-on-Hudson.[10] It is a designated Bird Conservation Area that affords birders the opportunity to sight bald eagles, cerulean blue warblers, green-

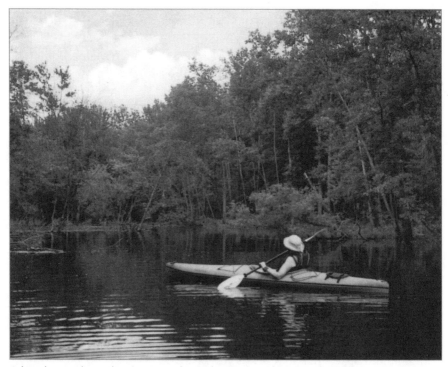

A kayaker explores the river's nooks and crannies. Photograph 2006.

▶ **Schodack Island**

backed heron, spotted sandpiper, mallards, American black duck, marsh wren, American woodcock, and swamp sparrows. During spring migration, osprey can be seen feeding there.[11]

At one time all three islands, plus Mull Island and Mull's Plat (Dutch for "Mill Plot"), were distinct bodies of land that divided the Hudson River into two flows. They were joined together during the twentieth century when dredged material from the bottom of the river was deposited on and between the islands.

The area now covered by the main parking lot was formerly one of these open channels. It was used as a landfill to ensure that no Native American artifacts would be inadvertently buried, as might have happened if dredged earth were deposited on dry land.[12] The islands have been visited by humans for millennia, starting in 1,000 AD, but possibly as far back as 4,000 BC. The word "Schodack" comes from the Mahican *ischoda*, meaning "fire plain" or "place of fire"—a reference to the permanent council fire that the Mohicans (a later name for the Mahicans) maintained in this area.[13]

The Mahicans' first encounter with Europeans was in 1609 when Henry Hudson and his crew appeared suddenly on the river. Subsequent encounters occurred with increasing rapidity. A mere twenty-one years later, the Dutch purchased land in the area. In 1650 part of Upper Schodack Island was acquired; then, between 1663 and 1670, further purchases were made, including the rest of Upper Schodack Island and all of Lower Schodack Island.[14]

Ampamit, the Mohicans' chief sachem, is known to have lived on Lower Schodack Island between 1730–1742 when the island was called Moesimus Island. New Baltimore Town Historian Clesson Bush suggests that Ampamit may very well have been the real-life model for the "last of the Mohicans."[15]

Richard Smith, a New Jersey lawyer who came up the river in 1769, had this to say about Schodack Island, which had already been stripped of its trees and was being cultivated: "The upper end of Scotoc's Island [Schodack Island] is a fine cleared Bottom not in Grass but partly in Wheat and partly in Tilth."[16]

During the nineteenth and early twentieth century, the Hudson Valley was a vital center for ice harvesting and the marketing of ice for refrigeration. Many local farmers were involved in harvesting ice during the winter as a way to augment their income. The first icehouse was established in 1872 by the Knickerbocker Ice Company[17] on lower Schodack Island. Soon after, thirteen icehouse complexes were operating on Schodack Island and Houghtaling Island alone, with a total of 135 major icehouse complexes lining the Hudson River from New York City to Albany by the 1880s. A great number of these were concentrated on both sides of the river in the general area of New Baltimore.

On the southeastern end of Schodack Island State Park is a well-preserved chimney from the Miller & Witbeck Icehouse. This is just one of several ruins found on the islands that may one day be made accessible to the public as new trails are established.

With the advent of modern refrigeration, the ice harvesting industry along the Hudson River went into sharp decline. It is quite likely, however, that the industry would have collapsed anyway, for winters in modern times are not as severe as they were a hundred years ago, and the Hudson River is less likely to freeze over today, and if so, not to the same thickness. Until the 1930s some of the former icehouses were used for growing mushrooms.

▶ **Schodack Island**

Introduction to the Champlain Canal

With a dash of imagination, a little sparkle, and an unforgivable play on words, the Champlain Canal could just as easily have been named the Champagne Canal, for in its time it was the toast of the town, linking the Hudson River and Erie Canal at Albany with Lake Champlain at Whitehall. Until then the only feasible northbound water route involved traveling up the Hudson River and then a laborious overland carry from Fort Edward to Lake George, and from there continuing north to Lake Champlain.

From a military standpoint, the route proved crucial during the seventeenth and early eighteenth centuries as France and Great Britain battled for control over North America. Each country understood that the nation that dominated the rivers and lakes would ultimately control the region. By the end of the French and Indian War (the Seven Years War in Europe), Great Britain had emerged as the clear winner.

In the late eighteenth century the rivers and lakes once again became a battleground between competing powers—this time between the thirteen British colonies and Great Britain, and this time it was Great Britain who met defeat. The water routes along eastern New York State at last were free for commerce. But more waterways were needed to make them truly efficient.

The Champlain Canal was completed in 1823 to create one continuous water route between the Hudson River at Albany and Lake Champlain at Whitehall (the village that proudly proclaims itself the birthplace of the United States Navy), thus eliminating the need for long overland carries. The canal negotiated sixty-three miles through a total of twenty-three locks. By 1828 the canal was moved to the east side of the river, where it paralleled the Hudson north to Fort Edward, then veered northeast to Wood Creek, and finally ran due north to Lake Champlain. In the process, boats were raised from nearly sea level at Cohoes to a height of 140 feet, and then down to the surface of Lake Champlain, roughly 96 feet above sea level.[1]

Even though the canal's significance was eventually eclipsed by trains and, later, the internal combustion engine, significant parts of the canal have survived into modern times. Several old sections can still be kayaked today, and extensive parts of the canal farther north remain in use, having been incorporated into New York State's modern canal system. Today there are eleven locks (numbered 1 through 12, with no #10) to be transited between the Hudson River and Lake Champlain, a trip of nearly sixty-four miles—forty miles from Troy to Fort Edward, and another twenty-four miles from Fort Edward to Whitehall at the head of Lake Champlain following a dug channel.

The village of Waterford, reportedly the oldest incorporated village (1794) in the United States,[2] contains two short but interesting paddles, both of which are found near the beginning of the historic Champlain Canal (or Northern Canal, as it was originally called).

Western Shore: Saratoga County

18

Champlain Canal: Paddle #1 (South Waterford)
The Old Champlain Canal

Western Shore: Saratoga County

▪ **Launch Site:** Historic Champlain Canal in Waterford (Saratoga County). Burton Ave.—50-foot carry up slope to towpath next to canal, informal launch. Fulton Street Bridge—50-foot carry to canal, informal launch. For more information: The Waterford Historical Museum & Cultural Center, (518) 238-0809, waterfordmuseum.com.

▪ **Delorme NYS Atlas & Gazetteer:** p. 67, B4–5; **Estimated GPS:** From 42°46.931′N; 73°41.655′W to 42°47.394′N; 73°41.167′W

▪ **Destinations:** Along canal, principally between Burton Avenue Bridge and Fulton Street Bridge

▪ **Mileage:** *From Burton Avenue:* South to Fulton Street Bridge—0.8 mile (one-way); north to intersection of the Champlain Canal and the New York State Barge Canal—0.1 mile (one-way). *From Fulton Street:* North to Burton Avenue Bridge—0.6 mile (one-way) with portage

▪ **Comments:** Read "Caution" beginning on page xxii. There is no current except when Lock 2 is drawing water from the canal to help refill the lock. Winds tend to be quietest in the early morning and evening. Go no farther north than the underwater barrier before Lock 2. A bike path parallels the east side of the canal, following the original towpath. This part of the canal was restored to its present condition in 1999.

▪ **Directions:** From the terminus of I-787 at Cohoes, turn right onto Rt. 32 to reach the following access points:

   Burton Avenue Put-in—Drive north on Rt. 32 for 1.3 miles. Turn right onto Burton Avenue, drive over a small bridge spanning the Champlain Canal, and pull into a small parking area on your right as soon as the road takes you downhill to your right. Follow a path uphill for 50 feet to the bike path and canal.

   Fulton Street Put-in—Drive north on Rt. 32 for 0.5 mile. Turn right onto Fulton Street and proceed east for 0.1 mile. At the end of the bridge, turn left and park in the area provided. Put in along the east bank of the canal just beyond the three posts where the bike path enters the woods. Or, once you cross the Fulton Street bridge, you can turn right and follow the road to its end. From there, put in next to old Lock #4.

The Paddle:

South from Burton Avenue—Head south on the canal waterway, passing behind a series of houses and backyards on the west bank where the faint but constant sound of cars traveling along Route 32 can be heard. Despite the intrusions of civilization, the canopy of trees makes for a bucolic setting.

   When you reach O'Connor Street, at 0.4 mile, you will find that the bridge spanning the canal is too low to pass under. To continue, portage around the

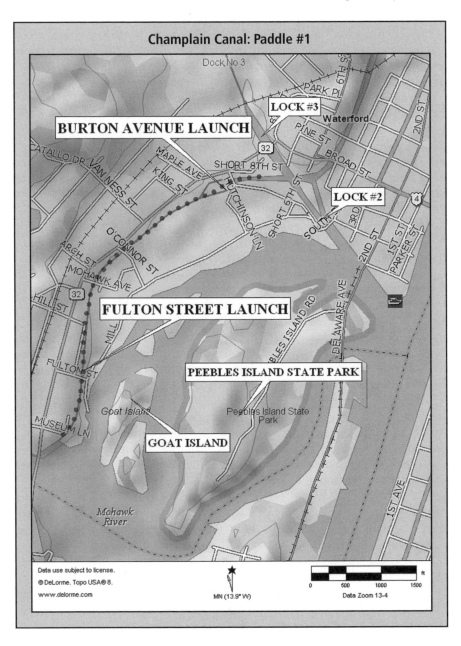

Champlain Canal: Paddle #1

bridge by lifting your watercraft up onto the towpath, carrying it across O'Connor Street, and putting it back in on the other side.

The section of the canal between O'Connor and Fulton streets is more difficult to negotiate, with occasional pieces of driftwood that have to be bypassed or pushed through. Also noticeably different is that the bank on the canal's west side begins to increase significantly in height, rising up to fifteen feet or more where the canal had to be dug out of the side of a hill. At 0.5 mile you will pass under an abandoned bridge whose height allows for easy passage.

In another 0.3 mile you will reach the Fulton Street Bridge, which also can be paddled under without any hindrance. From here the canal continues for another 0.1 mile farther, coming suddenly to an abrupt end at a guard lock, which served to protect the canal from being washed out or filled with silt when the Mohawk River was overflowing. The flight of wooden steps going up the bank from the canal to your right leads to the White Homestead, home of the Waterford Historical Museum and Cultural Center. You may wish to drive up to the museum afterwards rather than leaving your canoe or kayak unattended.

In earlier times there was no interposing cement wall by the guard gate to block the way, and the canal continued south, crossing the Mohawk River via a slack water pool.

North from Burton Avenue—This is a very short route, not much longer than 0.1 mile each way. Begin by putting in along the towpath immediately north of the bridge, and then head north. The water current will only be detectable if the locks are in operation. When Lock 2 is filling up, it will draw down the canal's water level several inches, causing the stream to flow north. When the lock has refilled, the water level in the canal will rise several inches, causing the stream to momentarily flow south until equilibrium is reached again. At these times the canal is acting as a "surge basin."

After you have gone 0.1 mile north, stop when you come to the top of a small barrage normally a couple of inches under water. While it is possible to continue paddling straight ahead, crossing through the intersection of Lock 2 to your right and Lock 3 to your left, the canal dead-ends within a hundred feet. There the water, blocked from continuing north, pours over a six-foot-high dam on the right and then proceeds to drop over a series of artificial falls ("side-cut" locks #2, #3, and #4) on the Waterford side of the Champlain Canal. The water finally comes out into the Mohawk River next to the bottom of Lock 2. Although there is not much of a pull on the canoe from the water going over the dam, it is best to stop before reaching the intersection of the two canals.

Keep in mind that the canal does resume north again on the other side of Division Street (see following chapter for a description of that paddle).

North from Fulton Street—This is essentially the reverse of the paddle from Burton Avenue. Put in along the east bank of the canal just past the three posts where the bike path enters the woods. Head north, bypassing or pushing through occasional pieces of driftwood. In over 0.2 mile you will pass under an abandoned bridge. In another 0.1 mile you will come to the O'Connor Street Bridge. You can either turn around here or portage across the road to the other side and resume your trip north along the canal for another 0.3 mile. The Burton Avenue Bridge makes a good turnaround point.

▶ **Champlain Canal: Paddle #1**

From the put-in at the Fulton Street bridge, you can also travel south, but not much farther than 0.1 mile. At the canal's end you will come to a guard lock. Beyond is a huge cement wall, which ends any further exploration—and just as well, for behind it is the full force of the Mohawk River.

A wooden footbridge at the south end of the canal leads across the lock, turns right, and then proceeds up a flight of wooden stairs to the Waterford Historical Museum and Cultural Center, located in the 1830 White Homestead.

Scenic Walks: From the Fulton Street parking area there are two short walks that provide views of the north (fourth) sprout of the Mohawk River, which the canal parallels:

View #1—Follow the road downhill for 100 feet to reach the edge of the north (fourth) sprout of the Mohawk River. In the past this sprout was used by the Dutch as they colonized the area. If you look upstream you will see small cascades in the distance. Immediately downstream, less than 0.05 mile away, the top of a dam that extends from both sides of Bock Island to the opposite banks of the river is visible. Directly east is Goat Island. Although you may be tempted to launch your canoe or kayak here, it is inadvisable. The current at times can be strong, and if you were to lose the battle against it, you would be instantly swept downstream and over the dam. Furthermore, there is really nowhere to go. Immediately upstream are small cascades that create an impasse, and immediately downstream is a red buoy line that warns of the danger in trying to edge between Bock Island and Goat Island.

View #2—Walk south, staying on the road as it parallels the river. In 0.05 mile you will approach a cul-de-sac near the end of the road. Look to your left for a faint path leading down to the river, where there are close-up views of a breached dam and small but well-defined cascades. The island that you are looking at directly across the river is Goat Island.

Continue walking south. In another several hundred feet you will reach the Boralex NYS Dam Hydro Electric Project (which is owned by NYSD Limited Partnership, an independent company). Walk to the right of the hydroelectric project and proceed over to a huge cement wall. On the other side of the wall is the Mohawk River which, having gone under the Rt. 32 bridge, now drops over a long dam.

An earlier version of this dam played a vital role during the Champlain Canal's heyday. It created a "slack-water pool" (an area of relatively calm water) that boats could cross without being swept downstream by the Mohawk River's fast current. At that time the canal, instead of abruptly ending near the Fulton Street Bridge, continued south across the Mohawk River into Cohoes. The guard locks, located on both sides of the Mohawk, assured that the canal would not sustain any damage when the Mohawk River was running too high, and also that adequate water levels would be maintained when the Mohawk was running abnormally low. This slack-water pool was located at the end of the Cohoes Falls gorge where the river still had another thirty-five feet of descent to go before reaching the Hudson River, farther east.[1]

History: Waterford is appropriately named, fortuitously located next to a shallow portion of the Mohawk where the river could be forded.[2] Its strategic location at the confluence of the Mohawk River and Hudson River assured that the town would be a center of commerce. By the early 1800s the village was heavily involved in industry, including a flour mill, tannery, twine factory, dye works, brush-making factory, knitting mill, flax mill, pearling mill (for making thread), and a whiskey plant.[3]

The Waterford Historical Museum & Cultural Center is located in the former White Homestead, which was constructed in 1830 by Hugh White, a railroad builder and congressman who helped to establish Cohoes as an industrial power. White was also the brother of Canvass White, whose development of hydraulic cement helped facilitate the building of the Erie Canal.

In 1964 the White Homestead was moved to its present location, where it now overlooks the north (fourth) sprout of the Mohawk River. The house, which has been turned into a museum, is open May through October or by appointment. To be safe, it is best to either call for current hours or consult the Web site. If you are interested in the history of the Champlain Canal, you will be pleased with the wealth of information contained in the museum, particularly regarding the sections of the canal you have just paddled. The museum is located at the end of Museum Lane off of Rt. 32, 0.3 mile north of the junction of Rt. 32 & I-787.

Champlain Canal: Paddle #1

Champlain Canal: Paddle #2 (North Waterford)
Another Section of the Old Champlain Canal

19

■ **Launch Site:** Historic Champlain Canal at Waterford (Saratoga County); informal put-in along Canal Towpath next to Division Street.

■ **Delorme NYS Atlas & Gazetteer:** p. 67, B4–5; **Estimated GPS:** 42°47.52′N; 73°40.79′W

■ **Destination:** Along section of canal north of Waterford

■ **Mileage:** 1.6 miles (round-trip) + optional 1.0-mile walk (round-trip)

■ **Comments:** Read "Caution" beginning on page xxii. There is no current. Winds tend to be quietest in the early morning and evening.

■ **Directions:** From the terminus of I-787 at Cohoes, turn right onto Rt. 32 (Saratoga Street) and drive north. At 1.4 miles you will cross over a bridge spanning the New York State Barge Canal. Continue following Rt. 32 as it bears to the right and enters the village of Waterford. At 1.5 miles turn left onto 6th Street and drive north for 0.1 mile. Then turn right onto Division Street and proceed east. In less than 0.05 mile you will cross over the Champlain Canal. Park on the north side of the bridge, close to the bike/footpath that parallels the canal's east bank. This is an area that was once called Slade's Hill.1 Put in next to the bike path (the canal's former towpath).

   From the village of Waterford (junction of Rtes. 4 & 32), drive west for 0.1 mile and turn right onto 6th Street. When you come to Division Street, turn right and park where the road crosses over the Champlain Canal.

   Carry your watercraft over to the northeast side of the bridge and put in next to the bike path. This part of the canal goes no farther south than Division Street.

The Paddle:

This delightful paddle quickly leaves the village behind, unlike the south section of the canal described in the last chapter. The canal is easy to paddle for most of its length. Take note that a number of early mills that once existed downhill to your right were powered by water from the canal.

   Heading north for less than 0.1 mile, you will pass by the former site of the power take-off dam for these now-vanished mills and then a narrow island of rock near the left bank. At one time this oblong-shaped island formed the east wall of the "Weigh Station" lock, where boats would be weighed in order to determine the toll charge. The weighing system didn't work all that well, however; as a result, a stick gauge was substituted and used to determine how deeply the barge sat in the water, and from that the weight was calculated. The lock tender's house, located on the west side of the canal, was made primarily of wood and brick and lasted long after the demise of the canal, but was finally consumed by fire in 1959.[2]

   At 0.2 mile you will reach and pass under the Hudson Valley Railroad Bridge (informally called the Black Bridge today).[3]

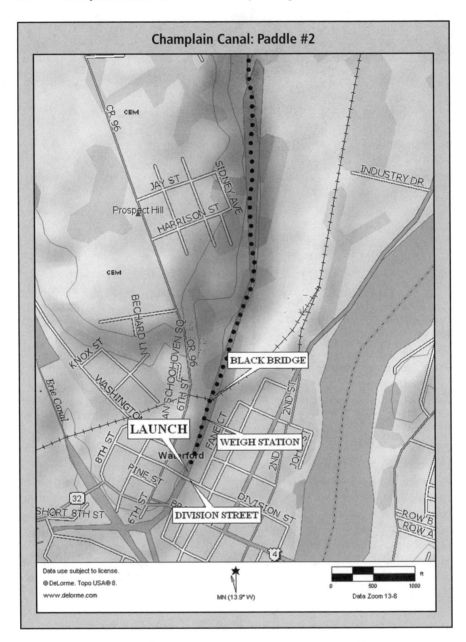

Champlain Canal: Paddle #2

Look for a trapezoid-shaped cement wall along the west bank at roughly 0.4 mile into the trip.

In 0.8 mile you will reach the end of the canoeable waterway. This is where the walk begins.

▶ **Champlain Canal: Paddle #2**

A blue heron strikes a pose before taking flight. Photograph 2002.

Walk: From the canoeable end of the canal, secure your watercraft and continue on foot north, following the bike path (which is the old canal towpath). Although the canal can still be vaguely seen on your left, it is essentially marshland, filled with reeds and traversable only by small animals and birds. In 0.3 mile you will reach Lock 5 (Lower Lock 2) where a historic plaque states that the John E. Matton boatyard once operated several hundred feet from the canal. Eventually Matton relocated his boatyard to the north end of Van Schaick Island, where it is now part of Peebles Island State Park (see chapter "Lansingburgh Boat Launch").

If you continue north for another 0.2 mile, you will arrive at the Waterford Landfill. Since most of Lock 6 (Upper Lock 2) is buried under fill and no longer visible, this is as good a point as any to turn around.

20

Champlain Canal Lock C-1 (Waterford)
Accessing the Hudson above Lock C-1

- **Launch Site:** Champlain Canal Lock C-1 (Saratoga County); cement ramp & dock at north end of parking area; Designated Greenway Water Trail Site with picnic tables.
- **Delorme NYS Atlas & Gazetteer:** p. 67, B4–5; **Estimated GPS:** 42°49.54'N; 73°39.91'W
- **Destinations:** Deep Kill, McDonald Creek, Lock C-2
- **Mileage:** To Deep Kill—0.5 mile (one-way); to McDonald Creek—2.0 miles (one-way); to Lock 2—3.8 miles (one-way)
- **Comments:** Read "Caution" beginning on page xxii and "The Hudson River: Caution" on page 1. Stay a safe distance back from the Lock C-1 dam.
- **Directions:** From Waterford (junction of Rtes. 4 & 32), drive north on Rtes. 4/32 for 2.5 miles and turn right onto Lock One Road.
    From south of Mechanicville (junction of Rtes. 146 & 32/4), drive south on Rtes. 4/32 for roughly 5.0 miles and turn left onto Lock One Road.
    From either direction, go east on Lock One Road for 0.1 mile. Turn left into a large parking area and drive to the north end to park. A cement ramp leads down to the water.

The Paddle:

Take note that the put-in is just upstream from the entrance channel to Lock C-1, which raises the height of the river from 15 feet to 29.5 feet above sea level. By heading north along the west bank, you will pass by the Deep Kill coming into the Hudson River on your right at 0.5 mile. In 2.0 miles you will pass by McDonald Creek to your left. Lock C-2 & dam is reached in 3.8 miles.

▶ **Champlain Canal Lock C-1**

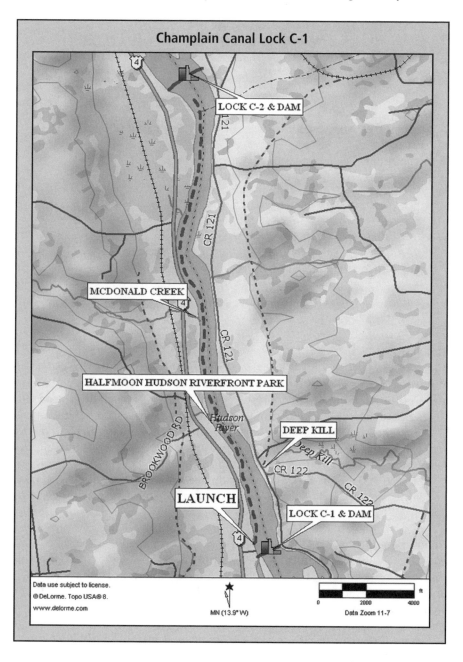

Champlain Canal Lock C-1

LOCK C-2 & DAM

CR 121

MCDONALD CREEK

CR 121

HALFMOON HUDSON RIVERFRONT PARK

Hudson River

DEEP KILL

Deep Kill

CR 122

BROOKWOOD RD

LAUNCH

LOCK C-1 & DAM

CR 122

Data use subject to license.
© DeLorme. Topo USA® 8.
www.delorme.com

MN (13.9° W)

0   2000   4000   ft

Data Zoom 11-7

21 Halfmoon Hudson Riverfront Park (Halfmoon)
Access from the Hudson's Newest Park (to open in late 2010)

- **Launch Site:** Halfmoon Hudson Riverfront Park (Saratoga County); put-in along shoreline. Designated Greenway Water Trail Site with picnic area, restrooms, waterfront overlook, and pavilion.
- **Delorme NYS Atlas & Gazetteer:** p. 67, B4–5; **Estimated GPS:** 42°50.36'N; 73°40.32'W
- **Destinations:** Champlain Lock C-2, Champlain Lock C-1
- **Mileage:** To Lock C-2—2.7 miles (one-way); to Lock C-1—1.1 miles (one-way)
- **Comments:** Read "Caution" beginning on page xxii and "The Hudson River: Caution" on page 1. Stay a safe distance back from the Lock C-1 dam and Lock C-2 dam.
- **Directions:** From Waterford (junction of Rtes. 4 & 32) drive north on Hudson River Road (Rt. 4/32) for 3.7 miles. Just before you reach Brookwood Road (on your left), turn right into the park.

  From south of Mechanicville (junction of Rtes. 146 & 4/32) turn onto Rt. 4/32 and drive south for approximately 3.6 miles. Turn left into the park just after you pass by Brookwood Road.

The Paddle:

North—Head north as you follow along the west shoreline of the Hudson River. You will immediately pass by Owl Creek to your left, and then McDonald Creek, also to your left, roughly 0.9 mile later. After 1.1 miles, Hudson River Road (Rt. 4/32) becomes visible to your left, paralleling the river for over 0.5 mile. Lock C-2 is reached in 2.7 miles. Look for the Halfmoon Hydroelectric Plant by the lock, which has been in continuous operation for over a century. Stay a safe distance back from the dam.

South—In 0.5 mile you will pass by the Deep Kill, which comes in on your left along the east bank. Lock C-1 is reached in 1.1 miles. Stay a safe distance back from the dam.

History: The Halfmoon Hudson Waterfront Park consists of 2.5 acres of land with 270 feet of waterfront. It was created through the collaborative efforts of the Town of Halfmoon, the Local Waterfront Revitalization Program (LWRP), and the Water Trail Program of the Hudson River Valley Greenway.[1] A multiuse trail connects with the Champlain Canal Towpath, located on the west side of Hudson River Road (Rt. 4/32).

The park is located next to historic Brookwood Manor, which was built by Thomas Peebles in 1766. The building served as a tavern and was patronized by such distinguished figures as George Washington, Alexander Hamilton, and Governor Dewitt Clinton in 1783.[2]

▶ **Halfmoon Hudson Riverfront Park**

Halfmoon Hudson Riverfront Park

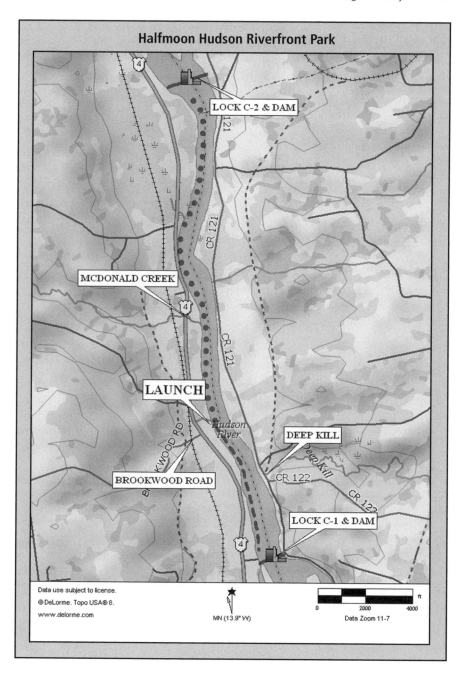

LOCK C-2 & DAM

CR 121

MCDONALD CREEK

LAUNCH

Hudson River

DEEP KILL

BROOKWOOD ROAD

CR 122

LOCK C-1 & DAM

Data use subject to license.
© DeLorme. Topo USA® 8.
www.delorme.com

MN (13.9° W)

0   2000   4000   ft

Data Zoom 11-7

22 Champlain Canal Lock C-2 (Mechanicville)
Accessing the Hudson River below Lock C-2

- **Launch Site:** Champlain Canal Lock C-2 (Saratoga County); 50-foot carry with some scrambling required to get to informal access at river's edge.
- **Delorme NYS Atlas & Gazetteer:** p. 67, AB4–5; **Estimated GPS:** 42°52.59'N; 73°40.58'W
- **Destination:** Deep Kill, Champlain Canal Lock C-1
- **Mileage:** To Deep Kill—3.1 miles (one-way); to Champlain Canal Lock C-1— 3.8 miles (one-way)
- **Comments:** Read "Caution" beginning on page xxii and "The Hudson River: Caution" on page 1. Stay a safe distance back from the Lock C-1 dam and Lock C-2 dam.
- **Directions:** From Waterford (junction of Rtes. 4 & 32), drive north on Rtes. 32/4 for 6.3 miles.

   Turn right onto Lock Two Road. From south of Mechanicville (junction of Rtes. 146 & 32/4), drive south on Rtes. 32/4 for roughly 1.2 miles.

   Turn left onto Lock Two Road. From either direction, drive east on Lock wo Road for 0.2 mile. Just before crossing over a bridge that leads to Lock 2, turn right into an informal parking area. Put in your watercraft at the side of the bridge.

The Paddle:

From Lock C-2 head downriver along the west bank of the river. There are no islands to explore, only shoreline. However, you will pass by a myriad of tiny streams dropping into the Hudson from the east hills. Of these, the most prominent is the Deep Kill, which is reached at 3.1 miles. Under most conditions the Deep Kill can be explored for nearly 0.2 mile of its length by heading under the Route 121 bridge and continuing east.

   At approximately 3.4 miles you will pass by the Lock 1 Marina, a private marina, on the west side. Finally, at 3.8 miles, you will come to Lock C-1 and dam, a natural turnaround point. Stay a safe distance back from the dam.

History: Lock C-2 and dam raise the river from a height of 29.5 feet to 48 feet above sea level.

   The town of Halfmoon was named for its crescent-shaped border with the Mohawk River.[1] The surface of the area is described by one writer as "undulating and contains several small streams running in places through narrow ravines."[2]

   The Halfmoon Hydroelectric plant at Lock C-2 is the oldest continuously operating hydroelectric plant in the United States, having started up in 1898. It was designed by Charles Steinmetz, an electrical genius who worked for General Electric. The plant generates 4.5 megawatts of power.[3]

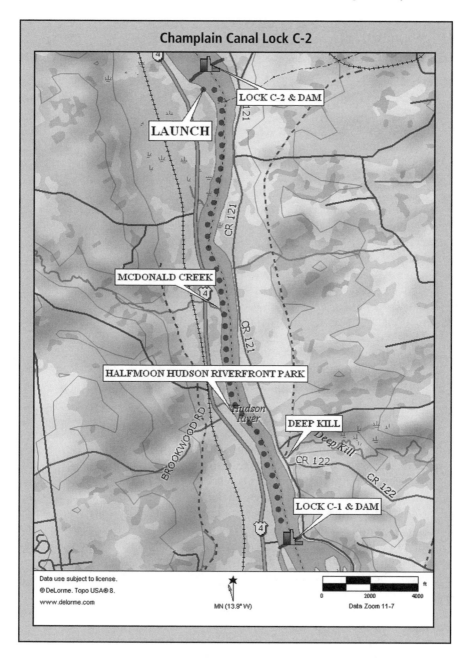

Champlain Canal Lock C-2

LOCK C-2 & DAM

LAUNCH

CR 121

CR 121

MCDONALD CREEK

CR 121

HALFMOON HUDSON RIVERFRONT PARK

Hudson River

DEEP KILL

BROOKWOOD RD

Deep Kill

CR 122

CR 122

LOCK C-1 & DAM

Data use subject to license.
© DeLorme. Topo USA® 8.
www.delorme.com

MN (13.9° W)

0   2000   4000   ft

Data Zoom 11-7

23 | Terminal Street Launch (Mechanicville)
Accessing the Hudson River & Several Islands

- **Launch Site:** Terminal Street Launch at Mechanicville (Saratoga County). Access from the wharf is challenging at present. In 2010 a kayak dock will be set into place at the north end of the wharf using a grant from the Hudson River Greenway Water Trail Grant Program, greatly facilitating small-craft access. This is a designated Greenway Water Trail Site with lockable kayak storage racks, picnicking, bus service, fishing, and retail/supplies.
- **Delorme NYS Atlas & Gazetteer:** p. 66, A4; **Estimated GPS:** 42°54.21′N; 73°41.04′W
- **Destinations:** Champlain Canal Lock C-3, First and Second Islands, Quack Island
- **Mileage:** To Champlain Canal Lock C-3—0.6 mile (one-way); to First & Second islands—0.3 (one-way); around First and Second islands—1.3 miles; to Quack Island—1.3 miles (one-way)
- **Comments:** Read "Caution" beginning on page xxii and "The Hudson River: Caution" on page 1. Stay a safe distance back from the Lock C-2 dam and Lock C-3 dam.
- **Directions:** From Mechanicville (junction of Rtes. 67 West & 4/32), drive east for 0.1 mile and turn right onto North Main Street (which initially is Rt. 67 east). Proceed south for over 0.3 mile and then turn left onto Terminal Street just before crossing over the Anthony Kill. Follow the street east for 0.05 mile to a long parking area paralleling the river. Park at the south end of the wharf.

The Paddle:

Directly across the river from the Mechanicville Terminal is Hemstreet Park, a small village community. The Mechanicville Terminal dates back to the early twentieth century. It was one of fifty-six terminals built by New York State connecting ports at Buffalo, Rochester, Oswego, Woodsport, Brockport, and other sites along the New York State Barge Canal system.

North—Head upstream, passing under the Route 67 Bridge (connecting Mechanicville and Schaghticoke) in less than 0.2 mile. In 0.6 mile you will reach Champlain Canal Lock C-3 and Riverside Dam, a natural turnaround point. Stay a safe distance back from the dam to avoid hydraulics.

Along the west bank next to the dam is NYSEG—a Rochester-based subsidiary of Energy East Corporation.

Lock C-3 is the highest lift lock on the Champlain Canal, raising the height of the river by another 19.5 feet to 67.5 feet above sea level.

South—Paddling downstream along the west shore, you will immediately pass by the Anthony Kill, to your right, which comes in along the south end of the wharf. A series of small cascades gives the stream a final dash of individuality before it merges with the Hudson and loses its identity.

In 0.3 mile you will reach the north end of a 0.6-mile-long, low-lying island

▶ **Champlain Canal Lock C-2**

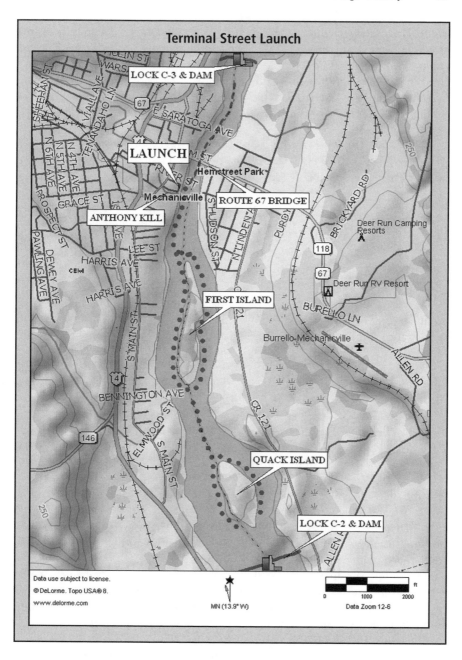

consisting principally of alluvial soil with a smattering of trees. Just to the west is a second, much smaller and narrower, island that is also low-lying. (It is so small that it does not even appear on the Delorme map.) First and Second islands can be circumnavigated in 1.3 miles. The large smokestack prominently visible along the west shore during most of the paddle belongs to the former Tagsons Paper Co., now called Cascades. It is passed in 1.1 miles.

When you reach the south end of the First & Second islands complex, you will enter an area of the Hudson that is noticeably wider and considerably more circular. Whereas the river was 0.1 mile wide at the put-in, it has now increased to 0.5 mile in width.

Proceed farther downriver, reaching the north end of 0.3-mile-long Quack Island in 0.4 mile. The Half Moon Hydroelectric Plant and Champlain Canal Lock C-2 are clearly visible nearby to the right of Quack Island, just a short distance beyond.

Paddling along the west side of Quack Island, you will reach the island's south end in 0.3 mile. This side of Quack Island is characterized by prominent cliffs that rise up steeply 20–25 feet above the water. Orange warning buoys lead away from the south end of the island diagonally across to Champlain Canal Lock C-2, ensuring that boaters don't stray too far to the east from their course and run afoul of the dam.

If you paddle along the east side of Quack Island, you will find that the cliffs are not as high and are considerably more inclined. Looming prominently in the distance is the east bank of the Hudson, which rises up sharply to a height of more than seventy feet.[1]

Unlike on the west side of Quack Island, the east side contains no orange buoys to warn of the dam's presence a scant 0.1 mile downstream. For this reason, go no farther south than the island's south end.

On the way back upriver be sure to paddle over to the enormous boulder located in the middle of the river between the southeast end of First Island and the east shore. The surprise of coming upon such an anomaly is part of what makes outdoors adventures so much fun.

History: Mechanicville was noted in the past for its brickyards, paper mills, knitting mills, and later as a railroad center.

The city's Main Street is part of the old King's Highway, a seventeenth-century trail that extended between Fort Orange (Albany) and Canada. Later, this route was heavily used during the Revolutionary War.

Allegedly, the first canal in the United States was constructed between Mechanicville and Stillwater in 1800.[2] It was part of a grand scheme envisioned by Philip Schuyler for interconnecting major waterways, but it never reached completion. More a ditch than anything resembling a canal, it provided a way for bypassing a series of rapids on the Hudson.

The Anthony Kill, also known as Tenandaho Creek, flows out of Round Lake and enters the Hudson River near the end of Terminal Street in Mechanicville. The first sawmill on the Anthony Kill was established around 1783; it was quickly followed by a forge.[3] Harold Sheehan, former Mechanicville his-

▶ **Terminal Street Launch**

The Hudson River is forced to go around several islands as it flows past Mechanicville. Postcard ca. 1910.

torian, speculates that it was likely that it was the erection of a woolen mill later, at the mouth of the Anthony Kill, and the proliferation of mechanics that gave Mechanicville its name.[4] Earlier, the tiny hamlet was known as "the Borough."[5]

Interestingly, the area around the Anthony Kill was considered militarily significant, but it was never used during wartime. In 1780, Francois-Jean, Marquis de Chastellux, wrote: "I saw, on my left, an opening in the wood, and a pretty extensive plain, below which runs a creek. I told General Schuyler that there must be a good [military] position there. He told me I was not mistaken, and that it had been reconnoitered for that purpose in case of need. The creek is called Anthony Kill."[6]

24

Mill Creek: Lewis A. Swyer Preserve (Stuyvesant)
One of Only Five Freshwater Tidal Swamps & Forests in New York State

- **Launch Site:** Lewis A. Swyer Preserve (Columbia County); challenging put-in along boardwalk near Rt. 9J bridge. For more information: nature.org/wherewe-work/northamerica/states/newyork/preserves/art12198.html.
- **Delorme NYS Atlas & Gazetteer:** p. 52, A3–4; **Estimated GPS:** 42°24.98′N; 73°46.15′W
- **Destinations:** Mill Creek, Houghtaling Island, Stuyvesant Landing
- **Mileage:** Down Mill Creek to Hudson River—0.5 mile (one-way); from mouth of Mill Creek to south tip of Houghtaling Island—0.9 mile (one-way); from mouth of Mill Creek to Stuyvesant Landing—1.8 miles (one-way)
- **Comments:** Read "Caution" beginning on page xxii and "The Hudson River: Caution" on page 1. Take note that Mill Creek is tidal. The depth of the stream can increase by 4–5 feet at high tide, nearly cresting the top of the bank; at other times the creek can be undesirably shallow. It's best to undertake this paddle when high tide is approaching. Check tides at: tidesandcurrents.noaa.gov. You may wish to first survey the stream by walking along the boardwalk to ensure that Mill Creek is not blocked by fallen trees and contains a sufficient volume of water. Remain on boardwalk unless you are in your watercraft.
- **Directions:** From the blinking traffic light at Stuyvesant, drive north on Rt. 9J for 2.0 miles to reach the Lewis A. Swyer Preserve, to your left. If the tiny parking area by the preserve is full, continue farther up the road for less than 0.1 mile and turn into a larger pull-off on your left. From Castleton-on-Hudson (junction of Rtes. 9J & 150), proceed south on Rt. 9J for 8.2 miles and park to your right just before the stream. If there is no room to park, drop off your watercraft, turn around, and drive back north for less than 0.1 mile to use the upper pull-off. From Rt. 9J, carry your watercraft down the nature trail for several hundred feet. Thirty feet beyond the kiosk, you will come to a deck that overlooks the stream. With considerable effort, a canoe or kayak can be launched from here.

Eastern Shore: Columbia County

The Paddle:

West—Paddle southwest down Mill Creek for 0.5 mile. The nature boardwalk, paralleling the stream, will remain on your right. As soon as you pass under the railway bridge, you will come out onto the Hudson River.

North—From the mouth of Mill Creek, paddle upstream for 0.9 mile to the southern tip of Houghtaling Island. If you bear right, you can follow Schodack Creek north for over 5.0 miles (see chapter "Schodack Island State Park").

South—From the mouth of Mill Creek, head downstream for 1.8 miles to reach Stuyvesant Landing. Along the way you will pass by a tiny, 150-foot-long island at 0.1 mile. The stone base of the old Stuyvesant Lighthouse can be seen at the island's south end. The island is separated from the mainland by a mere fifty feet of water.

 Mill Creek

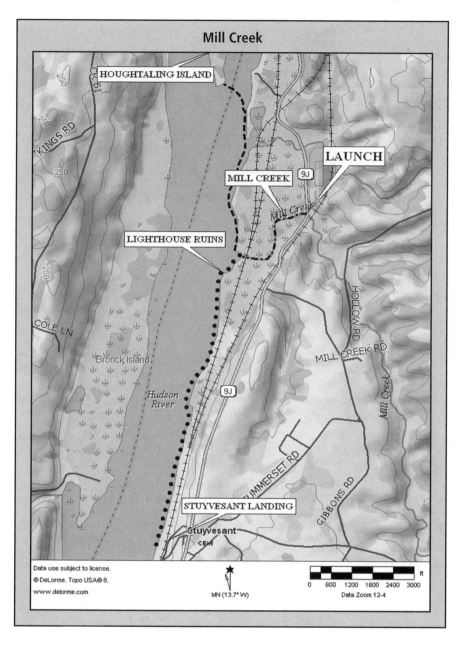

Mill Creek

HOUGHTALING ISLAND

LAUNCH

MILL CREEK   9J

LIGHTHOUSE RUINS

KINGS RD

COLE LN

Bronck Island

Hudson
River

9J

Mill Creek

HOLLOW RD

MILL CREEK RD

Mill Creek

SUMMERSET RD

GIBBONS RD

STUYVESANT LANDING

Stuyvesant
CEM

Data use subject to license.
© DeLorme. Topo USA® 8.
www.delorme.com

MN (13.7° W)

0   600   1200   1800   2400   3000   ft
Data Zoom 12-4

At 0.7 mile south of the lighthouse ruins, you will pass by a small bay to your left, the interior of which can be explored east for up to 0.1 mile to the Amtrak rail tracks. Watch out for a dike that extends south from the northwest end of the bay for 0.1 mile, terminating at a large boulder.

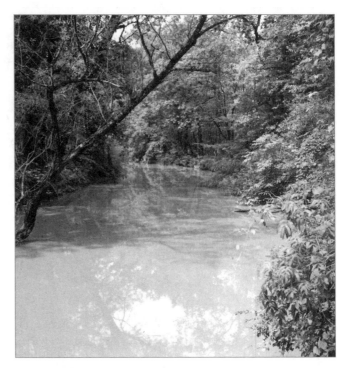

The first half mile of Mill Creek is tidal, rising and falling in lockstep with the Hudson River. Photograph 2008.

History: The nature preserve is named after a regional patron of the arts and former Eastern New York Chapter Trustee of the Nature Conservancy.[1] Swyer's name is familiar to many residents of the Capital Region because of the 450-seat Lewis A. Swyer Auditorium at the Empire State Plaza's Performing Arts Center (an oblate spheroid better known as "The Egg").

Back in the mid-1600s, a sawmill operated upstream on Mill Creek making use of the creek's waters for hydropower. During high tide, boats could make their way up the creek from the Hudson River to the mill. The return trip had to be timed to coincide with the next high tide. Mill Creek has been known by several other names—*Pittannoock* (Native American), Frank Peiteers (or Frans Peters) Clover's Saw Kill, and Light House Creek.[2]

Just upstream from its confluence with the Hudson River, Mill Creek passes under the former New York–Penn Central railroad bridge, now used by Amtrak for its runs between New York City and Rensselaer. When the first bridge was built in the 1850s, no thought was given as to future unintended consequences. The raised bedding supporting the tracks subsequently created a barrier that not only reduces the flow of nutrients between the Hudson River and the swamp, but limits the wetlands' ability to filter out pollutants.

Because the 95-acre tidal freshwater wetland is bisected by the railroad's raised bedding, an artificial division in the swamp's flora has been created. East

▶ **Mill Creek**

of the tracks, the land is principally a freshwater tidal swamp; to the west, the land consists of subtidal shallows, intertidal mudflats, and tidal marshes.

A variety of bird species can be seen in the preserve, including nesting birds like the green-backed heron, spotted sandpiper, wood duck, mallard, belted kingfisher, and blue-winged teal. Passerine species (birds that typically can perch), such as veery, swamp sparrow, white-eyed vireo, blue-gray gnatcatcher, and cerulean warblers can also be observed.[3]

Stuyvesant Lighthouse—The original lighthouse was built in 1829 and lasted until 1832, when an ice jam gave way upriver, destroying the structure and killing four members of the keeper's family. A new four-room lighthouse was built in 1836 and rebuilt in 1868. The last keeper to occupy the house was a man named Reilly.[4] Shortly after 1933 the lighthouse was torn down and replaced by an automatic light.[5] All that remains today of the original thirty-two-foot-high structure[6] is the circular stone base. The huge foundation stones were moved to the Stuyvesant Post Office to support the porch.[7]

Unlike most lighthouses, which are separate from the mainland and reachable in the winter only by boat or by crossing ice, the Stuyvesant Lighthouse was accessible by a footbridge that connected it to the mainland.[8]

25 Stuyvesant Landing (Stuyvesant)
The Hudson River, Several Islands, and Two Tributaries

■ **Launch Site:** Riverview Park at Stuyvesant Landing (Columbia County); dirt ramp. This is a designated Greenway Water Trail Site.

■ **Delorme NYS Atlas & Gazetteer:** p. 52, AB3–4; **Estimated GPS:** 42°23.35′N; 73°46.06′W

■ **Destinations:** Coxsackie Creek, Bronck Island, Rattlesnake Island, Coxsackie Island, Mill Creek

■ **Mileage:** West to Coxsackie Creek—0.5 mile (one-way); to navigable end of creek—0.5 mile farther (one-way); north along Bronck Island—1.0 mile from mouth of Coxsackie Creek (one-way); to Rattlesnake Island—0.8 mile from mouth of Coxsackie Creek (one-way); around Rattlesnake Island—1.2 miles; to Coxsackie Island—0.1 mile from south tip of Rattlesnake Island (one-way); to circumnavigate Coxsackie Island—1.8 miles; north to Mill Creek—1.8 miles (one-way); 0.5 mile farther (one-way) to navigable end of Mill Creek

■ **Comments:** Read "Caution" beginning on page xxii and "The Hudson River: Caution" on page 1. It is best to paddle up Coxsackie Creek at high tide. Check tides at: tidesandcurrents.noaa.gov. Stay vigilant when paddling along the east side of Coxsackie Island and Rattlesnake Island where the main shipping channel is. The upper section of Mill Creek may become impassable at low tide. Drive carefully across the railroad tracks to access the riverfront park.

■ **Directions:** From north of Stockport (junction of Rtes. 9J & 9), drive north on Rt. 9J for 5.1 miles and turn left when you reach a blinking light at Stuyvesant. From Castleton-on-Hudson (junction of Rtes. 9J & 150), drive south on Rt. 9J for 10.3 miles to Stuyvesant and turn right at the blinking traffic light. Proceed downhill on Rt. 26A for 0.2 mile. When the road veers to the left, continue straight across the railroad tracks into Riverview Park. Turn right after you cross the railroad tracks and head north over to the inclined river access, about 100 feet away. Take note of the numerous "No Parking" and "Private" signs displayed in the park. Drop off your watercraft here and park back on the main road. Don't block the access, which is used by the fire department.

The Paddle:

West to Coxsackie Creek—Paddle straight across the Hudson River for 0.5 mile, veering slightly to the south of a marshy area along the west bank. You will come to the mouth of Coxsackie Creek where a small bay provides respite from the river's current and the wind. Paddle northwest into the bay for 0.2 mile until you reach its end, where Coxsackie Creek visibly emerges from a gorge. Proceed west up the creek for 0.3 mile until you come to the confluence of Coxsackie Creek and Sickles Creek. Route 61 will be visible above the west bank, where a roadside pull-off is used by fishermen. At this point no further progress upstream is possible because of rapids.

▶ **Stuyvesant Landing**

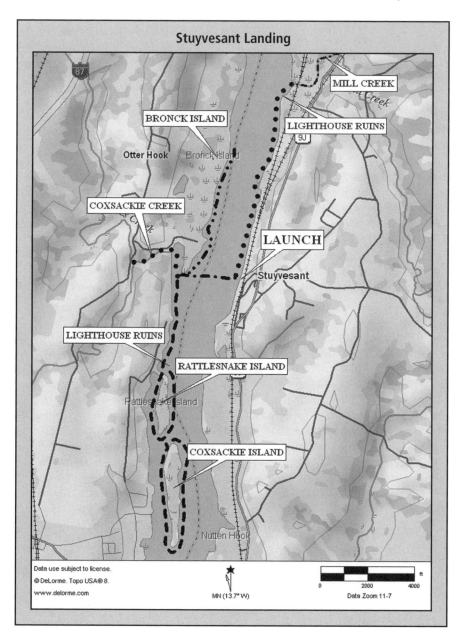

Coxsackie Creek is a medium-sized stream that rises in the hills west of Coxsackie and flows into the Hudson River several miles north of the village. It possesses a number of small cascades beyond its canoeable section.[1] At one time the creek was called the Clove Kill.[2]

Interestingly, unlike most streams, which develop gradually through the merger of tiny rivulets to form a brook, Coxsackie Creek spurts out full-formed from the base of a huge cliff visible from roadside along Rt. 49, 1.4 miles from the junction of Rtes. 49 & 9W, northeast of Lime Street. Coxsackie Creek is closely associated with the name Bronck. In 1663, Pieter Bronck built his home (today called the Bronck House) close to the creek. It remains the oldest surviving dwelling in upstate New York. Pieter also established the first mill in the town of Coxsackie, in 1670,[3] on Sickles Creek.

North along Bronck Island—Starting from the mouth of Coxsackie Creek, proceed upriver on the Hudson following its west bank along Bronck Island—an island only in name, having been connected to the mainland by dredged fill many years ago. At 0.4 mile you will pass by a tiny peninsula to your left, where a two-story gazebo, topped by a crow's nest, overlooks the river. The land is privately owned and posted, so remain in your watercraft. The cement wall partially extending around the peninsula is a reminder of times when the land was used for other purposes.

At 0.5 mile you will pass by a green-colored automatic light, numbered 169. Using this beacon as a marker, continue upriver along the west bank for another 0.5 mile. You will come to the Van Schaack campsite, a twenty-five-acre parcel of land on your left. From the shore, a raised wooden walkway leads uphill to the top of a small rise. The land was donated to the Hudson River Watertrail Association by Wilbur & Ruth Van Schaack. There is a composting toilet at the far end of the ramp and two tent platforms just south of the landing beach. Lockable kayak storage racks are located near the ramp. This site is a designated Greenway Water Trail Campsite, built using a Greenway Water Trail Grant and much volunteer labor.

South to Rattlesnake Island—From the mouth of Coxsackie Creek, paddle downriver along the west bank of the Hudson for 0.8 mile until you reach the north end of 0.5-mile-long Rattlesnake Island. Look for the stone base of a former lighthouse on the small circular island of rock just before Rattlesnake Island.

Rattlesnake Island can now be circumnavigated, because a tiny, water-filled ditch was created across the causeway connecting the island to the mainland.

South to & around Coxsackie Island—Once you clear the south tip of Rattlesnake Island, it is only another 0.1 mile south before you arrive at the north end of 0.6-mile-long Coxsackie Island, which can be circumnavigated in 1.8 miles.

North to Mill Creek—Staying on the east side of the Hudson River, paddle upstream from the boat launch for 1.8 miles. You will come to Mill Creek, which can be explored eastward for over 0.5 mile of its length (see chapter "Mill Creek" for specific details). Look for the stone base of an old lighthouse at the south end of a tiny island just before reaching the mouth of Mill Creek.

History: Riverview Park is overseen by the Nature Conservancy, Hudson River Foundation, and Stuyvesant Fire District #1. Access to the river was made possible through a 1988 conservation easement granted by Margaret & William See.

▶ **Stuyvesant Landing**

The old railroad station next to the park is a second-generation relic from the nineteenth century. The original station was destroyed in 1880 by a devastating fire that consumed most of the buildings in town. In 1881 the railroad station was rebuilt and continued operating until 1956. It was then bought by a local man who used it for storage. Unfortunately, the building was allowed to deteriorate further during this time. In the 1990s the Stuyvesant Railroad Restoration Committee came together to save the historic building, and federal and state grant money was obtained for its preservation. Today the station is listed on the National Register of Historic Places.[4]

Stuyvesant Landing was originally called Kinderhook Landing and has the distinction of being one of several sites visited by Henry Hudson during his historic voyage along the Hudson River. It was named Stuyvesant Landing after Governor Peter (Pieter or Petrus) Stuyvesant, who was Dutch Director-General of the colony of New Netherlands (New York) from 1647 until it was ceded provisionally to the English in 1664.

The landing was one of the first river ports on the Hudson. By 1820 freight sloops were making regular trips to and from New York City.[5] For a time it served as the port for Kinderhook.

Stuyvesant Landing was also part of the Underground Railroad, providing a way station for escaped slaves fleeing north.

26   Nutten Hook Reserve (Nutten Hook)
Accessing the Hudson River near Ruins of a Historic Icehouse

■ **Launch Site:** Hudson River National Estuarine Research Reserve at Nutten Hook (Columbia County); 0.3-mile carry along dirt road to put-in along rocky shore. Designated Greenway Water Trail Site with picnicking, hiking trails, fishing, hunting, and trapping. The reserve provides a field laboratory for estuarine research, stewardship, and education.

■ **Delorme NYS Atlas & Gazetteer:** p. 52, AB3–4; **Estimated GPS:** 42°21.49′N; 73°47.30′W

■ **Destinations:** Coxsackie Island, Rattlesnake Island, Little Nutten Hook, Gay's Point, Stockport Middle Ground

■ **Mileage:** To Coxsackie Island—0.5 mile (one-way); around Coxsackie Island— 1.7 miles; to Rattlesnake Island—1.2 miles (one-way); around Rattlesnake Island—1.2 miles; to Little Nutten Hook/Fordham Point—1.1 miles (one-way); up tributary to Rt. 9J—0.4 mile (one-way); to Gay's Point—2.4 miles (one-way); to Stockport Middle Ground—2.6 miles (one-way); around Stockport Middle Ground—1.7 miles

■ **Comments:** Read "Caution" beginning on page xxii and "The Hudson River: Caution" on page 1. Be extra cautious when paddling along the east side of Coxsackie Island and Rattlesnake Island where the main shipping channel is. A canoe carrier would be helpful for reaching the launch site. Walk carefully across railroad tracks to reach the reserve. Be prepared for an increase in boat traffic near the Coxsackie Riverside Park & State Boat Launch and the boat launch at Stockport Station.

■ **Directions:** From north of Stockport (junction of Rtes. 9 & 9J), drive northwest on Rt. 9J for 2.7 miles. If you are approaching from Castleton-on-Hudson (junction of Rtes. 9J & 150), drive south on Rt. 9J for 12.6 miles (or 2.3 miles south from the blinking traffic light at Stuyvesant). Coming from either direction, turn west onto a dirt road where you will see a sign for the Nutten Hook Reserve. Park immediately at a small parking area to your left before crossing over the railroad tracks. No automobile traffic is allowed beyond this point. Walk west along the road for 0.3 mile until you reach the river. What makes this access so appealing is that you will pass by the ruins of an old icehouse, where there are opportunities for exploration and hiking.

The Paddle:

Before starting, take a moment to look across the river and slightly to the left to the village of Coxsackie, where Coxsackie Riverside Park is located. The river at this point is nearly 0.5 mile wide.

North to Coxsackie Island and Rattlesnake Island—Head upriver to arrive at Coxsackie Island in less than 0.5 mile. The island can be circumnavigated in 1.7 miles.

▶ **Nutten Hook Reserve**

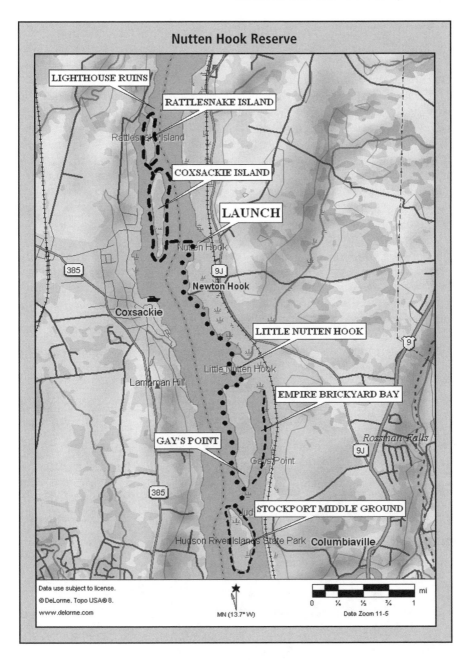

Nutten Hook Reserve

LIGHTHOUSE RUINS

RATTLESNAKE ISLAND

Rattlesnake Island

COXSACKIE ISLAND

LAUNCH

Nutten Hook

385

9J

Newton Hook

Coxsackie

LITTLE NUTTEN HOOK

Little Nutten Hook

9

Langman Hill

EMPIRE BRICKYARD BAY

GAY'S POINT

Gay's Point

Rossman Falls

9J

385

STOCKPORT MIDDLE GROUND

Hudson River Islands State Park Columbiaville

Data use subject to license.
©DeLorme. Topo USA® 8.
www.delorme.com

MN (13.7° W)

0   ¼   ½   ¾   1   mi

Data Zoom 11-5

From the north end of Coxsackie Island, continue north to reach Rattlesnake Island in over 0.1 mile. It is now possible to paddle around the island despite its northwest end having been joined to the mainland years ago by a causeway.

A tiny, water-filled ditch, wide enough to permit the passage of a canoe, spans the causeway at a narrow point. At low tide you may need to portage your watercraft if there is insufficient water in the ditch. (See chapter "Coxsackie Riverfront Park" for further details on these two islands.)

South to Stockport Middle Ground—Heading south along the east shore, you will pass by Lampman Hill to your right at 0.8 mile, and Little Nutten Hook to your left in 0.9 mile, reaching the tip of Gay's Point in 2.2 miles. By rounding the tip of Gay's Point and bearing left (north), you can paddle up through Empire Brickyard Bay for nearly a mile, depending upon tidal conditions. Lampman Hill (elevation 270 feet) is associated with Leonard Bronck Lampman,[1] who willed the Bronck estate—the Hudson Valley's oldest home and now a museum—to the Greene County Historical Society as a permanent memorial to his mother, Adelaide Ely Bronck Lampman.

From Gay's Point, if you continue south for 0.2 mile you will reach Stockport Middle Ground, which can be circumnavigated in 1.7 mile. Gay's Point and Stockport Middle Ground together make up the Hudson River Islands State Park, a designated Greenway Water Trail Campsite. These two sites have over thirty campsites that are accessible only by boat. Outhouses are available in a number of locations, particularly at the main dock on Gay's Point.

Hike: While you are at the reserve, be sure to take a short, 0.5-mile-long hike along the yellow-blazed trail that leads off from the southwest end of the ice-

The Scott Ice House is gone, but its brick powerhouse still rises above the tree line at Nutten Hook Reserve. Photograph 2008.

Nutten Hook Reserve

house foundation to the top of a very pronounced small knob, then down the other side, around, and back to the southeast corner of the icehouse foundation. There are nice views from the top of the hill, where a dance hall once stood.[2]

History: Nutten Hook is an anomaly. It contains a 0.2-mile-long knob of rock that has resisted the river's erosive power from all sides. Little Nutten Hook, a short distance to the southeast, is similarly formed. Nutten Hook was formerly known as Newton Hook and also Newton Hook Station. At one time a ferry connected Nutten Hook with Coxsackie.[3]

Nutten Hook's most prominent historical feature is the Robert & William Scott Ice House, which was constructed in 1885 and whose foundation lies at the end of the 0.3-mile-long road leading into the Nutten Hook Reserve. The icehouse stood six stories high and was 300 feet long and 200 feet wide (other estimates put it at 350 feet by 270 feet). When filled to capacity, it could hold 52,880 tons of ice.[4] During its later years, it was used for growing mushrooms. It burned down in 1934.

You can see the block outline of this building and walk around its perimeter. The series of parallel abutments next to the foundation were supports for a train track that led from the icehouse to the main railroad line. Most noticeable is the surviving powerhouse structure, whose brick walls remain surprisingly intact. It stands between the icehouse foundation and the river, and is impossible to miss thanks to its high red smokestack made of brick. It was used as a power source for conveying ice blocks up from the river into the storage house.[5]

Two historic markers provide information on the ice harvesting industry. One tells of the many hazards endured by the workers.

It is said that the ice harvesting industry on the Hudson came about through providence and good fortune. In 1824 an early breakup of ice on the river led some to realize that harvesting blocks of ice could be a profitable venture.[6] By 1880 there were 135 icehouses along the river. By 1900 the number had increased to over 200. Icehouses were amazingly efficient at keeping in the cold. Blocks of ice, covered by sawdust, could last nearly three years.

	Ferry Road Access (Nutten Hook)
27	*Accessing the Hudson from a Former Ferry Slip*

- **Launch Site:** Hudson River National Estuarine Research Reserve (Columbia County); 100-foot carry to beach slip-in. Designated Greenway Water Trail Site with picnicking, hiking trails, fishing, hunting, and trapping.
- **Delorme NYS Atlas & Gazetteer:** p. 52, AB3–4; **GPS:** 42°21.23'N; 73°47.32'W
- **Destinations:** Coxsackie Island, Rattlesnake Island, Little Nutten Hook, Gay's Point, Stockport Middle Ground
- **Mileage:** To Coxsackie Island—0.7 mile (one-way); around Coxsackie Island—1.7 miles; to Rattlesnake Island—1.4 miles (one-way); around Rattlesnake Island—1.2 miles; to Little Nutten Hook & Fordham Point—0.7 mile (one-way); up tributary to Rt. 9J—0.4 mile (one-way); to Gay's Point—2.0 miles (one-way); to Stockport Middle Ground—2.2 miles (one-way); around Stockport Middle Ground—1.7 miles
- **Comments:** Read "Caution" beginning on page xxii and "The Hudson River: Caution" on page 1. Be extra cautious when paddling along the east side of Coxsackie Island and Rattlesnake Island where the main shipping channel is. Drive carefully across the railroad tracks to reach the launch site. Be prepared for an increase in boat traffic near the Coxsackie Riverside Park & State Boat Launch and the boat launch at Stockport Station.
- **Directions:** From north of Stockport (junction of Rtes. 9 & 9J), drive northwest on Rt. 9J for 2.4 miles. Approaching from Castleton-on-Hudson (junction of Rtes. 9J & 150), drive south on Rt. 9J for 12.9 miles (or 2.6 miles south from the blinking traffic light at Stuyvesant). Coming from either direction, turn west onto Ferry Road at the blinking light, cross over the railroad tracks, and continue for 0.2 mile. Park on your right at the base of a steep, rock-faced hill. From here, follow a path to the left of the roadside kiosk that leads down to the shore in 100 feet. If you wish, you can follow Ferry Road west for another 0.1 mile, where there is a larger parking area and additional opportunities to launch your watercraft.

The Paddle:

North to Rattlesnake Island—Heading upriver, you will arrive at Coxsackie Island in 0.7 mile. The island can be circumnavigated in 1.7 miles.

From the north end of Coxsackie Island, you can reach Rattlesnake Island in over 0.1 mile. It is possible to circumnavigate Rattlesnake Island despite its northwest end having been joined to the mainland years ago. A small water-filled ditch now connects Rattlesnake Cove with the river proper. (See chapter "Coxsackie Riverfront Park" for further details on these two islands.)

South to Stockport Middle Ground—Heading south, at 0.1 mile you will pass by a stream that is not navigable at low tide. At 0.7 mile you will reach Little Nutten Hook. The westernmost part of Little Nutten Hook was once a separate point of land called Fordham Point, but it is now joined to the mainland by a marshy

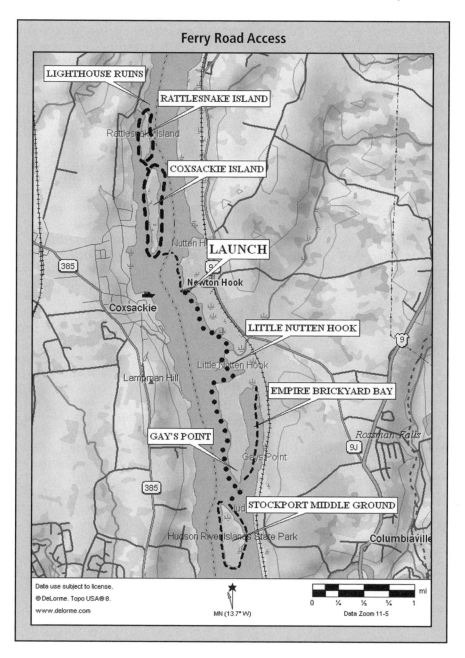

area. Turn left here and follow the shoreline east for 0.2 mile. You will come to the entrance of a twenty-foot-wide creek that goes east for over 0.4 mile. You can easily paddle up the stream to the Amtrak railroad bridge, and then continue for a short distance farther to the Rt. 9J bridge. These are low bridges, so high tide could present a problem here.

Paddling south from Little Nutten Hook, you will pass by a bay in 0.1 mile. Although a dike extends across the front of the bay, a break midway allows for ready entry, enabling you to explore the bay's interior east for up to 0.2 mile. This is part of Hudson River Islands State Park, a designated Hudson River Greenway Water Trail Campsite. Look for a secluded campsite along the shore just after entering the bay.

By proceeding farther south on the Hudson River, you will reach the tip of Gay's Point in 2.0 miles. By rounding the tip of Gay's Point and bearing left (north), you can paddle up Empire Brickyard Bay for nearly a mile.

Stockport Middle Ground (an island) is reached at 2.2 miles and can be circumnavigated in 1.7 miles.

History: Ferry Road is at the eastern terminus of a ferry service that once ran between Nutten Hook and Coxsackie. Until the nineteenth century, ferries provided the only means for crossing the Hudson River. Bridges simply could not be built strong enough to withstand the Hudson River's relentless onslaught.

 **Ferry Road Access**

Stockport Station (Columbiaville)
Accessing the Hudson River from Stockport Creek

28

■ **Launch Site:** Boat Launch onto Stockport Creek at end of Station Road at Stockport Station (Columbia County); inclined dirt ramp next to railroad bridge. Designated Greenway Water Trail Site with fishing and water trail kiosk.

■ **Delorme NYS Atlas & Gazetteer:** p. 52, B3–4; **GPS:** 42°18.55'N; 73°46.31'W

■ **Destinations:** Stockport Creek, Stockport Middle Ground, Gay's Point, Empire Brickyard Bay, Middle Ground Flats

■ **Mileage:** East up Stockport Creek—0.9 mile to Rt. 9 bridge (one-way), 1.8 miles to confluence with Kinderhook Creek and Claverack Creek (one-way); north to Stockport Middle Ground—0.5 mile (one-way), around Stockport Middle Ground—1.7 miles; to Gay's Point from north end of Stockport Middle Ground—0.2 mile (one-way); up Empire Brickyard Bay to end—0.9 mile (one-way); south to Middle Ground Flats—2.5 miles (one-way); around Middle Ground Flats—4.5 miles

■ **Comments:** Read "Caution" beginning on page xxii and "The Hudson River: Caution" on page 1. *Stockport Creek*—Even though Stockport Creek is not as heavily traveled as the Hudson, watch out for boat traffic, particularly fast-moving boats whose wakes can capsize a small watercraft. A short portage will be required in order to continue farther than 0.9 mile up Stockport Creek. *Hudson River*—When heading over to Stockport Middle Ground, look carefully both ways to make sure no oncoming boats are in sight and then paddle straight across quickly. Be extra cautious when paddling along the west side of the island where the main shipping channel is. By early summer, choking plants can make paddling difficult along the east shore of the Hudson River opposite Stockport Middle Ground. Stockport Middle Ground is off-limits during nesting season for bald eagles. At such times paddlers should keep a responsible distance from the island, recognizing that the silent and sudden appearance of a canoe or kayak can be more startling and disruptive to nesting birds than the gradual, noisy approach of a motorboat. Landing on the shore by the Empire Brick Supply Company ruins is restricted from January 1 through September 30. The Amtrak railway passes directly in front of the parking lot, just east of the Hudson River. Stay back from the tracks. High-speed trains frequently pass by.

■ **Directions:** From Stottsville (junction of Rtes. 9 & 20), drive north on Rt. 9 for 3.3 miles. As soon as you cross over Stockport Creek, turn left onto Station Road (Rt. 22). From north of Stockport (junction of Rtes. 9J & 9), drive south on Rt. 9 for 1.1 miles and turn right onto Station Road (Rt. 22) just before crossing over Stockport Creek. From either direction, drive west on Station Road for 1.0 mile. When you come to the long parking area next to the Amtrak railway, bear left and park near the south end of the parking area, close to the railroad bridge. From here it is a short, 100-foot carry down a gravelly incline to the edge of Stockport Creek.

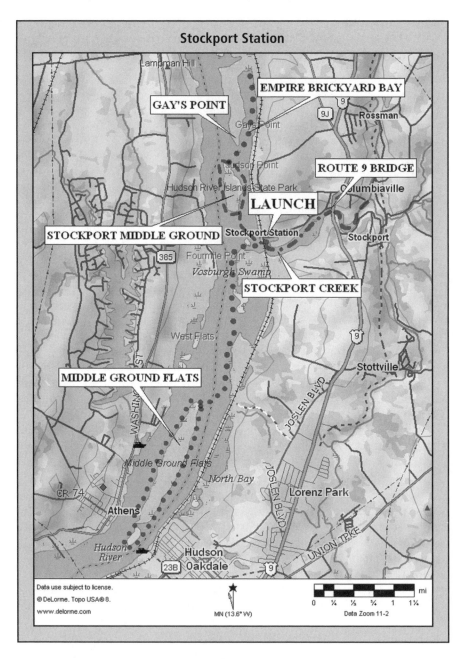

Stockport Station

The Paddle:

East on Stockport Creek—This paddle provides the opportunity to explore not only the Hudson, but also one of its main tributaries, Stockport Creek. Stock-

The historic Abram Staats House, near the confluence of Stockport Creek and the Hudson River. Photograph 2007.

port Creek is made up of two main branches—Claverack Creek, entering from the south, and Kinderhook Creek, entering from the north. Stockport Creek drains a watershed of 500 square miles, making it one of the ten largest tributaries entering the middle Hudson River.[1] At one time the stream was known as Major Abraham's Creek.

Follow Stockport Creek upstream, east, for 0.9 mile to the Rt. 9 bridge or 1.8 miles to its confluence with Claverack and Kinderhook creeks. During the first part of the trip, the creek is wide and fairly deep, with houses and docks scattered about along the north shoreline. The creek is broken up by a number of small islands.

For the second part of the trip, the stream becomes much rockier and shallower. You may want to turn around when you reach the Rt. 9 bridge. Several hundred feet of substantial rapids and tiny cascades have to be portaged around in order to continue farther upstream.

North to Stockport Middle Ground—Head west on Stockport Creek, immediately passing under a railroad bridge and then out onto the Hudson River. You will see a small island straight ahead. Veer to the right, paddling north, and within 0.5 mile you will be parallel to the south end of Stockport Middle Ground. This is an artificial island created by an overlay of dredge materials from the Hudson River. The island is held together by the forest and brush that have tenaciously taken hold along the island's entire length. At its south end the land rises up to a height of nearly twenty-five feet.

You will find yourself far away from the east shore as you maneuver to get around tangles of water chestnuts. Continue paddling upriver between Stockport Middle Ground (to your left) and the east bank of the Hudson River (to your right). These waters are weed-choked. Rounding the north end of Stockport Middle Ground, at 1.3 miles, you will spot a primitive campsite. You will pass by a sliver of an island created by dikes just north of the tip of Stockport Middle

Ground. Continue south along the island's west side. Stockport Middle Ground can be circumnavigated in 1.7 miles.

North to the end of Empire Brickyard Bay—Gay's Point is roughly 0.2 mile north of Stockport Middle Ground and consists of a mile-long peninsula with much potential for wilderness camping along the west shore. Gay's Point, like Stockport Middle Ground, is artificially made. It is accessible only by water; overland access is not permitted. At one time it was an island. Paddlers will find that the shorelines of both Stockport Middle Ground and Gay's Point are sandy and beach-like. This is the result of intertidal vegetation being unable to take root, partially because of boat-generated waves pounding the shoreline. A 1.0-mile-long nature trail follows around the perimeter of Gay's Point. Empire Brickyard Bay is on the east side of the peninsula.

Gay's Point and Stockport Middle Ground together make up Hudson River Islands State Park, a designated Greenway Water Trail Campsite. The two bodies of land contain over thirty campsites accessible by boat only. The park is managed by Schodack Island State Park in the Saratoga-Capital District Region.

Starting from the railroad bridge at the mouth of Stockport Creek, paddle north, paralleling the east shore of the Hudson River. Don't be surprised to see high-speed Amtrak trains racing by along the east bank during your paddle, for the tracks lie close to the river.

At 1.0 mile you will come to Judson Point on your right, where cement ruins can be seen. At 1.3 miles you will pass by the tip of Gay's Point, off to your left. You are now entering what duck hunters refer to as Empire Brickyard Bay.[2]

After 1.6 miles the channel ahead is marked by a series of wooden posts on both sides that protrude above the water line. At 1.9 miles you will come to an artificial, square-shaped inlet on your right that extends east for several hundred feet. During high tide you can paddle in, if you wish. A duck blind has been erected next to the entrance. At 2.0 miles the channel narrows considerably and is demarcated by a sliver of land on your left containing a row of trees. To your right are the ruins of the Empire Brick Supply Company. A long narrow cement wharf is surprisingly still intact. Red bricks engraved with the word "Empire" are strewn about everywhere.

A sign posted on a tree reminds visitors that this is a restricted area from January 1 to September 30 because it is the habitat for endangered species, including bald eagles. Paddlers should stay in their watercraft and not step ashore between those dates.

By 2.1 mile the way ahead becomes impassable and the end of Empire Brickyard Bay is clearly visible just beyond.

This paddle is best enjoyed by venturing out at low tide when many of the interesting features are at maximum visibility. On the other hand, if you wish to go under and through several railway culverts that lead to tidal ponds on the east side of the railroad causeway, you will need to head out at high tide.[3] (Check tides at: tidesandcurrents.noaa.gov.)

▶ **Stockport Station**

A surviving pier from the Empire Brick Supply Company. Photograph 2009.

South to Middle Ground Flats—Head downriver for 2.5 miles to the northern tip of Middle Ground Flats. Along the way, at 0.5 mile, you will pass by a substantial, 0.5-mile-long bay and marshland to your left.

You can use Middle Ground Flats either as a turnaround point or you may circumnavigate the island first (an additional 4.5 miles) before returning to your starting point.

History: Stockport Station is located at the confluence of the Hudson River and Stockport Creek and is historically significant because Henry Hudson came ashore here on September 17, 1609. Stockport is named after Stockport, England.

The house located just before the end of Station Road is the historic Staats House, built in 1664 by Major Abram (Abraham) Staats,[4] who was a surgeon and trader at Fort Orange (now Albany). This structure replaced an earlier house that was used by Staats for trading. That building was burned down by Indians in 1654 during the Esopus Wars.

The Empire Brick Supply Company/Empire Brickyard began operating in the 1880s and was a large manufacturer. The brickyard closed in 1940 after having exhausted all available clay. All that remains of the brickyard today are shoreline artifacts visible from the water and ruins farther into the woods and not visible from the shore. These interior ruins consist of six enduring kiln walls, in addition to a number of smaller surviving structures.[5]

The Empire Brickyard was the site of the "Battle of Stockport." It started in June 1900 when one of the employees developed the "Cuban Itch," which was quickly diagnosed as smallpox. The New York State Board of Health determined that the factory should be quarantined, but some of the workers, fearing contagion, fled the facility. The National Guard from Hudson was then called in to round up the escapees, and the affair became known as the Battle of Stockport.[6]

29 Hudson Waterfront Park (Hudson)
A Lighthouse, Bays, and Nearby Islands

■ **Launch Site:** Hudson Riverfront Park off of Ferry Street at Hudson (Columbia County); cement ramp. Designated Greenway Water Trail Site with picnicking, bus, train, and tour boat services, and public bathrooms and showers located at the tour boat dock to the south.

■ **Delorme NYS Atlas & Gazetteer:** p. 52, BC3; **GPS:** 42°15.36′N; 73°47.87′W

■ **Destinations:** Middle Ground Flats, North Bay, South Bay, Hudson-Athens Lighthouse, Rogers Island

■ **Mileage:** Northwest to Middle Ground Flats—0.2 mile (one-way); around Middle Ground Flats 4.5 miles; northeast to North Bay south entrance—0.4 mile (one-way); around North Bay—variable mileage; northeast to North Bay north entrance—1.0 mile (one-way); around bay—variable mileage; south to South Bay—0.5 mile (one-way); up South Bay—0.3 mile (one-way); southwest to Hudson-Athens Lighthouse—0.5 mile (one-way); southwest to Rogers Island—2.5 miles (one-way); around Rogers Island—3.0 miles

■ **Comments:** Read "Caution" beginning on page xxii and "The Hudson River: Caution" on page 1. Use care when you're on the main part of the Hudson, as the shipping channel wanders back and forth across the river. Expect an increase in boat traffic near Hagar's Harbor Marina, Athens State Boat Launch, and Dutchman's Landing.

■ **Directions:** From the south—Entering Hudson on Rt. 9G/23B, turn left at the first stoplight onto Allen Street and drive northwest for 0.3 mile. Cross over South Front Street and continue straight onto Ferry Street. Within several hundred feet you will cross over a small bridge. Immediately turn right into the Hudson Riverfront Park, and park at the north end near the boat launch.

From the north—Entering Hudson on Rt. 9, proceed west until you come to the junction of Rtes. 9 & 9G/23B at the town square. From there, follow Rt. 9G/23B (Columbia Street) northwest. After 0.5 mile turn left onto North 3rd Street, following Rt. 9G/23B as it proceeds south. Go over 0.1 mile and turn right at a stoplight onto Allen Street. When you reach South Front Street, continue straight across onto Ferry Street. Cross over a small bridge and then turn right into Hudson Riverfront Park. Park near the boat launch site.

The Paddle:

Northwest to Middle Ground Flats—Head straight (northwest) across the river for 0.2 mile to reach the east side of Middle Ground Flats. From here circle around the island's 4.5-mile perimeter and return to the boat launch, a round-trip of about 5.0 miles. As you proceed along the island's east side, don't be surprised to see a number of shanty-like camps near the shoreline, even in places where state land markers are prominently displayed on trees.

▶ **Hudson Waterfront Park**

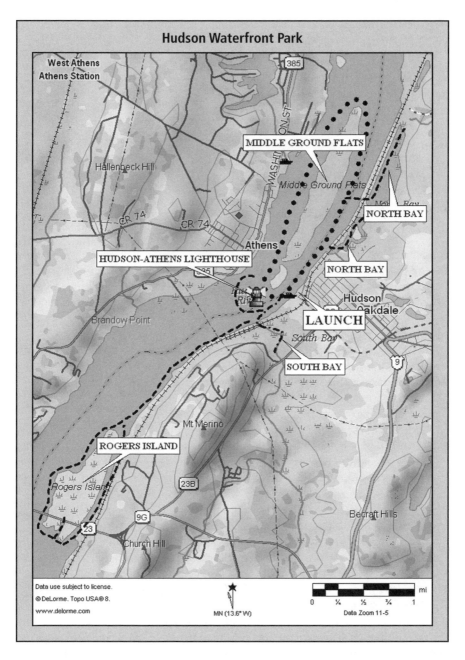

Be sure to look for the marshy treeless area along the south half of Middle Ground Flats. At one time a channel here divided Middle Ground Flats into two sections. By taking advantage of this channel, a ferry line was able to transport

Small camps on stilts can be seen at the south end of North Bay. Photograph 2009.

customers directly between Hudson and Athens. The ferry operated without the help of poles, ropes, or steam power. Six horses in harness would plod along on a large turntable, with power from the revolving turntable transmitted through gears to a vertical paddle wheel that in turn drove the boat through the water. This system generally worked well except when the current was especially strong, in which case it would out-perform the horses and sweep the ferry miles downstream.[1]

In 1845 the steamer *Swallow* rammed into a small, rocky section just offshore from the south end of Middle Ground Flats while racing two other boats downriver. Out of three hundred passengers, fifty died in the disaster.[2]

Northeast to North Bay—From the launch site, head northeast along the east bank, paralleling a dock that extends along the riverfront for 0.2 mile.

North Bay, as you will soon discover, is a fascinating place to explore. A narrow strip of land divides the bay into two halves. Nineteenth-century railroad engineers also erected a causeway between the bay and the Hudson River, setting the two bodies of water apart. Fortunately, culverts, which were installed to allow the exchange of water between the Hudson and the bay, now provide entry points into the bay for paddlers. Access to the south half of North Bay is reached in 0.4 mile; access to the north half is reached in 1.0 mile.

North Bay encompasses 125 acres of marshland and is part of the 714-acre Greenport Conservation Area, which is owned by the Open Space Institute (OSI) and managed by the Columbia County Land Conservancy.

North Bay South Entrance—Heading northeast from the boat launch, you will reach the first railroad culvert in 0.4 mile, shortly after passing by the end of the long waterfront dock. Even at high tide the culvert is high enough for a kayak to slip through (although some ducking may be required). Paddle through the culvert and you will come out into the south portion of North Bay, where a number of shanty-like camps, many on stilts, are visible at the bay's south end.

Once inside the bay, proceed north, following either the channel closest to the railroad causeway or the one farther to the east. The two are separated by

▶ **Hudson Waterfront Park**

Downriver views
from Hudson
Riverfront Park.
Photograph 2009.

a mass of dense weeds, cattails, and grasses, hundreds of feet wide and impenetrable except at the two ends of the bay.

As you paddle through these marshlands, you will discover a seemingly endless number of side passages and channels—some wide, some narrow—all formed by towering walls of cattails and high grasses. This is particularly true at the north end, where the channels become narrower and more labyrinthine. You can have much fun as you explore this maze of waterways, tracking down dead-end channels, retracing your path and finding new leads.

North Bay North Entrance—Once you have explored the south section of North Bay, return to the culvert and paddle back out onto the Hudson River. From here, paddle north, upriver, for another 0.5 mile until you come to a large culvert leading into the north section of North Bay. This section is wider and more expansive than the south section and its claustrophobic labyrinth of channels. Leads can be followed north for over 0.7 mile.

South to South Bay—Although South Bay was essentially filled in and made impassable many years ago, there are still sections that can be paddled. From the boat launch, head south down the Hudson along the east shore. In 0.2 mile you will pass by the dock for the *Spirit of Hudson*—a commercial liner that takes passengers on river excursions. Immediately past the dock are three tiny inlets, none of which go inland for more than several hundred feet, followed by a huge wharf owned by the St. Lawrence Cement Company. In 0.5 mile you will reach a culvert under the railroad track. The culvert is less than 0.2 mile from the Hudson-Athens Lighthouse, directly to the west. Turn left and paddle through the culvert into South Bay. A wide channel can now be followed south for over 0.2 mile. Once a fork is reached, the waterway becomes narrower. Going left leads quickly to a dead end. Veering right extends the paddle for another 0.1 mile, depending upon such variables as blowdown and the tides.

Southwest to Hudson-Athens Lighthouse—Head southwest, downriver, for 0.5 mile to reach the Hudson-Athens Lighthouse. The lighthouse is one of seven on the Hudson River that have survived into the twenty-first century. It is listed on the National Register of Historic Places and has become a museum chartered by the State of New York. The tiny island supporting the lighthouse can be circled, but landing on it is not permitted.

Southwest to Rogers Island—Proceed downstream for 2.5 miles until you reach the northeast tip of Rogers Island. Continue downriver along the island's west side, rounding the south end at 1.6 miles, then proceed upstream along Hallenbeck Creek for 1.4 miles, following along the island's east side. When you reach the northeast tip of Rogers Island, you will have completed a 3.0-mile circumnavigation of the island.

Take note that at the south end of Rogers Island is a small channel that leads nearly 0.5 mile north into the island's interior, inviting exploration. Rogers Island is a substantial island, covering 650 acres and possessing one of the largest tidal swamp forests in the Hudson estuary. It is also notable for being the site of a climactic battle between the Mohawks and Mohicans in which the Mohicans were resoundingly defeated.

As you circle around the island, you will pass under the Rip Van Winkle Bridge twice—four times if you paddle up and down the 0.5-mile-long interior channel. The Rip Van Winkle Bridge is a nearly mile-long cantilever bridge built in 1935 by the Frederick Share Corporation. Tolls are charged for eastbound traffic only.[3]

History: Despite being far removed from the Atlantic Ocean, the City of Hudson at one time was a major whaling port settled by New England whalers and merchants.[4] In 1800, John Maude (an English traveler) observed that there was a windmill above the city,[5] something not commonly encountered inland from the ocean and perhaps symbolic of Hudson's position as a prominent seaport.

Until the Hudson River was dredged and substantially deepened, the city of Hudson was as far upriver as large ships could venture. Postcard ca. 1900.

► **Hudson Waterfront Park**

In the latter part of the twentieth century, Hudson reinvented itself, becoming a notable antique center.

The boat launch is located near the base of a tall, sixty-foot-high[6] slate bluff that rises abruptly from the river. At the top of the bluff is Promenade Park (Parade Hill), once favored by Victorian strollers for its panoramic views of the Hudson River, Mount Merino, the Helderbergs, and the Catskills.

Until the Hudson River was dredged and deepened, South Bay (just downstream from the put-in) was the last upriver stop for ocean-going ships. Cargo bound for the north would be taken off these large seafaring ships and then transported upriver by land.[7] At the time Hudson was founded, in 1785, South Bay covered 110 acres and was a significant tidal estuary as well as an emerging port of major significance. This changed radically, however, as the city underwent a period of heavy industrialization. The Hudson Iron Company constructed piles on South Bay and filled its waters with slag.[8] Other businesses soon followed, expanding their warehouses and docks into the bay, with the result that the bay was gradually turned mostly into a semisolid land mass.

In 1851 the Hudson River Railroad built a narrow causeway across the bay, which further isolated South Bay from the river, closing it off with additional earth and rubble. Then, in the 1920s, when dredging resumed on the Hudson, more fill was added to the Greenport shoreline, the south side of South Bay.[9] Today, South Bay is essentially a swamp.

Fortunately, North Bay (north of Hudson) remains a body of water, though marshy.

Western Shore: Greene County

30 | Cornell Park (New Baltimore)
Accessing the Hudson River opposite Houghtaling Island

■ **Launch Site:** Cornell Park at New Baltimore (Greene County); gravelly inclined road to water's edge. Designated Greenway Water Trail Site with port-a-sans (chemical toilets), fishing, and hiking trail.

■ **Delorme NYS Atlas & Gazetteer:** p. 52, A3; **GPS:** 42°26.72'N; 73°47.21'W

■ **Destinations:** Hannacroix Creek, Matthews Point, Houghtaling Island

■ **Mileage:** To Hannacroix Creek—1.1 miles (one-way); up Hannacroix Creek—0.2 mile (one-way); to Matthews Point—1.1 miles (one-way); to south tip of Houghtaling Island—1.5 miles (one-way)

■ **Comments:** Read "Caution" beginning on page xxii and "The Hudson River: Caution" on page 1. Watch out for the dike at the south end of Hannacroix Bay that becomes evident at low tide. Be prepared for an increase in boat traffic near the Schodack Island State Park Boat Launch, and Shady Lane Marina.

■ **Directions:** From Coxsackie (junction of Rt. 385 and Main Street), drive northwest on Rt. 385 for 0.7 mile. Turn right onto Lawrence Avenue just before reaching an underpass and proceed north for 6.3 miles. The road turns into Rt. 61 after 0.3 mile. When you arrive at Rt. 144 in New Baltimore, turn right and drive east for 100 feet. Then turn right onto Church Street and go downhill for 0.1 mile. When you come to Main Street, turn left, drive north for 100 feet, and then turn right onto Mill Street. Cornell Park is on your left, 100 feet down the road.

From Coeymans (junction of Rtes. 144 & 143), drive south on Rt. 144 for 1.7 miles, turn left onto Main Street just before entering the village, and go downhill for 0.3 mile. Then turn left onto Mill Street and continue downhill for less than 100 feet to Cornell Park, on your left.

The Paddle:

North—Head upstream for 1.1 miles to the bay formed by the mouth of Hannacroix Creek. Along the way you will pass by the Shady Harbor Marina with its extensive docks at roughly 0.4 mile. Watch out for the dike that spans the south end of Hannacroix Bay and is revealed during low tide. Hannacroix Creek can be paddled upstream for 0.2 mile before rapids and shallows force a turnaround.

South—Going downriver, you will reach Matthews Point at 1.1 miles and, in another 0.4 mile, the south tip of Houghtaling Island, which extends nearly into the middle of the river. Do not attempt to paddle to the south tip of Houghtaling Island unless the weather is calm, no boats are coming from either direction, and you are confident in your abilities to paddle across open waters. If you choose to round the tip of the island to paddle north up Schodack Creek, be sure to paddle over to the navigational light before turning; otherwise you may run into a submerged line of piles that extends from the land to this point (see chapter "Schodack Island" for more details).

▶ **Cornell Park**

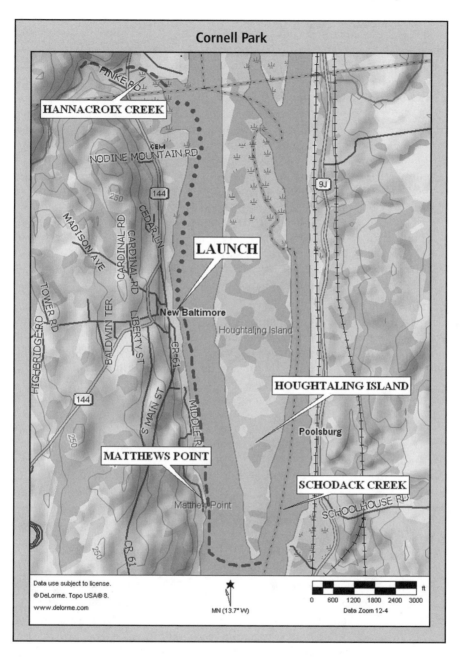

Cornell Park

History: After the Revolutionary War, New Baltimore was heavily involved in the shipbuilding industry. The shoreline above today's Cornell Park's gazebo, as you headed south, was full of warehouses and wharfs, humming with human activity as sloops, schooners, steam-driven tugboats, barges, and other passenger and cargo vessels were built. This continued right into the 1920s. Clesson Bush, New Baltimore Historian, states, "The Sherman family and others operated active trading businesses, shipping and receiving agricultural and other goods up and down the Hudson and as far away as the West Indies and Europe."[1]

Today a majority of the hamlet is listed as a National Register Historic District because of its collection of eighteenth- and nineteenth-century buildings. According to local kayaker Mark Peckham, "The quiet hamlet . . . paints a memorable and picturesque scene deeply evocative of an earlier era."[2] New Baltimore is built on the side of a steep, sloping hill, with Cornell Park resting on the bottommost terrace, directly facing the river and Houghtaling Island. Many of the houses are over a hundred feet above the park.

Cornell Park is named after the Cornell brothers—Theodore, a prominent local physician, and James, a Reformed Church minister. Look for the big yellow building directly across from the park—a former residence of the Cornells.[3] Cornell is a historic name along the Hudson River. The Cornell Steamboat Company out of Kingston, owned by Thomas Cornell, was one of the largest steamboat lines in the nineteenth century.

As a point of interest to cinema fans, the movie *Little Old New York*, starring Fred McMurray and Alice Faye, was filmed in New Baltimore in 1939.[4] It is the story of Robert Fulton's attempt to convince skeptical old New York that a ship without sails could be made to go up and down the Hudson River.

By the time Hannacroix Creek reaches the flat waters near New Baltimore, it has dropped precipitously over a half-dozen waterfalls. Postcard ca. 1920.

Cornell Park

Coxsackie Riverside Park (Coxsackie)
Island-Hopping along the Hudson River

31

■ **Launch Site:** Coxsackie Riverside Park & State Boat Launch, off of South River Street, Coxsackie (Greene County); hard-surface ramp with parking for over thirty cars. Designated Greenway Water Trail site with lockable kayak storage racks, restrooms, picnicking, dining/restaurant, retail/supplies. For more information: coxsackie.org/park.html.

■ **Delorme NYS Atlas & Gazetteer:** p. 52, AB3; **GPS:** 42°21.19'N; 73°47.75'W

■ **Destinations:** Coxsackie Island, Rattlesnake Island, Little Nutten Hook, Gay's Point, Stockport Middle Ground

■ **Mileage:** North to Coxsackie Island—0.5 mile (one-way); around Coxsackie Island—1.9 miles; from Coxsackie Island to Rattlesnake Island—over 0.1 mile (one-way); around Rattlesnake Island—1.2 miles; northeast to Nutten Hook—0.5 mile (one-way); south to Little Nutten Hook—1.0 mile (one-way); south to Gay's Point—2.2 miles (one-way); south to Stockport Middle Ground—2.4 miles (one-way); around Stockport Middle Ground—1.7 miles

■ **Comments:** Read "Caution" beginning on page xxii and "The Hudson River: Caution" on page 1. Expect a small increase in boat traffic as you pass by the Coxsackie Yacht Club. Be extra cautious when paddling along the east side of Coxsackie and Rattlesnake islands where the main shipping channel is. Watch out for occasional eddies around the foundation ruins of the Coxsackie Lighthouse.

■ **Directions:** From the NYS Thruway (I-87), take Exit 21B for Coxsackie & Ravena. Turn left onto Rt. 9W and drive south for over 2.1 miles. Turn left onto Rt. 385 and drive east for 1.6 miles into Coxsackie. When you come to Mansion Street (where Rt. 385 bears right), proceed straight ahead and downhill on Mansion Street for 0.4 mile. At Reed Street turn left and drive east for 0.05 mile. Turn left onto South River Street and drive north 0.05 mile to the entrance to Riverside Park, on your right.

The Paddle:

Before leaving Coxsackie Riverside Park take note that the wreck of the 180-foot-long packet boat *Storm King* lies underwater along the north side of the park at the boat landing.[1] The wooden hull steamer was built in Wilmington, Delaware, in 1911. It ran on the Catskill Evening Line until 1931. The boat was broken up in 1936.[2]

Also take a look across the river and slightly north along the riverbank. You will see rising above the trees the brick chimney of the powerhouse that once served the Robert & William Scott Ice House.

North to Coxsackie and Rattlesnake Islands—Head up the Hudson River for roughly 0.5 mile until you reach the south end of Coxsackie Island. The island has also been known as "Budd's Island" and "Hauver Platte."[3] It can

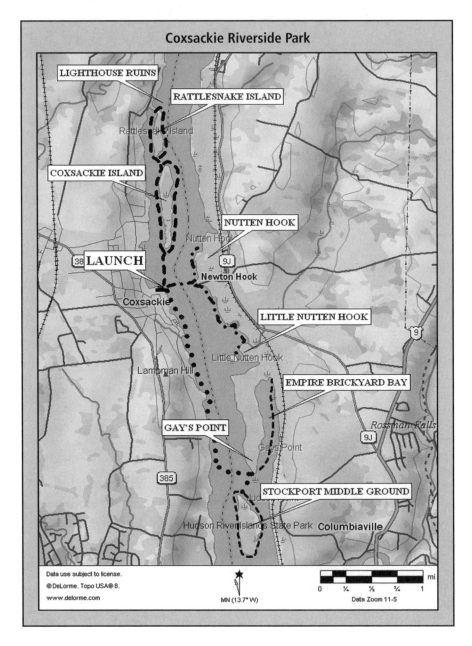

be circumnavigated in 1.9 miles. Sandy beaches are visible along the island's east shore.

Paddling north along the island's west shore, you will pass by the Coxsackie Yacht Club (a private marina) in 0.3 mile. Opposite the yacht club is a

▶ **Coxsackie Riverside Park**

docking area on Coxsackie Island's west shore where members of the club and their guests can debark and follow a boardwalk that leads to a rustic pavilion on the island's east side. The lower half of Coxsackie Island is owned by the Town of Coxsackie, the upper half by the yacht club.

As you approach the island's northwest side, you will observe hundreds of feet of wooden dikes that protect the island's exposed flank from the erosive power of the Hudson. Across the bay, on the Hudson's west shore, is a tiny man-made peninsula of rocks where an Adirondack-style lean-to overlooking the river has been erected by a private landowner.

From the north tip of Coxsackie Island, paddle over 0.1 mile farther north to reach the south tip of Rattlesnake Island. Although a causeway joins the north end of the island to the mainland, a tiny channel has been created that is more than wide enough to allow the passage of a canoe when the river level is sufficiently high. For this reason it is possible to circumnavigate Rattlesnake Island either by using the tiny channel or, if the river level is unusually low, by portaging your watercraft a very short distance across a narrowing in the causeway. Rattlesnake Island was earlier known as Lighthouse Island, after the lighthouse near its north end. The island probably never harbored rattlesnakes—only copperheads.[4]

Just 0.05 mile north of the island's north end is a circular conglomeration of rocks on which can be seen the cut-stone foundation of the old lighthouse with its intact, integrated stone stairway. Watch out for eddies around this obstruction that can be strong at times. The island is now used as an aid to navigation.

The Coxsackie Lighthouse was built in 1830 and then significantly rebuilt in 1868.[5] In 1903 the structure sustained major damage when its northern wall was repeatedly hit by onrushing blocks of ice. Despite structural damage, the lighthouse was propped back up and made operational again.[6] In 1940, however, the lighthouse was replaced by a steel skeletal structure, and later demolished.[7]

In earlier times it was known as "Old Maid's Light," after two spinsters who staffed it.[8] According to legend, the two women didn't have a bell handy to warn approaching ships in the fog, so they would bang a clunky spoon against a large frying pan to sound the alarm. An old postcard (circa 1910) shows the lighthouse on a tiny island barely larger than the building itself.

Northeast to Nutten Hook—Paddle across the Hudson and slightly upriver to reach Nutten Hook, 0.5 mile away. Do not attempt this unless the weather is calm, no boats are coming from either direction, and you are confident in your abilities to paddle across open waters. The ruins that you see along the east shoreline belong to the Robert & William Scott Ice House, which was constructed in 1885 (see chapter "Nutten Hook" for more details). Continue south for another 0.5 mile to reach Little Nutten Hook.

South to Little Nutten Hook, Gay's Point, and Stockport Middle Ground—Heading downriver will take you to the Hudson River Islands State Park, consisting of Gay's Point, a 1.0-mile-long peninsula that contains a landing, restrooms, and

Foundation ruins on Lighthouse Island. Photograph 2009.

campsites, and Stockport Middle Ground, a size-able island. Do not cross over to these sites unless the weather is calm, no boats are coming from either direction, and you are confident in your abilities to paddle across open waters. Both of these bodies of land were created from dredged materials when the Hudson River was deepened during the 1930s and 1940s. What keeps these land masses from breaking apart more quickly now is the proliferation of cottonwood and locust trees whose root systems create a patchwork holding the sandy soil together.[9]

Leaving Riverside Park behind, you will pass by Little Nutten Hook at 1.0 mile, and then Gay's Point at 2.2 miles. By rounding Gay's Point you can head northeast into a 1.0-mile-long cove called Empire Brickyard Bay if you wish to extend your paddle further. From Gay's Point, Stockport Middle Ground is reached in another 0.2 mile.

History: The word Coxsackie is possibly Algonquin for "place of owls," "cut banks,"[10] "migrating geese," or a corruption of the Dutch word *koeksrackie*, meaning "Cook's Little Reach."[11]

Coxsackie was settled in 1661 by Pieter Bronck of Albany. In 1663, Bronck built a home near present-day Route 9W that is now used as a museum by the Greene County Historical Society (gchistory.org/barns.php). In 1867 the village became incorporated. The historic Reed Street District in the village, listed on the National Register of Historic Places, is named after Eliakim Reed, who established a small wharf by the river in the early 1800s. The port developed into a major business district shipping farm goods and ice, principally to New York City. In 1864 fire severely damaged much of Reed Street.[12]

In 1854, Isabella Bird Bishop (the first female Fellow of the Royal Geographical Society) traveled up the Hudson and saw this section of the river as "a succession of small wild lakes, connected by narrow reaches, bound forever between abrupt precipices. ... At Coxsackie the river expands into a small lake, and the majestic Catsgill [*sic*] Mountains rise abruptly from the western side."[13]

▶ **Coxsackie Riverside Park**

Four Mile Point Preserve (Coxsackie)
Near Site of Historic Lighthouse

32

■ **Launch Site:** Four Mile Point Preserve, off of Four Mile Point Road, Coxsackie (Greene County); 0.1-mile carry down a graded trail from parking area to beach. For more information: scenichudson.org/oldsite/parks/shparks/fourmile/index. html.

■ **Delorme NYS Atlas & Gazetteer:** p. 52, B3; **GPS:** 42°19.05′N; 73°47.17′W

■ **Destinations:** Stockport Middle Ground, Gay's Point, Stockport Creek, Hudson Anchorage/Vosburgh Marsh

■ **Mileage:** East to Stockport Middle Ground—0.2 mile (one-way); around Stockport Middle Ground—1.7 miles; from north end of Stockport Middle Ground to Gay's Point—0.2 mile (one-way); up east side of Gay's Point to end of Empire Brickyard Bay—1.0 mile (one-way); from south tip of Stockport Middle Ground to Stockport Creek—0.8 mile to creek (one-way); up Stockport Creek to Route 9 bridge—1.0 mile (one-way), to confluence with Kinderhook Creek & Claverack Creek from Rt. 9 bridge—0.8 mile farther (one-way); southwest to Four Mile Point—0.8 mile (one-way), to Hudson Anchorage/Vosburgh Marsh—2.1 miles (one-way)

■ **Comments:** Read "Caution" beginning on page xxii and "The Hudson River: Caution" on page 1. Be extra cautious when paddling along the east side of Stockport Middle Ground where the main shipping channel is. Stay clear of Stockport Middle Ground during nesting season. A kiosk near shoreline contains relevant historical information about the preserve. By early summer, choking water plants can make paddling difficult near the east bank of the Hudson River opposite Stockport Middle Ground. A short portage will be required in order to continue farther than 0.9 mile up Stockport Creek. Be prepared for an increase in boat traffic near the boat launch at Stockport Station.

■ **Directions:** From Athens (junction of Second Street & Rt. 385), drive north on Rt. 385 for over 4.1 miles and turn right onto Four Mile Point Road. From Coxsackie (junction of Mansion Street and Rt. 385), drive south on Rt. 385 for 2.7 miles and turn left onto Four Mile Point Road. From either direction, drive east downhill on Four Mile Point Road for 0.5 mile and continue straight into the parking area for the preserve where the main road bears to the right. Follow a wide trail downhill for 0.1 mile to the beach. Along the way you can detour momentarily, following a secondary trail that leads uphill to a nearly 100-foot-high area called Barker Hill for views of the Hudson River.

The Paddle:

East to Stockport Middle Ground—Paddle straight across the river for less than 0.2 mile to the west side of Stockport Middle Ground (an island). From there, Stockport Middle Ground can be circumnavigated in 1.7 miles. You will notice that the southwest end of the island is steeply walled and earthen. This bank is a

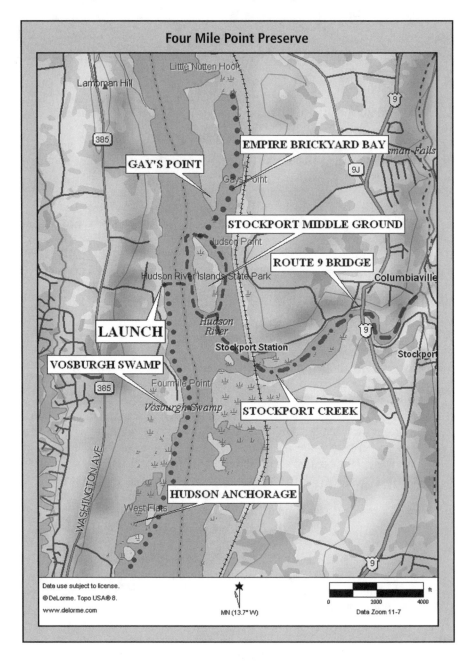

nesting site each spring for a colony of bank swallows. The rest of the shoreline around the island is fairly flat. At the north end of Stockport Middle Ground, opposite a narrow, artificial island, is a primitive campsite.

▶ **Four Mile Point Preserve**

North from Stockport Middle Ground to Gay's Point—Head north from the north tip of Stockport Middle Ground to reach Gay's Point in 0.2 mile; from here, you can paddle east around Gay's Point into a cove called, by local fishermen, Empire Brickyard Bay that goes north for up to 1.0 mile (tidal conditions permitting).

Southeast from Stockport Middle Ground to Stockport Creek—From the south tip of Stockport Middle Ground, travel diagonally southeast (left), heading toward the rust-colored railroad bridge about 0.6 mile away that marks the beginning of Stockport Creek. Once you reach Stockport Creek, it can be followed upstream for 1.0 mile to the Route 9 bridge or, with much more difficulty and portages, 1.8 miles to the confluence of Kinderhook Creek and Claverack Creek.

South to Four Mile Point and Hudson Anchorage/Vosburgh Marsh—Head downstream. In 0.8 mile you will pass by Four Mile Point, a high bluff to your right. At 2.1 miles you will reach a shallow area of the river, called Hudson Anchorage, in the West Flats, which are part of Vosburgh Marsh. Entering near the yellow buoy, you can explore the marsh through its various channels. At one time three separate islands existed here, but they now have all been incorporated into the marshlands.

History: The 7.6-acre Four Mile Point Preserve was developed jointly in 1992 by Scenic Hudson, the Town of Coxsackie, and the Greene County Soil & Water Conservation District. It is presently owned by Scenic Hudson and is part of 279.6 acres of protected lands.

Scenic view near Four Mile Point. Postcard ca. 1920.

A nineteenth-century lighthouse stood on top of a nearby rocky bluff to the south. The bluff was called Echo Hill, so-named because skippers bounced echoes off the fifty-foot-high cliffs at night and during fog to help them navigate. The bluff was also known as Paddock's Island. Although not strictly an island, it did have a marshy area behind it[1] called Vosburgh Swamp. The lighthouse was built in 1831 and consisted principally of a round tower[2] that in 1880 was replaced by a twenty-five-foot-high iron structure.[3] All traces of the lighthouse are gone today, the structure having been dismantled around 1928.[4] The early lighthouse was manned by Jacob Hallenbeck, whose dwelling was nearby.[5] A small lighthouse along Four Mile Point Road was constructed in 2008.

During the heyday of ice harvesting on the Hudson River, the Knickerbocker Ice Company leased nearby Lampman's Dock in order to ship blocks of ice to downstate customers.[6] Some of the icehouses grew to enormous size. The Tillie Littlefield—the Knickerbocker Ice Company's largest icehouse—contained twelve rooms and three double elevators, and could hold up to sixty tons of ice.[7]

Archaeological digs have determined that, much earlier, the site was used by Native Americans for fishing. Then, in 1665, the property was purchased as part of the Loonenburgh Patent from Native Americans.

Stockport Middle Ground was artificially created in the 1930s and 1940s when the river was dredged to deepen the main channel. The fact that the island is of fairly recent origin has not stopped life from proliferating on it, as you will see from the large population of cottonwoods and locust trees. The island's north end allows for picnicking and some camping, except during nesting season when bald eagles take over and access to the island is restricted.[8] Stockport Middle Ground is part of the Hudson River Islands State Park.

▶ **Four Mile Point Preserve**

Athens State Boat Launch (Athens)
A Large Earthen Dam and Spillway

33

- **Launch Site:** Athens State Boat Launch north of Athens (Greene County); cement ramp and parking for over twenty-five cars. Designated Greenway Water Trail Site with lockable kayak storage racks, picnicking, dining/restaurant, retail/supplies, lodging, and fishing. The Athens State Boat Launch is managed by Schodack Island State Park in the Saratoga-Capital District Region.
- **Delorme NYS Atlas & Gazetteer:** p. 52, BC3; **GPS:** 42°16.33′N; 73°48.12′W
- **Destinations:** Sleepy Hollow Reservoir Dam, Middle Ground Flats
- **Mileage:** Up Murderer's Kill to Sleepy Hollow Reservoir Dam—1.0 mile (round-trip); to Middle Ground Flats—0.2 mile (one-way); around Middle Ground Flats—4.4 miles; to village of Athens—0.9 mile (one-way)
- **Comments:** Read "Caution" beginning on page xxii and "The Hudson River: Caution" on page 1. *Murderer's Kill*—When paddling up the Murderer's Kill, choose a calm day and watch the weather. The current is generally mild to moderate except during the early spring. Since the creek is affected by tides, plan to paddle upstream at high tide. Check tides at: tidesandcurrents.noaa.gov. *Hudson River*—Be extra cautious when paddling along the east side of Middle Ground Flats where the main shipping channel is. Be prepared for an increase in boat traffic near Hagar's Harbor Marina and the Hudson Riverfront Boat Launch & Marina.
- **Directions:** From Athens (junction of Rt. 385 & Second Street), drive north on Rt. 385 for over 1.0 mile. Turn right into the Athens State Boat Launch just before crossing over Murderer's Kill. The launch is virtually at the confluence of Murderer's Kill and the Hudson River. From Coxsackie (junction of Rt. 385 & Mansion Street), drive south on Rt. 385 for 5.8 miles. As soon as you cross over Murderer's Kill, turn left into the Athens State Boat Launch site.

The Paddle:

Northwest—Paddle upstream on Murderer's Kill, quickly passing under Route 385 and then a smaller, abandoned bridge whose narrow opening constricts the creek. The second bridge was built for the abandoned Athens Branch of the West Shore Railroad, established in 1883.[1]

Once you clear the second bridge, the creek widens appreciably. In another 0.4 mile you will reach the base of the Sleepy Hollow Reservoir Dam, about 30–40 feet high, with its wide, inclined spillway. The dam is quite impressive, particularly when seen from the level of the creek. The Sleepy Hollow Reservoir is an artificial, 2.5-mile-long, 324-acre lake[2] created by damming the Murderer's Kill. The lake is quite substantial in size, lying within the boundaries of both Athens and Coxsackie,[3] and is ringed by numerous private homes.

East—From the mouth of Murderer's Kill, paddle straight across the Hudson River for 0.2 mile to the west shore of Middle Ground Flats, a narrow, slender

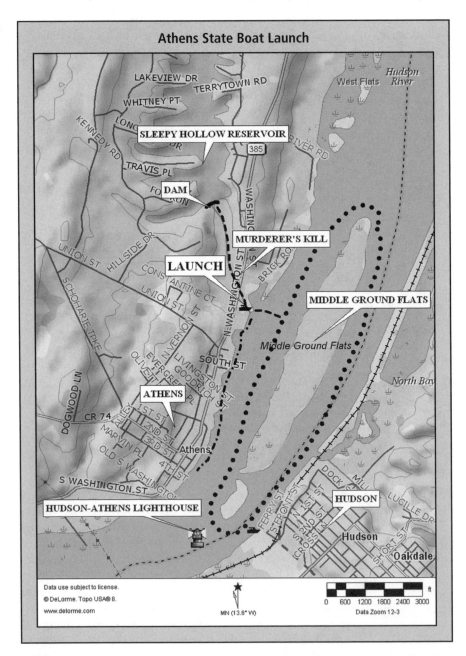

island. Head upstream for 0.8 mile, clearing the north end of the island where a small beach area can be seen. Continue downriver along the east shore of the island, undoubtedly sharing this part of the Hudson with a few passing boats,

▶ **Athens State Boat Launch**

and round the south end in 3.0 miles, where an uninviting marsh is passed. The island, as the name suggests, is essentially flat, but heavily forested.

South—Heading downstream you will reach the village of Athens in 0.9 mile. Along the way you will pass by a tiny cove to your right at 0.3 mile, where the shoreline facilities of Peckham Industries can be seen as well as a number of old barges that have been abandoned and left to disintegrate in the water. At 0.5 mile the old stone Albertus Van Loon house, whose back faces the river, can be glimpsed to your right. The *Half Moon* is frequently docked at the marine repair business here when it needs work.

The Van Loon house, a stone Dutch Colonial structure, was built in 1724 by Albertus, son of Jan Van Loon (the area's first patentee) and has been lived in ever since. It is listed on the National Register of Historical Places.

History: In 1999 major improvements were made at the Athens State Boat Launch, including dredging the lower part of Murderer's Kill near its mouth. Murderer's Kill is a medium-sized stream that rises in the hills northwest of the Sleepy Hollow Reservoir near Route 9W. Early records indicate that the stream was known by the Dutch as the Mudenaer (Kill) and Mudder Creek.[4] The stream may have been named to memorialize a massacre.[5]

Murderer's Kill is part of the Vosburgh Swamp & Middle Ground Flats preserve. The preserve encompasses 1,200 acres and has roughly 4 miles of shoreline along the Hudson River's west bank. The area includes mudflats, freshwater marshes, freshwater tidal marshes, paludal (marshy) hardwood swamps, and islands created from dredged materials, as well as a Murderer's Kill (a freshwater stream).[6] Scenic Hudson bought the 112-acre Vosburgh Swamp in 2006.[7]

Murderer's Kill starts at the Sleepy Hollow Reservoir dam, 0.5 mile upstream from the Hudson River. Photograph 2007.

Athens Kayak Launch (Athens)
A Historic Lighthouse Looms Invitingly in the River

34

- **Launch Site:** Athens Kayak Launch at end of Fourth Street in Athens (Greene County). Designated Greenway Water Trail Site with restrooms, picnicking, dining/restaurant, retail/supplies, and fishing.
- **Delorme NYS Atlas & Gazetteer:** p. 52, BC3; **GPS:** 42°15.49′N; 73°48.57′W
- **Destinations:** Hudson-Athens Lighthouse, Middle Ground Flats
- **Mileage:** To Hudson-Athens Lighthouse—0.6 mile (one-way); to Middle Ground Flats—0.2 mile (one-way); around Middle Ground Flats—4.4 miles
- **Comments:** Read "Caution" beginning on page xxii and "The Hudson River: Caution" on page 1. Be prepared for an increase in boat traffic near the Athens State Boat Launch, Dutchman's Landing, and Hudson Riverfront Boat Launch & Marina.
- **Directions:** From north of Catskill (junction of Rtes. 23A & 385), drive north on Rt. 385 for 4.0 miles. From Coxsackie (junction of Rt. 385 & Mansion Street), drive south for 6.8 miles. At the center of Athens, turn east off Rt. 385 onto Second Street and drive downhill for 0.05 mile. At the end of Second Street, turn right onto South Water Street and drive southwest for 0.05 mile. Park at the end of Fourth Street where a pier and river access has been recently created.

The Paddle:

Head east across the river for 0.2 mile until you reach the west side of Middle Ground Flats, a heavily forested island. Middle Ground Flats is believed by some to be the hidden shoal that caused Henry Hudson's ship, the *Half Moon*, to momentarily run aground, forcing Hudson and his crew to wait until high tide before resuming their travels.[1] Two centuries later, dredging began on the Hudson River, and Middle Ground Flats was transformed from a shallow mud bar into an island.

North—Middle Ground Flats can be circumnavigated in 4.4 miles, going either clockwise or counterclockwise.

Southeast—From Middle Ground Flats, proceed downriver, veering east, until you reach the Hudson-Athens Lighthouse, a paddle of roughly 0.3 mile from the southwest tip of Middle Ground Flats. Be alert for boat traffic once you leave the southern end of the island.

The towering hill visible southeast of the Hudson-Athens lighthouse is 540-foot-high Mount Merino, named after the Merino sheep that once grazed on its slopes. The city of Hudson becomes evident once you clear Middle Ground Flats.

On a hill just beyond Mount Merino is Olana (meaning "our castle on high"[2]), the thirty-five-room Persian-style home of Frederic Edwin Church, the renowned Hudson River School painter and student of Thomas Cole. The mansion was completed in 1872. Perhaps Church's most magnificent accomplishment was when he turned his grand estate into a living "landscape painting." Church was meticulous in the placement of every tree, shrub, and rock on his land. The

▶ **Athens Kayak Launch**

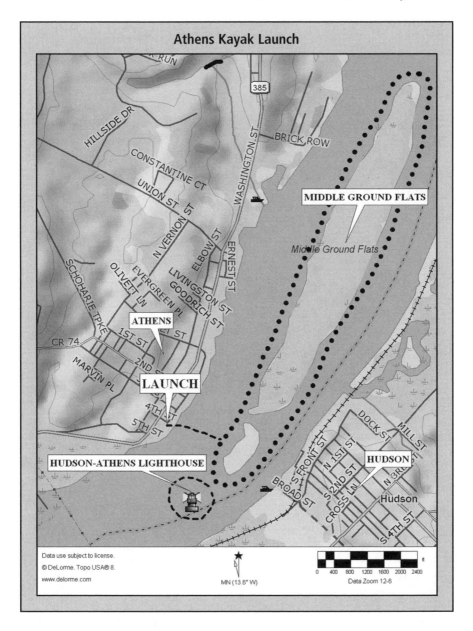

home is now a historic site and open to the public year-round. For further information, see olana.org.

Looking downriver farther south, you will see the 5,041-foot-long Rip Van Winkle Bridge, which links the village of Catskill with the city of Hudson. Farther southwest is the beautiful soaring skyline of the Catskill Mountains, which

Having saved many lives, The Hudson-
Athens Lighthouse now needed rescu-
ing itself. Photograph 2007.

Native Americans aptly called the
"Mountains of the Sky." Two of its high
peaks, Slide Mountain and Hunter
Mountain, tower over 4,000 feet.

History: Athens was initially known as
Loonenburgh (or Lunenberg) after the
Van Loon family, who were early settlers. It has also been called Esperanza and
Algiers, the latter name arising because some of the early inhabitants engaged
in piracy.[3] Athens became a port for whalers and sailing ships, and later became
a shipbuilding center. Hudson River day liners, transporting goods and passengers along the river, would stop frequently, and a variety of businesses developed
including the Athens Shipyard, Every & Eichhorn Ice House, Howlands Coal
Yard, and Clark Pottery. A waterfront fire in 1935 permanently changed the character of the village's riverfront.

The year 1935 proved to be fateful in other ways. It was the year that the Rip
Van Winkle Bridge connecting Hudson and Catskill was completed, resulting in
the sudden and rapid decline of the once-prosperous ferry business near Athens.[4]

Athens's most recent claim to fame is that it provided the background for a
dramatic scene in the 2005 movie version of *The War of the Worlds*, wherein the
Martian tripods with their death rays appeared as people fleeing New York City
were trying to cross the Hudson River by ferry.

The Hudson-Athens Lighthouse, originally called the Hudson City Lighthouse, became operational in 1874. Pilings were driven fifty feet down into the
riverbed and capped by granite piers. The two-story, fifty-four-foot-high, Empire-
style brick structure that you see today sits atop those piers.[5] The northern base
of the lighthouse is shaped like the prow of a ship in order to deflect spring's
rampaging volley of ice blocks and floodwaters.

The lighthouse was manned until the late 1940s. After 1949 automation
eliminated the need for a caretaker, and the building began to fall into neglect. In
1982 a group of concerned citizens from Greene and Columbia counties formed
the Hudson-Athens Lighthouse Preservation Society to ensure that the lighthouse
would be preserved. The building was originally leased in 1984 to the Lighthouse
Preservation Society; then, in 2000, the organization acquired full ownership of
the property.[6] For further information see hudsonathenslighthouse.org.

Like all lighthouses, the Hudson-Athens Lighthouse is unique, individual-
ized by the pulses of its green flashing light powered by a solar panel connected
to batteries. The Fourth Street launch site is located at the former boat inlet for
Elco Electric Launch Incorporated.

▶ **Athens Kayak Launch**

Cohotate Preserve (Athens/Catskill)
Accessing the Hudson River between Catskill and Athens   **35**

- ■ **Launch Site:** Cohotate Preserve off of Rt. 385 (Greene County); 0.4-mile carry to informal put-in at site of old icehouse. For more information: Greene County Soil & Water Conservation District, 907 Greene County Office Building, Cairo, NY 12413, (518) 622-3620, gcswcd.com/education/cohotate.html.
- ■ **Delorme NYS Atlas & Gazetteer:** p. 52, BC3; **GPS:** 42°14.66′N; 73°50.35′W
- ■ **Destinations:** Hudson-Athens Lighthouse, Rogers Island
- ■ **Mileage:** To Hudson-Athens Lighthouse—1.6 miles (one-way); to Rogers Island—0.6 mile (one-way); around Rogers Island—3.0 miles
- ■ **Comments:** Read "Caution" beginning on page xxii and "The Hudson River: Caution" on page 1. Be prepared for an increase in boat traffic near the Athens State Boat Launch, Dutchman's Landing, and Hudson Riverfront Boat Launch & Marina. Bring along a canoe/kayak carrier for this paddle. Beware of poison ivy.
- ■ **Directions:** From north of Catskill (junction of Rtes. 23 & 385), proceed northeast on Rt. 385 for 1.8 miles and turn right into the parking area for the Cohotate Preserve. Approaching from Athens (junction of Rt. 285 & Second Street), drive southwest for 2.2 miles and turn left into the preserve. Once you have parked, be prepared for a carry of roughly 0.4 mile to reach the river. A canoe/kayak carrier would be advisable here. Follow the main path (an old road) downhill as it descends fairly steeply to the river. Look for the Columbia-Greene Community College Environmental Field Station on your right as you reach the bottom. The flat area next to the river is the site of an old icehouse whose foundation can still be partially seen.

The Paddle:

Northeast—Head upriver, veering slightly east, to reach the Hudson-Athens Lighthouse in 1.6 miles. This is one of seven surviving lighthouses on the Hudson River and makes for a wonderful destination paddle (see previous chapter "Athens Kayak Launch" for more history).

The large hill to your right along the east side of the river is Mount Merino, a 540-foot-high rounded hill named after the Merino sheep introduced to the area in the nineteenth century.

Circle around the lighthouse (but don't land on it!) and return the way you came, a round-trip of 3.2 miles. Middle Ground Flats is only 0.3 mile northeast of the lighthouse and can be easily reached if you wish to lengthen your trip.

South—Paddle downstream, heading southeast, to reach the northeast tip of Rogers Island in 0.6 mile. To circumnavigate the island, continue down the Hudson River along the island's west side and then back up along its east side via Hallenbeck Creek, a paddle of roughly 3.0 miles. Near the island's south end you will pass under the Rip Van Winkle Bridge twice as you make your way around and back up.

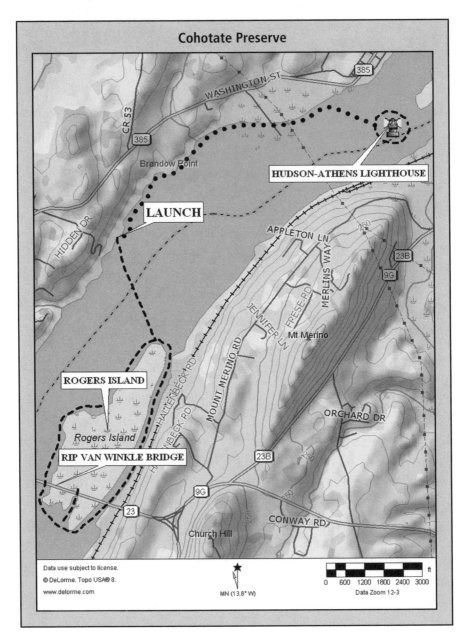

The trip is best taken in a counterclockwise fashion, since you will benefit from the Hudson's current paddling downstream (unless you are encountering a flood tide), and then enjoy its absence as you proceed upstream on Hallenbeck Creek.

▶ **Cohotate Preserve**

Rogers Island, 1.2 miles long and 0.4 mile wide, is owned by the New York State Department of Environmental Conservation (DEC). Its 650 acres of land include tidal forested wetlands and mudflats.[1] It was on this island that a decisive battle was fought between the Mohawks and the Mohicans, resulting in the Mohicans being badly beaten and ultimately banished to western Massachusetts. Today the island is a fertile spawning ground for American shad, striped bass, blueback herring, white perch, and alewife.[2]

Hike: The Cohotate Preserve offers some great opportunities for hiking, particularly along the Riverside Trail. A large portion of the trail parallels the Hudson River shoreline, crossing over several tiny gullies whose rushing streams are breathtaking to behold in the early spring. A total of nine footbridges provide traverses over the little ravines.

History: *Cohatatea* (cohotate) is an Iroquois language word for "water that flows two ways," an apt enough description of the tidal Hudson River, which reverses its direction several times a day. The Cohotate Preserve contains 52.5 acres of land with over 3,000 feet of river frontage. In 1978, Charles and Louise Gardner bequeathed the land to the Nature Conservancy, which then gifted it to Greene County in 1984. Since 1990 the preserve has been managed by the Greene County Soil & Water Conservation District.[3]

The Columbia-Greene Community College Environmental Field Station is a 30-foot-by-40-foot structure that contains a lab, classroom, and prep space. It is used as an adjunct for college programs and other environmental education programs.[4]

36 Dutchman's Landing (Catskill)
Confluence of the Hudson River & Catskill Creek

■ **Launch Sites:** Hudson River—Dutchman's Landing near end of Main Street in Catskill (Greene County); cement ramp. Catskill Creek—Kiwanis Park off of West Main Street in Catskill (Greene County); shore launch.

■ **Delorme NYS Atlas & Gazetteer:** p. 52, C3; **Estimated GPS:** Dutchman's Landing—42°12.68'N; 73°51.24'W; Kiwanis Park—42°13.10'N; 73°52.070'W

■ **Destinations:** Rogers Island, Catskill Creek, Dubois Creek, RamsHorn Creek

■ **Mileage:** To Rogers Island—0.7 miles (one-way); around Rogers Island—3.0 miles; up Catskill Creek—2.6 miles (one-way); up Dubois Creek—0.5 mile (one-way); to RamsHorn Creek—1.0 mile (one-way); up RamsHorn Creek—variable, depending upon tide; up Catskill Creek from Kiwanis Park—1.5 miles (one-way); down Catskill Creek from Kiwanis Park—1.1 miles (one-way)

■ **Comments:** Read "Caution" beginning on page xxii and "The Hudson River: Caution" on page 1. *Hudson River*—Be prepared for an increase in boat traffic near the Athens State Boat Launch and Hudson Riverfront Boat Launch & Marina. *Catskill Creek*—When heading out onto Catskill Creek, choose a calm day and watch the weather. Current and winds can be severe at times. Watch out for boat traffic, particularly fast-moving boats whose wakes can capsize a small watercraft. Turn around upstream when rapids and shallows are encountered. *RamsHorn Creek & Dubois Creek*—These creeks are tidal and therefore best paddled when the tide is high. Check tides at: tidesandcurrents.noaa.gov. Current is generally mild to moderate. The wind tends to be quietest in the early morning and evening.

■ **Directions:** From the NYS Thruway (I-87), get off at Exit 21 for Catskill & Cairo. At 0.1 mile past the Thruway tollbooth, turn left onto Rt. 23B and follow it southeast for a total of 3.1 miles. (As you approach the village of Catskill, Rt. 23B becomes the town's Main Street).

To Dutchman's Landing—At 3.1 miles (0.1 mile before the road's terminus), turn left where signs indicate the way to Dutchman's Landing. Drive northeast for 0.1 mile and park in the area provided to your left, directly in front of the boat launch.

To Kiwanis Park—At 2.4 miles turn right onto Bridge Street (Rt. 385), approximately midway through the village of Catskill. Drive west for over 0.1 mile, crossing over Catskill Creek in the process. At the end of the bridge, turn right onto West Main Street and drive northwest for 0.1 mile. Turn right into a long parking area next to Catskill Creek, where two gazebos can be seen. The kayak launch site is at the east end of the parking area. Kiwanis Park, overlooking Catskill Creek, memorializes Vincent Sheridan, who was charter president of the organization from 1986 to 1987.[1]

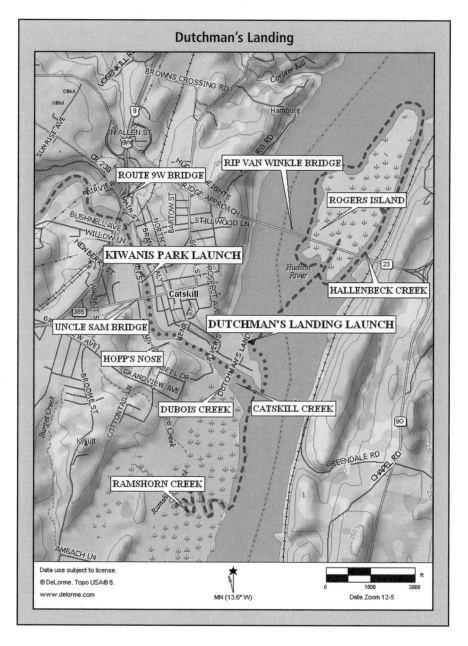

The Paddles:

From Dutchman's Landing Access

    Northeast—Head upstream on the Hudson River, veering slightly east, until you reach the south end of Rogers Island at 0.7 mile. Huge pillars supporting the

The Rip Van Winkle Bridge crosses over historic Rogers Island. Postcard ca. 1940.

east section of the Rip Van Winkle Bridge visually dominate this point as they rise up from the island's south end. You will quickly come to a 0.5-mile-long narrow channel leading north into the island's interior that can be leisurely explored.

Rogers Island (formerly known as Vastrack Island[2]) is an oval-shaped body of land, 1.2 miles long and 0.4 mile wide. It was the scene of an epic battle between the Mohawks and Mohicans in 1628 in which the Mohicans were resoundingly defeated. Artifacts from this fateful battle once lay scattered about on the island, but a procession of eighteenth- and nineteenth-century treasure hunters removed them and obliterated whatever traces of history remained.

Continuing counterclockwise around the island, proceed east around the southeast tip and then head north up Hallenbeck Creek for 1.4 miles, following along the island's east shoreline. During the Revolutionary War, American vessels hid in Hallenbeck Creek behind Rogers Island to evade detection in the event the British navy began advancing upriver.[3] British forces never appeared this far north on the Hudson, however, leaving historians and military strategists to ponder whether this ruse indeed would have actually worked.

When you clear the northeast end of Rogers Island, head back downriver on the Hudson, reaching the island's south end again in roughly 1.6 miles. From there it is a reasonably short paddle back to Dutchman's Landing—a round-trip of nearly 4.5 miles.

Northwest—Paddle 0.2 mile down the Hudson River until you reach its confluence with Catskill Creek. Bear right and head northwest up Catskill Creek. At 0.2 mile you will pass by the mouth of Dubois Creek, to your left, which can be explored for up to 0.5 mile south. At 0.7 mile you will pass by Hop-O-Nose

▶ **Dutchman's Landing**

(also called Hopp's Nose),[4] a rock formation projecting out onto the stream like an enormous wedge or nose.

From there you will pass under a number of bridges: at 1.0 mile the Uncle Sam bascule bridge (drawbridge); at 1.3 mile an old crossing that has been converted into a footbridge; at 1.5 miles the high trestle of the old West Shore Railroad bridge, now used by CSXT freight trains; then, finally, before 1.6 miles, the Route 9W bridge, whose southern pier rests on a 0.1-mile-long island near the south bank of the stream. Up to this point the village of Catskill has paralleled the river for most of the distance. Continue upstream, following the contortions of the river for 2.6 miles until rapids and shallows force you to turn around.

Catskill Creek is a large stream, nearly thirty-eight miles long. It rises south of Middleburgh and flows into the Hudson River at the village of Catskill. It is fed by four major tributaries—Kaaterskill Creek and the Shingle Kill from the south, and Basic and Potic creeks from the north.

In 1912, Dubois Creek was described as flowing "through a well-nigh impenetrable marsh. It is bordered by heavy growths of alders and shrubs."[5] You can judge for yourself whether this description has changed much over the last century. The creek is likely named after Benjamin, Cornelius, and Huybartus DuBois whose stone house is located on West Main Street in Catskill.

South—Paddle downriver for 1.0 mile until you reach RamsHorn Creek at the 480-acre RamsHorn-Livingston Sanctuary. The creek, which meanders considerably, can be followed west for an appreciable distance. It starts wide and gradually narrows. The RamsHorn-Livingston Sanctuary is co-owned by the Scenic Hudson Land Trust and the National Audubon Society. It is the Hudson River's largest tidal swamp forest.

From the Kiwanis Park Access

You can paddle up Catskill Creek for 1.5 miles to where further progress is halted by rapids and shallows, or downstream for 1.1 miles to the creek's confluence with the Hudson River.

History: According to a historic marker near Dutchman's Landing, an "Indian village" once stood on the north bank of Catskill Creek across from Hop-O-Nose (the rock protuberance on the south bank). The land was later purchased from Indians, in 1682, under the Loveridge Patent.[6] A ferry that crossed the Hudson River in the eighteenth century had its landing place opposite Hop-O-Nose.[7]

The first European settler in Catskill was Claes Uylenspiegel, who erected a hut by Hopp's Nose prior to 1650.[8] A hamlet slowly grew along the north side of Catskill Creek, west of Het Strand (Dutchman's Landing), becoming incorporated as a village in 1806. The port became a bustling center for commerce, providing a main point of entry into the Catskills. From here a great tourism industry developed as a series of hotels opened up southwest of the village in the area of North and South Lake and Platte Clove. It was the golden age of elegant Catskill Mountain hotels and the Victorian pursuit of nature at its most sublime.

The Uncle Sam Bridge is named after Sam Wilson, who lived in Catskill on West Main Street from 1817–1824.[9] This is the same "Uncle Sam" whose caricature became a symbol of the United States government and who was buried at Oakwood Cemetery in Lansingburgh, New York. The Uncle Sam Bridge was built in 1930 as a drawbridge and then renovated in 1990.[10]

Thomas Cole, a famous nineteenth-century landscape painter and "founder" of the Hudson River School, lived in Catskill and painted some of the memorable scenes you can still enjoy as you paddle along the Hudson River. Cedar Grove, Cole's home in Catskill, has been preserved as the Thomas Cole National Historic Site (thomascole.org).

In days past when the Hudson River would freeze over solidly, ice yacht racing was a favorite pastime. People have always been drawn to speed, and during the nineteenth century ice yachts were the "fastest vehicles on the face of the earth," achieving velocities in excess of 70 MPH.[11] Just to prove the point, in 1871 the *Icicle* (the largest ice yacht of its time) raced against the Chicago Express (one of America's fastest trains) and won.[12]

Postscript

Chapters on paddling the Hudson River from Stillwater to Hadley/Lake Luzerne will be included in the companion volume to this book, *A Kayaker's Guide to Lake George & the Saratoga Region*. That book will also include the lakes, ponds, and secondary rivers of the Capital District Region.

▶ **Dutchman's Landing**

PART II

The Mohawk River:
From Waterford & Cohoes
to Fort Hunter

Do not venture out onto the Mohawk River unless you are at least an intermediate-level paddler, capable of handling a variety of water and weather conditions and able to self-rescue.

Caution

When heading out onto the river, choose a calm day and watch the weather. Current and winds can be severe at times. In early spring, the stronger, snowmelt-fed currents can make these paddles significantly more difficult. The wind tends to be quietest in the early morning and evening. Always check the forecast and weather before setting out. Do not leave shore if storms and/or high winds are predicted or if the weather forecast is at all questionable. Be aware that the weather can change abruptly, often with little warning and in spite of the forecast. Wind and current increases as you move away from the shoreline.

Watch out for boat traffic, particularly large ships and barges whose wakes can capsize a small watercraft. When close to a rocky section of shoreline, stay alert for rebounding waves as well as incoming waves. The Mohawk River experiences heavy boat traffic. Operators of small watercraft like kayaks and canoes must be ever-vigilant. Don't assume boats can see you. Wear bright colors. Paddle close to shore unless you need to cross the river or wish to visit an island. Cross in a group and keep the group together. If you see a boat in the distance, let it pass before you set out. Some large boats move surprisingly fast, and distance can be hard to judge. Take into account current and wind when planning your trajectory.

Stay a safe distance back from all dams.

Be prepared for an increase in boat traffic as you pass by harbors, marinas, docks, or wharves.

Memorize the shoreline as you leave so that you can return to the same starting point.

Introduction

The Mohawk is a large and powerful river, second in New York State only to the Hudson River. Rising from the sparsely populated Tug Hill Plateau in the western Adirondacks, the Mohawk makes its way east for over 150 miles[1] until it reaches the Hudson River between Waterford and Cohoes. Along the way it is fed by a number of large tributaries, including West Canada Creek and East Canada Creek from the north and Schoharie Creek from the south, draining a total watershed of 3,456 square miles.[2]

In earlier times the Mohawk River was called the *Maasquas*, after a tribe of Native Americans who lived along its banks.[3] It has also been called *Tenonanatche*, meaning "the river that flows through the mountains," an apt description for a river that heads east through the only notch in an otherwise impregnable northeastern section of the Appalachian Plateau.[4] For this reason the valley, right from the beginning, became the "gateway to the west," with the valley and river later being named for its primary Native American residents—the Mohawks.

Despite its size and power today, the Mohawk River is but a shadow of its former self. Thousands of years ago, the Iro-Mohawk River (ancestor to today's Mohawk River) was bigger than the Niagara River, which drains four of the Great Lakes and powers Niagara Falls today. Fed by the meltwaters of retreating, mile-high glaciers, the Iro-Mohawk River drained glacial Lake Iroquois (which was larger than all of the Great Lakes combined), carrying this huge outflow east into Lake Albany, whose dry basin is now occupied by the Capital District. In the process, it carved out the Mohawk Valley.

In the Mohawk Valley. — On the "New York Central"

The Mohawk River as it looked over one hundred years ago. Postcard ca. 1900.

This was quite temporary, however. As the glaciers continued their relentless retreat northward toward Canada, new land was exposed, and the waters of Lake Iroquois that fed the Iro-Mohawk River were eventually pirated away by the St. Lawrence River. Left behind was the Mohawk River that we see today, still an enormously powerful river fully capable of going on rampages, which it does periodically in the Stockade section of Schenectady as well as along a number of other low-lying areas. During flood conditions the Mohawk carries so much water that at the confluence of the Mohawk and the Hudson rivers it can look as though the Hudson is flowing into the Mohawk, rather than the other way around.[5]

In 1825 engineers took advantage of the deep valley cut through central New York State by the Iro-Mohawk River and established a canal linking the Hudson River at Albany with Lake Erie at Buffalo. The canal paralleled the Mohawk River for the most part, crossing it via aqueducts only when necessary.

It wasn't until 1918, when the New York State Barge Canal was created, that engineers turned the river itself into one extended canal by interposing a series of locks and dams along the way to raise the water level. Prior to that, the section of the river west from Schenectady to Fort Stanwix at Rome was manageable for canoes and small boats that could overcome ninety sets of rifts and rapids, but travel east (downriver) from Schenectady was very difficult.[6]

Paddlers should be advised that in the early spring, before the Barge Canal begins operating, the river level can be variable. Lack of water in some areas can increase the carry to the river's edge, as well as making it muddier and less pleasant to traverse. When walking across mudflats, bear in mind that river mud is more slippery and clay-like than lake mud, a fact you can only fully appreciate after you begin sinking into it.

Also bear in mind that plant life along the shallows of the river begins to proliferate rapidly with the approach of summer, the result being that open water areas turn into virtually impassable mats of water chestnuts and like nuances.

From the height of the industrial revolution until very recent times, boaters and swimmers have been dissatisfied with the Mohawk's water quality. At its worst, the river was an open sewer. Fortunately, matters began changing in the 1950s as New Yorkers developed a newfound appreciation for the river's unique history. In 1965, New York State issued its billion-dollar Pure Waters Bond Act, augmented in 1973 by the federal Clean Waters Act, and the river has sprung back to life.

The eighteen-mile stretch of the Mohawk River between the Niskayuna Hamlet Railroad Station and Lock 9 was designated the Blueway Trail by Schenectady County. For more information about the trail, contact the Chamber of Schenectady County (sayschenectady.org) or Schenectady County Department of Economic Development & Planning (schenectadycounty.com).

It cannot be emphasized enough that the Capital District occupies a special place topographically—at the confluence of New York State's two mightiest rivers. When it comes to water, there is indeed much to see and do in the Capital Region.

Southern Shore: Albany County

37 Cohoes Falls (Cohoes)
A Natural Wonder That Once Rivaled Niagara Falls as a Tourist Attraction

- **Launch Site:** Mohawk River recreational area established by Boralex Operations off of North Mohawk Street in Cohoes (Albany County); slip-in at water's edge. The site is open from April 15–Oct. 15. For more information: cohoes.com/Cit-e-Access/webpage.cfm?TID=34&TPID=9360.
- **Delorme NYS Atlas & Gazetteer:** p. 66, B4; **Estimated GPS:** 42°46.71′N; 73°41.02′W
- **Destinations:** Cohoes Falls, Route 32 bridge
- **Mileage:** To Cohoes Falls—0.4 mile (round-trip); to Route 32 bridge—0.4 mile (round-trip)
- **Comments:** Read "Caution" beginning on page xxii and "The Mohawk River: Caution" on page 147. As you head upstream you will find that the current gets stronger as the water gets shallower; the river is impassable after 0.2 mile. Stay a safe distance back from a huge dam 0.2 mile downstream. Don't put in at the launch site if the current seems unusually strong.
- **Directions:** From the terminus of I-787 at Cohoes, drive straight across Rt. 32 and proceed northwest on New Courtland Street (which turns into North Mohawk Street) for 0.2 mile. Turn right at a traffic light just before a sign stating "Col. Robert R. Craner Parkway" and proceed downhill on a paved road for less than 0.05 mile. Park at the northwest end of a parking area next to the Mohawk River.

The Paddle:

Rapids and shallows limit the upstream paddle to 0.2 mile under normal conditions. The fact that this paddle is even possible is the result of a massive dam that was erected across the Mohawk River downstream from the Route 32 bridge, causing the river to back up and deepen for 0.4 mile.

Northwest—Heading upstream you will be awed by the enormity of the gorge whose walls rise over 100 feet above you. Ahead in the near distance looms Cohoes Falls. Although it is not possible by paddling to get much closer than 0.3 mile from its base, it is still a thrilling experience to view this historic waterfall from the level of the river.

At the top of the cliffs to the left is Harmony Mills; no longer a mill, it is now a residential housing complex. As soon as you are nearly parallel with Harmony Mills, no further progress upstream is possible because of a line of rapids extending across the entire width of the river. This is the turnaround point. Sit back and simply let the power of the river sweep you downstream back to your launching point.

Southeast—Heading downriver for less than 0.2 mile, go under the old railroad bridge and then no farther than the Route 32 bridge, where a string of buoys farther downstream warns of the presence of an impending large dam.

 **Cohoes Falls**

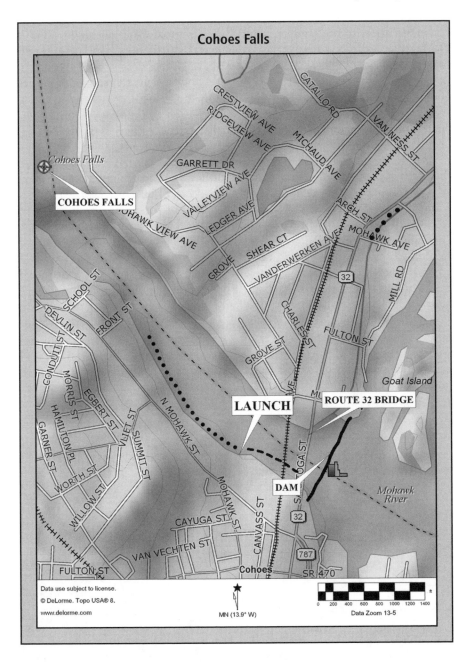

Cohoes Falls

History: Cohoes Falls is a 70-foot high, 600-foot wide, massive wall of black Snake Hill shale (named after a hill overlooking Saratoga Lake)[1] that extends across the full length of the Mohawk River, roughly 0.7–0.8 mile upstream from its confluence with the Hudson River. The falls' most distinguishing feature is The Nose, a projecting mass of rock that extends from the main face approximately one-third of the way from the north bank. Generally, even when substantial amounts of water are racing over the falls, The Nose is left exposed. Potholes abound in the bedrock both above and below the waterfall.

At one time Cohoes Falls was 2,000 feet farther downstream from its present location,[2] not far from where you initially launched your watercraft. Over the last few millennia the waterfall has eroded its way upstream, and will continue to do so for many millennia to come. Its recession, however, has been slowed by the fact that the bedrock is tipped at a 70-degree angle instead of lying horizontally, which makes it more difficult for the bedrock to be worn away.[3]

Cohoes Falls once rivaled Niagara Falls as New York State's premier scenic wonder, in part because of its more prominent and accessible location at the confluence of New York State's two largest river-valley systems. It even had a fashionable hotel, called the Cataract House, which overlooked the falls near where the new Cohoes Falls Overlook Park is located. The hotel was constructed in 1860, then rebuilt and enlarged after a fire engulfed it. The hotel survived until after 1912.[4] Cohoes Falls, on the other hand, became a victim of eighteenth-century industrialization when its waters were harnessed to power numerous mills and factories that lined the banks of the gorge. Later, a hydroelectric plant was constructed by the falls, with a 0.8-mile-long canal siphoning off water from an upriver dam, severely compromising the aesthetic value of the falls for the sake of driving turbines.

Seventy-foot-high Cohoes Falls formed an impassable barrier that prevented boats from advancing up the Mohawk River until 1825. Photograph 2009.

 **Cohoes Falls**

Today, between the hydroelectric plant and, to a much lesser degree, the New York State Barge Canal, vast amounts of water continue to be diverted from Cohoes Falls, causing the waterfall to routinely appear anemic except during early spring or following periods of exceptionally heavy rainfall. So much water is diverted that it is even possible at times during the summer to walk across the Mohawk River below the fall.[5]

Even in the past, however, little water would run through the gorge after spring's snowmelt was over. In 1749, Peter Kalm, a Swedish naturalist, had this to say about the falls: "The bed of the river, below the falls, was quite dry, there being only a channel in the middle fourteen feet broad, and a fathom or somewhat more deep, through which the river passed which came over the falls. We saw a number of holes in the rock below the falls, which bore a perfect resemblance to those in Sweden which we call giants' pots, or mountain kettles."[6]

The word "Cohoes" has a number of possible origins. Some contend that it was a Native American word for "falling canoe" or "shipwrecked canoe,"[7] or "salmon" or "shad," which were plentiful at the fall at one time. Cohoes may even have meant the area "beyond the falls,"[8] but no one knows for sure.

The Route 32 bridge is not the first to cross the Mohawk River between Cohoes and Waterford. The first bridge, 900 feet long and 24 feet wide, was built in 1795 and crossed over just west of the railroad bridge that is presently upstream from Route 32.[9]

The Harmony Mills buildings, which overlook the gorge from the south bank, once comprised the largest cotton manufacturing complex in the United States, a distinction the company retained from the 1860s through the 1880s.[10]

The Craner Parkway memorializes Col. Robert R. Craner, who was held prisoner in Hanoi, North Vietnam, after his plane was shot down in 1967. Craner survived five years of captivity—three of them in isolation—before returning stateside and being awarded numerous military honors. He died in 1980 at the age of forty-seven.[11]

The launch site is located on city property and maintained by Boralex (a power provider in Waterford). The road in and the parking lot are privately owned, but access to the shore is permitted.[12]

Gorge below Cohoes Falls—From the perspective of a kayaker or canoeist traveling virtually at eye level with the river, the 120-foot-high vertical walls of the gorge are nearly as impressive as Cohoes Falls itself.

For those who have already paddled a variety of sections of the Mohawk River, it is impossible not to be struck by how extraordinarily different this part of the river looks as opposed to the part of the river above Rexford. The section of the river downstream from Rexford is deeply cut, with vertical walls that look as though they were chiseled out of stone by the hand of a giant. Upstream from Rexford (going west), the banks of the Mohawk are more rounded. The reason for this difference is that the section of the Mohawk below Rexford is much younger. When the Mohawk River was prevented by a large delta from flowing into the Hudson River at Albany, it first detoured north to Ballston Lake, following Ballston Creek and the Anthony Kill into the Hudson River. When a second channel opened up at Rexford, the river detoured again, this time cutting out a huge gorge to the Hudson River through Rexford many millennia after the rest of the Mohawk Valley had formed.

Viewing Cohoes Falls from Cohoes Falls Overlook Park—From the terminus of I-787 at Cohoes, drive straight across Rt. 32 and proceed northwest on New Courtland Street / North Mohawk Street for 1.0 mile. Park to your left in an area designated for Cohoes Falls. Walk across North Mohawk Street and then over a footbridge that spans the raceway leading to the hydroelectric plant at Cohoes Falls. You will come out onto a spacious, inlaid-stone viewing area overlooking the fall. This area was opened in 2008 and the views are spectacular. A long flight of stairs that will take you down to the base of the fall has recently been added.

 **Cohoes Falls**

Crescent Plant (Crescent Station)
Access to Mohawk River between the Crescent Plant and Cohoes Falls

38

■ **Launch Site:** Fishing access site next to Crescent Plant off of Mohawk Street (Albany County); slip-in at water's edge.

■ **Delorme NYS Atlas & Gazetteer:** p. 66, B4; **Estimated GPS:** 42°48.29'N; 73°43.37'W

■ **Destinations:** Paradise Island, Cohoes Company Dam (0.9 mile above Cohoes Falls)

■ **Mileage:** To Paradise Island—0.2 mile (one-way); to Cohoes Company Dam—1.2 miles (round-trip)

■ **Comments:** Read "Caution" beginning on page xxii and "The Mohawk River: Caution" on page 147. Watch out for energetic waters released from the Crescent Plant 100 feet upstream from the slip-in. Stay a safe distance back from the upstream Crescent Dam and from the lower Cohoes Company Dam, 0.7 mile downstream.

■ **Directions:** From the terminus of I-787 at Cohoes, cross over Rt. 32 and continue straight ahead on New Courtland Street (which quickly becomes Mohawk Street), driving northwest for 2.5 miles. As soon as you see the sign on your right for "Crescent Plant: New York Power Authority," turn right and follow a side road that leads down in less than 0.05 mile to a fishing access site just downriver from the power plant. From 0.2 mile south of the Crescent Bridge on Rt. 9, turn onto the Cohoes-Crescent Road and drive southeast for 0.9 mile. When you see the sign for "Crescent Plant, New York Power Authority," turn left and follow a dirt road down to the fishing access site just downriver from the power plant.

The Paddle:

This scenic part of the Mohawk River receives little if any boat traffic because the river here is truncated by two dams separated by only 0.8 mile. There simply is little room for motorboats to maneuver.

At the put-in, look for potentially fast-moving waters. The flow can vary depending upon the hydroelectric plant's hours of operation.

Directly across the river to the left is the long, crescent-shaped dam that extends to both shores from a mid-river island.

Northeast—Staying back a safe distance from the Crescent Dam, paddle northeast directly over to Paradise Island (the 0.3-mile-long island that lies midway between the two sections of the dam). If you wish, you can debark and bushwhack up to the top of the island for more elevated views (see chapter "Paradise Island" for further details).

East—Head directly across the river for 0.2 mile to old ruins by the south end of the Crescent Dam. The ruins stand today as a vivid reminder of the river's industrial past.

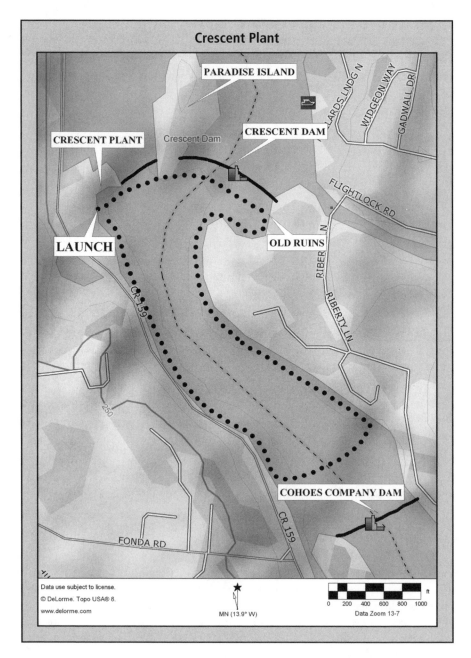

Southeast—Paddling downriver, you will quickly see that an obvious dichotomy exists here. The left (east) bank is partially rimmed with houses and camps, with an occasional stairway leading down to the water's edge. The right (west)

▶ **Crescent Plant**

bank remains undeveloped and pristine. Why? The west bank's lack of development is the result of the Cohoes-Crescent Road having been built closely paralleling the river. This has left little room for houses to be built.

In season, wild yellow irises can be seen growing along the banks. Take note of the vertical rock walls that rise up twenty feet or higher above sections of the river.

At 0.6 mile you will be approximately 0.1 mile from the top of the Cohoes Company Dam, which diverts a substantial portion of the Mohawk's water toward the west bank where it is then carried down a 0.9-mile-long sluiceway to the power plant next to Cohoes Falls. Go no farther. Turn around here.

History: The Crescent Plant was built in 1925, one hundred years after the Erie Canal was opened. In 1987 the plant was expanded, with two new turbines added to the original, now-rehabilitated unit. The plant became fully operational again in 1993 and is currently able to generate 9,948 kilowatts of power.[1]

A nearby historic marker states: "Loudon's Ford. British and Continental Army ford protected August–September 1777 by Generals Enoch Poor and Benedict Arnold."[2] In the 1700s, any place that could be forded (or crossed) along a large river like the Mohawk was always of military significance. Although Generals Poor and Arnold were prepared to defend the crossing in 1777, the British army never advanced far enough to be engaged; it had been defeated at the Battle of Saratoga. The crossing is also known as Loudon's Ferry.

The Crescent Dam, consisting of two curved sections separated by a rocky island, is spectacular when viewed from the water. The west section (closest to the power plant) is 537 feet long; the east section (the more dramatic of the two) is 907 feet long.[3]

The Cohoes Company Dam was constructed in 1866 and serves to divert water from the river into the 4,500-foot-long power canal that feeds the School Street Powerhouse next to Cohoes Falls.[4]

The hamlet of Crescent Station was earlier called Lower Aqueduct. It received its present name from a train station that was established along the Troy & Schenectady Railroad Branch of the New York Central Railroad.[5] Today the rail line is gone, but the rail bed remains and is part of the Mohawk-Hudson Bikeway.

<table>
<tr><td>39</td><td>**Freddie's Park (Crescent)**
Along the Path of the Old Erie Canal</td></tr>
</table>

- ■ **Launch Site:** Freddie's Park, off of Albany Marine Service Lane by Crescent Bridge (Albany County); 60-foot carry to put-in at water's edge.
- ■ **Delorme NYS Atlas & Gazetteer:** p. 66, B4; **Estimated GPS:** 42°49.18′N; 73°43.82′W
- ■ **Destinations:** Island on Mohawk River, Crescent Dam
- ■ **Mileage:** To island—0.2 mile (one-way); around island—1.3 miles; to Crescent Dam—1.4 miles (one-way)
- ■ **Comments:** Read "Caution" beginning on page xxii and "The Mohawk River: Caution" on page 147. Be prepared for an increase in boat traffic as you pass by the Albany Marine Service. By early summer, choking water plants can make paddling difficult along the south shore of the Mohawk River between the Albany Marine Service and Crescent Dam. Stay a safe distance back from the Crescent Dam.
- ■ **Directions:** Heading north on the Adirondack Northway (I-87), get off at Exit 7 for Latham & Cohoes. Stay to the right as you head east on Rt. 7, then turn immediately right onto a ramp, following signs to Rt. 9, which leads you up and around to Rt. 9. Turn right and proceed north on Rt. 9. At 4.4 miles you will pass by Crescent Road. In another 0.2 mile, just before reaching the Crescent Bridge (which spans the Mohawk River), turn right onto Albany Marine Service Lane. In several hundred feet you will arrive at a small parking area on your left for Freddie's Park.

The Paddle:

Standing by the shoreline at a grouping of limestone blocks, take a moment to look out across the river. You will see similar blocks of stone on the opposite side, relics from an old aqueduct that once spanned the Mohawk River. You will also see the steel abutment from a former Crescent bridge on the opposite shore. You are at a very historic spot on the river.

Southwest—Head upstream, passing under the Crescent Bridge, and then continue for 0.2 mile farther until you come to a 0.5-mile-long island, just past where the river does an abrupt U-turn as it changes direction from northeast to southeast. There are many opportunities for exploration here. You can paddle around the island, a circumnavigation of 1.3 miles, lingering momentarily on its east side where motorboats are less likely to enter because of shallow waters. For a few moments of quiet contemplation, you can paddle into a tiny, 0.1-mile-long cove at the northeast end of the island, but be prepared to paddle through marshy waters.

Southeast—Paddling downstream, you will immediately see 15-foot-high, vertical walls that have been cut into the south bank by the river. These walls end within less than 0.1 mile as the river bends southward, passing by the Albany Marine Service.

▶ **Freddie's Park**

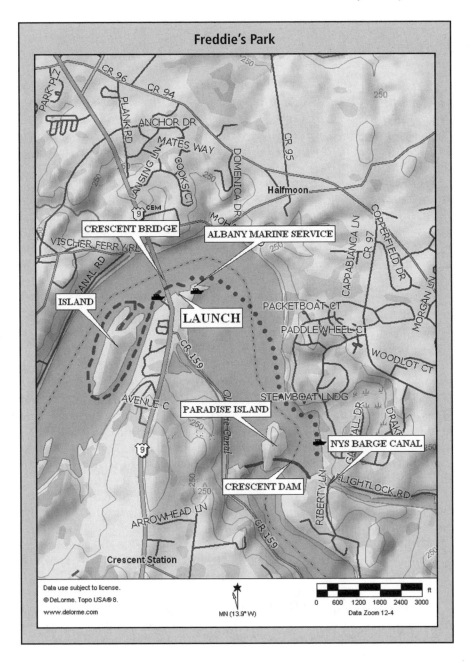

Freddie's Park

Shortly after passing by the marina, turn right and paddle into a cove created by several islands. This area becomes even more cove-like as the summer progresses and underwater growth becomes denser.

Today's Crescent Bridge crosses the Mohawk River where the Erie Canal aqueduct once did. Photograph 2008.

It is another 1.2 miles to reach Paradise Island (near the center of the river) and Guard Gate 2 of the New York State Barge Canal (along the east shoreline), both just upstream from the Crescent Dam.

History: When the Erie Canal was constructed in 1825, the Mohawk River's solid bedrock and shallow waters at Crescent (Fonda's Ferry) provided the logical place to erect the Lower Mohawk Aqueduct to carry the canal across the river to the north bank. The Upper Mohawk Aqueduct, in turn, constructed farther upstream at Rexford, returned the canal to the south side of the river. The crossings were conceived by Canvass White as a way of bypassing a section of particularly rocky, steep terrain on the river's south side.[1]

In 1842 the original Lower Mohawk Aqueduct was replaced by an enlarged one. The new aqueduct was constructed just several feet downstream from the old one, and it is the blocks of the old aqueduct that are visible today at the launch site and across the river between the Crescent Bridge and the old steel abutment. The old aqueduct was not totally discarded. Its piers were used as a foundation for a plank road and then, later, to support an iron toll bridge. The new aqueduct, 1,840 feet long with twenty-six arched piers,[2] was a phenomenon of engineering, considered to be the longest of its kind in the world when it was built. It proved to be equally as durable as the original, lasting for seventy-three years until the New York State Barge Canal rendered the old Erie Canal obsolete. The structure was torn down when it became a navigational hazard.

The Mohawk River can be readily traveled by boats today because of having been dredged and deepened through a series of locks and canals. Without the elevated waters to support the New York State Barge Canal, the river would

▶ **Freddie's Park**

be of variable depth with shallows and riffs. The Crescent Dam raised the river at Crescent by an additional twenty-seven feet, turning parts of the river into miniature lakes.

The first twentieth-century Crescent Bridge, a five-span steel truss, lasted from around 1915 to 1957. It was replaced by a steel girder bridge.[3] In 1966, the 1950s bridge was replaced by the present Crescent Bridge, consisting of a five-span, twin-arched girder 1,229 feet long.

Freddie's Park was named in honor of Alfred (Fred) Valentini for his years of dedicated service in helping to improve Colonie's environment.[4] The Empire Dry Dock and a blacksmith's shop once stood close to where the park is now located.

The Dutch called this area The Boght, which referred to the sharp bend in the river opposite Crescent[5] (which in itself is an obvious reference to the curvature in the river).

40 Colonie Mohawk River Park (Dunsbach Ferry)
Between Bridges

■ **Launch Site:** Colonie Mohawk River Park off of Schermerhorn Road (Albany County); cement ramp. Modest boat launch fee for Town of Colonie residents; higher fee for nonresidents; restrooms available. Use of the pool and athletic fields is restricted to town residents only. For more information: Town of Colonie Parks & Recreation, 71 Schermerhorn Road, Cohoes, NY 12047, (518) 783-2760, parks@colonie.org.

■ **Delorme NYS Atlas & Gazetteer:** p. 66, B3-4; **Estimated GPS:** 42°47.92′N; 73°44.85′W

■ **Destinations:** Adirondack Northway Twin Bridges, Crescent Bridge, Delphus Kill, Mohawk View, Shaker Creek

■ **Mileage:** Southwest to Adirondack Northway Twin Bridges—0.9 mile (one-way); to Delphus Kill—1.4 miles (one-way); to Mohawk View—2.2 miles (one-way); to Shaker Creek—3.2 miles (one-way); up Shaker Creek—0.1 mile (one-way); northeast to Crescent Bridge—1.8 miles (one-way)

■ **Comments:** Read "Caution" beginning on page xxii and "The Mohawk River: Caution" on page 147. Be prepared for an increase in boat traffic from Blains Bay Marina, Diamond Reef Marina, Klamsteam Marina, and Crescent Boat Club.

■ **Directions:** From the Adirondack Northway (I-87) get off at Exit 7 for Troy & Cohoes and proceed east on Rt. 7. Within 0.3 mile from where the Northway crosses over Rt. 7, bear to your right and follow an exit ramp where signs point to "Latham & Cohoes. Rtes. 9 & 9R." When you reach the stoplight at Rt. 9, turn right and follow Rt. 9 north for nearly 2.4 miles. When you come to a stoplight at Old Loudon Road (0.1 mile past the first left-hand turn for Old Loudon Road), turn left and then immediately bear right, following Old Loudon Road for less than 0.05 mile. When you come to Schermerhorn Road, turn left and drive northwest for over 0.5 mile. The entrance to Colonie Mohawk River Park on Ballenberg Blvd. will be directly to your right. From the entrance gatehouse, follow the paved path as it takes you through the park and down to the ramp site by the Mohawk River.

The Paddle:

Southwest—Heading upstream, you will come to a small island in 0.2 mile and then pass by Blains Bay Marina, along the south bank, at 0.8 mile. The Twin Bridges (I-87) are reached at 0.9 mile.

For the next 0.4 mile, the houses on both sides of the river are worth a look. Along the twenty-foot-high south bank can be seen modern, expensive homes with stairways leading down to the water's edge. Along the north bank are older, more modest and camp-like homes sitting closer to the water. It is an interesting study in contrast between the old and the new.

At 1.3 miles you will come to a small, rocky island whose flat, slab-like west end allows for easy docking for those who wish to get out for a stretch and have

▶ **Colonie Mohawk River Park**

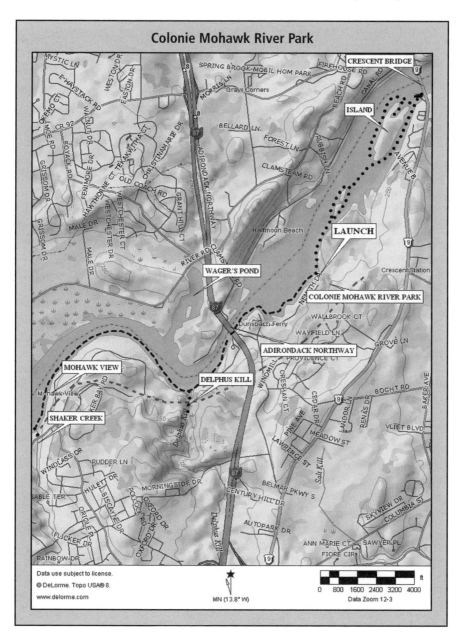

Colonie Mohawk River Park

a look around. Gazing upstream it is easy to think that the river is rapidly turning into a lake as it widens markedly.

At 1.4 miles the Delphus Kill empties into a tiny bay along the south bank. Although worth exploring, the creek unfortunately becomes unnavigable within

The Twin Bridges of the Adirondack Northway. Photograph 2008.

about 0.1 mile from its confluence with the Mohawk River.

By the time you have gone 2.2 miles, you will see to your left, looking south, an area of flatlands called Mohawk View (the name of a summer cottage colony).[1] A water treatment plant is located there, but is not all that visible.

At 3.2 miles you will come to the mouth of Shaker Creek, which comes in on your left. You can paddle south up the creek for less than 0.1 mile before being stopped by a huge drainpipe that carries Shaker Creek under River Road. Just before the drainpipe you will pass under the Mohawk-Hudson Bikeway footbridge.

Northeast—Proceeding downstream, you will pass by a group of small islands in 0.5 mile. None of these are much longer than 0.1 mile. At 1.0 mile you will reach the south end of a 0.5-mile-long island (which can be circumnavigated in 1.3 miles), and then the Crescent Bridge at 1.8 miles. (For more details, see chapter "Vandenburgh-Dunsbach Ferry.")

History: Colonie Mohawk River Park is a 160-acre town park and nature preserve that opened in 1967. It is bordered to the west by the Mohawk River and to the east by the Mohawk-Hudson Bikeway. Until fairly recently the park was known as the Colonie Town Park.

The hamlet of Dunsbach Ferry is named after J. H. Dunsbach and family, who operated a local river crossing.[2] Later the hamlet became an important stop on the Troy & Schenectady branch of the New York Central Railroad.

Mohawk View, a flat sweep of land near the river, was once used for growing broom corn (not truly a corn plant, but a grass-like, sorghum plant that was used in the production of natural-bristled brooms). During winter, ice was harvested from this section of the Mohawk River.

Shaker Creek is a small stream that rises from Ann Lee Pond several miles south of the Mohawk River. The pond and stream are associated with the Watervliet Shaker community, which left the area in the twentieth century.

▶ **Colonie Mohawk River Park**

Peebles Island (Waterford/Cohoes)
An Island with Centuries of History

41

▦ **Launch Site:** Battery Park at end of First Street in Waterford (Saratoga County); concrete ramp, parking for 15 cars. For more information: Waterford Harbor Visitors Center, One Tugboat Alley, Waterford, NY 12188, (518) 233-9123; Visitors Center at Peebles Island State Park, One Delaware Avenue, Waterford, (518) 237-7000 x220, nysparks.state.ny.us/parks/info.asp?parkID=120.
▦ **Delorme NYS Atlas & Gazetteer:** p. 67, B4; **GPS:** 42°47.06'N; 73°40.73'W
▦ **Destinations:** Buttermilk Falls, Polderump Island, south sprout of Mohawk River, Simmons Island
▦ **Mileage:** Middle Branch to Buttermilk Falls—0.8 mile (one-way); North Branch to Polderump Island—0.6 mile (one-way); to south sprout of Mohawk River—2.4 miles (one-way); up south sprout to Simmons Island—1.2 miles (one-way)
▦ **Comments:** Read "Caution" beginning on page xxii and "The Mohawk River: Caution" on page 147. In early spring the stronger, snowmelt-fed currents can make these paddles significantly more difficult. Stay a safe distance back from Buttermilk Falls and the Polderump Island dam.
▦ **Directions:** From the terminus of I-787 at Cohoes, turn right onto Rt. 32 and drive northeast for 1.7 miles until you reach a traffic light at the junction of Rtes. 4 East & 32 North in the middle of Waterford. Continue east, on Rt. 4, for another 0.1 mile and then turn right onto First Street. Drive south for 0.2 mile until you reach Battery Park and a large parking area located near the east end of a long docking area for large boats. A cement ramp at the east end of the parking lot provides ready access to the Mohawk River.

The Waterford Visitor Center (at the end of Second Street) is just a short distance west of the parking lot.

The Paddle:

This paddle begins at the confluence of the Hudson River and Mohawk River. Directly east of the boat launch is the Hudson River; straight ahead (south) and to the west are branches of the Mohawk River; the land due south is Van Schaick Island, and the land slightly southwest is Peebles Island.

To Buttermilk Falls—Head south across the Mohawk River to the east side of Peebles Island, where the middle branch of the Mohawk comes into the Hudson River. Look for an observation deck and dock along the island's northeast side as you paddle by. Beyond the deck are a pavilion, picnic area, and the park's main recreational area. The visitor center is located by the main building, just beyond the recreational area.

Continue upstream, keeping close to Peebles Island on your right. You will pass under a former railroad bridge (now used for automobile traffic) at 0.2 mile, and then pass a massive inclined cement wall to your right that was erected years ago to shore up the bank of the island. The building that you see to your

Northern Shore: Saratoga County

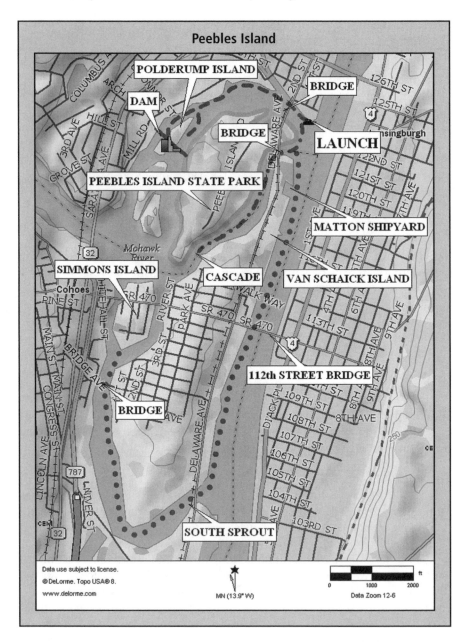

Peebles Island

right is the former Cluett, Peabody & Company Factory, now home to the New York State Department of Parks, Recreation, and Historical Preservation.

As you proceed upstream, the west bank of the Mohawk momentarily becomes earthen and only several feet in height. The east bank (along Van

Schaick Island), in contrast, remains noticeably higher and rockier, littered with large boulders and cement blocks. The boulders and blocks were placed there to keep the bank stable during the days when the Delaware & Hudson railroad tracks went along Delaware Avenue paralleling the Mohawk River.

At 0.1 mile beyond the bridge, you will pass by a large sandbar on your left composed of stones and pebbles. The flatness of this sandbar ensures that it will be swept over by the rippling Mohawk River during each spring's freshet. By the time you reach this sandbar you will notice that the composition of the banks on both sides of the river has begun to change from earth and loose stones to solid shale, and the banks continue to rise up higher as you make your way upstream. Buttermilk Falls is also visible, approximately 0.3 mile in the distance.

This is the part of the trip where the views start to get exciting. You have now entered into a wide, deep gorge with walls over twenty-five feet high. Take note of the gorge's somewhat circular appearance—evidence of Buttermilk Falls' earlier location before it slowly moved upstream to its present site. Stay close to the towering west bank on your right as you continue upstream. You will pass by two small sea-cave-like cavities near the base of the escarpment, further evidence of the Mohawk's powerful erosive force.

Once you reach the cascade, you have gone nearly 0.8 mile from the put-in. It is important to remain at a safe distance from the base of the falls. Looking left (east), you will notice that the river has worn a very pronounced semicircle into the east wall of the gorge at the base of the falls, almost as if someone took a larger-than-life-sized buzz saw and cut right into the bedrock.

After you have had a chance to look at the waterfall close-up, stop paddling and let the current sweep you away from the cascade. Return the same way you came, this time staying to the right along the east bank for a slight change in perspective.

Upstream to the dam between Peebles Island and Polderump Island—From Battery Park, follow the north branch of the Mohawk River west. You will immediately pass under a 670-foot-long, double-span, steel-truss bridge built in 1913 by the Delaware & Hudson Railroad.[1] The bridge has just recently been reconditioned for automobile and pedestrian traffic. This rail line was originally opened in 1835 by the Rensselaer and Saratoga Railroad.

Uphill from the flat areas of land along both sides of the south end of the bridge is the site where Revolutionary War breastworks were constructed on Peebles Island (earthen structures that survive to this day).

Within 0.1 mile after going under the bridge, you will pass by a small sandbar to your right whose flatness ensures that it will be periodically overrun by the Mohawk River during times of heavy water flow. A small channel to your left is often navigable for a short distance, allowing you to approach wildlife more closely.

You will also notice to your right a very prominent, five-story-high, red brick building with tower and steeple. This is a former knitting mill currently

Rocky islands dominate the confluence of the Mohawk and Hudson rivers. Postcard ca. 1910.

occupied by the Ursula Company. There are no foundation ruins or cement walls to be seen along Peebles Island, but you will notice several ruins along the north bank of the Mohawk.

If you look at the Peebles Island shoreline here, you can often see turtles sunning themselves on logs. They have been occupants at this site for decades.

In another 0.1 mile you will reach a point where the river veers southwest (left). Peebles Island has now become a massive block of rock with steep walls rising up as high as 30–40 feet. You will observe that Polderump Island (straight ahead) divides the river into two flows like the prow on a ship. To the left of the divide, the water becomes shallow quickly and the riverbed flatter, with sections that can easily snag a canoe or kayak. No matter how carefully you proceed upstream, you can get no farther than to a half-foot-high shelf of bedrock that spans the stream before you reach the base of the dam. At this point you have gone nearly 0.6 mile from Battery Park.

If you choose to go to the right of the divide, it is best to wait until summer. Until then the flow can be very swift and choppy. By summer the force of the river will have ebbed substantially, and it becomes much easier to paddle upstream. You will pass by the massive vertical walls of Polderump Island to your left and the continuous cement walls of factories to your right. A New York State Permitted Discharge Point is one of the factories you will pass.

In 0.2 mile you will reach another split in the river, where going right leads to impassable waters downstream from a dam and veering left takes you into calmer waters between two islands where the shallow bottom makes continuation impossible.

A faint path from the west end of Polderump Island leads northeast to views from the island's high bluffs.

Return back to Battery Park the same way you came.

Up the South Sprout of the Mohawk River—From Battery Park head south, downstream, on the Hudson River for 2.4 miles, paralleling the east side of Van Schaick Island. At the south end of Van Schaick Island you will see the rusted

▶ **Peebles Island**

skeletal structure of an old railroad bridge that spans the south sprout of the Mohawk's entrance chasm.

Bear right and begin following the south sprout west, heading upriver. You will pass by a small island in 0.2 mile and then negotiate a sharp right-angled bend in the river at 0.4 mile. The sounds of I-787 are clearly audible in the distance. Now, proceeding north, you will pass two small islands at 0.5–0.6 mile. By the time you approach the cement bridge ahead, the water has become appreciably shallower and the current more noticeable.

At 1.0 mile you will pass under Bridge Avenue, which connects Van Schaick Island to the mainland. A new bridge is presently being constructed at this site. From here upstream, the current becomes considerably stronger. In another 0.2 mile you will reach the south tip of Simmons Island, where the Mohawk is divided into two channels that rejoin at the north end of the island. Because of shallows and rapids, however, it is doubtful that you will be able to continue past this point.

Although the paddle along the south sprout runs through a heavily populated area, the riverfront is surprisingly free of development and almost bucolic in setting. In large part this is because of the Van Schaick Island Country Club (a private nine-hole golf course) occupying the south end of the island.

History: Peebles Island is replete with history, from Native American "castles" to Revolutionary War fortifications and from farming and agriculture to the industrial revolution. Since 1972 the island, including also part of Van Schaick Island, has been owned by New York State, which has converted it into a state park.

Known earlier as Haver Island and Oat Island, Peebles is one of several islands that have been carved out at the terminus of the Mohawk River by the river's four sprouts (or branches). The word "sprout" is derived from the Dutch word *spreutum,* for stream.[2] At one time there were at least fourteen islands, but erosion has taken its toll on their numbers.

One of the first descriptions of the confluence of the Hudson and Mohawk rivers was by Jasper Dankers, an early explorer, who in 1680 wrote: "The river begins above Fort Albany to divide itself, first by islands, and then by the main land, into two arms or branches, one of which turns somewhat toward the west [the Mohawk]. ... The other preserves the course of the main river for the most part."[3]

The Mohicans, who first occupied the island, called the area *Nachtenac,* or "excellent land" and referred to the junction of the two rivers as *Tiogaronda.* The first white men to see the island were sailors from Henry Hudson's *Halve Maen* (*Half Moon*). Hudson had been able to advance up the Hudson River to just south of Albany, but faced with shallow water ahead decided to send an exploratory party upstream on a much smaller boat to see if the river deepened again. The men probably got as far as the present Champlain Canal Lock before rapids and shallows forced them to retreat[4]—but no one knows for certain how far they went.

Buttermilk Falls makes for a scenic destination. Photograph 2004.

In the nineteenth century Peebles Island was owned by the Peebles family of Halfmoon and Lansingburgh.

The building that you will see to your right as you paddle along the northeast sweep of Peebles Island was originally the bleachery for Cluett, Peabody, and Company, where textiles were bleached from 1911 to 1972. At the time this was a fairly vital area of commerce, with a railroad line crossing the island's north end (which has been turned into an automobile road today). The abandoned factory is now occupied by the New York State Department of Parks, Recreation, and Historical Preservation[5] and is the headquarters for researching, restoring, and preserving historic sites and artifacts. The former summer home of Anthony A. Peebles stands at the rear of the bleachery building complex.

Buttermilk Falls has also been known in past times as Whirlpool Falls, Little Cohoes Falls, Little Falls, and Horseshoe Falls.[6]

Simmons Island may have been named after Daniel Simmons, whose company, D. Simmons & Co., built a dike across the sprout from his lower forge in the late 1850s. The island was earlier called Demilt's Island.[7]

The Van Schaick Country Club was founded in 1895 and incorporated as the Island Club in 1900. The name changed to the Van Schaick Island Country Club in 1916, the year after Jack Gormley designed the present nine-hole course.[8]

Peebles Island Cartop Launch Site: There is also a launch site for paddlers on Peebles Island, less than 0.2 mile from the Waterford Launch at Battery Park. The Peebles Island site essentially duplicates the paddle described above.

To get there from Waterford, take Second Street (one block east of the junction of Rtes. 4 East and 32 North) south across the Mohawk River to Peebles Island and pull into the large parking area to your right. Be prepared to pay a modest seasonal day-use fee. Carry your watercraft east across the open lawn for less than 0.1 mile to a launch site with aluminum dock 100 feet past the red-brick pavilion building.

▶ **Peebles Island**

Paradise Island (Waterford)
Island Hopping near the Crescent Dam

42

■ **Launch Site:** State Boat Launch at end of Flight Lock Road (Saratoga County); cement ramp, parking for fifty cars & trailers.
■ **Delorme NYS Atlas & Gazetteer:** p. 66, B4; **Estimated GPS:** 42°48.43′N; 73°42.89′W
■ **Destinations:** Paradise Island and its satellite island, Crescent Bridge
■ **Mileage:** To Paradise Island—0.2 mile (one-way); to satellite island and back—0.5 mile (round-trip); to Crescent Bridge—1.5 miles (one-way)
■ **Comments:** Read "Caution" beginning on page xxii and "The Mohawk River: Caution" on page 147. Stay a safe distance back from the Crescent Dam, 0.1 mile downstream from the launch site. Don't put in at the launch site if the current seems unusually strong. Be prepared for an increase in boat traffic as you pass near the Albany Marine Service.
■ **Directions:** From the terminus of I-787 at Cohoes, turn right onto Rt. 32 and drive north for over 1.4 miles. As soon as you cross over a bridge spanning the Barge Canal, turn left onto 8th Street and drive north for 0.2 mile. Turn left onto Washington Avenue (Rt. 97) and proceed northwest for 0.5 mile. This was an old colonial military road. When you come to a "V" in the road, bear left onto Flight Lock Road and drive west for 1.6 miles. Along the way you will parallel the Barge Canal and its series of locks.

The road ends at a large parking area just north of the junction of the Barge Canal and the Mohawk River. Park at the north end of the parking area where a cement ramp and dock provide ready access to the river. A new housing development is directly behind the parking area.

The Paddle:
Southwest—Head straight across the Mohawk River to Paradise Island, a distance of less than 0.2 mile. Just downstream is the 0.4-mile-long Crescent Dam, which must be given wide berth. For those who need it spelled out, a large red sign with big white letters on top of a cement block at the southeast end of Paradise Island warns of the upcoming dam.

Once you reach the east shore of Paradise Island (directly across from the put-in), you may secure your craft and explore the island on foot if you wish. A path leads uphill from the water line. Near the beginning of the trail you will come across a plaque set into the ground containing the curious words "Paradise Island. Rye Bread. 1977–1997." Follow the path uphill for 100 feet and then left (south) for another couple of hundred feet. Although the path never ends up going to anywhere of particular interest, it does lead past several makeshift campsites. You may even glimpse a marshy pond in the woods. Considerable debris and junk lies scattered about the trail.

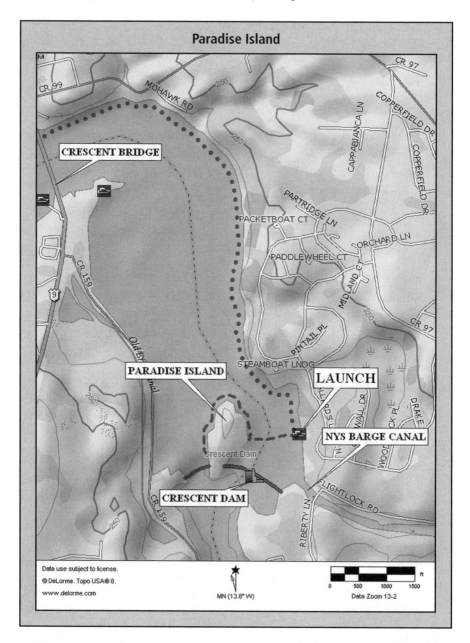

Returning to your watercraft, head north along the island's perimeter where vertically cut walls of shale loom over ten feet above you. Round the north end of Paradise Island, going between the tip of the island and a tiny, twenty-foot-wide satellite island, and continue south following the island's perimeter. The

▶ **Paradise Island**

enormous mound of land you can see way off in the distance to the west is the Cohoes landfill. Continue paddling along the perimeter of Paradise Island, now passing between Paradise Island (to your left), and a smaller island (to your right). Old rusted power towers are visible on both islands. Paddle south for a short distance between the two islands, turning back long before you reach the Crescent Dam and the south end of the satellite island.

North—Proceed upstream for 1.5 miles to reach the Crescent Bridge. The east side of the river is definitely more interesting, with its ten-foot-high rocky shoreline and private homes. The west shoreline is shallow and heavily infested with weeds. Along the way you will pass by the Albany Marine Service, at 1.1 miles, at a point where the river alters direction dramatically from north to southwest as you continue upstream.

Hike to Crescent Dam: From the parking area, drive back (east) for 0.2 mile and then turn right, crossing over the Barge Canal at Guard Gate 2. At the end of the bridge, turn right and park immediately at a small area for visitors.

From the parking area, walk west along the edge of the canal toward the Mohawk River. As you continue, a dirt road will slowly take form. Follow the dirt road (called Guard Gate Road) as it bears left to parallel the east bank of

The Crescent Dam extends to Paradise Island. Photograph 2005.

the Mohawk River, heading south. Soon the road will turn right, bearing west, and in less than 0.1 mile you will come out to a point overlooking the Mohawk River and the Crescent Dam. From there you can clearly see the full sweep of the dam as it arcs northwest to Paradise Island and then southwest to the Crescent Plant/New York Power Authority on the west bank. Directly below the cement overlook are old factory ruins.

History: The paddle begins near the upper terminus of the 1.4-mile-long Waterford Flight of Locks, whose five concrete step-locks (numbered 2 through 6) lift and lower boats a total of 170 feet to bypass the nearby 70-foot-high Cohoes Falls. On the drive up to the Crescent Dam parking area, you will pass by several of these locks. It is said that the Waterford Flight offered the greatest rise over the shortest distance of any lift lock in the world, two times higher than the Panama Canal locks.[1]

In case you're wondering why the Waterford Flight begins at Lock 2 in Waterford, the answer lies at the Federal Dam, farther downstream on the Hudson (not on the Mohawk), which is counted as Lock 1.[2]

At one time it was possible to ford the Mohawk River near where today's Crescent Dam is located. This made the site militarily significant during the Revolutionary War, since the Mohawk River otherwise presented a natural barrier to an advancing army. From August through September of 1777, Benedict Arnold and Enoch Poor and their men guarded the crossing, but they never had to defend it against an invading British force.[3] In the 1800s the ford became known as Loudon's Ford.

 **Paradise Island**

Halfmoon Crescent Park (Crescent)
Put-in near Site of a Historic Aqueduct

43

- **Launch Site:** Halfmoon Crescent Park off of Canal Road (Saratoga County); 20-foot carry to river.
- **Delorme NYS Atlas & Gazetteer:** p. 66, B4; **Estimated GPS:** 42°49.36'N; 73°44.13'W
- **Destinations:** Island on Mohawk River, Crescent Dam
- **Mileage:** To island—0.2 mile (one-way); around island—1.3 miles; to Twin Bridges (Adirondack Northway)—2.6 miles (one-way); to Crescent Dam— 1.5 miles (one-way)
- **Comments:** Read "Caution" beginning on page xxii and "The Mohawk River: Caution" on page 147. Stay a safe distance back from the Crescent Dam downstream. Be prepared for an increase in boat traffic near the Albany Marine Service.
- **Directions:** Heading north on the Adirondack Northway (I-87), get off at Exit 7 for Latham & Cohoes. Stay to the right as you head east on Rt. 7, then turn immediately right onto a ramp, following signs to Rt. 9, which leads you up and around to Rt. 9. From there, turn right and proceed north on Rt. 9. In 4.4 miles you will come to the Crescent Bridge, which spans the Mohawk River. Continue north on Rt. 9 for another 0.2 mile to the north end of the bridge, then turn left at the traffic light onto River Road. Go west for 0.1 mile and turn left onto Canal Road. Almost immediately you will come to a parking area on your left for Halfmoon Crescent Park. An informal put-in at the east end of the parking area involves a twenty-foot carry.

The Paddle:
Most of the paddle duplicates the one described in the chapter "Freddie's Park." However, if you wish to extend your journey farther up the Mohawk, continue southwest for a total of 2.6 miles to the Adirondack Northway's Twin Bridges. Along the way you will pass by several small islands between 1.1 miles and 1.4 miles, and the easternmost projection of Halfmoon Beach, at 1.7 miles. (See chapter "Vandenburgh-Dunsbach Ferry" for further details.)

History: Canal Road follows along the path of the historic old Erie Canal. The water level at the Crescent Bridge was raised by twenty-eight feet when the downstream Crescent Dam was constructed circa 1910.

A historic marker near the end of a tiny, 100-foot-long inlet on the northeast end of the Crescent Bridge states that the "stone remnants mark the northern end of the Aqueduct which carried the Erie Canal over the Mohawk River between 1825 to 1915."[1] The aqueduct was the longest of its kind in the state and contained twenty-six stone arch supports.

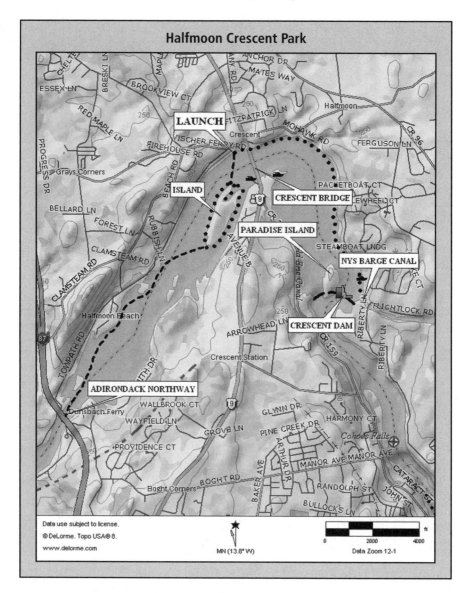

The house with the iron stairs in front, near the northeast end of the bridge, is the Noxon Bank building. It was owned by Alfred Noxon, an entrepreneur who established a foundry, paint works, hotel, and several stores here.

The town has created a lovely park. A walkway leads east to a sheltered viewing area, complete with railings and a bench, directly under the Crescent Bridge. Going west, the walkway follows along the Mohawk River for well over one mile. The Halfmoon Crescent Park is part of the Mohawk Towpath Scenic Byway.[2]

▶ **Halfmoon Crescent Park**

Vandenburgh-Dunsbach Ferry (Halfmoon Beach)
Accessing the Mohawk River at Site of Historic Ferry

44

■ **Launch Site:** Slip-in at water's edge at end of short dirt road off of Canal Road (Saratoga County). This is the site of the northwest terminus of the historic Vandenburgh-Dunsbach Ferry and is now owned by the Town of Halfmoon.

■ **Delorme NYS Atlas & Gazetteer:** p. 66, B3–4; **Estimated GPS:** 42°47.80′N; 73°45.65′W

■ **Destinations:** Adirondack Northway's Twin Bridges, Halfmoon Beach, several small islands opposite the Crescent Boat Club, large island near Crescent Bridge, Crescent Bridge

■ **Mileage:** South to Adirondack Northway's Twin Bridges—0.3 mile (one-way); northeast to Halfmoon Beach—0.3 mile (one-way); to several small islands near Crescent Boat Club—0.9 mile (one-way); to south end of large island near Crescent Bridge—1.5 miles (one-way); around large island near Crescent Bridge—1.3 miles; to Crescent Bridge—2.3 miles (one-way)

■ **Comments:** Read "Caution" beginning on page xxii and "The Mohawk River: Caution" on page 147. Be prepared for an increase in boat traffic as you pass by the Klamsteam Marina, Diamond Reef Yacht Club, Crescent Boat Club, and Blains Bay Marina. Access to the river is also permitted from the Klamsteam Tavern & Marina (32 Clamsteam Road, Clifton Park, NY 12065, 518-373-9409), but fairness dictates that you should stop in at the restaurant for a drink or meal if you use their facilities.

■ **Directions:** From the Adirondack Northway (I-87) take Exit 8 for Crescent & Vischer Ferry. Proceed east on Crescent Road for 0.4 mile, turn right onto Dunsbach Road, and drive south for nearly 0.8 mile. When you come to Clamsteam Road, turn right and go southwest for 0.9 mile. At the junction of Clamsteam Road and Canal Road, turn left onto Canal Road and then immediately right onto a short dirt road that descends to the river in a couple of hundred feet, dead-ending at the water's edge. Park along the side of this road or unobtrusively along Canal Road. Park by the Klamsteam Tavern & Marina only if you are planning to have a meal or drink there afterwards.

The Paddle:

From the slip-in, head southwest for 0.2 mile, paddling by numerous boats docked at the Klamsteam Marina and then the Diamond Reef Yacht Club. Pass to the left of a tiny island at the end of the bay and you will immediately be out on the Mohawk River. At one time the land to the east of the slip-in was an island, but years of sediment buildup have filled in the space between the island and the shore with reeds and cattails. Thus, today you must follow the passageway past the two marinas in order to access the Mohawk River.

South to Twin Bridges—The Twin Bridges are quickly reached in less than 0.3 mile. Be prepared for the sound of endless heavy traffic that emanates from the

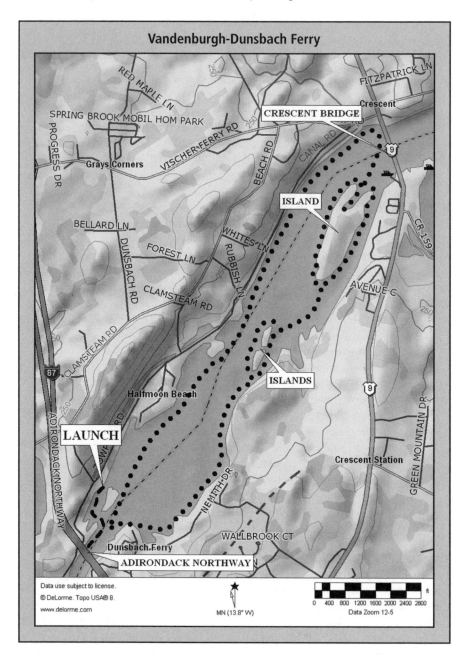

Vandenburgh-Dunsbach Ferry

bridges. From the Twin Bridges it is another 0.6 mile to the Delphus Kill, coming in on your left. The creek can only be explored south for 0.1 mile of its length under normal conditions. (See chapter "Colonie Mohawk River Park.")

▶ Vandenburgh-Dunsbach Ferry

East—Head straight across the Mohawk River to the east shore, turn left, and then follow the shoreline downstream. You will quickly pass by Blains Bay Marina on your right and then, within another 0.3 mile, a small island, also on your right. Near the northwest end of the island is a small overhang of rock where you can seek shelter from the sun on a hot day. The 0.1 mile of water between the island and the shore is usually congested with weeds.

In another 0.3 mile from the first island, you will pass by Halfmoon Beach to your left, once occupied by an establishment called Klause's, but now abandoned.

Go 0.3 mile farther and you will encounter several small islands that are formed opposite the Crescent Boat Club (a private boating club located along the west shore). The first island, closest to the east bank, is by far the largest of the group. It consists of two medium-sized islands that were once separated but are now joined together by a lowland section. At the island's south end is a ten-foot-high rocky bluff. You can debark onto the island from your watercraft once you pass to the right of the bluffs.

The islands closest to the west shore and the Crescent Boat Club are much smaller. Several are treeless and consist only of a small outcropping of brush.

In 1.5 miles you will reach the south end of an island that can be circum-navigated in 1.3 miles.

The Crescent Bridge is reached at 2.3 miles from the put-in.

History: Cornelius Claes Vandenburgh established a rope ferry at this site before 1705, following an old Indian trail that led across the river from the south to Round Lake or east to the Hudson River. It was here that Henry Knox crossed the Mohawk River in January 1776 with fifty-nine cannons as he made his way from Fort Ticonderoga to Boston.

The Vandenburghs built a stone house on this site in 1718, and it lasted until 1917 when it was demolished after the New York State Barge Canal was created.

In 1813 Henry Dunsbach purchased the ferry and stone house and operated the ferry until 1873, at which time the business was sold to the Emerich family, who then operated the ferry until around 1912, when it was acquired by the State of New York. The only time the ferry didn't run was between 1898 and 1900, when a toll bridge replaced it. The toll bridge, however, only lasted for a short period of time. It was washed away by a spring freshet and the ferry, after being reestablished, continued for another decade.[1]

The Old Erie Canal

The following chapters, "Wager's Pond" and "Vischer Ferry Nature & Historic Preserve," provide canoeists and kayakers with an opportunity to paddle on a small section of the old Erie Canal that has survived into this century. The fact that any part of the canal still exists after nearly 200 years may be a surprise to those who confine themselves to the cities and suburbs. Most sections of the canal in these built-up areas have been buried under streets and new development. Head out into the country, however, and vast sections of the canal await exploration.

The Erie Canal's demise was as inevitable as its birth and, regardless of its monumental impact on American history, its life was no longer than that of a modern-day human. It was a canal born out of necessity. By the start of the nineteenth century, New York State was in the midst of the industrial revolution and in desperate need of a state-wide system of transportation faster and more efficient than horse and wagon.

Although the Mohawk River had cut a natural corridor through central New York State, its waters were too shallow and inconsistent to permit boat travel for any appreciable distance other than by canoe or raft. An artificial river, however, if cut deeper than the Mohawk, would not have the shoals and riffs that plagued water travel on the river. It could be made to parallel the Mohawk River, following the course of the wide valley that the river had cut; it could even crisscross the Mohawk via an aqueduct whenever insurmountable obstacles were encountered. Thus was born the concept of the Erie Canal, moving from imagination to initiation in 1817, and to inauguration in 1825.

The canal was an immediate success, transporting passengers and cargo a distance of 363 miles[1] between Albany and Buffalo in a comparatively short length of time (although a slow crawl by today's standards, of course). The canal was 40 feet wide and 4 feet deep; crossing it were 300 bridges and viaducts, averaging nearly one crossing to every mile.[2]

Called "the mother of cities," the Erie Canal single-handedly put Utica, Syracuse, Rochester, and Buffalo on the map and changed New York City from the fourth-largest port in the nation to the largest.

In its time the Erie Canal was the longest artificial waterway in either the New World or Europe and was truly one of the man-made wonders of the world. But within just a decade, the canal could no longer keep pace with the growing demands placed upon it by a quickly multiplying number of boats. Starting in 1835, major modifications were made to improve the waterway. The canal was deepened to 7 feet and widened to 70 feet, and 90-by-15-foot single locks were replaced with 110-by-18-foot double locks so that traffic could be kept moving steadily in both directions.[3] Thus, the old Erie Canal ("Clinton's Ditch") became the new (enlarged) Erie Canal and, because it had been made straighter in the process, shrank in length from 363 miles to 350 miles.

But even as the canal adapted to the times by increasing its efficiency, there was a new revolution in transportation. The canal had replaced roads as the primary avenue of transportation; now, the focus switched back from water to the land. The age of the locomotive had arrived.[4] Steam engines could transport goods and passengers many times faster than the swiftest mule-hauled canal boat, and they could carry loads heavier than those managed by the largest barge coming through the locks. Perhaps most significantly, they could go wherever tracks were laid; they were not longer dependent, as canals were, on stream-cut corridors.

By the beginning of the twentieth century, the Erie Canal's days were over, superseded by both the locomotive and the New York State Barge Canal, which turned the Mohawk River into one long channel.

45 **Wager's Pond (Vischer Ferry)**
A Pond with History

- **Launch Site:** Wager's Pond adjacent to Riverview Road (Saratoga County); 20-foot carry to slip-in at water's edge.
- **Delorme NYS Atlas & Gazetteer:** p. 66, B3–4; **Estimated GPS:** 42°47.93′N; 73°46.06′W
- **Destinations:** Wager's Pond along section of the abandoned Erie Canal, Adirondack Northway Twin Bridges, Railroad Station Park
- **Mileage:** Across Wager's Pond—0.6 mile (one-way); from Wager's Pond to Clute's Dry Dock—0.4 mile (one-way); to Lock 9—2.5 miles with portage (one-way); from south end of Wager's Pond to Adirondack Northway Twin Bridges—0.7 mile (one-way); from south end of Wager's Pond to Railroad Station Park—3.0 miles (one-way)
- **Comments:** Read "Caution" beginning on page xxii and "The Mohawk River: Caution" on page 147.

  Wager's Pond—When heading out onto the pond, choose a calm day and watch the weather. By early summer, choking plants can make paddling across the pond challenging.

  Old Erie Canal—There is no current. The wind tends to be quietest in the early morning and evening. A short portage will be required to do the entire length of this section of the canal.

  Mohawk River—Expect an increase in boat traffic near Blains Bay Marina, Klamsteam Marina, and Diamond Reef Marina.
- **Directions:** From the Adirondack Northway (I-87) get off at Exit 8 for Crescent & Vischer Ferry. Go east on Crescent Road for 0.4 mile, turn right onto Dunsbach Road and drive south for nearly 0.8 mile. When you come to Clamsteam Road, turn right and go southwest for 0.6 mile. Turn right onto Riverview Road and drive west for 0.3 mile (at 0.1 mile you will cross over the Adirondack Northway). As soon as you pass by Boyack Road (to your right), pull over to the side of the road. There is parking available on both sides. The bay is to your left.

The Paddle:

Old Erie Canal/Wager's Pond—Head southwest across Wager's Pond, keeping toward the west shore. You will see a forested island at 0.3 mile. Keep to the right as you pass by it. In another 0.3 mile you will come to the cove's inlet where the old Erie Canal crosses, forming a four-way intersection.

Turning left onto the old Erie Canal will take you northeast for 0.4 mile to a dead end at the Adirondack Northway (I-87). A secondary channel to your left from the dead end also terminates within 0.05 mile (just before breaking into Wager's Pond). On the east side of the Northway, the old Erie Canal resumes its course northeast, immediately passing by the Diamond Reef Yacht Club & Marina.

 **Wager's Pond**

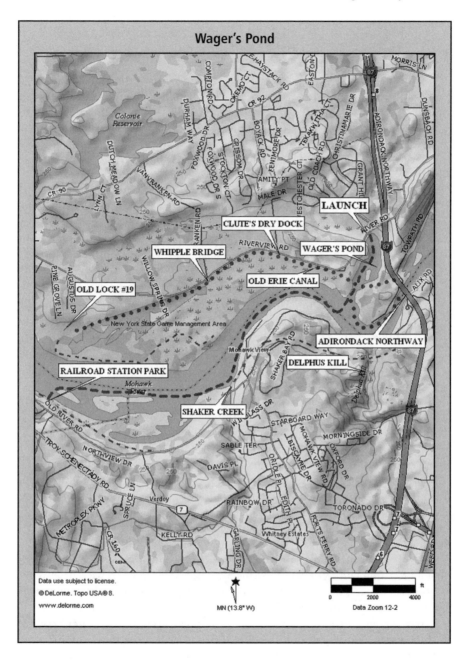

Wager's Pond

The better route at the end of Wager's Pond is to turn right at the intersection onto the old Erie Canal. As you proceed northwest up the old Erie Canal, the Mohawk River will be visible directly to your left, separated from the canal by a tiny strip of land. After paddling over 0.4 mile you will reach Clute's Dry Dock on your right (see following chapter), which provides a momentary side diversion.

Continue northwest for another 0.7 mile to where the canal's direction changes from northwest to southwest. A brief portage over a narrow strip of land will be necessary if you want to continue farther. For most, this will prove to be the ideal point to turn around and head back. If you elect to portage over the causeway and continue west, you will reach the Whipple Bridge (see following chapter) in 0.4 mile and old Lock 19 after another 1.3 miles (the last 0.1 mile of which can only be traversed by walking along the towpath).

Mohawk River—When you reach the inlet of Wager's Pond, instead of veering right or left onto the old Erie Canal, continue straight ahead (south) for 0.2 mile, passing under power lines and paralleling the land mass on your left until you come to the main sweep of the Mohawk River. The river at this point has the appearance of a lake.

East—Turn left and head downstream. You will reach the Twin Bridges in 0.7 mile, where the Adirondack Northway crosses the Mohawk River. Along the way you will pass by a small, rocky island 0.4 mile before arriving at the Twin Bridges. Unlike many of the islands, which are overgrown or provide insubstantial footing, it is possible to get out and walk along the spine of this island for a short distance.

West—Turn right and head upstream, quickly passing by a small island. In a mile or two you will reach a section where the river widens considerably; then, at 3.0 miles, you will reach Railroad Station Park on your left (see chapter "Railroad Station Park").

History: At one time the State University of New York at Albany (SUNYA) owned 100 acres of land by Wager's Pond. The plot was called the Mohawk Campus and featured a white house, swimming pool, outdoor pavilion, and picnic facilities. Even though the bay was periodically dredged, it generally proved too reedy for swimming; however, it was usually traversable by boats and canoes. The Mohawk Campus no longer exists, the land having been sold by SUNYA during the 1980s. The house is now privately owned and is the first house encountered on your left after you cross over the causeway and begin heading west. The swimming pool, located on the opposite side of Riverview Road, was filled in years ago and is now part of a sheep farm.

As a topographical map or gazetteer will show, the body of water between the Adirondack Northway and Riverview Road is large enough to be considered a lake, and many who came to visit the Mohawk Campus in years gone by were probably fooled into thinking that it *was* a lake, for the side wall of the old Erie Canal and the islands to the south obscured the fact that Wager's Pond is connected to the Mohawk River and is therefore part of the river.

▶ **Wager's Pond**

There has been some discussion about reestablishing the old canal towpath across Wager's Pond. Should this happen in years to come, the character of Wager's Pond will change again.

Additional point of interest: To view a portion of the Erie Canal northeast of the Twin Bridges, get back in your car and drive east on Riverview Road from Wager's Pond for 0.3 mile. At the junction of Riverview Road and Clamsteam Road, turn right onto Clamsteam Road and drive south for 0.2 mile, then turn either right or left onto Canal Road. Going either way will provide views of the old Erie Canal, which Canal Road parallels.

46 Vischer Ferry Nature & Historic Preserve (Vischer Ferry)
Paddling along a Section of the Erie Canal

- **Launch Site:** Vischer Ferry Nature & Historic Preserve along Riverview Road (Saratoga County). Clute's Dry Dock access to the old Erie Canal—100-foot carry to dock put-in; Whipple Bridge access to the old Erie Canal—100-foot carry to put-in under bridge; Mohawk River access near Forts Ferry—0.5-mile carry to slip-in on Mohawk River; Ferry Drive access to the Mohawk River—15-foot carry down steep embankment to river's edge. For more information: Clifton Park Town Hall, One Town Hall Plaza, Clifton Park, NY 12065, (518) 371-6651, byways.org/explore/byways/57185/places/62397/, mohawktowpath.homestead. com/naturepreserve.html.
- **Delorme NYS Atlas & Gazetteer:** p. 66, B3; **Estimated GPS:** Clute's Dry Dock—42°47.74'N, 73°46.95'W; Whipple Bridge—42°47.55'N, 73°47.75'W; Mohawk River—42°47.22'N, 73°47.51'W; Ferry Drive—42°47.65'N, 73°49.88'W
- **Destinations:** Along sections of the old Erie Canal, Railroad Station Park, Lock E-7, Adirondack Northway Twin Bridges
- **Mileage:** Along Erie Canal—variable, up to 5.0 miles with portages (round-trip); to Railroad Station Park—1.8 miles (one-way); to Lock E-7—3.7 miles (one-way); to Adirondack Northway Twin Bridges—1.9 miles (one-way)
- **Comments:** Read "Caution" beginning on page xxii and "The Mohawk River: Caution" on page 147.

  Old Erie Canal—There is no current. The wind tends to be quietest in the early morning and evening. A short portage will be required to do the entire length of this section of the canal.

  Mohawk River—Stay a safe distance back from the Lock E-7 dam.
- **Directions:** From the Adirondack Northway (I-87) get off at Exit 8 for Crescent & Vischer Ferry. Proceed east on Crescent Road for 0.4 mile, turn right onto Dunsbach Road and drive south for nearly 0.8 mile. When you come to Clam-steam Road, turn right and go southwest for over 0.6 mile. Turn right onto Riverview Road. There are three access points:

  Clute's Dry Dock—Drive west for 0.9 mile and turn left into a small parking area for Clute's Dry Dock. Walk several hundred feet over to the rectangular-shaped inlet of water (the dry dock), where a modern dock allows easy access to the dry dock and canal.

  Whipple Bridge—Drive west for 2.0 miles (or 1.1 miles past Clute's Dry Dock) and turn left into a roadside parking area next to a kiosk. Continuing on foot, cross over the Whipple Bridge:

  To Old Erie Canal: At the end of the Whipple Bridge, turn right, and then right again to put in directly under the bridge.

  To Ponds: From the end of the Whipple Bridge, follow the dirt road south for 100 feet and slip in to the pond on your right. This pond is fairly narrow, probably less than 0.1 mile wide, but its length extends for over 1.0 mile,

▶ **Vischer Ferry Nature & Historic Preserve**

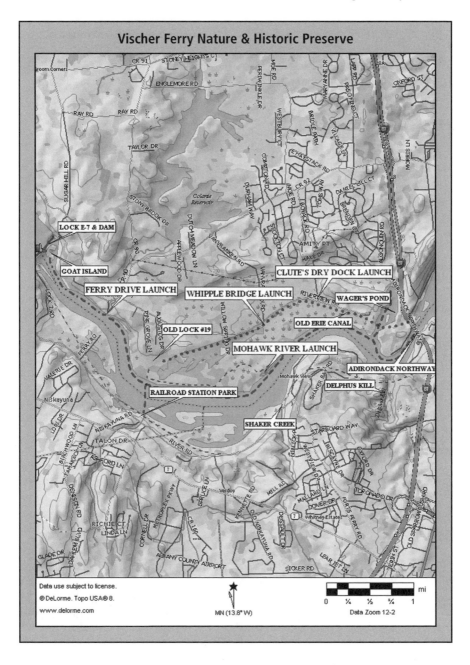

Vischer Ferry Nature & Historic Preserve

paralleling the Erie Canal to your right and separated from the canal by a tiny strip of land (which forms the former towpath). The pond can get pretty reedy during the summer. There are additional smaller bodies of water that can be slipped into from the dirt road as you head south. These also become progressively reedier with the arrival of summer.

To Mohawk River near Forts Ferry: A canoe/kayak carrier is advisable here. From the Whipple Bridge, follow the level, well-packed footpath/road south for 0.5 mile to the Mohawk River, where you can slip in at the river's edge, pushing through 50 feet of weeds until you are clear. This dirt road was once called the "Public Bridge Road" and is the oldest road in Clifton Park. The settlement of Forts Ferry is gone, becoming uninhabitable with the creation of the New York State Barge Canal, which raised the level of the river and the ferocity of its floods.

Ferry Drive—Drive west for nearly 4.0 miles and turn left onto Ferry Drive, approximately 0.2 mile after passing by Vischer Ferry Road (on your right). Head south for 0.1 mile to a cul-de-sac parking area. You have reached the site of an early ferry crossing, where a bridge later spanned the Mohawk only to be washed away after two years' use. You will see bridge abutments on both sides of the river. The put-in involves a 15-foot descent down a steep gully in the embankment to the river's edge.

Approaching these three access sites from Rexford (junction of Rt. 146 & Riverview Road)—Drive southeast on Riverview Road, paralleling the Mohawk River to your right. At 5.6 miles you will come to Ferry Drive, at 7.4 miles the Whipple Bridge pull-off, and at 9.0 miles the parking lot for Clute's Dry Dock.

The Paddle:

It is exciting to dip into the historic Erie Canal and to imagine what it must have been like during the nineteenth century for canal boatmen and travelers making their way between Albany and Buffalo. During the 1800s it was not uncommon for travelers to also walk along the towpath, for the footpath provided an efficient pedestrian route across the state and was used by those who couldn't afford passage on conventional transports.[1] Today the towpath is still steadily used by walkers, bicyclists, and anglers. Bear in mind that the trees lining the canal have only existed since the old Erie Canal was abandoned; their presence earlier would have snagged the tow lines extending from the boats to the mules.

You will find that the waters are fairly murky year-round, but turn green and in some places become algae-covered and more viscous with the approach of summer.

From Clute's Dry Dock

Paddle east and you will reach the point where the canal enters the Mohawk River, in 0.4 mile. From here it is possible to go north (left) onto Wager's Pond or south (right) onto the main part of the Mohawk River.

If you paddle west along the canal, you can go as far as 0.7 mile before it becomes necessary to portage over a causeway. Once you put back into the canal, it is 0.4 mile to the Whipple Bridge, and from there roughly 1.2 miles to a point where

▶ **Vischer Ferry Nature & Historic Preserve**

Clutes Dry Dock. Photograph 2007.

the waters become too shallow to proceed any farther. If you go that far, it makes sense to leave your canoe momentarily and follow the towpath west on foot for another 0.1 mile to reach Lock 19, which is worth visiting.

From the Whipple Bridge
Old Erie Canal Access—Head east for 0.4 mile to reach a causeway, which you must portage over to continue 0.7 mile to Clute's Dry Dock or 1.1 miles to where the canal enters the Mohawk River.

If you paddle west toward Lock 19, which is 1.3 miles away, you will be able to go roughly 1.1 miles before shallow waters prevent further advancement. Along the way you will pass by a couple of old bridge abutments. When you reach the navigable end of the canal, you may wish to pull over to the south bank and walk the remaining 0.1 mile to see old Lock 19, which remains fairly well preserved.

Pond Access—Head west for up to 1.1 miles, paralleling the Erie Canal and towpath to your right.

Mohawk River Access—Before starting, look directly across the river to see where the ferry service once brought passengers and cargo to Forts Ferry Road. Paddle east for 1.9 miles to reach the Twin Bridges where the Adirondack Northway spans the Mohawk River. Along the way you will pass by numerous private homes lining the south shore.

Head west for 1.8 miles to reach Railroad Station Park, or 3.7 miles to reach Lock E-7.

From Ferry Drive
Paddle east for 1.2 miles to reach Railroad Station Park on the south bank of the river. Head northwest for 1.1 miles to reach Lock E-7. Directly across the river from Ferry Drive is Ferry Road. A bridge once connected the two.

History: The Vischer Ferry Nature & Historic Preserve is cooperatively managed by the Town of Clifton Park and the New York State Department of Transporta-

Lock 19 at the
Vischer Ferry
Nature & Historical
Preserve. Photo-
graph 2006.

tion.[2] Contained
in the park is a
long section of
the Erie Canal
and its towpath, a
double-chamber lock from when the Erie Canal was enlarged in 1842, Clute's
historic dry dock, and the site of two, nineteenth-century ferry crossings.

In 1825 the first dry dock was constructed near the east end of the preserve
by a man named Volvyder. It was reestablished in 1852 by Nicholas J. Clute, and
from that time on became known as Clute's Dry Dock. Boats were repaired and
built at the site. Clute also established a home and general store here, an ideal
location because canal boatmen would frequently stop at the store for supplies.
The settlement was abandoned in 1907,[3] partly as a result of the Barge Canal
raising the river level.

The cast-iron Whipple Bridge, which crosses the Erie Canal on what used
to be an extension of Van Vranken Road, was built in 1869 by Squire Whipple,
a Union College graduate who is considered to be the father of iron bridges.[4]
The bridge originally spanned the Erie Canal in Fultonville. It was brought to its
present location in 1997.[5] The stone blocks that support the bridge were taken
from the old aqueduct canal at Rexford.

Roughly 0.4 mile south of the Whipple Bridge is the site of the now-vanished community of Fort's Ferry. A historic marker there reads: "Fort's Ferry: Site
of oldest settlement in Clifton Park. Known as Canastigione, settled 1672. Nicholas Fort established a rope ferry in 1728." By 1765 fifteen farmhouses formed
a coherent settlement.

In another 0.1 mile from this site, the Mohawk River is reached, where Fort's
ferry operated. On the opposite side of the river can be seen the connecting road
coming down to the edge of the river.

Lock 19, located 1.3 miles west of the Whipple Bridge, is exceptionally well
preserved and worth visiting. The lock was built in 1842 when the Erie Canal
was being enlarged to accommodate the growing number of boats traveling
between Albany and Buffalo. The lock had three compartments, raising or lowering boats a total of 8.5 feet. Forty-three years later, the lock was once again
enlarged, becoming a double-chamber lock to accommodate two boats simultaneously. The stones for the lock were quarried from Rotterdam Junction (west
of Schenectady).

▶ **Vischer Ferry Nature & Historic Preserve**

Mohawk Landing (Grooms Corner)
An Historic Lock & a Scenic Gorge

47

■ **Launch Site:** Riverview Public Access Project, Town of Clifton Park, off of Riverview Road (Saratoga County); 0.2-mile carry along wide walkway made of stone dust, with boardwalk sections bridging wet areas. A rock cut at the end of the walkway leads down to the river's edge. Wheelchair-accessible.

■ **Delorme NYS Atlas & Gazetteer:** p. 66, B2–3; **Estimated GPS:** 42°49.43′N; 73°51.55′W

■ **Destinations:** Lock E-7; Rexford Bridge

■ **Mileage:** Downriver to Lock E-7—1.1 miles (one-way); upriver to Rexford Bridge—3.0 miles (one-way)

■ **Comments:** Read "Caution" beginning on page xxii and "The Mohawk River: Caution" on page 147. Stay a safe distance back from the Lock E-7 dam. A canoe carrier would be helpful.

■ **Directions:** From Rexford (junction of Rt. 146 & Riverview Road), turn onto River-view Road and drive southeast for 2.9 miles. Turn right onto an unpaved road that leads immediately down to a parking area large enough to hold about eight vehicles. If you go past Brian Drive, on your right, then you have just missed the turn.

From Vischer Ferry (junction of Riverview Road and Vischer Ferry Road), drive northwest for 2.7 miles (or 1.3 miles past Sugar Hill Road). As soon as you drive by Brian Drive, on your left, turn left onto an unpaved road that takes you immediately down to a medium-sized parking area.

From the parking area, follow a wheelchair-accessible walkway west for 0.2 mile and then descend to the river's edge via a gravel incline through a rock cut.

The Paddle:

The paddle begins 0.3 mile downstream from the Knolls Atomic Power Laboratory (KAPL), located on the opposite side of the river. From the launch, look directly across the river to the west bank and you will see a seasonal cascade.

By heading downstream you will reach the Lock E-7 dam at 1.1 miles. Stay a safe distance back from the dam and the power plant on the northeast bank. If you wish, you can paddle over to the southwest bank and the put-in at the boat launch by Lock E-7.

Paddling upstream takes you through a more dramatic portion of the Rexford Gorge, with towering walls on both sides of the river. After 3.0 miles you will reach the Rexford Bridge, a good place to turn around.

Refer to chapters "Lock E-7 Boat Launch" and "Kiwanis Aqueduct Park Cartop Launch" for more specific details about the sights seen along this trek.

History: The land at Mohawk Landing was initially owned by Bill Leversee, who built three riverfront camps and rented them out to vacationing families. Years later, Howard Barrett purchased the property and continued renting

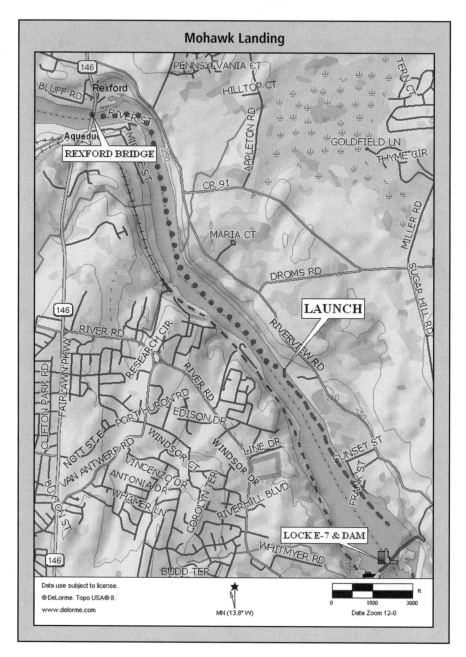

out the camps until 1964, when they were abandoned. In 2006 the Town of Clifton Park purchased the six-acre property from Isabel and Joel Prescott— Bill Leversee's daughter and son-in-law—for $202,000, of which $100,000 was

▶ **Mohawk Landing**

obtained through the country's open space protection program.[1] Developing the park required an additional expense of $288,000; $180,000 of that sum came through the New York State Canal Corporation's Erie Canal Greenway Grant Program; the rest of the money came out of the town's surplus funds.

Lock E-7—one mile downriver from Mohawk Landing. Photograph 2002.

48

Alplaus Creek (Alplaus)
One of the Mohawk River's Most Historic Tributaries

■ **Launch Site:** Mohawk Valley Marine off of Maritime Drive (Saratoga County); ramp. There is a modest launch fee. Restrooms are available. Open spring, summer & fall, Mon.–Fri. 9 AM–6 PM, Sat. & Sun. 9 AM–4 PM. For more information: Mohawk Valley Marine (mohawkvalleymarine.com).

■ **Delorme NYS Atlas & Gazetteer:** p. 66, AB2; **Estimated GPS:** 42°51.00'N; 73°54.31'W

■ **Destinations:** Alplaus Creek, island on Mohawk River, Great Western Gateway Bridge, Rexford Bridge

■ **Mileage:** North and up Alplaus Creek—1.0 mile (one-way); southwest to island on Mohawk River—0.4 mile (one-way); around island—0.7 mile; to Great Western Gateway Bridge—3.4 miles (one-way); east to Rexford Bridge—0.8 mile (one-way)

■ **Comments:** Read "Caution" beginning on page xxii and "The Mohawk River: Caution" on page 147.

Alplaus Creek—The current is generally mild to moderate because of the backing up of the Mohawk River at the Lock E-7 dam. Short portages will be required in order to continue the paddle after 1.0 mile.

■ **Directions:** From east of Schenectady (junction of Rt. 7 and Balltown Road [which quickly becomes Rt. 146]), drive north on Balltown Road/Rt. 146 for over 4.2 miles until you come to a stoplight at the top of a long hill 0.3 mile after crossing over the Mohawk River. Turn left onto Alplaus Avenue (opposite Riverview Road) and drive west for 1.0 mile. Turn left onto Maritime Drive and follow it south for over 0.3 mile. You will come to a stop sign at the intersection with Mohawk Avenue. Continue straight ahead for 0.05 mile and then turn left into the marina. The main office is located next to the river. The put-in ramp is to the right (south) of this building.

The Paddle:

North and up Alplaus Creek—Leaving the marina, paddle downstream on the Mohawk River for less than 0.1 mile and turn left (north) into Alplaus Creek. The water at the creek's mouth is very deep because the Mohawk River is backed up by the Lock E-7 dam. In 0.3 mile you will pass under the Alplaus Avenue bridge. Continue paddling north. Within 1.0 mile you will start to encounter rapids and shallow waters. It is probably best to turn around here. If you decide to continue ahead, it will be necessary to repeatedly get out of your watercraft to portage past each new set of rapids. If you continue upstream, the railroad bridge is reached at 1.2 mile. It was near here that French and Native Americans are believed to have camped while readying for a late-evening surprise attack on Schenectady during the French and Indian wars.

Southwest—From the marina, paddle upstream on the Mohawk River, heading southwest. In 0.4 mile you will come to the east end of a 0.4-mile-long

▶ **Alplaus Creek**

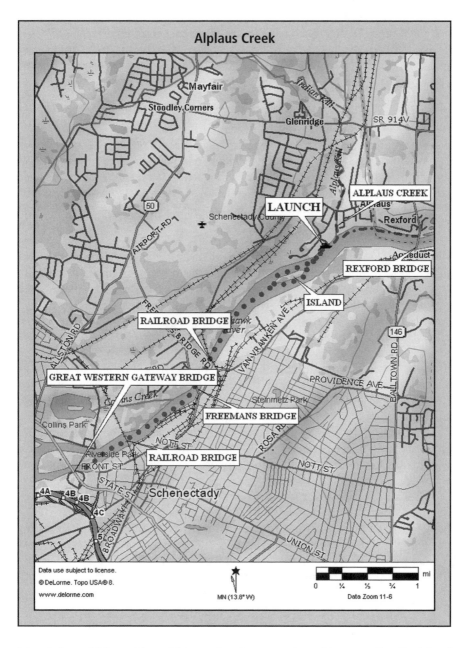

Alplaus Creek

island shaped like a ship, which can be circumnavigated in 0.7 mile. The island is crossed by power lines and, like a number of islands on the Mohawk, rises only several feet above the water line. Visible on the north bank of the river, opposite the island, is the Mohawk Valley Rowing Club.

Continuing farther upriver, the Mohawk narrows considerably. You will pass under a railroad bridge at 1.6 miles, under Freemans Bridge at 1.9 miles, and then past Collins Creek, on your right, at 2.2 miles. When you reach 2.8 miles, you will go under a second railroad bridge. After another 0.3 mile the river widens appreciably again, leading you past the Isle of the Cayugas and to the Great Western Gateway Bridge, 3.4 miles upriver from the marina.

East—Proceed downstream from the marina. In 0.2 mile you will pass by a series of piers, remnants of a former bridge that crossed the Mohawk River. You will also pass by a 0.4-mile-long sliver of earth and rocks to your left that is the result of dredging. In 0.8 mile you will reach the Rexford Bridge, which is a good turnaround point unless you plan to venture farther downstream into the Rexford Gorge (see chapters "Kiwanis Aqueduct Park Cartop Launch," "Mohawk Landing," and "Lock E-7 Boat Launch").

History: "Alplaus" is a corruption of the Dutch words *Aal Plaats*, meaning "place of eels." Up until the creation of the Federal Dam at Troy, Jamaican eels were able to swim up the Mohawk River from the Hudson and then up Alplaus Creek to spawn. It was the bountiful harvest of eels that gave this stream its name.

Alplaus Creek rises from the Consaul Vly, producing twelve-foot-high Krystal Falls in the High Mills area as it wends its way down toward the Mohawk River. For many years it was a main water trail north for Native Americans and trappers. Travelers would follow the stream up to High Mills and then portage across land to Ballston Lake; from there they would make their way across successive streams and bodies of water to the Canadian border near northern Lake Champlain. Some called the route the Saratoga Trail.[1]

The most famous person to travel this route was Sir William Johnson, who was taken to Saratoga Springs in 1767 by his Mohawk friends so that his wounded leg could benefit from the supposed curative powers of the mineral waters. Apparently, in Johnson's case it worked.

Alplaus Creek is also associated with infamy. On the night of February 8, 1690, in what came to be known as the Schenectady Massacre, a party of 114 Frenchmen, 80 Mohawks, and 16 Algonquins left their camp at Alplaus during a raging blizzard and attacked and burned the settlement in Schenectady.[2] Sixty settlers were killed and ninety prisoners were taken, with the attackers losing only two of their own. The original target had been Fort Orange (Albany), but the long cold march south had sapped the war party's strength and convinced them that Schenectady would be the easier target.[3]

During the last several centuries a number of mills have operated along the creek, many in the area by High Mills (five miles upstream from the mouth of Alplaus Creek). In the mid-1700s, Peter Brummaghin operated a gristmill at the site where Glenridge Road crosses Alplaus Creek,[4] 1.4 miles from the mouth of the river.

Mohawk Valley Marine has been family-owned and operated since 1986.

▶ **Alplaus Creek**

Railroad Station Park (Niskayuna)
Islands in the Mohawk River

49

■ **Launch Site:** Railroad Station Park (aka Lions Station Park) off of River Road (Schenectady County); slip-in at river's edge. For more information: niskayuna.org.
■ **Delorme NYS Atlas & Gazetteer:** p. 66, B3; **Estimated GPS:** 42°46.66'N; 73°49.36'W
■ **Destinations:** Niska Isle, Lisha Kill Bay, Goat Island and other islands, Shaker Creek, Adirondack Northway Twin Bridges
■ **Mileage:** To Niska Isle—1.0 mile (one-way); to Ferry Road bridge at Lisha Kill Bay—1.0 mile (one-way); to Goat Island—2.2 miles; around the downstream islands and back—2.5 miles (round-trip); to Shaker Creek—1.6 miles (one-way); up Shaker Creek—0.1 mile (one-way); to Adirondack Northway Twin Bridges—3.7 miles (one-way)
■ **Comments:** Read "Caution" beginning on page xxii and "The Mohawk River: Caution" on page 147. By early summer, choking plants can make paddling along the south shoreline challenging. Expect an increase in boat traffic from Blains Bay Marina, Klamsteam Marina, and Diamond Reef Marina by the Adirondack Northway Twin Bridges.
■ **Directions:** From the Adirondack Northway (I-87), get off at Exit 6 for Schenectady/Troy and drive northwest on Rt. 7 (which is the old Schohanna Trail between Troy and Schenectady)[1] for approximately 3.2 miles. When you come to the stoplight at Rosendale Road, turn right and drive northwest on Rosendale Road for 0.3 mile. Turn right onto a short road leading to Railroad Station Park, where joggers, walkers, and bikers park their cars while exercising along the rail bed of the old Troy-Schenectady Railroad Line, which was converted into a paved bikeway.

From the west (junction of Rosendale Road and River Road), drive east on Rosendale Road for 2.2 miles and turn left into the area for the Niskayuna Railroad Station Park.

From either direction, once you have turned off of Rosendale Road, drive down to the lower right corner of the parking area, cross over the Mohawk-Hudson Bikeway (looking out for bicyclists and pedestrians), and continue down a dirt road for less than 100 feet to the edge of the river, where a canoe or kayak can be launched directly next to a tiny stream that comes into the Mohawk River on your right.

The Paddle:

Northwest—Head upstream to Niska Isle (a peninsula), approximately 1.0 mile distant. You will pass by a partially forested 0.2-mile-long island in 0.2 mile. When you reach the south tip of Niska Isle, you can either veer left into a marshy area where the Ferry Road bridge crosses over the bay and bikeway, or to the right, following along the main sweep of the Mohawk River. You will discover that cattails and purple loosestrife grow abundantly in this area.

Southern Shore: Schenectady County

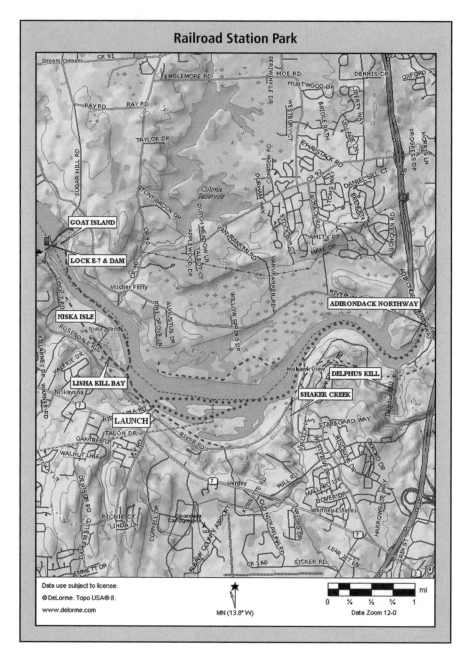

Railroad Station Park

Leaving the mouth of Lisha Kill Bay behind, continue northwest for another 1.6 miles to reach Goat Island. Along the way you will pass by the site of the old Vischer Ferry Bridge, at 0.5 mile. The name Goat Island is not an uncommon

▶ **Railroad Station Park**

one. A second Goat Island can be found farther downstream next to Peebles Island at the confluence of the Mohawk and Hudson rivers. There is also the world-famous Goat Island above the American Falls at Niagara Falls. The name suggests that the islands were once used to herd goats and sheep, for what could better serve as a natural fence than water?

East—To the right of the old train station, heading downstream, are two islands, separated by a channel that cuts across diagonally. The main one is called Shaker Island. The south sides of the islands are weedy and impenetrable, but you can easily put-in on the north side of the easternmost island.

The islands can be circumnavigated as a group, a round trip of 2.5 miles.

At 1.6 mile, continuing east, you will reach the mouth of Shaker Creek along the south bank of the Mohawk. You can paddle south up the creek for 0.1 mile until further continuation is blocked by River Road.

If you continue farther down the Mohawk River, you will reach the Adirondack Northway Twin Bridges in 3.7 miles.

On both paddles be prepared for shallow waters between and along some of the land masses. If you are wearing rubber water shoes and go ashore, watch out for the tetrahedral-shaped water chestnuts. Their spiny, thorny bodies can easily penetrate thin rubber materials.

History: The railroad station is the lone surviving structure from the Troy-Schenectady Railroad, which established a rail line along the south bank of the Mohawk River in 1843. The station was constructed by the Shakers with help from the Van Vranken family. The Van Vrankens, who owned a nearby sawmill, wanted to ensure that an adequate rail system was set up to transport their produce, which included seeds, canned goods, and brooms.[2]

Directly across the tracks from the train station stood a water tank, essentially where the parking lot is now located. It was dismantled in 1925 and no trace of it remains today.[3]

At one time this section of the Mohawk River was divided up by numerous small islands, many of which have disappeared since the creation of the Barge Canal and the deepening of the river. One of the islands near the railroad station is of fairly recent origin, however, perhaps built up through an accumulation of dredged material. Named Marite Damen Island, it honors a seventeenth-century Dutchwoman who owned property in Niskayuna.[4]

The word "Niskayuna" comes from the Mohawk word *Canastigione* for "field of corn." The fertile islands and land next to the river were used extensively by natives to grow corn, beans, and pumpkins.[5]

The unusually high narrow bridge crossing over the Lisha Kill inlet is called the Niska Isle Bridge. It was built in 1916 and serves a neighborhood of ten residents and one farm. Plans are currently underway to replace the bridge with a 588-foot-long span that will be lower to the ground. Work may commence as early as 2010.[6]

A Mohawk village (called a "castle") thrived on Niska Isle, occupying the area, roughly, from Lock E-7 to the Lisha Kill. The land was fertile and defensible because of its ideal location at the confluence of the Lisha Kill and the Mohawk River.

The Lisha Kill, earlier known to the Dutch as the "Lysjens,"[7] is a small stream that rises south of Schenectady and meanders for nine miles before flowing into

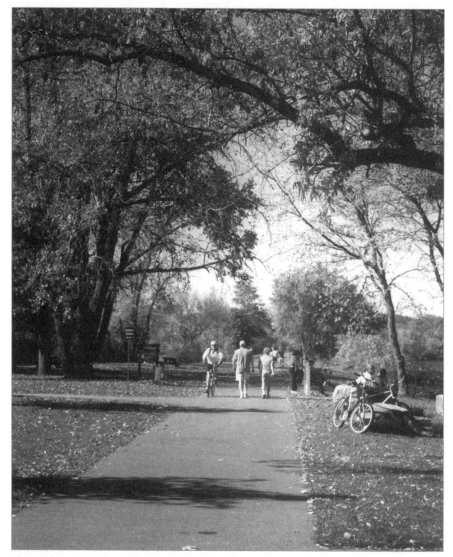

The Mohawk-Hudson Bikeway, once a railroad bed, closely follows along the shoreline of the Mohawk River. Photograph 2007.

 **Railroad Station Park**

Niska Isle Bay. Along the way the stream passes through the 109-acre Lisha Kill Preserve, owned by the Nature Conservancy, whose hiking trails can be accessed off of Rosendale Road. Long ago the Lisha Kill was part of a trail system used by the Mohawks to travel between the Normans Kill and the Mohawk River.[8] The trail passed over the south end of the Lisha Kill.

Vischer Ferry is named after Eldert Vischer, who operated a rope ferry in 1790 at this site. The Vischer Ferry Bridge underwent construction in 1901 and was 790 feet long.[9] In the spring of 1901, ice floods washed out two sections of the bridge. It was decided then to build the bridge three feet higher. Raging floodwaters, however, permanently swept away the bridge in 1902 before that work was completed.[10]

Invasive, non-native species—When you paddle into Niska Isle Bay or near the old railroad station farther east, you will encounter a proliferation of water chestnuts, which are indigenous to Asia, Europe, and tropical Africa. It is believed that the water chestnuts were inadvertently introduced into New York State in the late 1800s and only recently spread upstate into northern waters. The problem with water chestnut plants is that they thrive without opposition and create a mat-like layer of dense plant material that has to be paddled through in order to make headway. This can feel like dragging an anchor behind your watercraft. The spiny chestnuts are also rather unpleasant to step on if you are barefoot or wearing rubber-soled water shoes.

50 | Lock E-7 Boat Launch (Niskayuna)
Vertical Walls of Rock

■ **Launch Site:** Lock E-7 Boat launch at terminus of Lock 7 Road (Schenectady County); concrete ramp.

■ **Delorme NYS Atlas & Gazetteer:** p. 66, B3; **Estimated GPS:** 42°48.20'N; 73°50.91'W

■ **Destination:** Rexford Bridge

■ **Mileage:** 4.2 miles (one-way)

■ **Comments:** Read "Caution" beginning on page xxii and "The Mohawk River: Caution" on page 147. Keep a safe distance back from the Lock E-7 dam. Don't put in at the launch site if the current looks unusually strong. Expect an increase in boat traffic from the Schenectady Yacht Club near the Rexford Bridge.

■ **Directions:** From the Adirondack Northway (I-87), get off at Exit 6 for Schenectady/Troy and drive northwest on Rt. 7 for 3.2 miles. When you come to the stoplight at Rosendale Road, turn right and drive northwest on Rosendale Road for 2.0 miles until you come to Lock 7 Road on your right.

From Schenectady (junction of Union Street and Rosendale Road), go east on Rosendale Road for 2.3 miles until you come to Lock 7 Road.

Approaching from either direction, turn onto Lock 7 Road and drive northwest for 0.8 mile. When you come to a fork in the road, bear left and continue up a small hill to a parking lot in front of the boat launch, at 0.9 mile.

If you wish to make this a one-way paddle, with cars stationed at each end of the trek, position the second car at the Kiwanis Aqueduct Park. To get there from Lock 7 Road, drive northwest on Rosendale Road for 0.5 mile, then turn right onto River Road and continue northwest for 3.3 miles until you reach Balltown Road (Rt. 146). Turn right onto Balltown Road and drive north for 1.5 miles until you come to a stoplight south of the Rexford Bridge. Turn left onto Aqueduct Road, and then immediately turn right onto a tiny road between the Boat House (a store that sells muscle-powered watercraft and related paraphernalia) and the Aqueduct Rowing Club. Park at the end of this road, several hundred feet away from a public dock.

The Paddle:

Head upstream (northwest) on the Mohawk River, staying close to the rocky walls along the west bank, which gradually increase in height and grandeur as you proceed northwest. After 1.5 miles you will enter a deeply cut gorge, with towering walls on both sides of the river, separated by a distance of over 0.1 mile. The gorge runs for over 2.0 miles of the trip's length.

Along the way, to your left, are: the Mohawk River State Park (formerly the Schenectady Museum Nature Preserve); KAPL (Knolls Atomic Power Laboratory), at 1.8 miles; and the General Electric Research and Development Center, built in 1947, at 2.5 miles. Note that the Mohawk-Hudson Bikeway runs con-

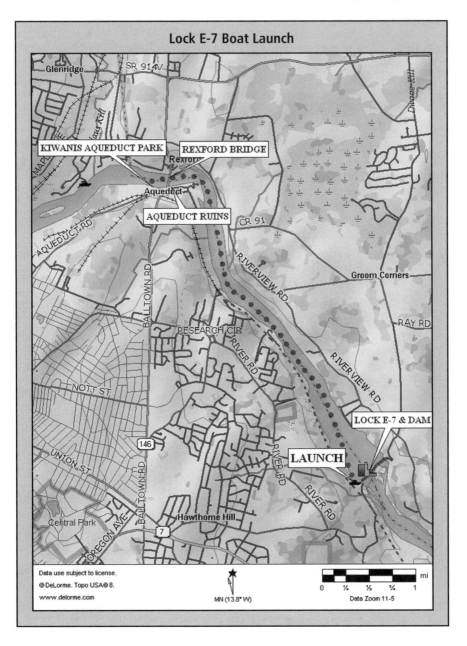

Lock E-7 Boat Launch

KIWANIS AQUEDUCT PARK

REXFORD BRIDGE

AQUEDUCT RUINS

LOCK E-7 & DAM

LAUNCH

Glenridge

SR 914V

Rexford

Aqueduct

CR 91

Groom Corners

RAY RD

RIVERVIEW RD

RESEARCH CIR

RIVERVIEW RD

BALLTOWN RD

AQUEDUCT RD

NOTT ST

RIVER RD

UNION ST

146

RIVER RD

RIVER RD

BALLTOWN RD

Central Park

OREGON AVE

Hawthorne Hill

7

Data use subject to license.
© DeLorme. Topo USA® 8.
www.delorme.com

MN (13.8° W)

0   ¼   ½   ¾   1   mi

Data Zoom 11-5

tinuously from Lock E-7 to Rexford, paralleling the river, but remains out of sight for most of the distance.

The grand estate on the high bluffs to your right—you'll know it when you see it!—once belonged to the insurance magnate Albert W. Lawrence. He called it Llenroc, after his alma mater, Cornell University (Llenroc is Cornell spelled backwards). The estate is roughly 0.1 mile upstream from the Knolls Atomic Power Laboratory, on the opposite side of the river.

At 3.1 miles you will pass by a tiny cove on your left that conceals a pretty, twenty-five-foot-high waterfall.

In 3.7 miles the river changes direction from northwest to west, and you will pass by the Schenectady Yacht Club on your right.

At 4.2 miles you will reach the public dock and exit site on your left (if you are making this a one-way trip), 0.2 mile past the Rexford Bridge and just past the dock used by the Rowing Club. If making a round-trip, turn around at the Rexford Bridge and paddle back, returning to the boat launch at Lock E-7.

History: Lock E-7 and the dam were constructed from 1910 to 1913 and serve as part of the New York State Barge Canal system. The powerhouse on the north bank of the Mohawk River opposite Lock E-7 was constructed in 1925.[1] In 1989 it was enlarged by the New York State Power Authority, more than doubling its power capacity.

The Rexford Gorge is of recent geologic origin compared to the rest of the Mohawk Valley. Its youthful age is revealed by the gorge's sharply cut, vertical walls, which will need thousands of years more to be eroded into the mature, sloping hills that characterize the upper part of the Mohawk Valley. The walls of the gorge are formed out of sandstone and shale, sedimentary rocks that came into existence around 400 million years ago.

▶ **Lock E-7 Boat Launch**

Kiwanis Aqueduct Park Cartop Launch (Rexford)
Walls of Rock, an Old Aqueduct, and the Ruins of a Trolley Bridge

51

■ **Launch Site:** Kiwanis Aqueduct Park off of Aqueduct Road (Schenectady County); 150-foot carry to ramp leading to dock on Mohawk River.
■ **Delorme NYS Atlas & Gazetteer:** p. 66, B2; **Estimated GPS:** 42°50.96'N; 73°53.42'W
■ **Destinations:** Lock E-7, Alplaus Creek
■ **Mileage:** To Lock E-7—4.2 miles (one-way); to Alplaus Creek—0.7 mile (one-way); up Alplaus Creek—1.0 mile (one-way)
■ **Comments:** Read "Caution" beginning on page xxii and "The Mohawk River: Caution" on page 147.
   Mohawk River—Stay a safe distance back from the Lock E-7 dam.
Expect an increase in boat traffic from the Schenectady Yacht Club and Mohawk Valley Marina.
   Alplaus Creek—When heading up the creek, choose a calm day and watch the weather. Current tends to be mild to moderate because of the backing up of the Mohawk River at the Lock E-7 dam. The wind tends to be quietest in the early morning and evening. Short portages will be required in order to continue the paddle after 1.0 mile.
■ **Directions:** From the Adirondack Northway (I-87), get off at Exit 6 for Schenectady/Troy and drive northwest on Rt. 7 for 3.2 miles. When you come to the stoplight at Rosendale Road, turn right and drive northwest on Rosendale Road for 2.5 miles. Turn right onto River Road and drive northwest for 3.3 miles until you reach Balltown Road (Rt. 146). Turn right onto Balltown Road and drive north for 1.5 miles. At a stoplight just south of the Rexford Bridge, turn left onto Aqueduct Road and then drive west for 100 feet. Quickly turn right onto a tiny road between the Boat House (which sells kayaks, canoes, and boating parapher-nalia) and the Aqueduct Rowing Club. Go less than 0.1 mile to the end of the road and park.
   From the center of Schenectady (junction of State Street/Rt. 5 & Erie Blvd.), drive northeast on Erie Blvd. for 1.3 miles. Just before crossing over the Mohawk River, turn right onto Maxin Road Extension and drive northeast for 0.8 mile. When you come to Van Vranken Avenue, turn left (the road quickly changes to Aqueduct Road). Drive 1.8 miles northeast on Aqueduct Road. Just before reach-ing Balltown Road (Rt. 146), turn left onto a tiny road between the Boat House and the Aqueduct Rowing Club, and follow it 0.1 mile to a small parking area. From either direction, carry your canoe or kayak back down the road for less than 100 feet. At a break in the wooden railing, turn left and head down to a dock where a sign states: "Aqueduct Rowing Club: This dock is available to the public for launching muscle-powered boats only and for other recreational activities." A short distance farther downstream is the private dock used by the rowing club. It is not open to the public.

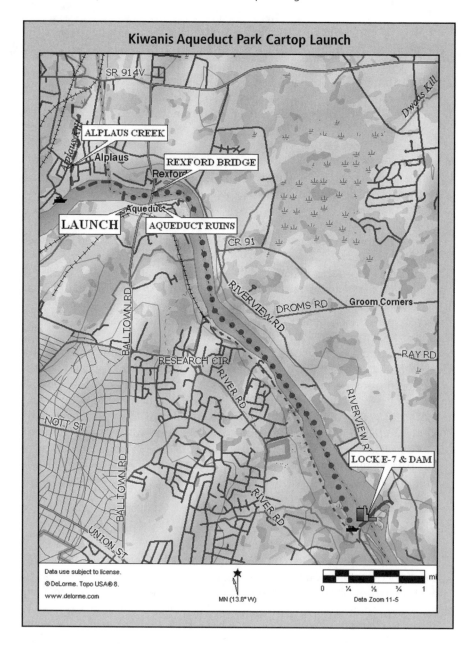

Kiwanis Aqueduct Park Cartop Launch

If you are planning a one-way paddle to Lock E-7, position a second car in the parking area at Lock E-7. Lock E-7 can be reached from Aqueduct Road by driving south on Balltown Road for 1.5 miles. At a stoplight turn left onto River Road and drive southeast for 3.2 miles. Then turn left onto Rosendale Road and continue

▶ **Kiwanis Aqueduct Park Cartop Launch**

southeast for 0.5 mile. When you reach Lock 7 Road, turn left and drive north for 0.9 mile to Lock E-7. Park in the upper parking area.

The Paddle:

Southeast—Paddle downstream, quickly passing under the Rexford Bridge, where remnants of the old aqueduct can be seen next to the southeast end of the bridge, and you can even paddle through its two arches. If you cross over to the northeast end of the Rexford Bridge, you will see an intact, surviving single-arch section of the old aqueduct.

Take note of the towering north wall of the gorge as you continue paddling from the Rexford Bridge and pass by the Schenectady Yacht Club, to your left at 0.4 mile. Right after this point the river dramatically changes direction, going from east to southeast. A couple of houses have been erected near the rim of the high cliffs overlooking the gorge, as if no thought or concern need be given to these mighty cliffs breaking apart one day from the incessant wear of the river against the underpinning rock.

If you cross over to the north bank of the river by the yacht club, you can turn into the old Erie Canal channel and follow it back west for 0.1 mile to old Lock 21, which the club uses for getting boats in and out of the water.

Heading east from the Schenectady Yacht Club you will immediately pass by a little island near the shoreline whose north side once formed part of the channel for the Erie Canal. During times of heavy rainfall, a tall, narrow cascade is produced from a tiny creek that drops over the top of the cliffs overlooking this small island. Look for the drainpipe near the top of the cliffs. Roughly 0.1 mile farther downriver is another seasonal cascade that sometimes runs down the cliff face. (You will only see these cascades during times of heavy rainfall and runoff.)

Across the river, along the south bank, is the hamlet of Aqueduct, where Williams Street parallels the river for 0.6 mile.

In 1.1 miles you will pass by a tiny, grotto-like cove on your right (along the west bank) where a twenty-five-foot-high waterfall cascades down.[1] The General Electric Research & Development Center is passed at 1.8 miles, and the Knolls Atomic Power Laboratory (KAPL) at 2.4 miles.

At 2.7 miles you will exit from the gorge, but rocky walls still rise up on your right as you continue paddling downstream. Finally you will reach Lock E-7, 4.2 miles from where you started. This is the turnaround point unless you are planning to take out here.

West to Alplaus Creek—From the launch site, head straight across the Mohawk River for 0.2 mile to the north bank, where you'll see a stone block wall that is part of old canal Lock 22. Take a moment to paddle into the west end of the lock for several feet.

Next, head upstream, going west. You will paddle along the base of a thirty-foot-high escarpment where one home after another can be seen on top. Catwalks and stairways lead steeply down to the water's edge, connecting the homes to the river.

To your left, several hundred feet from the shore, is a finger-like projection of rocks and earth extending upriver for 0.4 mile, remnants from earlier days of river dredging.

At roughly 0.4–0.5 mile you will pass by a series of piers across the width of the river and extending into the woods on the south side.[2] These are relics from an old steel bridge built by the Schenectady Railroad Company. The bridge carried a trolley line across the Mohawk from Aqueduct Road to Snyder Street in Alplaus and was one of the principal routes for accessing Luna Park (an amusement park). Having crossed the Mohawk River, the trolley would then swing right and continue west up to the park, which was only a short distance away. In its time, this 1,800-foot-long bridge was considered by some to be the longest trolley bridge in the world. The bridge was dismantled in 1942, and the steel was used for weapons in World War II.

North up Alplaus Creek—At 0.7 mile you will reach the mouth of Alplaus Creek. Turn right and begin following the creek north. In 0.3 mile you will pass under Alplaus Road. After another 0.7 mile of paddling, you may be unable to continue farther before rapids and shallows bring you to a standstill. Further progress can only be made if you are willing to portage repeatedly.

At Rexford, the Erie Canal crossed over the Mohawk River before continuing its journey westward. Postcard ca. 1900.

▶ **Kiwanis Aqueduct Park Cartop Launch**

Remnants of the Rexford Aqueduct continue to resist the relentless onslaught of the Mohawk River. Photograph 2007.

History: The name "Rexford" comes from Edward Rexford, who settled in the area of Rexford Flats around the time of the American Revolution. His son Eleazar carried on the family name, and is considered to be the real founder of Rexford Flats.[3]

The Rexford (Upper) Aqueduct was the upstream counterpart to the Lower Mohawk Aqueduct at Crescent. The first aqueduct was built in 1824 near Alexander's Mills,[4] only to be replaced in 1842 by a much larger structure. The second aqueduct was 1,160 feet long with 14 gracefully curved arches.[5] The towpath was constructed along the aqueduct's west side, where mules and horses would walk as they pulled the boats along the canal.

The trough of the canal was made of sturdy wooden planks that could be readily dismantled each fall, thus sparing the aqueduct from the inevitable damage that would have occurred with the arrival of spring's freshets.

The Erie Canal, after crossing the Mohawk River at Rexford, continued southwest, following essentially the same route that Aqueduct Road now follows into Schenectady. If you have driven through Schenectady on Erie Boulevard, then you have driven on top of the old Erie Canal, which was buried and turned into a roadway following its demise. During the canal's heyday, an average of ninety-five boats a day passed through Rexford. Sections of the old canal can be seen on your left by following a wide path that leads west from the parking area. Large piles of stone blocks were deposited into the old canal bed when the aqueduct was dismantled.[6]

Luna Park was a favorite destination for Schenectadians, many of whom arrived by trolley. Postcard ca. 1900.

The aqueduct's usefulness came to an end when the Barge Canal opened in 1918. By 1964 only three of the aqueduct's arches were still standing, the rest having been dismantled to clear the river of navigational hazards. If you stand by the dock and look downstream, you will notice two of the old arches on the south bank just east of the Rexford Bridge. Parts of the old bridge are also visible across the river.[7]

Between the Mohawk River and Aqueduct Road, not visible from the water, runs the Mohawk-Hudson Bikeway.

The Schenectady Yacht Club is located next to a small cove near the northeast end of the Rexford Bridge. The club is imbued with history. Its main building is a reincarnation of Mickey Travis's Restaurant, Saloon & Feed Store, a twentieth-century business that catered to customers coming through the locks.[8] Lock 21, which was built when the Erie Canal was enlarged, is now used by the club to raise boats in and out of the river.[9]

Luna Park was a popular twentieth-century amusement park located west of the aqueduct. The park was named after the famous amusement park in Coney Island. Built in the early 1900s, Luna Park offered a variety of rides including a roller coaster, merry-go-round, whip, airplane, and "Shoot-the-chute" (a toboggan-like run down a long incline into a pond of water). It had a penny arcade, house of mirrors, skating rink, and a dance hall. People from Schenectady traveled to the park on the Van Vranken Trolley Line.[10]

The park was known by a variety of other names during its more than twenty-five-year existence—River View Park, Luna Park, Dolle's Park (after Fred Dolle, one of its owners), Colonnade Park, Palisades Park, and Rexford Park.[11] While under the management of the Riverside Operating Company of New York, the park closed in 1933, during the Great Depression, never to open again.[12]

▶ Kiwanis Aqueduct Park Cartop Launch

Gateway Landing–Rotary Park (Schenectady)
Five Islands Named after the Iroquois Nation

52

■ **Launch Site:** Gateway Landing–Rotary Park near east end of the Great Western Gateway Bridge in Schenectady (Schenectady County); short carry to put-in by gazebo. For more information: schenectadycounty.com/FullStory.aspx?m=193.

■ **Delorme NYS Atlas & Gazetteer:** p. 66, B2; **Estimated GPS:** 42°49.07′N; 73°57.11′W

■ **Destinations:** Binne Kill, New York Central Railroad Bridge, Collins Creek, the Isle of the Cayugas, the Isle of the Onondagas

■ **Mileage:** South to Binne Kill—0.1 mile (one-way); east along Riverside Park to New York Central Railroad Bridge—0.5 mile (one-way); to Collins Creek—1.1 miles (one-way); up Collins Creek—0.3 mile (one-way); around the Isle of the Cayugas—1.4 miles; around the Isle of the Onondagas—1.6 miles

■ **Comments:** Read "Caution" beginning on page xxii and "The Mohawk River: Caution" on page 147.

    Collins Creek—The current is generally mild to moderate because of the backing up of the Mohawk River at the Lock E-7 dam.

■ **Directions:** Heading west on I-890, get off at Exit 4C for Scotia and Rt. 5. When you come to the stoplight by Schenectady Community College, turn left onto Rt. 5 and begin to head northwest across the Great Western Gateway Bridge, which connects Schenectady and Scotia. After 0.1 mile turn right at a green-colored sign for "Schenectady Community College and Gateway Landing" and drive down an exit ramp for less than 0.05 mile to a roadside pull-off on your right for Gateway Landing.

The Paddle:

The paddle begins on the south channel of the Mohawk River where the riverbed was deepened to accommodate the Barge Canal. Gateway Landing lies just south of the Isle of the Cayugas (Hog Island)[1] which, along with several other islands, has divided the river into two channels on this stretch of the Mohawk.

    South—From the launch site, bear right, turning away from the main part of the river, and enter a shallow bay. Head immediately over to the east side of the inlet where the water is slightly deeper. The bay was created by the Binne Kill, a major Schenectady stream that now issues unceremoniously from a large pipe running under Route 5 at the southeast end of the Great Western Gateway Bridge. Paddle south following the old streambed of the Binne Kill.

    As you approach the end of the bay, you will see two small drainpipes protruding from the east bank, where tiny streams of water emerge. These are smaller creeks that have been diverted underground through a drainage system. Straight ahead and to the right is a massive drainpipe, well over ten feet in diameter, which carries the waters of the Binne Kill. As you head up to the drainpipe,

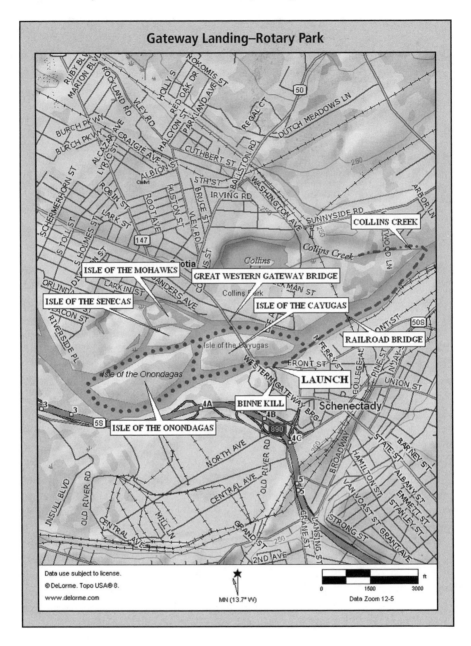

Gateway Landing–Rotary Park

you will notice that a fairly noticeable current can be felt. By this time you have gone less than 0.1 mile.

From here, it is possible to paddle into the pipe for perhaps twenty-five feet before it is too dark to continue farther. At this point you can either turn around

▶ **Gateway Landing–Rotary Park**

Mohawk Bridge, Schenectady, N. Y.

The Mohawk River has been paddled for centuries. Postcard ca. 1920.

(yes—the pipe is so large that a kayak can rotate 180 degrees inside it) or just let the current sweep you back out into the daylight and the waters of the bay. This little adventure affords you the opportunity to do a bit of "urban caving."

East—Paddle downstream along the south bank of the Mohawk River. In 0.2 mile you will see Riverside Park, also known as Rotundo Park in past years, on your right. The park parallels the riverbank for nearly 0.3 mile from the end of Washington Avenue to the end of Ingersoll Avenue. At one time Riverside Park was one of only several waterfront parks that existed along the entire Hudson River watershed. The park occupies the site of what was once the Yates Boathouse, named after V. Hanson Yates, who ran the business from 1894–1915.[2] In times past, ice-skating on the Mohawk River was a popular winter activity at the park.[3]

Queen Anne's Fort was located in this general vicinity, overlooking the river from a high point.

Along the way you will pass by an old bridge abutment to your right, a remnant of a historic bridge that once connected Washington Avenue in Schenectady to Washington Avenue in Scotia. If you look across the river to the north bank, you will observe a matching abutment.

Continue paddling east for a total of 0.5 mile to reach the old New York Central Railroad Bridge, which spans a narrower portion of the river. If you wish, you can continue downstream, heading northeast, for a total of 1.1 miles to reach Collins Creek, which comes in on the left (north) side of the river. It can be explored upstream for 0.3 mile (see chapter "Freemans Bridge Boat Launch").

Around the Isle of the Cayugas—From the launch site, head northeast (downstream) for 0.2 mile to clear the east end of the Isle of the Cayugas. Paddle around the tip of the island and then head back west. Continuing in this vein you can circumnavigate the island in 1.4 miles. While doing so you can also paddle around the Isle of the Onondagas, just southwest of the Isle of the Cayugas, which will add on an additional 1.6 miles to your trek. It is quite possible that it was by the Isle of the Onondagas or just farther upstream by the Isle of the Oneidas that a famous eighteenth-century rapid called "Knock 'em Stiff" could be found.[4]

History: Schenectady was considered to be the head of navigation on the Mohawk River, and Gateway Landing was a major harbor from 1660 to 1820, where goods, soldiers, settlers, and traders were constantly embarking and disembarking. Schenectady became famous for its river bateaux (a kind of double-ended flat-bottomed rowboat) and later for its "Schenectady Boats."[5] These Mohawk River bateaux were fairly substantial in size—up to thirty feet long, five feet wide, and capable of carrying 3,000 pounds of cargo and crew.

In 1792, General Philip Schuyler departed from Schenectady and headed upriver to survey the Mohawk River for possible future development. From 1792 to 1820, Schuyler's company, the Western Inland Lock Navigation Company, did much to make the Mohawk more navigable and led the way for what would eventually become the Erie Canal and then, later still, the New York State Barge Canal.

The harbor in Schenectady came to an end when the harbor facilities were destroyed by the Great Fire of 1819.[6]

The Binne Kill, Dutch for "inner stream,"[7] was once a major creek that ran past the west side of Schenectady's historic Stockade section and entered the

The Hotel Van Curler eventually became part of the Schenectady County Community College. Postcard ca. 1940.

▶ **Gateway Landing–Rotary Park**

Mohawk between Van Slyke Island and the Schenectady mainland.[8] Its banks were lined with warehouses filled with salt, grains, potash, furs, and a variety of other goods. The Binne Kill was particularly noted for the "Durham boats" that were constructed in the boatyards along its banks. These boats were forty feet long and capable of carrying loads of up to four tons. They were generally propelled by small sails or oars, but they could be poled like a gondola or pulled over rapids using ropes if need be.[9]

The Binne Kill is now an underground stream and is no longer visible as a surface feature in Schenectady, and Van Slyke Island (named after Jacques Cornelyssen Van Slyck), once separated from the mainland by the Binne Kill, no longer exists, having been turned into the parking lot and fields of the Schenectady Community College in the 1900s. But Van Slyke Island, too, had its moment of glory. In the early 1900s the island was connected to the mainland by a pontoon bridge, and thousands of people would cross it to reach the state league baseball diamond and grandstands.[10] At that time it was known as Island Park. After World War I the island was taken over by the Knights of Columbus Athletic Association and was then known as Columbus Park.[11]

In 1809 the first bridge between Schenectady and Scotia was constructed by Theodore Burr, cousin of Aaron Burr.[12] Until then the only way to cross the Mohawk River was by ferry. The Mohawk Bridge (also called the Burr Bridge, Glenville Bridge, and Washington Avenue Bridge)[13] spanned the river from Washington Avenue in Schenectady to Washington Avenue in Scotia. It had three piers and was 900 feet long. Four additional piers were added in the 1830s to carry the additional weight of railroad cars.[14] In this same period of time, the bridge was enclosed so that its life expectancy would be extended. By 1874, however, the Mohawk Bridge had outlived its usefulness and was replaced by a new bridge made out of iron. Scrap wood from the old bridge ended up being used for manufacturing matchsticks.

In 1925 a much larger bridge was constructed upstream from the Mohawk Bridge. Formally known as the Great Western Gateway Bridge (and by some the "Bridge of Fame"), it connected State Street in Schenectady with Mohawk Avenue in Scotia and opened up central and western New York State to westbound traffic on Route 5. In doing so, engineers fulfilled a vision first established by the Mohawks, who called the valley *Schonowee*, or "the gate."[15]

In 1925 the six-story-high Hotel Van Curler (now Elston Hall and part of the Schenectady County Community College) also opened its doors. Located at the east end of the Great Western Gateway Bridge, it was ideally sited to accommodate Route 5 travelers needing lodging.

In 1926 the Mohawk Bridge was permanently closed off and, within several years, dismantled to keep it from becoming a navigational hazard. All that remains today are the abutments visible on opposite sides of the river.

The present Great Western Gateway Bridge was built in 1973 after the old Great Western Gateway Bridge was deemed unsuitable and in need of replacement. The bridge was erected on fill that was used to buttress the river islands and proved to be five times as expensive as the first bridge.

Queen Anne's Fort was one of several fortifications that were built in the Mohawk Valley by the British for defensive purposes. It stood near Riverside Park, lasted from roughly 1704 to 1795,[16] and was situated just south of the famous Indian Statue near the junction of Front, Ferry, and Green streets, overlooking the Mohawk River from a slight rise of ground. The fort had 12-foot-high, 100-foot-long walls, with two-story-high blockhouses at each of the four corners. It occupied the same site as the earlier Dongan Fort (named after Governor Thomas Dongan), which was burned down in the Schenectady massacre.[17]

Geology—Thousands of years ago the Iro-Mohawk River flowed straight east into Lake Albany at Schenectady. When Lake Iroquois (which comprised the totality of the Great Lakes, and then some) was bled away by the St. Lawrence River, the Iro-Mohawk River lost much of its power and became the Mohawk River of today. Weakened, it could no longer push through a large delta that had formed at the inlet to Lake Albany and was diverted northeast. All of this becomes apparent when you study the shape of the land near the Great Western Gateway Bridge. If you look south toward the steeply rising hills by Mt. Pleasant, you will see the ridgeline that forced the river to bend 90 degrees and head northeast. At the large bend in the river near the Great Western Gateway Bridge, the Mohawk River was broken into a series of islands.

Island Park & Mohawk River looking West, Schenectady. N. Y.

People once gathered by the thousands to watch sporting events at Island Park. Postcard ca. 1920.

▶ Gateway Landing–Rotary Park

Lock E-8 (Rotterdam)
Accessing the Mohawk River and Islands
53

■ **Launch Site:** Lock E-8 at end of Rice Road (Schenectady County). Upriver launch from Lock E-8—0.1-mile carry to north end of wharf, rocky put-in; downriver launch from Lock E-8—0.1-mile carry to sheltered area at south end of wharf.

■ **Delorme NYS Atlas & Gazetteer:** p. 66, B1–2; **Estimated GPS:** Upriver—42°49.78′N, 73°59.51′W; Downriver—42°49.74′N, 73°59.46′W

■ **Destinations:** Dalys Island, I-890 bridge, Isle of the Oneidas, Isle of the Ononda-gas, Isle of the Cayugas, Great Western Gateway Bridge

■ **Mileage:** Upriver to south end of Dalys Island—0.3 mile (one-way); around Dalys Island—1.5 miles; to I-890 bridge—1.5 miles (one-way); downriver to and around the Isle of the Oneidas—1.6 miles; to Isle of the Onondagas—1.3 miles (one-way); around the Isle of the Onondagas—1.6 miles; around Isle of the Cayugas—1.4 miles; to Great Western Gateway Bridge—2.3 miles (one-way)

■ **Comments:** Read "Caution" beginning on page xxii and "The Mohawk River: Caution" on page 147. Stay a safe distance back from the Lock E-8 dam. Don't put in at upper launch if the current seems unusually strong. A canoe/kayak carrier would be helpful to access either put-in.

■ **Directions:** Heading northwest on I-890, get off at Exit 2B for Rice Road and proceed northwest, staying close to the river. You will reach Lock 8 in 1.4 miles. Traveling southeast on I-890, get off at Exit 2 for Campbell Road & Rt. 337. At the end of the ramp, turn left onto Campbell Road and follow it northwest, stay-ing to your right as it becomes Rice Road. In 1.2 miles you will reach Lock E-8, on your right.

To put-in above Lock E-8—From the parking area, carry your watercraft north-west along the bike path for 0.1 mile and then descend to the north end of the wharf. Your watercraft can be launched from a tiny sliver of rocky shoreline next to the wharf. (It is also possible to lower a canoe into the water along the wharf next to one of the ladders, and then climb down into the canoe. The difficult part is getting your canoe out of the water and over the top of the wharf when the trip is done—an effort requiring two moderately strong adults.)

To put-in below Lock E-8—From the parking area, head southeast down a grassy hill, following the faint outline of a road for 0.1 mile. When you reach the end of the mowed lawn, follow a path straight ahead for another 100 feet, par-alleling the river. At the end of the wharf, you will reach a little shelter where you can put in your watercraft. Unlike the wharf above Lock E-8, this section of the wharf is considerably higher than the Mohawk River, making it impossible to put in or take out from the wharf itself.

The Paddle:
Upriver from Lock E-8—Head upstream, proceeding northwest for over 0.3 mile until you reach the south tip of Dalys Island, which comprises 208 acres. From

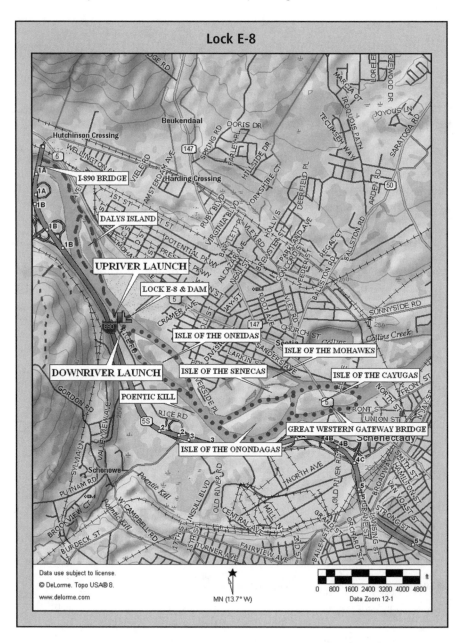

here you can either circumnavigate the island, in 1.5 miles, or continue upriver for another 1.2 miles until you come to the I-890 bridge.

As you paddle along the northeast side of Dalys Island, you will be struck by the height of the Mohawk River's north bank, which towers over thirty feet

Lock E-8

above the river. Steep wooden stairways descend to the river's edge from houses and camps that are invisible until you pull away from the shoreline and look back from the middle of the river. You may want to remember that the northeast channel around Dalys Island contracts significantly during the summer when the level of the water in the river drops.

If you paddle along the southwest side of Dalys Island, you will find yourself exposed to the unending sounds of I-890, which parallels the river just west of the bikeway.

After paddling by the north end of Dalys Island, you will reach the I-890 bridge in another 0.5 mile. Along the way you will pass by a huge section of the river's northeast bank that has been eroded, leaving behind a lofty bluff of exposed rock and sandstone.

Downriver from Lock E-8—From the launching site, paddle over to the north tip of the Isle of the Oneidas, which is close by. The island is heavily forested (as are most of the Mohawk's islands) and can be circumnavigated in 1.6 miles.

From the south tip of the Isle of the Oneidas, paddle downriver for 0.4 mile to the west tip of the Isle of the Onondagas (a total distance of 1.3 miles from your launch site). This island can be circumnavigated in 1.6 miles.

Continue east from the east end of the Isle of the Onondagas, paddling along the south shore of the Isle of the Cayugas (which can be circumnavigated in 1.4 miles) until you come to the Great Western Gateway Bridge, one of whose

Erosion continues to modify the banks of the Mohawk River. Photograph 2008.

pilings rests on this island. At this point you have gone 2.3 miles from your launch site. Along the way you will see the sprawling General Electric Company (GE) complex on your right, which evolved from the Edison Machine Works established by Thomas A. Edison in 1886. The plant today is but a shadow of its former self, having diversified to meet the demands of a global economy.

History: See "Rotterdam Kiwanis Park" and "Gateway Landing–Rotary Park" chapters for further details.

 Lock E-8

Rotterdam Kiwanis Park (Rotterdam)
Between Locks and Dams

54

■ **Launch Site:** Rotterdam Kiwanis Park off of Rt. 5S (Schenectady County); cement ramp, dock. Restrooms available seasonally.

■ **Delorme NYS Atlas & Gazetteer:** p. 66, AB1–2; **Estimated GPS:** 42°50.83′N; 74°00.80′W

■ **Destinations:** Washout Creek, Lock E-9, Lock E-8

■ **Mileage:** To Washout Creek—1.6 miles (one-way); to Lock E-9—2.8 miles (one-way); to Lock E-8—2.1 miles (one-way); around Dalys Island—1.5 miles additional

■ **Comments:** Read "Caution" beginning on page xxii and "The Mohawk River: Caution" on page 147. Stay a safe distance back from the Lock E-8 dam and Lock E-9 dam. Expect an increase in boat traffic from the Arrowhead Marina, directly across the river.

■ **Directions:** Heading northwest on I-890, get off at Exit 1A for Rt. 5S & Rotterdam Junction. Set the odometer to 0.0 as you head down the ramp. At 0.8 mile, turn right off of Rt. 5S into the entrance to the Rotterdam Kiwanis Park, just after crossing over the Plotter Kill.

Approaching from Rotterdam Junction (junction of Rt. 5S & 103), head southeast on Rt. 5S for 2.6 miles. Turn left into Rotterdam Kiwanis Park.

From the upper parking lot continue driving northeast, immediately crossing over the bikeway, and then head down to a lower parking area next to the river. You can put in either at the main access point on the Mohawk River, or at the mouth of the Plotter Kill at the east end of the parking area.

The Paddle:

Before starting off, take a look upriver and you will see the sloping south wall of the valley, which Native Americans called *Yantapuchaberg* (John-Ear-of-Corn-Hill). Its highest point is 1,160 feet.[1] To the north is *Touereuna* (a Native American word for "neighboring hills"),[2] 1,097 feet above sea level. It is better known today as the Glenville Hills.[3] Downriver can be seen the I-890 bridge. Directly across the river is the Arrowhead Marina and RV Park.

Northwest—Begin heading upstream. At 1.0 mile you will pass under the Boston & Maine railroad bridge, near where SI Group is located, occupying sixty acres of land. The company was founded in 1906 by W. Howard Wright, who named it the Schenectady Varnish Works. As the company grew, eventually becoming global, its name changed to Schenectady Chemicals, then Schenectady International, and finally to SI Group.

At 1.6 miles you will go past the tiny bay created at the mouth of Washout Creek, to your right. Washout Creek acquired its name following a cloudburst in 1885 that severely damaged the New York Central Railroad bridge crossing over the stream. Earlier the creek was called Arent Mebie's Kill, and also Walton Creek.

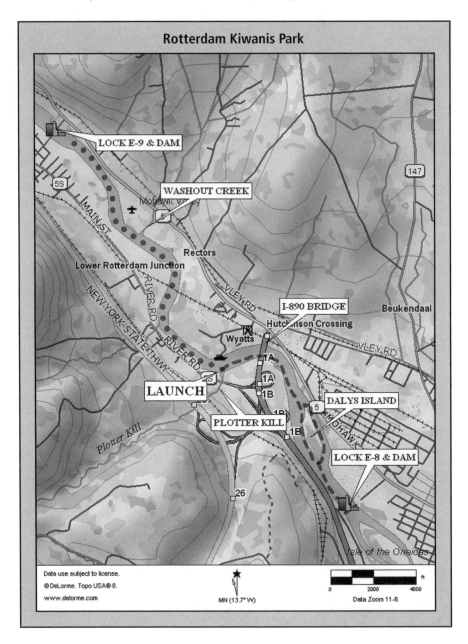

After 2.8 miles you will reach Lock E-9, which is a good place to turn around and begin making the return trip.

East—There is more of interest to see paddling downstream. Proceeding east, you will immediately pass by the mouth of the Plotter Kill, next to the

Rotterdam Kiwanis Park. Look to your right to glimpse a tiny, three-foot-high cascade formed out of stone block. Visible just upstream from the cascade is a triple-arch bridge that once carried the Erie Canal across the Plotter Kill; it is now used by the Mohawk-Hudson Bikeway.[4]

At 0.4 mile you will pass beneath a towering bridge that was built in 1999 to allow I-890 to be extended across the Mohawk River and joined with Route 5 and Vley Road Extension. In another 0.5 mile you will come to the north tip of 0.5-mile-long Dalys Island, which can be circumnavigated in 1.5 miles.

If you continue downstream for a total of 2.1 miles, you will reach Lock E-8 & dam. Roughly 0.5 mile before the lock is the site where Dr. Charles Steinmetz had a camp (called Camp Mohawk), which once stood at the river's edge along the north bank next to the mouth of Viele's Creek.[5] Steinmetz achieved worldwide renown as an electrical engineering wizard at General Electric.[6] It was at Camp Mohawk that a serendipitous event with lightning inspired Steinmetz to build the world's first lightning generator, a feat that the press rightly heralded, calling Steinmetz "The Thunderer," a "Modern Jove," and "The man who tamed lightning."[7]

History: Rotterdam Kiwanis Park was established by the Kiwanis Club in the early 1980s.[8] A 1986 plaque in front of the upper parking lot next to the bikeway reads: "Dedicated to Margaret Lordi & Eleanor Brown for their stewardship of the Mohawk River and for their leadership in establishing this bikeway." The park is located on the Great Flats Aquifer, which the Dutch called *groote vlachte* for "great flats."[9] The Mohawks grew corn on the flats.[10] Later, after the Native Americans were displaced by Europeans, broom corn became the main crop locally, with Schenectady County producing more broom corn than any other county in the nation.[11] More recently the flats have proven to be an inexhaustible supply of unusually pure water for Schenectady, Rotterdam, and parts of Niskayuna. The aquifer came into existence at the end of the last ice age when retreating glaciers left behind 80-to-200-feet-deep glacial till covering a two-mile tract of land in the Mohawk Valley.[12]

Just south of Lock E-8, along the west bank of the river adjacent to the bikeway, is the red-brick Rotterdam pumping station, which extracts 20 million gallons of pure water a day[13] and shunts it off to nearby communities. The pumping station is not visible from the river, but it is visible from the bikeway.

55

Freemans Bridge Boat Launch (Scotia)
A Tiny, Seldom-Visited Tributary of the Mohawk River

■ **Launch Site:** Freemans Bridge Boat Launch next to northeast end of Freemans Bridge (Schenectady County); cement ramp.

■ **Delorme NYS Atlas & Gazetteer:** p. 66, B2; **Estimated GPS:** 42°49.89'N; 73°55.80'W

■ **Destinations:** Collins Creek, Delaware & Hudson Railroad bridge, island, Alplaus Creek

■ **Mileage:** Southwest to Collins Creek—0.4 mile (one-way); up Collins Creek—0.5 mile (round-trip); northeast to Delaware & Hudson Railroad bridge—0.2 mile (one-way); to downriver island—1.2 miles (one-way); to Alplaus Creek—2.0 miles (one-way)

■ **Comments:** Read "Caution" beginning on page xxii and "The Mohawk River: Caution" on page 147.

   Mohawk River—Expect an increase in boat traffic from the Mohawk Valley Marina near mouth of Alplaus Creek.

   Collins Creek—This small creek can only be followed upstream for a short distance. The current is generally weak. The creek is navigable only because of the backing up of the Mohawk River at the Lock E-7.

   Alplaus Creek—This medium-sized stream can be followed upstream for about 1.0 mile. The current is generally mild to moderate because of the backing up of the Mohawk River at Lock E-7. Short portages will be required in order to continue the paddle after 1.0 mile.

■ **Directions:** Heading west on I-890, get off at Exit 4B for Erie Boulevard and General Electric. Follow the exit ramp as it goes around and under I-890 and then becomes Erie Boulevard. When you reach the stoplight at the main intersection in Schenectady (the junction of Erie Boulevard and Rt. 5 (State Street), continue driving northeast on Erie Boulevard for 1.3 miles. Turn left onto Freemans Bridge Road and cross over the Mohawk River, heading north. As soon as you are at the north end of the bridge, take your first right, marked by a sign stating, "Freemans Bridge Access Site."

   The road immediately leads to a parking area at a boat launch site. Be sure to park in the gravel area closest to the bridge, designated for cartop boats. From here, it is only a 100-foot carry to the cement ramp. You may also drop off your watercraft there first before you park.

The Paddle:

Before you begin, take a look downriver. Roughly 0.2 mile distant, spanning the Mohawk River, is the old D&H (Delaware & Hudson) Railroad bridge. Directly across the river, just downstream from the present Freemans Bridge (built in 1984)[1] is the surviving abutment from the previous bridge, erected in 1917.[2]

▶ **Freemans Bridge Boat Launch**

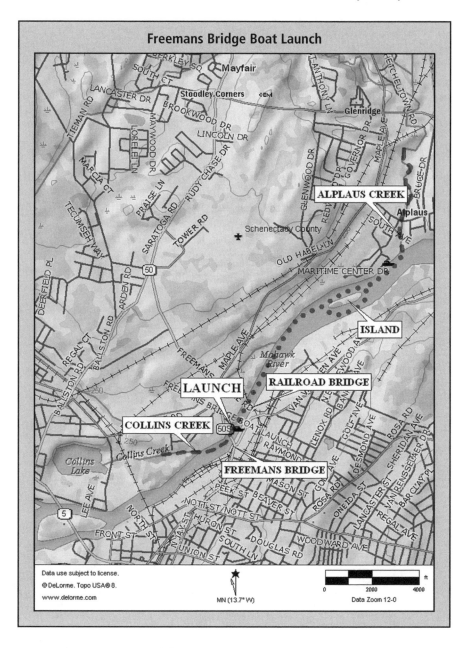

Freemans Bridge Boat Launch

Southwest—Begin paddling upstream. You will immediately pass under Freemans Bridge, named after Volney Freeman, who built the first bridge on this site in 1855. Off in the distance, approximately 0.9 mile farther upstream, can be seen the old New York Central Railroad bridge.

Within 0.4 mile you will arrive at the mouth of Collins Creek, on your right, which is the outlet stream from Collins Lake, located approximately 0.7 mile upstream from the Mohawk River. It is unlikely that you will be able to reach Collins Lake, however. Under most conditions Collins Creek can be navigated for only 0.2–0.3 mile. The fact that the creek is navigable for even that distance is undoubtedly thanks to the backing up of waters from the Lock E-7 dam.

As soon as you begin paddling up Collins Creek you will pass under a bike path footbridge. The bridge was constructed by faculty and students at nearby Union College, duplicating a design created by Squire Whipple.[3] After passing under the bridge, you can continue upstream for 0.1–0.2 mile farther before the creek becomes too shallow to continue. The buildings on your right, visible at times, belong to Tryon Avenue Apartments.

Northeast—Heading downriver from Freemans Bridge, you will pass under the D & H Railroad bridge in 0.2 mile. While the southeast shore of the river appears significantly industrialized, the northwest shore remains in a natural state. It is only after you hear the sound of a passing train to your left that you realize that the railroad tracks from Schenectady, after crossing over the D & H bridge, continue northeast, paralleling the Mohawk River just a short distance away.

At 1.2 miles you will come to the west end of a 0.3-mile-long island that can be circumnavigated in 0.7 mile. Alplaus Creek, coming in on your left, is reached after 2.0 miles.

History: The boat launch occupies the site of the former Seeley Farmhouse, owned by John H. Seeley, a nineteenth-century broom corn grower and broom manufacturer.[4] During his time, broom manufacturing was a major industry in the area.

Just north of the boat launch is the Waters Edge Lighthouse, an attractive restaurant that overlooks the Mohawk River and is accessible by either boat or car.

▶ **Freemans Bridge Boat Launch**

Scotia Landing (Scotia)
A Forgotten Sports Island on the Mohawk River

56

- ◼ **Launch Sites:** Scotia Landing (Schenectady County)—0.05-mile carry from parking area to short flight of stairs down to a dock.
- ◼ **Delorme NYS Atlas & Gazetteer:** p. 66, B2; **Estimated GPS:** 42°49.30′N; 73°57.18′W
- ◼ **Destinations:** Reese Creek, Lock E-8, islands, New York Central Railroad bridge
- ◼ **Mileage:** West up Reese Creek—0.5 mile (one-way); northwest up Mohawk River past islands to Lock E-8—2.3 miles (one-way); around the Isle of the Onondagas—1.6 miles; around the Isle of the Cayugas—1.4 miles; east to New York Central Railroad bridge—0.5 mile (one-way)
- ◼ **Comments:** Read "Caution" beginning on page xxii and "The Mohawk River: Caution" on page 147. Stay a safe distance back from the Lock E-8 dam. There is minimal current on Reese Creek. Avoid Schonowee Avenue on Tuesday evenings during the summer (June, July & August) when the U.S. Water Ski Show Team is performing. Also check Freedom Park schedule to make sure that you don't arrive when a major outdoor event is being held.
- ◼ **Directions:** From the west end of the Great Western Gateway Bridge (Rt. 5) spanning the Mohawk River between Schenectady and Scotia (0.1 mile east of the junction of Rtes. 5 & 50), turn north onto Schonowee Avenue. Drive east for over 0.2 mile, passing by Freedom Park in the process. You will see a distinctive roadside sign on your right with the words "Scotia Landing." This is the launch site. To park, continue east for a couple of hundred feet farther and turn left onto Kiwanis Way. After driving 0.1 mile, park in an area to your left. From here, carry your watercraft back across the open field for over 0.05 mile to the landing site. Be careful crossing Schonowee Avenue. A short flight of steps takes you down to the river.

The Paddle:

If you are visiting while the U.S. Water Ski Show Team is set up behind Jumpin' Jacks, an eating establishment in business since the 1950s and reminiscent of that era, bear in mind that their dock is privately owned and off-limits. Shows are held Tuesday evenings in June, July, and August, so you may want to launch at another location during those days. It also makes sense to check the Freedom Park schedule to make sure that you don't arrive when an event is being held and the area is packed with people and cars.

West—Begin paddling upstream, heading southwest. Within 0.2 mile you will pass by Jumpin' Jacks, then underneath the Great Western Gateway Bridge, and finally past the Glen Sanders Mansion, one of the Capital Region's premier restaurants. After 0.4 mile turn right onto Reese Creek.

Reese Creek—It is possible to follow Reese Creek west for over 0.5 mile of its nearly 0.8-mile length because the stream is fairly wide and deep. Its water level

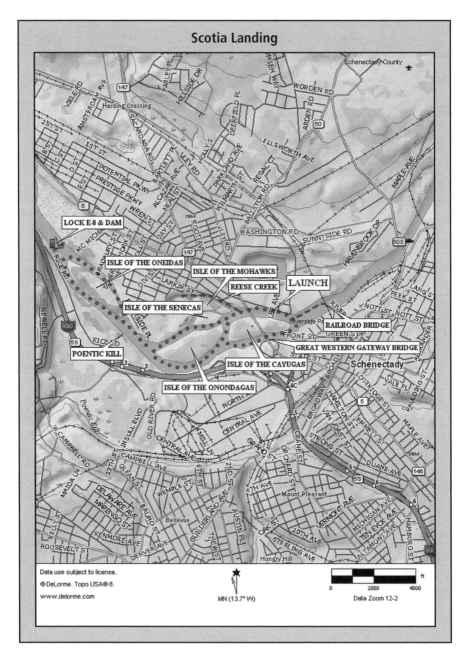

Scotia Landing

will vary somewhat depending upon the season and whether the New York State Barge Canal locks are in operation or not. The Isle of the Mohawks is directly on your left as you enter Reese Creek. It was on this island that an amusement park

▶ **Scotia Landing**

named Glenotia operated a century ago, accessible by a demountable (movable or capable of being disassembled) bridge that spanned the stream from the end of South Ballston Avenue to the island. No evidence of the bridge exists today, and the Isle of the Mohawks is overgrown with weeds and brush. Anyone setting foot on the island now would need to wear long pants and boots and be willing to thrash through the tangled vegetation.

In less than 0.3 mile you will pass by a little waterway that once separated the Isle of the Mohawks from the low-lying mainland of Scotia. The channel is now filled in with debris and sediment and is no longer navigable.

Proceeding west along Reese Creek, you will observe to the right an occasional dock or structure that was erected many years ago by village residents, only to be abandoned and reclaimed by dense vegetation. You will also pass by two tiny streams that enter Reese Creek along the north bank after making their way underground through Scotia. The second creek emerges from a drainpipe and drops six feet into the river.

Eventually you will reach a point where there are simply too many obstacles in the stream to continue any farther. This is the turnaround point.

Northwest—From the mouth of Reese Creek, round the east tip of the Isle of the Mohawks and proceed west. Although topographical maps suggest the possibility of continuing west between the Isle of the Mohawks and the Isle of the Senecas (the island to the south of the Isle of the Mohawks), the water is simply too shallow to allow the passage of a canoe or kayak. Perhaps such a side trip is possible at times when the river is running at high volume.

Continue on your voyage upstream, paralleling the south shore of the Isle of the Senecas. Soon you will follow a right-angle bend in the river, where the Mohawk, flowing southeast, alters course dramatically and proceeds northeast. Gaze up at the Mt. Pleasant Section of Schenectady and you will see high bluffs that form an enormous curve paralleling the bend in the river. At the end of the last ice age, the river was forced to bend here when its southeastward channel was blocked by the large delta that had formed at (former) Lake Albany.

At 1.2 miles you will reach the southeast tip of 0.7-mile-long Isle of the Onondagas. Stay to the left (southwest) side of the island and continue upstream.

At 1.5 miles you will pass by the Poentic Kill, a tiny stream that rises from east of Rynex Corners and enters the river on your left near a small white building. An ancient Mohawk-Iroquois campsite once stood on the south side of the Poentic Kill near this point.[1] During the twentieth century, a day camp called Tippecanoe could be found farther upstream in a ravine near the intersection of Putnam and Princetown roads.[2]

Looking back downstream, you should still be able to glimpse the east end of the Great Western Gateway Bridge.

At 1.7 miles, you will be nearing the end of the Isle of the Oneidas. Look to your left and you will see a huge towering block of cement on the southwest bank of the Mohawk River. On top of it is an observation deck that allows bicyclists and walkers on the Mohawk-Hudson Bikeway to gaze across at the Isle of the Oneidas and upstream to Lock E-8.

When you reach the west end of the Isle of the Oneidas, at 1.9 miles, take note that it is shored up by dikes, giving the island the appearance of a ship's prow facing into turbulent waters—in this case, the onslaught of water released from the Lock E-8 dam, less than 0.2 mile away.

You can round the northwest end of the Isle of the Oneidas and return back downstream along the northeast bank of the Mohawk River. A prehistoric fishing village flourished about 3,000 years ago near the Isle of the Oneidas on the river's north bank. The site was discovered in modern times after the Mohawk had eroded enough land to reveal a number of buried hearths. This spot is now referred to as "the Buried Village."

You can also circumnavigate the Isle of the Onondagas (a paddle of 1.6 miles), and the Isle of the Cayugas (a paddle of 1.4 miles), if you wish, before returning to the put-in by the Great Western Gateway Bridge.

East—Head downriver, passing by the east tip of the Isle of the Cayugas, at 0.3 mile, until you reach the old New York Central Railroad bridge at 0.7 mile. This makes for a good turnaround point. Heading back west, go around the south side of the Isle of the Cayugas and return to your starting point in a total of 2.1 miles.

History: Reese Creek is named after the Reese family, who lived in Scotia from 1820–1871. The junction of Mohawk Avenue (Rt. 5) and Sacandaga Road (Rt. 147) was at one time the center of Reeseville, prior to Scotia becoming incorporated. The Reeses were heavily involved in producing broom corn, for which Scotia and Schenectady were famous. Broom heads were created by using a specially grown twelve-foot-high sorghum crop. Even to this day a huge tract of land at the southern tip of Scotia is used for growing corn, which is irrigated by the periodic flooding of its lowlands when the Mohawk River becomes swollen and engorged by spring's release of snowmelt.

Most of Reese Creek remains hidden underground, the upper part having been paved over as the village of Scotia expanded. The wide section that you can paddle on today is actually more a part of the Mohawk River. The stream's west end has closed off over time, leaving the navigable section of the stream as an inlet.

Glenotia was an 8–10-acre twentieth-century amusement park located on a small island in the Mohawk River and accessible only by boat or by crossing a demountable bridge that abutted the end of South Ballston Avenue in Scotia. Every year the bridge would be set up and then dismantled before the arrival of winter.[3] The name "Glenotia" is a portmanteau word combining "Glenville" and "Scotia."

Established in 1907, Glenotia contained a dance hall, a baseball diamond, a one-eighth-mile-long racetrack, and bathing beaches. Concerts, picnics, cricket, tennis, and croquet were offered. A two-story wood pavilion was constructed

▶ **Scotia Landing**

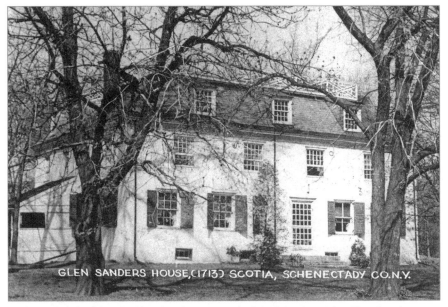

A picture of the historic Glen Sanders House before it became the Glen Sanders Mansion (restaurant). Postcard ca. 1940.

near the demountable bridge. It survived spring's annual flooding only because it was built on stilts.[4] On at least one occasion a major carnival made use of the island, offering rides on a Ferris wheel and a merry-go-ground.[5]

In 1912 a long gravel bar formed along the southeast side of the island after the Mohawk River was dredged to create the Barge Canal.[6]

Around 1914 the Mohawk Swimming School, sponsored by the Scotia Athletic Association, operated for a short time on the island.[7] The bridge to Glenotia was permanently dismantled in the early 1930s, isolating the island again. By then no surviving structures on the island remained, the beams of the dance pavilion having being cannibalized and used for timber in a house on South Ballston Avenue.

The Glen Sanders Mansion, before becoming a well-known restaurant in the 1980s, was a private residence for nine successive generations of direct descendants of Captain Johannes Glen. It is the oldest historical landmark in the village of Scotia. In 1658, Alexander Lindsey Glen built an earlier version of the house approximately 100 feet from the current site, but it was too close to the river and was demolished during a spring freshet. A second, more substantial house was constructed farther uphill, safe from the river's fury.[8] In 1685, Johannes Glen, Alexander Lindsey's son, inherited the home upon his father's death. George Washington is said to have been a guest at the house for tea (which may make it the only Revolution-era structure where Washington is not alleged to have slept). Louis Philippe is also said to have visited the mansion before he became King of France.

The Five Islands—To get a sense of the area's geography, it is helpful to have a mental picture of the islands' arrangement relative to one another. Directly south of the Isle of the Mohawks (at the entrance to Reese Creek) is the fourteen-acre Isle of the Senecas (also known as Little Island); farther south is the sixty-nine-acre Isle of the Onondagas (also called Big Island),[9] which is the largest island of the three. To the east of the Isle of the Onondagas is the Isle of the Cayugas (also known as Hog Island, The Plot, and Kruysbessen [Gooseberry] Island[10]), which is the body of land upon which some of the Great Western Gateway Bridge's pilings rest. Northwest, at a noticeable distance from the first four islands, is the Isle of the Oneidas (also called Eldrich Island).[11]

The names of the five islands came from five of the nations of the Iroquois, but the islands all belonged exclusively to the domain of the Mohawks, who were the guardians of the eastern Mohawk Valley.

 **Scotia Landing**

Maalwyck Park (Scotia/Glenville)
Accessing the Mohawk River across from Lock E-8

57

■ **Launch Site:** Maalwyck Park off of Rt. 5 in Scotia/Glenville (Schenectady County); 300-foot carry to shoreline below dam. For more information: townofglenville.org.
■ **Delorme NYS Atlas & Gazetteer:** p. 66, B1–2; **Estimated GPS:** 42°49.76′N, 73°59.31′W.
■ **Destinations:** Isle of the Oneidas, Isle of the Onondagas, Great Western Gateway Bridge
■ **Mileage:** To Isle of Oneidas—0.1 mile (one-way); around Isle of Oneidas— 1.6 miles; to Isle of the Onondagas—1.2 miles (one-way); around Isle of the Onondagas and Isle of the Cayugas—2.7 miles; to Great Western Gateway Bridge—2.3 miles (one-way)
■ **Comments:** Read "Caution" beginning on page xxii and "The Mohawk River: Caution" on page 147. Stay at a safe distance back from the Lock-8 dam.
■ **Directions:** Approaching from west of Scotia (junction of I-890 & Rt. 5), drive southeast on Rt. 5 for 1.7 miles and turn right onto Maalwyck Park Road. Approaching from Scotia (junction of Rtes. 5 & 50), proceed northwest on Rt. 5 (Mohawk Avenue) for 1.3 miles and turn left onto Maalwyck Road.

From either direction, drive southwest on Maalwyck Road for 0.3 mile until you reach the road's terminus, next to the north end of the Lock 8 dam. From the parking area, walk past the barrier toward the Lock 8 dam and then fol- low a gravel road that leads down to the edge of the river, a couple of hundred feet downstream from the dam. Be prepared for moderately choppy waters and strong current when the dam is releasing torrents of water. Turbulent waters can be minimized by staying close to shore as you head downstream. Within several hundred feet the waters become considerably calmer.

Additional paths also lead down to the water's edge farther downstream from the parking area. These are an option if the water is too choppy near the dam.

The Paddle:

Look directly across the river and you will see Lock E-8 and a long wharf for mooring boats. The wharf follows the bank of the river for hundreds of feet in both directions from the lock. The dam, which extends across the river to Lock E-8, should be avoided.

Heading downriver, you will arrive at the north end of 0.7-mile-long Isle of the Oneidas in 0.1 mile. An outcropping of rocks is encountered just before the tip of the island. The Isle of the Oneidas can be circumnavigated in 1.6 miles.

From the south tip of the Isle of the Oneidas, it is another 0.4 mile to the west end of the Isle of the Onondagas, at which point the river, flowing south- east, turns northeast. From here, you can continue downstream farther, circling around the Isle of the Onondagas and the Isle of the Cayugas if you wish to add

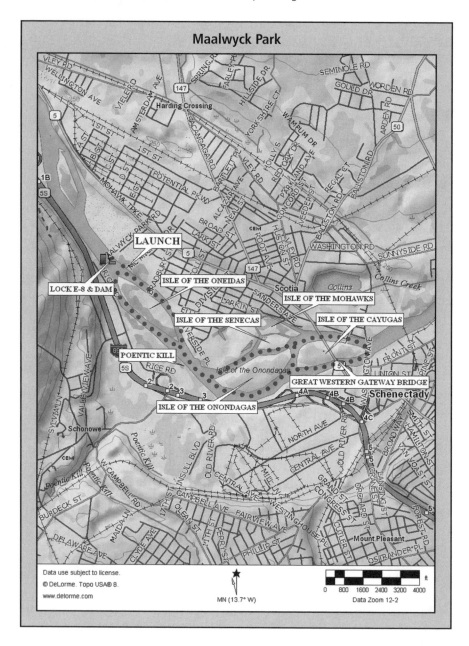

an extra 2.7 miles to the paddle. In doing so you will pass under the Great Western Gateway Bridge twice.

The site of a prehistoric fishing village, called the "Buried Village," was discovered along the north bank of the Mohawk River near Maalwyck Park when a

▶ **Maalwyck Park**

The dam at Lock E-8. Photograph 2007.

series of hearths, previously buried under the silt, were revealed by the river during one of its periodic floods. The village is believed to date back 3,000 years.

History: Maalwyck Park is a fifty-six-acre park[1] maintained under the auspices of the Town of Glenville. It has 1,600 feet of river frontage, both upstream and downstream from Lock E-8.[2]

The Lock E-8 dam is a movable dam (like many on the river), meaning that each of its seventeen sections can be raised or lowered individually by a trolley winch,[3] thus allowing the water to pass through in a measured, regulated way.

58 Lock E-9 State Canal Park (Rotterdam Junction)
Accessing the Mohawk River from Lock E-9

- **Launch Site:** Lock E-9 State Canal Park near Rotterdam Junction (Schenectady County); 200-foot carry to informal put-in.
- **Delorme NYS Atlas & Gazetteer:** p. 66, AB1; **Estimated GPS:** 42°52.68′N; 74°02.36′W
- **Destinations:** Washout Creek, Boston & Maine Railroad bridge, Rotterdam Kiwanis Park
- **Mileage:** To Washout Creek—1.2 miles (one-way); to Boston & Maine Railroad bridge—1.7 miles (one-way); to Rotterdam Kiwanis Park—2.7 miles (one-way)
- **Comments:** Read "Caution" beginning on page xxii and "The Mohawk River: Caution" on page 147. Stay a safe distance back from the Lock E-9 dam. Expect an increase in boat traffic from the Arrowhead Marina near Rotterdam Kiwanis Park.
- **Directions:** From west of Scotia (junction of Rt. 5 & the terminus of I-890), drive northwest on Rt. 5 for 2.6 miles until you reach a traffic light at the junction of Rtes. 5 & 103. Turn left onto Rt. 103 and then immediately left again before crossing bridge. Head southeast for 0.1 mile down to the Lock E-9 parking area, downstream from the dam.

  Approaching from Rotterdam Junction (junction of Rtes. 5S & 103), drive northeast on Rt. 103 for 0.4 mile. As soon as you cross over the Mohawk River, turn right into the Lock E-9 parking area.

  From either direction, at the south end of the parking area follow a fisherman's path for a couple of hundred feet to the water's edge, near the end of the wharf.

The Paddle:

Putting in 0.05 mile downstream from the Lock E-9 dam, proceed downriver, heading southeast. The paddle affords an opportunity to explore yet another part of the Mohawk River. At 0.8 mile you will pass by the boat dock for the historic Mabee House on your right. At 1.2 miles you will pass by Washout Creek on your left (named after an 1885 cloudburst that significantly damaged the New York Central Railroad bed and tracks). At 1.7 miles you will paddle underneath the Boston & Maine Railroad bridge. The Boston & Maine Railroad was the dominant railway of northern New England for a century. It is now known as the Boston & Maine Corporation. At 2.1 miles the Moccasin Kill will appear on your right, and then, at 2.7 miles, you will reach the Rotterdam Kiwanis Park, to your right, by the mouth of the Plotter Kill.

History: Lock E-9,[1] the dam, and the bridge were built between 1915 and 1916, raising the height of the river by 15 feet from 225 feet to 240 feet.[2] The bridge, which connected Rotterdam Junction with West Glenville, was the first to be

Lock E-9 State Canal Park

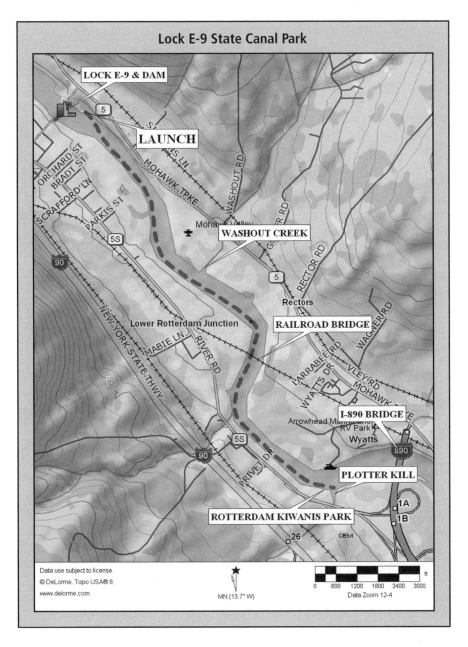

Lock E-9 State Canal Park

LOCK E-9 & DAM

LAUNCH

WASHOUT CREEK

RAILROAD BRIDGE

Lower Rotterdam Junction

Rectors

I-890 BRIDGE

Arrowhead Marina and RV Park

Wyatts

PLOTTER KILL

ROTTERDAM KIWANIS PARK

Data use subject to license.
© DeLorme. Topo USA® 8.
www.delorme.com

MN (13.7° W)

0   600   1200   1800   2400   3000   ft
Data Zoom 12-4

called the "Western Gateway Bridge."[3] A decade later the name was assigned to a new bridge constructed between Schenectady and Scotia, with "Great" added on to acknowledge its larger size. The lock is frequently referred to as the Rotterdam Lock and is contained in a twenty-one-acre park.

The Mabee House in Rotterdam Junction is the oldest home in the Mohawk Valley. Postcard ca. 1900.

The Mabee House is the oldest structure in the Mohawk Valley and one of the oldest in the state. It was built shortly after Daniel Janse Van Antwerp acquired the land in 1670.[4] In 1706, Jan Pieterse Mabee purchased the house from Van Antwerp, and it has been known as the Mabee House ever since. Successive generations of Mabees maintained it into the twentieth century.[5] It is now the property of the Schenectady County Historical Society, which provides tours of the home. Preservationists are currently hoping to acquire land on the opposite side of the Mohawk River to preserve the home's scenic view. For more information, contact (518) 887-5073, (518) 374-0263, or access the Web site at mabeefarm.org.

▶ **Lock E-9 State Canal Park**

Lock E-10 (Pattersonville)
Accessing the Mohawk River

59

■ **Launch Site:** Lock E-10 Fishing Access Site off of Rt. 5S (Montgomery County).
■ **Delorme NYS Atlas & Gazetteer:** p. 65, A7; **Estimated GPS:** 42°54.94'N; 74°08.31'W
■ **Destinations:** Swart Island, Sandsea Kill
■ **Mileage:** To Swart Island—1.9 miles (one-way); around Swart Island—0.7 mile; to Sandsea Kill—3.9 miles (one-way)
■ **Comments:** Read "Caution" beginning on page xxii and "The Mohawk River: Caution" on page 147. Stay a safe distance back from the Lock E-10 dam.
■ **Directions:** From Rotterdam Junction (junction of Rtes. 5S & 103), drive northwest on Rt. 5S for 5.8 miles and turn right onto a short access road to Lock E-10. Approaching from South Amsterdam (junction of Rtes. 5S & 30), drive southeast on Rt. 5S for 3.2 miles and turn left onto short access road to Lock E-10.
   From either direction, after driving 100 feet down the access road, turn right and proceed south on a tiny dirt road for 0.1 mile to a small parking area. A short flight of cement steps leads down to the put-in, which is enclosed in a tiny inlet.

The Paddle:
Begin paddling downstream (southeast). At 0.1 mile you will see the Evas Kill coming in on the north bank after passing through Crane Hollow and the tiny hamlet of Cranesville (named after its founder, David Crane).
   At 0.9 mile you will pass by Lewis Creek to your left. Like all of the small tributaries that flow into the Mohawk from the north, Lewis Creek has to run under Rt. 5 and then a line of railroad tracks to reach the river.
   At 1.9 miles you will reach 0.3-mile-long Swart Island, which can be circumnavigated in 0.7 mile. Like most of the islands, it is heavily forested. The Compaanen Kill, flowing down from the north, comes into the Mohawk River opposite the island's midpoint.
   Continuing still farther downstream, you will pass by the tiny village of Pattersonville, at 3.9 miles, where the mouth of the Sandsea Kill can be seen to your right. The Sandsea Kill is a small stream that rises in the hills southwest of Rotterdam Junction. It contains a series of cascading waterfalls farther upstream from its confluence with the Mohawk River. Just upstream from the mouth of the Sandsea Kill on the Mohawk are a railroad bridge and remnants of the old Erie Canal aqueduct.

History: Like bridges, locks can also sustain heavy damage when the Mohawk River runs amok. In July 2006, heavy rainfall produced unusually high waters, resulting in considerable damage to Lock E-10 (more so than to any of the other locks in the Barge Canal system). Work on restoring the grounds has continued right into 2010.

Southern Shore: Montgomery County

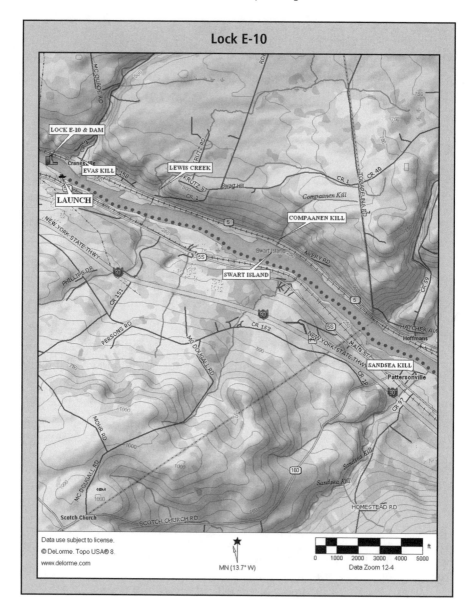

Swart Island is named after an early settler who built a mill on nearby Lewis Creek.[1] Lewis Creek rises from two main branches and is notable for its northernmost branch creating Adriutha Falls, one of the highest waterfalls in the Mohawk Valley.

The Evas Kill was named after Evas van Alstyne, who was killed near the stream by Indians.[2]

 Lock E-10

Port Jackson Boat Launch (South Amsterdam)
More Islands and Dams

60

■ **Launch Site:** Port Jackson Boat Launch at end of Erie Terrace in South Amsterdam (Montgomery County); cement ramp.

■ **Delorme NYS Atlas & Gazetteer:** p. 65, A7; **Estimated GPS:** 42°56.34'N; 74°12.04'W

■ **Destinations:** Bronson Island, Lock E-11, Davey Island, Lock E-10

■ **Mileage:** West to south end of Bronson Island—0.3 mile (one-way); around Bronson Island—0.7 mile; to Lock E-11—0.7 mile (one-way); southeast to Davey Island—0.8 mile (one-way); around island and its satellite—0.9 mile; to Lock E-10—3.5 miles (one-way)

■ **Comments:** Read "Caution" beginning on page xxii and "The Mohawk River: Caution" on page 147. Stay a safe distance back from the Lock E-10 dam and Lock E-11 dam.

■ **Directions:** From the NYS Thruway (I-90), get off at Exit 27 for Amsterdam. Turn right onto Rt. 30 and drive north for 0.4 mile. Before crossing over the Mohawk River, turn right onto Erie Street, which takes you down and under Rt. 30 in 0.2 mile to a stop sign at Bridge Street. Continue straight on Erie Street for another 0.1 mile and then turn right, following detour signs. In 0.1 mile you will come to Erie Terrace. Turn left and follow Erie Terrace northwest for 0.1 mile to the Port Jackson Boat Launch and Park, on your right. Along the way you will cross South Chuctanunda Creek.

The Paddle:

The put-in is nearly straight across the river from the Amsterdam Housing Authority (AHA) high-rise, which is several blocks north of the river. If you look upriver, you can make out the Lock E-11 (often referred to as the Amsterdam Lock) dam in the distance; downstream can be seen the Rt. 30 bridge.

Northwest—Head upriver and you will reach the southeast tip of 0.3-mile-long Bronson Island in 0.3 mile. Stay to your left, going around the island in a clockwise manner. In another 0.1 mile you will see along the south bank of the river an impressively constructed rope swing that hangs over the river. A path descends to the swing, presumably from the bikeway at the top of the hill.

Bronson Island can be circumnavigated in 0.7 mile.

Lock E-11 & dam are reached in 0.7 mile, at which point the dam raises the level of the river from 255 feet to 267 feet.[1]

Guy Park Manor, the mansion next to Lock E-11, dates back to 1766, when Sir William Johnson (arguably the Mohawk Valley's most famous and distinguished citizen) had the house built as a wedding present to his daughter Molly and her husband, Colonel Guy Johnson,[2] Sir William's nephew. The Georgian-style house built with limestone blocks now houses the Montgomery County Chamber of Commerce.

Port Jackson Boat Launch

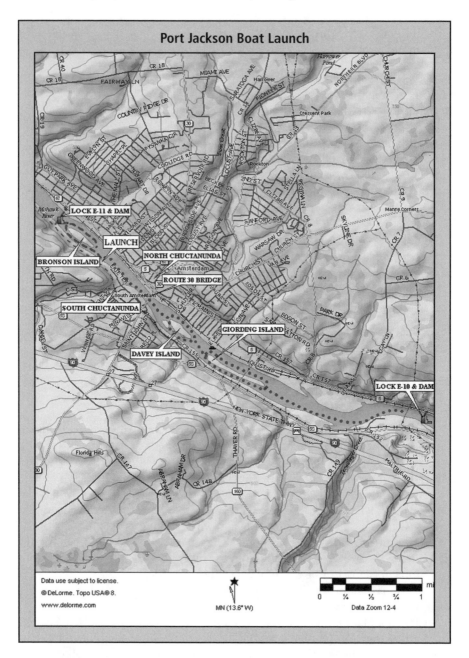

Southeast—Proceeding downstream, you will pass under the Route 30 bridge (connecting Amsterdam and South Amsterdam) in 0.5 mile. Immediately thereafter you will pass the Greater Amsterdam Riverlink Park (to your left), where

▶ **Port Jackson Boat Launch**

access to the river by canoe or kayak along the north bank is possible, but not practical at this time. However, you may want to stop at the park and get out for a stretch during your paddle. In another 0.2 mile, you will pass by a 100-foot-long rock ledge, 10–12 feet above the water, which historians believe was the site of the famous "painted rocks" (Native American petroglyphs). The Painted Rocks no longer exist, but were a familiar sight to eighteenth-and early-nineteenth-century boatmen. In Jeptha R. Simm's book, *Frontiersmen of New York* (1882), the petroglyphs are described as follows:

> Within the remembrance, possibly of some person still living, there was a large rock on the north shore of the Mohawk, near Amsterdam, to be seen at low watermark, that contained Indian Memorials, such as the figures of men and animals, and supposedly by some to have been traced with red chalk, although they may have been in vermilion, which the Whites bartered with the Natives for peltry.[3]

At 0.8 mile from the launch, Davey Island and a tiny satellite island are passed. The islands can be circumnavigated in 1.2 miles. At 1.3 miles you will come to Giording Island, a long, slender island opposite Fownes (a large building complex, complete with towering smokestack, standing on the north bank of the river).

You can continue farther downstream, paralleling Giording Island for part of the way, until you finally reach Lock E-10 at 3.5 miles. Shortly before Lock E-10, you will pass by the old Adirondack Power & Light Corporation (at one

Historic Guy Park Manor. Postcard ca. 1930.

time a steam plant) on your right. This is now the Cranesville Block Company. The plant was originally built to supplement the hydroelectric power generated by plants on the Hudson River and the East Canada Creek west of St. Johnsville.[4]

History: Port Jackson was incorporated in 1852 and became part of the City of Amsterdam when it was annexed in 1888.

The Port Jackson Boat Launch & Park was open in 1998. The park contains a gazebo and four covered bocci courts, and is located in close proximity to the canal bike path. The park is a popular site for anglers looking for walleye and bass.[5]

Bronson Island, before the creation of the Barge Canal, was a series of four to five small islands.[6]

Lock E-11 of the NYS Barge Canal, just north of Bronson Island. Postcard ca. 1920.

▶ **Port Jackson Boat Launch**

Schoharie Crossing (Fort Hunter)
Paddling Past a Section of the Old Erie Canal Aqueduct

61

- **Launch Sites:** East bank of Schoharie Creek near the Visitor Center at Schoharie Crossing (Montgomery County)—carry down a twenty-five-foot, moderately steep bank to the water's edge; west bank of Schoharie Creek at Schoharie Crossing State Historic Site Aqueduct Boat Launch & Picnic Area—cement ramp, seasonal boat launch with modest fee. For more information about Schoharie Crossing: eriecanal.org/Schoharie.html.
- **Delorme NYS Atlas & Gazetteer:** p. 65, A6; **Estimated GPS:** East bank put-in near Visitor Center at Schoharie Crossing—42°56.33′N, 74°16.88′W; Schoharie Crossing State Historic Site Aqueduct Boat Launch & Picnic Area—42°56.39′N, 74°17.45′W
- **Destinations:** Schoharie Creek, aqueduct ruins, Rt. 30A bridge
- **Mileage:** To aqueduct ruins—0.4 mile (one-way); up Schoharie Creek to Thruway bridge—0.6 mile (one-way); down Mohawk River to Lock E-12—0.2 mile (one-way); up Mohawk River to Route 30A bridge in Fonda—4.8 miles (one-way)
- **Comments:** Read "Caution" beginning on page xxii and "The Mohawk River: Caution" on page 147. Sections of the aqueduct have collapsed over time. Even though the arches look stable, caution should be exercised while navigating around or through them. Stay a safe distance back from the Lock E-12 dam.
- **Directions:** From the NYS Thruway (I-90), get off at Exit 27 for Amsterdam. Turn right onto Rt. 30 and then immediately right again onto an exit ramp leading up to Rt. 5S.

  East Bank of Schoharie Creek put-in: Visitor Center Launch—Head west on Rt. 5S for 4.0 miles. When you come to a fork where a green sign points to Fort Hunter, bear right onto Main Street. Drive downhill for 0.2 mile, going northwest. Then turn left onto Railroad Street, heading southwest. As soon as Railroad Street does a right-angle turn, at 0.2 mile (becoming Schoharie Street), look for a path on the left leading down to the river just before an old mule barn, also on your left. Park here momentarily to drop off your watercraft, then continue north for 0.2 mile to the Visitor Center, on the right, where parking is available.

  West Bank of Schoharie Creek put-in: Schoharie Crossing State Historic Site Aqueduct Boat Launch & Picnic Area—From South Amsterdam (junction of Rtes. 5S & 30) head west on Rt. 5S for 4.6 miles (or 0.6 mile southwest from the junction of Main Street and Rt. 5S at Fort Hunter). Turn right onto Hartley Lane and continue straight, heading north. In 0.5 mile you will reach the end of the road, where the parking area for the Schoharie Crossing State Historic Site Aqueduct Boat Launch & Picnic Area is located.

The Paddles:

The following paddles all begin from the visitor center put-in on the east bank of Schoharie Creek at Schoharie Crossing (Montgomery County). If you put in

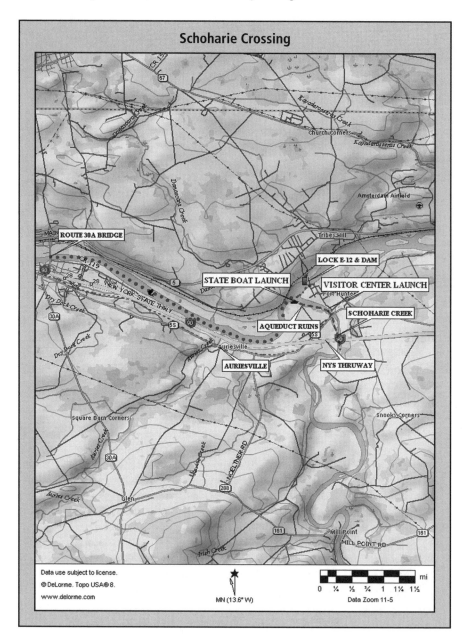

at the Schoharie Crossing State Historic Site Aqueduct Boat Launch, take into
account that the mileage will vary accordingly.

North—Paddle downstream for 0.4 mile to the historic Schoharie Aqueduct.
Along the way look straight down into the water for a possible glimpse of the

▶ **Schoharie Crossing**

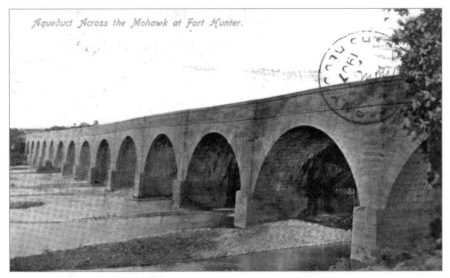

Aqueduct Across the Mohawk at Fort Hunter.

The aqueduct at Schoharie Crossing before a large section collapsed into the river. Postcard ca. 1900.

old "slack water dam" lying underwater near the east side of Schoharie Creek and opposite the visitor center. Old vestiges of the dam above water can be seen along the west bank shore.

Approaching the aqueduct, you will be impressed by its grandeur. Although the aqueduct's entire east section has collapsed into the deeper waters of Schoharie Creek, the west section remains standing defiantly where the river is shallower. It is possible to paddle through and around several of the arches for a closer look. Be cautious, however, for these are old ruins.

North of the aqueduct, you will likely encounter a sandbar. This can be paddled around during times when the water level is sufficiently high if you wish to head back upstream along the west bank. Doing so will provide closer views of the aqueduct's west end.

Continue downstream to the confluence of Schoharie Creek and the Mohawk River. From here, you can proceed downstream on the Mohawk River for 0.2 mile to near Lock E-12 and its dam,[1] where a bridge above the dam connects Fort Hunter to Tribes Hill. Every April the lock and dam are adjusted for the start of boat traffic season, causing waters from the Mohawk River to back up into Schoharie Creek, deepening it for a short distance. If you visit at a time of year when the Barge Canal is not in operation, be prepared for a much shallower Schoharie Creek.

You can also head west upstream on the Mohawk River for 4.8 miles, turning back when you come to the Route 30A bridge linking Fonda and Fultonville.

South—Heading upstream, you will quickly pass by the stone abutments of an old railroad bridge—now part of a bicycle pathway—and then under the Route 5S Bridge.

Continue upstream and in 0.6 mile (or 0.4 mile past Rt. 5S bridge) you will reach the new Thruway bridge. A tragic story accompanies this site. In April 1987 the raging waters of Schoharie Creek caused a former bridge here to collapse without warning, killing ten occupants of four cars and one tractor trailer that fell into the abyss. For months the Schoharie Creek section of the Thruway was closed off and vehicles were rerouted while the new bridge was under construction.

Those are not the only lives claimed by Schoharie Creek. A memorial for another tragedy can be seen at the end of the Schoharie Crossing parking lot—a grim reminder of the deadly power that Schoharie Creek can marshal. This memorial honors three local fishermen who were killed in the flood of June 1977.

From the Thruway bridge, it is possible to continue paddling upstream. You will immediately encounter shallow waters and tiny rapids, but these can be negotiated under most conditions.

History: The Erie Canal was completed in 1825 after eight years of intensive work. The canal took boats all the way from the Hudson River at Albany to Buffalo, negotiating 83 locks over a distance of 363 miles. The Schoharie Creek area portion of the canal was completed in 1823. Fort Hunter has the distinction of being known as "Canal Town USA."[2] The village is named after a Mohawk "castle" that once stood near the confluence of the Mohawk and Schoharie rivers.

Schoharie Creek is a substantial stream that rises southeast of Hunter in the Catskill Mountains and travels north for ninety miles to its confluence with the Mohawk River. It is the largest tributary to the Mohawk River entering from the south. The largest tributaries entering from the north into the Mohawk River are West Canada Creek and East Canada Creek.

During the 1800s a series of dams were constructed across Schoharie Creek, each one stronger than the one it replaced. The dams, known as slack water dams, served to back up the creek enough so that there would be little current to sweep boats downstream during river crossings when the boats were pulled across the creek using ropes and windlasses. Mules and horses were taken across by boat as well. It was still a difficult transit, however, because of the creek's power and unpredictability. Later, the windlass system was replaced with a bridge for mules to walk across while pulling boats behind them, but this was no less dangerous. It was from the crossing of boats near the slack water dam that the name Schoharie Crossing arose. The last dam, built in 1864, was 11 feet high and 436 feet long, and was formed out of rock rubble and lumber. It lasted into the twentieth century and the inception of the Barge Canal. A picture of the slack water dam can be seen in the visitor center.[3] Previous dams were constructed in 1822, 1832, and 1862.

▶ **Schoharie Crossing**

Two kayakers make their way up Schoharie Creek. Photograph 2008.

When the Erie Canal was enlarged to accommodate the increasing demands placed upon it by traffic and vessel size, a 624-foot aqueduct was built across the Schoharie Creek at Fort Hunter[4] in 1839–1841, and three new locks, including several miles of enlarged canal beds, were constructed. Water was held inside the stonework of the aqueduct by a wooden lining, which could be removed each year at the end of the season, to prevent damage to the lining, and then reintroduced in the spring.

The original canal was not abandoned in its entirety, however; rather, it ended up serving as a feeder for the enlarged canal, which explains why the 1862 and 1864 dams were created.

Despite all the intensive work to improve the Erie Canal through enlargements and modifications, the vast and intricate system of canals was ultimately abandoned. In part this was because of the arrival of the steam locomotive, which represented a newer and more efficient means of transportation. But the very success of the Erie Canal also led to its own demise; by demonstrating the feasibility of water-based travel through the central and western part of New York State, it encouraged the creation of its own successor—the more efficient New York State Barge Canal. The Barge Canal turned the Mohawk River into one long channel 160 to 200 feet wide with a minimal depth of 14 feet.

Additional Places of Interest—The Visitor Center and Canal Store Exhibit at Schoharie Crossing are open from the first Wednesday in May through the last Sunday in October, Wed.–Sat. from 10 AM–5 PM, and Sunday 1 PM–5 PM. The center is also open on Memorial Day, Independence Day, and Labor Day.

Contained in the center are exhibits that trace the history of the Erie Canal, particularly how it impacted the growth of New York State.

There are several other sites that are interesting to visit while at the Schoharie Crossing State Historic Site. They encompass an area approximately three miles in length from just west of Schoharie Creek to roughly one mile west of Amsterdam. These include:

1. The East Guard Lock and Lock #20 from the original Erie Canal, including 0.5 mile of waterway.

2. The Empire Lock (#29)—a lift-lock from the 1840s enlarged Erie Canal.[5]

3. The 220-foot-long Yankee Hill Double Lock #28 which, like all the locks along the Erie Canal, was expanded in 1889. Next to the lock is the preserved 1856 Putnam's Store, which operated until 1908.

The fertile plains of the Mohawk Valley are clearly evident in this scene. Postcard ca. 1930.

Schoharie Crossing

Quist Road Boat Launch (Amsterdam)
Accessing the Mohawk River near Amsterdam

62

■ **Launch Site:** Boat launch off of Quist Road near Amsterdam (Montgomery County); hard surface ramp and dock, parking area for up to twenty cars.
■ **Delorme NYS Atlas & Gazetteer:** p. 65, A7; **Estimated GPS:** 42°55.44'N; 74°10.30'W
■ **Destinations:** Three islands, Rt. 30 bridge, Lock E-10
■ **Mileage:** Around three islands (Davey, Giording, and a tiny satellite island)—2.5 miles (round-trip); to Rt. 30 bridge—1.4 miles (one-way); to Lock E-10—1.7 miles (one-way)
■ **Comments:** Read "Caution" beginning on page xxii and "The Mohawk River: Caution" on page 147. Stay a safe distance back from the Lock E-10 dam.
■ **Directions:** From the east side of Amsterdam, at the point where East Main Street (Rt. 5) becomes the Mohawk Turnpike (a four-lane road), drive southeast on Rt. 5 for over 0.2 mile and turn right onto Quist Road.

Approaching from West Glenville (junction of Rtes. 103 & 5), proceed northwest on Rt. 5 for 7.6 miles and turn left onto Quist Road just before reaching Amsterdam.

From either direction, follow Quist Road southeast for over 0.1 mile and then pull into a large parking area on your right before reaching the City of Amsterdam Waste Water Treatment Plant farther east.

The Paddle:

West—Paddle straight across the river for 0.1 mile until you reach Giording Island, which is the long, slender body of land directly in front of the launch site. The island can be circumnavigated in 1.4 miles. Davey Island and a smaller island slightly beyond it can also be explored, and circumnavigated in 0.8 mile.

The Rt. 30 bridge is reached in 0.3 mile from the west end of Davey Island (1.4 miles upriver from the launch site).

East—Going downstream you will pass by Degraff Creek at 0.5 mile on your left, and then Terwilleger Creek at 1.0 mile on your right. At 1.4 miles you will pass by the former Adirondack Power & Light Corporation to your right, which is now the Cranesville Block Company. Lock E-10 is reached at 1.7 miles.

History: The river town of Amsterdam was settled in 1710 by the Dutch. Early on it was known as Veeder Mills (and also Veedersburgh) after Albert Veeder, an early mill owner. The name changed to Amsterdam in 1803.

The North Chuctanunda Creek, which runs through Amsterdam, powered mills and factories and was an important factor in the rise of the city as a manufacturing center, particularly of carpets, during the nineteenth and twentieth centuries.

Northern Shore: Montgomery County

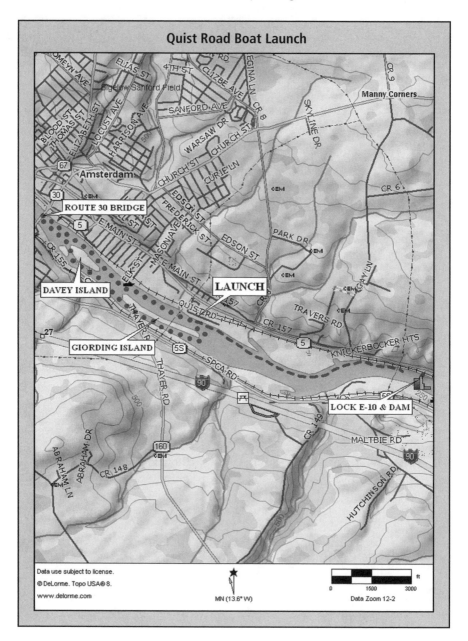

Quist Road Boat Launch

Lock E-12 Dam (Tribes Hill)
Accessing the Mohawk River at Lock E-12

63

- **Launch Site:** Lock E-12 at north end of Main Street bridge in Tribes Hill (Montgomery County). Fifty-foot carry to put-in at west end of wharf.
- **Delorme NYS Atlas & Gazetteer:** p. 65, A6; **Estimated GPS:** 42°56.70′N, 73°17.16′W
- **Destinations:** Schoharie Creek, Rt. 30A bridge at Fonda, Upper Pepper Island, Pepper Island, Robb Island, Lock E-11
- **Mileage:** To Schoharie Creek—0.2 mile (one-way); up Schoharie Creek—1.0 mile; to Rt. 30A bridge—5.0 miles (one-way); to Upper Pepper Island—1.6 miles (one-way); to Pepper Island—2.1 miles (one-way); to Robb Island—3.4 miles (one-way); to Lock E-11—4.5 miles (one-way)
- **Comments:** Read "Caution" beginning on page xxii and "The Mohawk River: Caution" on page 147.

  Keep a safe distance back from the Lock E-12 dam. Don't put in if the current seems unusually strong. Be prepared to "lock through" Lock E-12 in order to paddle to the downstream islands.
- **Directions:** From Amsterdam (junction of Rtes. 5 & 30), drive northwest on Rt. 5 for roughly 4.5 miles (or 1.8 miles west from the junction of Rtes. 5 and 67 West). When you come to Mohawk Drive, turn left and proceed southwest for 1.0 mile, then turn left onto Main Street and head south for 0.3 mile. Before crossing over the Mohawk River, turn left at Lock 12 and drive down to the main building, several hundred feet from the road. Bear right at the main building, and head west, immediately going under the bridge spanning the Mohawk River. In 0.1 mile you will reach the west end of the parking area. Park there, and put in at the end of the wharf.

The Paddle:

West—Heading upriver takes you immediately to Schoharie Creek (coming in from the south). Schoharie Creek can be paddled upstream to the NYS Thruway bridge, a distance of 1.0 mile.

From the mouth of Schoharie Creek, continue west on the Mohawk toward Fonda/Fultonville. You will reach the Rt. 30A bridge in Fonda at 5.0 miles. The first 1.2 miles of the paddle are in a southwest direction. Once you reach a point on the river south of the Auriesville Shrine, the river changes direction and heads west from that point on (see "Schoharie Crossing" chapter for map of upriver paddle to the Rt. 30A bridge in Fonda).

East (passing through Lock E-12)—Heading downriver, you will reach 0.4-mile-long Upper Pepper Island in 1.6 miles, then 0.6-mile-long Pepper Island in 2.1 miles. When you reach the east tip of Pepper Island (the second large island), you are nearly parallel to Fort Johnson—the eighteenth-century home of Sir William Johnson—which lies slightly inland to the north, at the junction of Rtes. 5

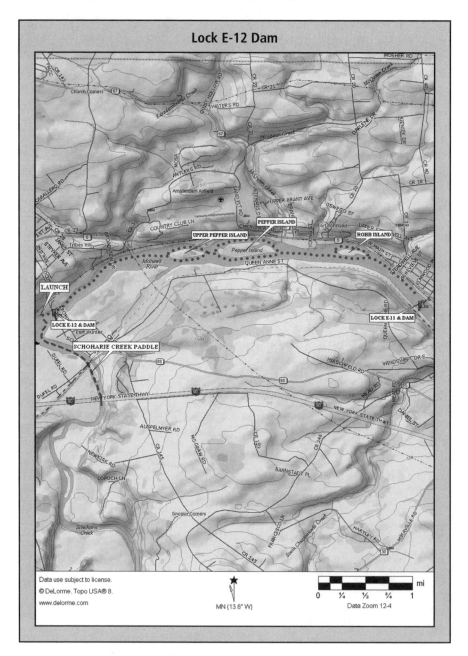

& 67 West. At 3.4 miles you will arrive at 0.3-mile-long Robb Island (located at a point where the river turns southeast). When you have paddled a total of 4.5 miles, you will be at Lock E-11.

▶ **Lock E-12 Dam**

History: Lock E-12 was designated the James Shanahan Lock in 1989, named after the man who served as superintendent of New York State Canals from 1878–1897.

The Auriesville Shrine (the Catholic Shrine of Our Lady of Martyrs) marks the spot where Father Isaac Jogues was slain by Native Americans in 1646. Father Jogues was one of twenty-six Jesuit missionaries who gave up their lives preaching the gospel in the North American colonies.[1]

Fort Johnson is the name of a large Georgian mansion built in 1749 by Sir William Johnson, the Mohawk Valley's most famous and illustrious resident. The home rested on 1,000 acres of land, which included about a mile and a half of waterfront along the Mohawk River. Today, only a small fraction of the land remains as part of the site.

After being made a baronet, Johnson built an even larger, more lavish home in nearby Johnstown in 1763, which came to be known as Johnson Hall. William's son John then took over Fort Johnson. During the Revolutionary War, John remained loyal to the king, which resulted in his lands being confiscated and sold after the war by the Tryon County Committee of Sequestration. At least seven other families have owned the house since then. In 1905, General J. Watts DePeyster deeded the property to the Montgomery County Historical Society with the provision that it be used strictly for historical purposes. Since then the house has been preserved, and underwent extensive restoration from 1979–1982. It was designated as a National Historic Landmark in 1974.[2] For more information: Old Fort Johnson, (518) 843-0300, museum@oldfortjohnson.org. Tours are conducted from May 17–October 15, Wednesday–Sunday, 1 PM–5 PM.

Anglers get to enjoy casting a line at Lock 12. Photograph 2008.

A quiet moment along the Mohawk River. Postcard ca. 1900.

▶ **Lock E-12 Dam**

Appendix A: Clubs & Agencies

- **Adirondack Mountain Club, ADK Member Services Center**
  814 Goggins Road, Lake George, NY 12845
  Phone: (518) 668-4447, Order, Join,
  Donate: 800-395-8080
  E-mail: adkinfo@adk.org: www.adk.org/

- **Adirondack Mountain Club (ADK), Albany Chapter**
  P. O. Box 2116, ESP Station, Albany, NY 12220, www.adk-albany.org

- **Adirondack Pirate Paddlers**
  www.adirondackpiratepaddlers.org

- **Albany Area Kayaking Meetup Group**
  www.meetup.com/Albany-Area-Kayaking

- **Appalachian Mountain Club (AMC), Mohawk-Hudson Chapter**
  5 Orchard Drive, Kinderhook, NY 12106, www.amcmohawkhudson.org

- **Catskill Mountain Club, P.O. Box 558, Pine Hill, NY 12465**
  www.catskillmountainclub.org

- **Erie Canalway National Heritage Corridor**
  PO Box 219, Waterford, NY 12188
  Visitor Center phone: (518) 237-7000
  www.nps.gov/erie

- **Greene County Canoe & Kayak Club, Coxsackie, NY**
  www.paddlegreene.com

- **Hudson River Greenway Water Trail**
  http://julie-elson.net/greenway-sites.html
  (for list of designated sites)

- **Hudson River Maritime Museum**
  50 Rondout Landing, Kingston, NY 12401
  (845) 338-0071   www.hrmm.org

- **Hudson River Watertrail Association**
  www.hrwa.org

- **Mohawk-Hudson Council of Yacht Clubs**
  www.angelfire.com/hi/grades/bridge.html,
  www.poughkeepsieyachtclub.org/.../
  Mohawk-Hudson

- **New York State Canals**
  www.nyscanals.gov

- **New York State Canal Corporation**
  200 Southern Blvd., Albany, NY 12201
  NY Tel. (518) 436-2700
  Toll Free 800-422-6254
  http://www.canals.state.ny.us

- **NYS Hudson River Valley Greenway**
  Capital Building, Capital Station, Room 254
  Albany, NY 12224 (518) 473-3835
  E-mail: hrvg@hudsongreenway.state.ny.us
  www.hudsongreenway.state.ny.us

- **Open Space Institute (OSI)**
  1350 Broadway, Suite 201
  New York, NY 10018
  (212) 290-8200   www.osiny.org/

- **Riverkeeper**
  828 South Broadway, Tarrytown, NY 10591
  800-21-RIVER E-mail: info@riverkeeper.org
  www.riverkeeper.org

- **Scenic Hudson, Inc.**
  One Civic Center Plaza, Suite 200
  Poughkeepsie, NY 12601
  (845) 473-4440   www.scenichudson.org

- **Schenectady County–Mohawk River Blueway Trail Plan**
  www.cityofschenectady.com/pdf/.../
  Blueway%20Trail%20Plan%202008.pdf

- **Taconic Hiking Club, 29 Campagna Drive, Albany, NY 12205**
  www.taconichikingclub.blogspot.com

- **Troy Motor Boat & Canoe Club, Troy, NY,**
  (518) 235-9697
  www.geocites.com/troyboatclub

Appendix B: Supplemental Reading

Hudson River, Champlain Canal, Lake Champlain

1. Arthur G. Adams, *The Hudson River Guidebook*, Second Edition (New York: Fordham University, 1996).
2. Walter F. Burmeister, *Appalachian Waters 2: The Hudson River and Its Tributaries* (Oakton, VA: Appalachian Books, 1974).

3. Ian H. Giddy, *The Hudson River Water Trail Guide: A River Guide for Small Boats*, Sixth Edition (New York: Hudson River Watertrail Association, 2003).
4. Catherine Frank & Margaret Holden, *A Kayaker's Guide to Lake Champlain: Exploring the New York, Vermont & Quebec Shores* (Hensonville, NY: Black Dome Press, 2009).
5. *Hudson River Waterfront Map* (Hudson Valley Tourism, 2001).
6. Alan & Susan McKibben, *Cruising Guide to the Hudson River, Lake Champlain, and the St. Lawrence River: The Waterway from New York City to Montreal and Quebec City* (Burlington, VT: Lake Champlain Publishing Company, 2006).
7. New York State Canal Corporation, *The Cruising Guide to the New York State Canal System: Champlain, Erie, Oswego, Cayuga-Seneca*, third edition (Albany, NY: New York State Canal Corporation, 2006).
8. Richard W. Wilkie, *The Illustrated Hudson River Pilot: Being a Small-Craft Sailor's Pictorial Guide to the Tidewater Hudson, Albany to New York* (Albany, NY: Three City Press, 1974).

Lower Hudson River
1. Shari Aber, *A Kayaker's Guide to the Hudson River Valley: The Quieter Waters, Rivers, Creeks, Lakes, and Ponds* (Hensonville, NY: Black Dome Press, 2007).

Mohawk River & Erie Canal (including other NYS canals)
1. The New York State Canal Corporation, *The Cruising Guide to the New York State Canal System, Third Edition* (Albany, NY: New York State Canal Corporation, 2006).

General
1. Kathie Armstrong & Chet Harvey, eds., *Canoe and Kayak Guide: East-Central New York State* (Lake George, NY: Adirondack Mountain Club, 2003).
2. Dave Cilley, *Adirondack Paddler's Guide* (Saranac Lake, NY: Paddlesports Press, 2008).
3. Jack Downs, *A Trail Marker Books Guide to Kayak and Canoe Paddles in the New York Champlain Valley* (Trail Marker Books, 2004).
4. Lawrence I. Grinnell, *Canoeable Waterways of New York State and Vicinity* (New York: Pageant Press, 1956). This book, over fifty years old, was superseded by Alec Proskine's *No Two Rivers Alike*.
5. John Hayes & Alex Wilson, *Quiet Water New York*, 2nd Edition (Boston, MA: Appalachian Mountain Club, 2007).
6. Paul Jamieson & Donald Morris, *Adirondack Canoe Waters: North Flow* (Glens Falls, NY: The Adirondack Mountain Club, 1987).
7. M. Paul Keesler, *Canoe-Fishing New York Rivers and Streams* (Prospect, NY: Mid-York Sportsman, 1995).
8. Barbara McMartin, *Fun on Flatwater: An Introduction to Adirondack Canoeing* (Utica, NY: North Country Books, 1995).
9. Alec C. Proskine, *Adirondack Canoe Waters: South and West Flow* (Glens Falls, NY: Adirondack Mountain Club, 1986).
10. Alec C. Proskine, *No Two Rivers Alike: 56 Canoeable Rivers in New York State*, New Edition (Fleischmanns, NY: Purple Mountain Press, 1995).
11. Kevin Stiegelmaier, *Canoeing & Kayaking New York* (Birmingham, AL: Menasha Ridge Press, 2009).

White-water paddling
1. Dennis Squires, *New York Exposed: The Whitewater State*, Volume 1 (Margaretville, NY: A White Water Outlaw Publishing, 2002).
2. Dennis Squires, *New York Exposed: The Whitewater State*, Volume 2 (Margaretville, NY: A White Water Outlaw Publishing, 2003).

Appendix C: Local Outfitters

- **Adirondack Paddle 'n' Pole**
  2123 Central Avenue, Schenectady, NY 12304
  (518) 346-3180 www.onewithwater.com

- **Adirondack Sports & Fitness Summer Expo**
  (held annually in early April at City Center in Saratoga Springs)
  (518) 877-8788 adksports.com

- **ADK Kayak Warehouse**
  4786 State Highway 30
  Amsterdam, NY 12010
  (518) 843-3232
  www.adkkayakwarehouse.com

- **The Boat House**
  2855 Aqueduct Road
  Schenectady, NY 12309
  (518) 393-5711
  www.boathousecanoeskayaks.com

- **B.S. Enterprises**
  PO Box 67, Coxsackie, NY 12051
  (518) 731-6286

- **Coxsackie Bike & Sport**
  369 Mansion St., W. Coxsackie, NY 12192
  (518) 731-9313

- **Dick's Sporting Goods**
  Crossgates Mall
  1 Crossgates Mall, Albany, NY 12203
  (518) 464-1948
  www.dickssportinggoods.com

- **Dick's Sporting Goods**
  Latham Farms
  579 Troy / Schenectady Road
  Colonie, NY 12110
  (518) 783-0701
  www.dickssportinggoods.com

- **Dick's Sporting Goods**
  Wilton Mall
  3065 Route 50,
  Saratoga Springs, NY 12866
  (518) 583-7218
  www.dickssportinggoods.com

- **Dick's Sporting Goods**
  Aviation Mall
  578 Aviation Road
  Queensbury, NY 12804
  (518) 743-8790
  www.dickssportinggoods.com

- **Eastern Mountain Sports (EMS) #136**
  Stuyvesant Plaza
  1475 Western Avenue, Albany, NY 12203
  (518) 482-0088 www.ems.com

- **Eastern Mountain Sports (EMS) #132**
  The Shoppes at Wilton
  3066 Route 50, Saratoga Springs, NY 12866
  (518) 580-1505 www.ems.com

- **Eastern Mountain Sports (EMS) #141**
  Mohawk Commons
  412C Balltown Road, Schenectady, NY 12304
  (518) 388-2700 www.ems.com

- **Goldstock's Sporting Goods**
  98 Freemans Bridge Road, Scotia, NY 12302
  (518) 382-2037
  www.goldstockssportinggoods.com

- **Kenco**
  1000 Hurley Mountain Road
  Kingston, NY 12401-7603
  (845) 340-0552 www.atkenco.com

- **Lake George Kayak Company**
  Main Street, Bolton Landing, NY 12814
  (518) 644-9366 www.lakegeorgekayak.com

- **LL Bean**
  131 Colonie Center, Suite 194
  Albany, NY 12205
  (518) 437-5460 www.llbean.com

- **Pine Lake Stoves of Saratoga**
  747 Saratoga Road (Route 9)
  Gansevoort, NY 12831
  (518) 584-9070
  www.pinelakestovesandspas.com

- **Schenectady Canoe Sales**
  502 Summit Avenue, Schenectady, NY
  (518) 370-0367

- **Steiner's Sports**
  329 Glenmont Street, Glenmont, NY 12077
  (518) 427-2406
  www.steinerssports.com/index.cfm

- **Steiner's Sports**
  301 Warren Street, Hudson, NY 12534
  (518) 828-5063
  www.steinerssports.com/index.cfm

- **Steiner's Sports**
  3455 U.S. 9, Valatie, NY 12184
  (518) 784-3663
  www.steinerssports.com/index.cfm

Notes

Caution and Safety Tips

1. Richard W. Wilkie, *The Illustrated Hudson River Pilot: Being a Small-Craft Sailor's Pictorial Guide to the Tidewater Hudson, Albany to New York* (Albany, NY: Three Cities Press, 1974), 1.

2. Ibid., 1.

3. www.ecostudies.org/images/education/chp/tides.pdf.

4. www.hudsonriver.com/almanac/0497alm.htm.

5. Peter Lourie, *Rivers of Mountains: A Canoe Journey down the Hudson* (Syracuse, NY: Syracuse University Press, 1995), 232.

6. Catherine Frank & Margaret Holden, *A Kayaker's Guide to Lake Champlain: Exploring the New York, Vermont & Quebec Shores* (Hensonville, NY: Black Dome Press, 2009), 3.

7. Kenneth Kamler, *Surviving the Extremes: What happens to the body and mind at the limits of human endurance* (London: Penguin Books, 2005), 91.

The Hudson River

Introduction

1. Informational sign, Corning Preserve. Estimates do vary. The U.S. Army Corps of Engineers in Vermont give a slightly lower figure of 12,650 square miles in their book *Water Resources Development: New England Division* (Waltham, MA: Department of Army New England Division, Corps of Engineers, 1979), 39. On the other hand, Stephen P. Stanne, Roger G. Panetta & Brian E. Forist give a comparable figure of 13,390 square miles in *The Hudson: An Illustrated Guide to the Living River* (New Brunswick, NJ: Rutgers University Press, 1996), 2.

2. Richard F. Ward, "Geology of the Hudson," *North Country Life and York State Tradition*, Vol. 13, no. 2 (Spring 1959), 44. "Even at sea the river maintains its identity for nearly 100 miles until it finally plunges off the Continental Shelf through a sub-surface gorge which rivals the Grand Canyon." Stanne et al., in *The Hudson*, mention that during the last glaciation, the ocean was 400 feet lower than today, forcing the Hudson River to cross an additional 120 miles of coastal plains before reaching the Atlantic Ocean.

3. Paul Grondahl, *Times Union*, December 12, 2007. Don Rittner, *Remembering Albany: Heritage on the Hudson* (Charleston, SC: History Press, 2009), 25.

4. Mrs. J. B. Vanderworker, *Early Days in Eastern Saratoga County* (Interlaken, NY: Empire State Books, 1994), 41.

5. Russell Dunn, *Hudson Valley Waterfall Guide: From Saratoga and the Capital Region to the Highlands and Palisades* (Hensonville, NY: Black Dome Press, 2005), 31.

6. Nathaniel Bartlett Sylvester, *History of Saratoga County, New York with Illustrations and Biographical Sketches of some of Its Prominent Men and Pioneers* (Philadelphia: Everts & Ensign, 1878), 14.

Western Shore: Albany County

Corning Preserve

1. Arthur G. Adams, *The Hudson River Guidebook*, 2nd edition (New York: Fordham University Press, 1996), 273.

2. Historic marker.

3. www.en.wikipedia.org/wiki/Maiden_Lane_Bridge.

4. Ibid.

5. Robert M. Toole, *A Lock at Metroland: A New Guide to Its History and Heritage* (Saratoga Springs, NY: Office of R. M. Toole, 1976), 36.

6. Roland Van Zandt, *Chronicles of the Hudson: Three Centuries of Travel and Adventure* (Hensonville, NY: Black Dome Press, 1992), 233.

7. Arnold W. Brunner, *Studies for Albany* (Albany, NY: n. p., 1914), 45. As far back as the beginning of the twentieth century, Albany's blighted riverfront was an acknowledged fact, and city officials were desirous of turning the riverfront into "an agreeable recreation ground, not only for children but for adults."

8. C. R. Roseberry, *Flashback: A Fresh Look at Albany's Past* (Albany, NY: Park Press, 1986), 79.

9. Historical Marker.

10. Tricia Barbagallo, Cynthia Sauer and John Warren (preparers), *A Historical Orientation to Albany, New York: Historic Crossroad, State Capital, City of Neighborhoods* (Albany, NY: n. p., 1997). A 1985 painting of the Albany Basin (circa 1868) by Len F. Tantillo is shown on page 9.

11. Amelia T. O'Shea, *Canals of Albany County* (Freehold, NY: Amelia T. O'Shea, 2006), 12, 16.

12. www.ulster.net/~hmm/halfmoon/manual.htm.

13. Don Rittner, *Images of America: Troy* (Charleston, SC: Arcadia Publishing, 1998). On page 69 can be seen a photo of the 1909 *Half Moon*.

14. Spindle City Historic Society, *Images of America: Cohoes Revisited* (Charleston, SC: Arcadia Publishing, 2005). On page 69 can be seen a photograph taken of the 1909 *Half Moon* while fenced in on Van Schaick Island.

15. J. A. van der Kooij, "Saga of the Half Moon of 1909," *de Halve Maen: Magazine of the Dutch Colonial Period in America*, Vol. LXVI, no. 3 (Fall 1993), 48–53.

16. Adams, 272. Benson J. Lossing, *The Hudson: From the Wilderness to the Sea* (1866; reprint, Hensonville, NY: Black Dome Press, 2000), 118.

17. Ibid., 119.

18. Amasa J. Parker, ed., *Landmarks of Albany County New York* (Syracuse, NY: D. Mason & Co., 1897), 282–283. Roseberry, 80. Some of these streams had grown fairly vile. The Rutten Kill (Dutch for "Rat Creek") had produced a sizable ravine that harbored rats, hence the name. There was also a gallows in the ravine where the last public execution in the city took place, in 1827.

Hudson Shores Park

1. Alan & Susan McKibben, *Cruising Guide to the Hudson River, Lake Champlain, and the St. Lawrence River: The Waterway from New York City to Montreal and Quebec City* (Burlington, VT: Lake Champlain Publishing Company, 2006), 63.

2. Green Island Bicentennial Commission, *Green Island Heritage and the Bicentennial* (n.p.: Green Island Bicentennial Commission, 1976), 15.

3. Arthur G. Adams, *The Hudson River Guidebook*, 2nd edition (New York: Fordham University Press, 1996), 277.

4. John C. Kacharian, "Watervliet Arsenal," *Mohawk Valley USA*, Vol. 3, no.10 (Fall 1982), 14. A picture of the Erie Canal passing in front of the arsenal can also be seen on page 14.

5. Francis P. Kimball, *The Capital Region of New York State: Crossroads of Empire*, Vol. II (New York: Lewis Historical Publishing Company, 1942), 317.

6. www.hudsonmohawkgateway.org/4_heritage_chron.html.

Green Island

1. Green Island Bicentennial Commission, *Green Island Heritage and the Bicentennial* (n. p.: Green Island Bicentennial Commission, 1976), 13.

2. Wikipedia.

3. www.bizjournals.com/albany/stories/2004/07/19/daily6.html.

The Little River

1. Arthur G. Adams, *The Hudson River Guidebook*, 2nd edition (New York: Fordham University Press, 1996), 273.

2. mstruct.neric.org/schuyler.

3. Historic marker.

4. Historic marker.

5. Anne Grant, *Memoirs of an American Lady with Sketches of Manners and Scenes in America as They Existed Previous to the Revolution* (1808; reprint, New York: D. Appleton & Co., 1845). In this book, Grant recalls her childhood during the 1760s when she was a guest and protégé

of Madame Margarita Schuyler at the Schuyler home.

Schuyler Flats

1. Historic marker.

2. Historic marker.

Island Creek Park

1. Claire K. Schmitt & Mary S. Brennan, *Natural Areas of Albany County*, fourth edition (Niskayuna, NY: The Environmental Clearinghouse, 2004), 21.

2. Arthur G. Adams, *The Hudson River Guidebook*, 2nd edition (New York: Fordham University Press, 1996), 261.

3. Amelia T. O'Shea, *Canals of Albany County* (Freehold, NY: Amelia T. O'Shea, 2006), 14.

4. Robert M. Toole, *A Lock at Metroland: A New Guide to Its History and Heritage* (Saratoga Springs, NY: Office of R. M. Toole, 1976), 39.

5. Adams, 262.

6. C. G. Hine, *Albany to Tappen: The West Bank of the Hudson River* (1906; limited edition facsimile reprint, Astoria, NY: J.C. & A. L Fawcett, n. d), 4.

7. Allison Bennett, *Times Remembered: Chronicles of the Towns of Bethlehem and New Scotland* (Delmar, NY: Newsgraphic of Delmar, 1984), 42.

8. Shirley W. Dunn, "Settlement Patterns in Rensselaerswijck: Godyns Burg, the Tobacco Experiment, and the Mills of Albert Andriessen," *de Halve Maen: Magazine of the Dutch Colonial Period in America*, Vol. LXXI, no. 2 (Summer 1998), 36. Dunn's article goes into detail about a failed experiment in the 1630s to raise tobacco near the mouth of the Normans Kill.

9. training.fws.gov/library/pubs5/web_link/text/upp_hud.htm.

10. Nelson Greene, ed., *History of the Valley of the Hudson: River of Destiny, 1609–1930*, Vol. I (Chicago: The S.J. Clarke Publishing Company, 1931), 114.

11. Russell Dunn, *Hudson Valley Waterfall Guide: From Saratoga and the Capital Region to the Highlands and Palisades* (Hensonville, NY: Black Dome Press, 2005), 142.

12. Jeffrey Perls, *Paths along the Hudson: A Guide to Walking and Biking* (Piscataway, NJ: Rutgers University Press, 1999), 377.

13. Arthur B. Reeve, "Three Hundred Years on the Hudson (1909)," Frank Oppel, compiler, *New York: Tales of the Empire State* (Secaucus, NJ: Castle, 1988), 224.

14. www.nyswaterfronts.com.

15. *This Guide to Albany* (Albany, NY: Cyrene Temple # 18, Daughters of the Nile, 1954), 7.

16. Hine, 6.

17. Amelia T. O'Shea, *Canals of Albany County* (Freehold, NY: Amelia T. O'Shea, 2006), 14.

18. Francis P. Kimball, *The Capital Region of New York State: Crossroads of Empire*, Vol. II (New York: Lewis Historical Publishing Company, 1942), 248.

Additional material on Port of Albany:

Port of Albany: Gateway of the World (Albany, NY: Albany Port District Commission, 1932).

NYS Bethlehem Fishing Access Launch

1. C. R. Roseberry, *Albany: Three Centuries a County* (Albany, NY: Argus Press, Inc., 1983), 17.

2. Nelson Greene, ed., *History of the Valley of the Hudson: River of Destiny, 1609–1930* (Chicago: The S.J. Clarke Publishing Company, 1931), 105.

3. Allison Bennett, *Times Remembered: Chronicles of the Towns of Bethlehem and New Scotland* (Delmar, NY: Newsgraphic of Delmar, 1984), 13.

4. Peter M. Kenny, "A New York Dutch Interior for the American Wing," *Magazine Antiques* (Jan. 2006) from Web site *findarticles.com*.

5. Ian H. Giddy and the Hudson River Watertrail Association, *The Hudson River Water Trail Guide*, sixth edition (New York: Hudson River Watertrail Association, 2003), 19.

Additional Material:

Alan Mapes, "Paddling the Hudson: Two Favorite Launches," *Adirondack Sports & Fitness* (October 2009), 11.

Coeymans Landing

1. Mark Peckham, National Register of Historic Places Coordinator.

2. Francis P. Kimball, *The Capital Region of New York State: Crossroads of Empire*, Vol. II (New York: Lewis Historical Publishing Company, 1942), 311.

3. Clesson Bush, New Baltimore Historian.

4. Peckham.

5. Russell Dunn & Barbara Delaney, *Trails with Tales: History Hikes through the Capital Region, Saratoga, Berkshires, Catskills & Hudson Valley* (Hensonville, NY: Black Dome Press, 2006), 202.

6. www.nysthruway.gov/environmental/recycling.html.

7. www.coeymans.org/history.htm.

8. Arthur G. Adams, *The Hudson River Guidebook*, 2nd edition (New York: Fordham University Press, 1996), 256.

9. Allison Bennett, *Times Remembered: Chronicles of the Towns of Bethlehem and New Scotland, New York* (Delmar, NY: Newsgraphics of Delmar, 1984), 1.

10. www.training.fws.gov.

11. Ibid.

12. C. G. Hine, *Albany to Tappen: The West Bank of the Hudson River* (1906; limited edition facsimile reprint, Astoria, NY: J.C. & A.L. Fawcett, Inc., n. d), 11.

13. O'Neil, *O'Neil's Guide Book of the Hudson River with Notes of Interest to the Summer Tourist*, 11th edition (Albany, NY: Walter S. Allen, 1892), 13.

14. Adams, 256.

15. Ernest Ingersoll, *Handy Guide to the Hudson River and Catskill Mountain* (1910; facsimile reprint, Astoria, NY: J.C. & A.L. Fawcett, Inc., 1989), 198. Maud Wilder Goodwin, *Dutch and English on the Hudson: A Chronicle of Colonial New York* (New Haven, CT: Yale University Press, 1919).

16. Edward D. Giddings, *Coeymans and Past* (Coeymans, NY: Tri-Centennial Committee, 1973), 108.

Additional Material:

Alan Mapes, "Paddling the Hudson: Two Favorite Launches," *Adirondack Sports & Fitness* (October 2009), 11.

Eastern Shore: Rensselaer County

Lansing's Ferry

1. Claire K. Schmitt, Norton G. Miller, Warren F. Broderick, John T. Keenan & William D. Niemi, *Natural Areas of Rensselaer County, New York*, 2nd edition (Schenectady/Troy, NY: The Rensselaer–Taconic Land Conservancy & Environmental Clearinghouse of Schenectady, Inc., 2002), 35.

2. Ibid., 35.

3. Edward T. Heald, *Taconic Trails: By Auto and Afoot* (Albany, NY: J. B. Lyon Company, 1929), 18. On pages 16–19, Heald devotes a chapter to Thieves' Hollow.

4. Warren Broderick, Senior Archives and Records Management Specialist at New York State Archives.

5. Schmitt et al., 39.

6. Sydney Ernest Hammersley, *The History of Waterford, New York* (Waterford, NY: Col. Sydney E. Hammersley, 1957), 122.

7. Hammersley, 122.

8. Broderick.

9. John J. Vrooman, *Forts and Firesides of the Mohawk County, New York* (Johnstown, NY: Baronet Litho Co., 1951), 40.

10. Hammersley, 122.

11. Violet B. Dunn, ed., *Saratoga County Heritage* (Saratoga County, NY: Saratoga County, 1974), 505.

12. www.nysm.nysed.gov/services/KnoxTrailkthistory.html.

Lansingburgh Boat Launch

1. Ian H. Giddy, *The Hudson River Water Trail Guide: A River Guide for Small Boaters*, sixth edition (New York: Hudson River Watertrail Association, 2003), 15.

2. Nelson Greene, ed., *History of the Valley of the Hudson: River of Destiny, 1609–1930*, Vol. I (Chicago: The S.J. Clarke Publishing Company, 1931), 121.

3. Arthur James Weise, *City of Troy and Its Vicinity* (Troy, NY: Edward Green, 1886), 185.

4. Sydney Ernest Hammersley, *The History of Waterford, New York* (Waterford, NY: Col. Sydney E. Hammersley, 1957), 113.

5. Violet B. Dunn, ed., *Saratoga County Heritage* (Saratoga County, NY: Saratoga County, 1974), 508, 509.

6. Don MacNaughton, "Troy," *Mohawk Valley USA*, Vol. 2, no. 8 (Spring 1982), 45.

7. www.vanschaickmansion.org.

8. "The History of a Forgotten Family," *The Van Schaick Story* (n. p: n. d).

9. Arthur G. Adams, *The Hudson River Guidebook*, 2nd edition (New York: Fordham University Press, 1996), 278.

10. Amelia T. O'Shea, *Canals of Albany County* (Freehold, NY: Amelia T. O'Shea, 2006), 126.

11. Warren Broderick, Senior Archives and Records Management Specialist at New York State Archives.

Ingalls Avenue Launch

1. Nelson Greene, ed., *History of the Valley of the Hudson: River of Destiny, 1609–1930*, Vol. I (Chicago: The S. J. Clarke Publishing Company, 1931), 784.

2. C. R. Roseberry, *Albany: Three Centuries a County* (Albany, NY: Argus Press, 1983), 38.

3. Don Rittner, *Images of America: Troy* (Charleston, SC: Arcadia Publishing, 1998), 69. Included is a photo of the first Federal Dam.

4. Warren Broderick, Senior Archives and Records Management Specialist at New York State Archives.

5. Alan & Susan McKibben, *Cruising Guide to the Hudson River, Lake Champlain, and the St. Lawrence River: The Waterway from New York City to Montreal and Quebec City* (Burlington, VT: Lake Champlain

Publishing Company, 2006), 71, 76.

6. Francis P. Kimball, *The Capital Region of New York State: Crossroads of Empire*, Vol. II (New York: Lewis Historical Publishing Company, 1942), 308.

7. Rittner, 110. A photograph is shown of the Green Island Bridge in collapse.

8. Arthur G. Adams, *The Hudson River Guidebook*, 2nd edition (New York: Fordham University Press, 1996), 277. Joseph A. Parker, *Looking Back: A History of Troy and Rensselaer County, 1925–1980* (Troy, NY: n. p., 1982), 41.

9. Parker, 40–41.

10. Arthur James Weise, *City of Troy and Its Vicinity* (Troy, NY: Edward Green, 1886), 56.

11. Kimball, 73. Don Rittner, *Remembering Albany: Heritage on the Hudson* (Charleston, SC: History Press, 2009), 19–25. Rittner recounts the story of the whale sightings in greater detail.

12. Irvin Richman, *Postcard History: Hudson River from New York City to Albany* (Charleston, SC: Arcadia Publishing, 2001), 123.

Madison Street Launch

1. Andrew Kreshik, Assistant Planner, City of Troy.

Rensselaer Boat Launch

1. Warren Broderick, Senior Archives and Records Management Specialist at New York State Archives.

2. Joseph A. Parker, *Looking Back: A History of Troy and Rensselaer County, 1925–1980* (Troy, NY: n. p., 1982), 150.

3. Brian & Becky Nielsen, *Postcard History Series: Troy in Vintage Postcards* (Charleston, SC: Arcadia Publishing, 2001), 99. Included is a photograph of the bridge.

Riverfront Park (Rensselaer)

1. Ian H. Giddy, *The Hudson River Water Trail Guide: A River Guide for Small Boaters*, sixth edition (New York: Hudson River Watertrail Association, 2003), 17.

2. Nelson Greene, ed., *History of the*

Valley of the Hudson: River of Destiny, 1609–1930, Vol. I (Chicago: The S.J. Clarke Publishing Company, 1931), 113.

3. Joseph A. Parker, *Looking Back: A History of Troy and Rensselaer County, 1925–1980* (Troy, NY: n. p., 1982), 154.

4. www.everything2.com.

5. Allison Bennett, *Times Remembered: Chronicles of the Towns of Bethlehem and New Scotland, New York* (Delmar, NY: Newsgraphics of Delmar, 1984), 1.

6. www.ussslater.org/history.html.

7. Ann Morrow, "A New Tour of Duty," *Metroland*, Vol. 31, no. 25 (June 19, 2008), 18.

8. www.nysparks.state.ny.us/sites/info. asp?siteID=7.

9. www.dmna.state.ny.us/forts/ fortsA_D/crailoFort.htm. Don Rittner, *Remembering Albany: Heritage on the Hudson* (Charleston, SC: History Press, 2009), 15–19. Rittner tells the story behind the Yankee Doodle mystery.

Papscanee Island Nature Preserve

1. www.powermag.com.

2. *Papscanee Island Nature Preserve Trail Guide.*

3. www.rensselaercounty.org/Environment.htm.

4. Claire K. Schmitt, Norton G. Miller, Warren F. Broderick, John T. Keenan & William D. Niemi, *Natural Areas of Rensselaer County, New York*, 2nd edition (Schenectady/Troy, NY: The Rensselaer-Taconic Land Conservancy & Environmental Clearinghouse of Schenectady, Inc., 2002), 68.

5. Jeffrey Perls, *Paths along the Hudson: A Guide to Walking and Biking* (Piscataway, NJ: Rutgers University Press, 1999), 371.

6. Shirley W. Dunn, "Settlement Patterns in Rensselaerswijck: Godyns Burg, the Tobacco Experiment, and the Mills of Albert Andriessen," *de Halve Maen: Magazine of the Dutch Colonial Period in America*, Vol. LXXI, no. 2 (Summer 1998), 45.

7. Perls, 371.

8. Raymond C. Houghton, *A Revolutionary Week along the Historic Champlain Canal* (Delmar, NY: Cyber Haus, 2003), 16.

9. Historic marker, Van Wies Point.

10. Houghton, 16. Houghton refers to it as Van Wie Point.

11. O'Neil, *O'Neil's Guide Book of the Hudson River with Notes of Interest to the Summer Tourist*, 11th edition (Albany, NY: Walter S. Allen, printer, 1892), 13.

12. Wallace Bruce, *The Hudson: Three Centuries of History, Romance and Invention* (1907; reprinted, New York: Walking News, 1982), 179.

13. Peter Lourie, *River of Mountains: A Canoe Journey down the Hudson* (Syracuse, NY: Syracuse University Press, 1995), 251.

Papscanee Creek

1. Arthur G. Adams, *The Hudson River Guidebook*, 2nd edition (New York: Fordham University Press, 1996), 261.

2. www.nyswaterfronts.com.

3. Wallace Bruce, *The Hudson: Three Centuries of History, Romance and Invention*. (1907; reprinted, New York: Walking News, 1982), 179. Peter Lourie, *River of Mountains: A Canoe Journey down the Hudson* (Syracuse, NY: Syracuse University Press, 1995), 249.

4. Francis P. Kimball, *The Capital Region of New York State: Crossroads of Empire*, Vol. II (New York: Lewis Historical Publishing Company, 1942), 145.

5. O'Neil, *O'Neil's Guide Book of the Hudson River with Notes of Interest to the Summer Tourist*, 11th edition (Albany, NY: Walter S. Allen, 1892), 13.

Schodack Island

1. Arthur G. Adams, *The Hudson River Guidebook*, 2nd edition (New York: Fordham University Press, 1996), 257.

2. Ibid., 257.

3. Claire K. Schmitt, Norton G. Miller, Warren F. Broderick, John T. Keenan & William D. Niemi, *Natural Areas of Rensselaer County, New York*, 2nd edition (Schenectady/Troy, NY: The Rensselaer–

Taconic Land Conservancy & Environmental Clearinghouse of Schenectady, Inc., 2002). A photograph of the Alfred E. Smith building under construction is shown on page 80.

4. Adams, 257.

5. Schmitt et al., 81.

6. Adams, 256.

7. The Center for Land Use Interpretation, American Regional Landscape Series, *Up River: Man-Made Sites of Interest on the Hudson from the Battery to Troy* (New York: Blast Books, 2008), 160.

8. Brian Nearing, "Saving Hudson Shoreline," *Times Union* (Thursday, November 15, 2007).

9. Schmitt et al., 76.

10. Ibid., 76.

11. www.training.fws.gov.

12. Rob Taylor, Park Manager.

13. Adams, 256.

14. Kiosk.

15. Clesson Bush, New Baltimore Historian.

16. Roland Van Zandt, *Chronicles of the Hudson: Three Centuries of Travel and Adventure* (Hensonville, NY: Black Dome Press, 1992), 77.

17. Schmitt et al. A photograph of the Knickerbocker Ice House is shown on page 79. A map revealing the location of the icehouses on the island can be seen on page 75.

Western Shore: Saratoga County

Introduction to the Champlain Canal

1. Alan & Susan McKibben, *Cruising Guide to the Hudson River, Lake Champlain, and the St. Lawrence River: The Waterway from New York City to Montreal and Quebec City* (Burlington, VT: Lake Champlain Publishing Company, 2006), 75.

2. Lois Ann Marquise, "A Ford across the Mohawk: Waterford, N.Y.," *Mohawk Valley USA*, Vol. 5, no.1 (Spring 1984), 4.

Champlain Canal: Paddle #1

1. Walter F. Burmeister, *Appalachian Waters 2: The Hudson River and Its tributaries* (Oakton, VA, Appalachian Books, 1974), 58.

2. Historic marker: "A Colonial Ford Across the Mohawk River From Which Waterford Derives Its Name."

3. Lois Ann Marquise, "A Ford across the Mohawk: Waterford, N.Y.," *Mohawk Valley USA*, Vol. 5, no.1 (Spring 1984), 7.

Champlain Canal: Paddle #2

1. Waterford Harbor Visitor Center, *Walking Tour of the Old Champlain Canal System* (brochure).

2. Ibid.

3. Ibid.

Halfmoon Hudson Riverfront Park

1. www.townofhalfmoon.org/pdf/842009.pdf.

2. www.townofhalfmoon.org/pdf/navigator2007.pdf.

Champlain Canal Lock C-2

1. The Saratogian (newspaper), *Saratoga County New York: Our County and Its People* (Boston: The Boston History Company, 1890), 353.

2. www.asm-easternny.org/docs/newsletters/2005-09.

3. Wallace E. Lamb, *Lake Champlain and Lake George* (New York: The American Historical Company, 1940), 468.

Terminal Street Launch

1. Walter F. Burmeister, *Appalachian Waters 2: The Hudson River and Its tributaries* (Oakton, VA, Appalachian Books, 1974), 57.

2. Violet B. Dunn, ed., *Saratoga County Heritage* (Saratoga County, NY: Saratoga County, 1974), 531.

3. Ibid., 528.

4. Ibid., 529.

5. Arthur James Weise, *City of Troy and Its Vicinity* (Troy, NY: Edward Green, 1886), 201.

6. Roland Van Zandt, *Chronicles of the Hudson: Three Centuries of Travel and Adventure* (Hensonville, NY: Black Dome Press, 1992), 114.

Eastern Shore: Columbia County

Mill Creek: Lewis A. Swyer Preserve

1. Scott Edward Anderson, *Walks in Nature's Empire: Exploring the Nature Conservancy's Preserves in New York State* (Woodstock, VT: The Countryman Press, 1995), 112.

2. www.kinderhooklanding.com/history.html. Francis P. Kimball, *The Capital Region of New York State: Crossroads of Empire*, Vol. II (New York: Lewis Historical Publishing Company, 1942), 344.

3. www.training.fws.gov.

4. Ruth R. Glunt, *Lighthouses and Legends of the Hudson* (Monroe, NY: Library Research Associates, 1990), 15.

5. Richard Tuers, *Lighthouses of New York: A Photographic and Historic Digest of New York State's Maritime Treasures* (Atglen, PA: Schiffer Publishing, 2007), 139.

6. www.usgennet.org. From the writings of Captain Franklin Ellis, *From Stuyvesant Landing: Stuyvesant, Columbia County, N.Y.*

7. Glunt, 15.

8. Patricia Edwards Clyne, *Hudson Valley Trails and Tales* (Woodstock, NY: The Overlook Press, 1990). A line drawing of the lighthouse by Roy Shannon accompanies an article by Harriet H. K. Van Alstyne in *Columbia County History & Heritage*, Vol. 3, no. 2 (Summer, 2004). The drawing, entitled "The Stuyvesant Lighthouse: Destruction by Ice and High Water," is on page 23.

Stuyvesant Landing

1. Walter F. Burmeister, *Appalachian Waters 2: The Hudson River and Its tributaries* (Oakton, VA: Appalachian Books, 1974), 63.

2. Arthur G. Adams, *The Hudson River Guidebook*, 2nd edition (New York: Fordham University Press, 1996), 255.

3. www.newyorkstatehistory.org/

4. www.books.google.com/books?isbn=1584655984. *Hudson Valley Ruins*, Thomas E. Rinaldi & Rob Yasinsac.

5. Francis P. Kimball, *The Capital Region of New York State: Crossroads of Empire*, Vol. II (New York: Lewis Historical Publishing Company, 1942), 362.

Nutten Hook Reserve

1. Arthur G. Adams, *The Hudson River Guidebook*, 2nd edition (New York: Fordham University Press, 1996), 255.

2. Chris DiCintio, Park Ranger.

3. Adams, 255.

4. Historical marker.

5. Mary Faherty-Sansaricq, "A Call for the Conservation of Nutten Hook," *Columbia County History & Heritage*, Vol. 3, no. 2 (Summer 2004), 21.

6. Francis P. Kimball, *The Capital Region of New York State: Crossroads of Empire*, Vol. II (New York: Lewis Historical Publishing Company, 1942), 374.

Stockport Station

1. www.training.fws.gov.

2. www.reel-time.com/forum/showthread.php?p=77038.

3. Ibid.

4. Historic marker. Arthur G. Adams, *The Hudson River Guidebook*, 2nd edition (New York: Fordham University Press, 1996), 254.

5. www.hudsonvalleyruins.org/yasinsac/columbia/empire.html.

6. www.freepages.genealogy.rootsweb.ancestry.com/~clifflamere/History/Col/ColumbiavilleColCo.htm.

Hudson Waterfront Park

1. From talk given on 7/19/09 by Len Tantillo, well-known regional painter, artist, and historian.

2. Arthur G. Adams, *The Hudson River Guidebook*, 2nd edition (New York: Fordham University Press, 1996), 253.

3. Ibid., 247.

4. Margaret B. Schram, *Hudson's Merchants and Whalers: The Rise and Fall of a*

River Port (Hensonville, NY: Black Dome Press, 2004). The history of Hudson as a whaling town is chronicled in detail.

5. Roland Van Zandt, *Chronicles of the Hudson: Three Centuries of Travel and Adventure* (Hensonville, NY: Black Dome Press, 1992), 134.

6. O'Neil, *O'Neil's Guide Book of the Hudson River with Notes of Interest to the Summer Tourist*, 11th edition (Albany, NY: Walter S. Allen, 1892), 14. Francis P. Kimball, *The Capital Region of New York State: Crossroads of Empire*, Vol. I (New York: Lewis Historical Publishing Company, 1942). On page 112 is a photograph depicting the view of the Hudson River from Promenade Park.

7. Don Christensen, "Hudson's South Bay: Landscape and Industry," *Columbia County History & Heritage*, Vol. 2, no. 1 (Summer 2003), 10–12.

8. Ian H. Giddy, *The Hudson River Water Trail Guide: A River Guide for Small Boaters*, sixth edition (New York: Hudson River Watertrail Association, 2003), 27.

9. Christensen, 10–12.

Western Shore: Greene County

Cornell Park

1. Clesson Bush, New Baltimore Historian.

2. Mark Peckham, National Register of Historic Places Coordinator.

3. Bush.

4. Irvin Richman, *Postcard History: Hudson River from New York City to Albany* (Charleston, SC: Arcadia Publishing, 2001), 57.

Coxsackie Riverside Park

1. Mark Peckham, National Register of Historic Places Coordinator.

2. From "Era of Romance," a series of articles that ran in the *Greene County Examiner-Recorder Newspaper* from May 28, 1959, to August 27, 1959.

3. Arthur G. Adams, *The Hudson River Guidebook*, 2nd edition (New York: Fordham University Press, 1996), 255.

4. Ruth R. Glunt, *Lighthouses and Legends of the Hudson* (Monroe, NY: Library Research Associates, 1990), 18.

5. Robert G. Muller, *Postcard History Series: New York State Lighthouses* (Charleston, SC: Arcadia Publishing, 2005). A postcard of the 1869 lighthouse is shown on page 58.

6. Richard Tuers, *Lighthouses of New York: A Photographic and Historic Digest of New York State's Maritime Treasures* (Atglen, PA: Schiffer Publishing, 2007), 139.

7. americahistory.si.ed/collections/lighthouses.

8. Adams, 255.

9. Ian H. Giddy, *The Hudson River Water Trail Guide: A River Guide for Small Boats* (New York: Hudson River Watertrail Association, 2003), 25.

10. Ernest Ingersoll, *Illustrated Guide to the Hudson River and Catskill Mountains* (1910; reprint, Astoria, NY: J.C. & A.L. Fawcett, 1989), 197.

11. Adams, 255.

12. www.hhr.highlands.com/lhouses.

13. Roland Van Zandt, *Chronicles of the Hudson: Three Centuries of Travel and Adventure* (Hensonville, NY: Black Dome Press, 1992), 284.

Four Mile Point Preserve

1. Ruth R. Glunt, *Lighthouses and Legends of the Hudson* (Monroe, NY: Library Research Associates, 1990), 18.

2. www.hhr.highlands.com/lhouses.

3. Richard Tuers, *Lighthouses of New York: A Photographic and Historic Digest of New York State's Maritime Treasures* (Atglen, PA: Schiffer Publishing, 2007), 130.

4. Robert G. Muller, *Postcard History Series: New York State Lighthouses* (Charleston, SC: Arcadia Publishing, 2005), 57. Included with the text is a postcard showing the lighthouse as it appeared from the Hudson River.

5. C. G. Hine, *Albany to Tappen: The West Bank of the Hudson River* (1906; limited edition facsimile reprint, Astoria, NY:

J.C. & A. L Fawcett, n. d.), 31.

6. Jeffrey Perls, *Paths along the Hudson: A Guide to Walking and Biking* (Piscataway, NJ: Rutgers University Press, 1999), 374.

7. Allison Bennett, *Times Remembered: Chronicles of the Towns of Bethlehem and New Scotland* (Delmar, NY: Newsgraphic of Delmar, 1984), 2.

8. Ian H. Giddy, *The Hudson River Water Trail Guide: A River Guide for Small Boats* (New York: Hudson River Watertrail Association, 2003), 25.

Athens State Boat Launch

1. Arthur G. Adams, *The Hudson River Guidebook*, 2nd edition (New York: Fordham University Press, 1996), 253.

2. www.greenecountyny-realestate.com/sleepyhollow.aspx.

3. www.query.nytimes.com.

4. C. G. Hine, *Albany to Tappen: The West Bank of the Hudson River* (1906; limited edition facsimile reprint, Astoria, NY: J.C. & A. L Fawcett, n. d.), 31.

5. Ian H. Giddy, *The Hudson River Water Trail Guide: A River Guide for Small Boats* (New York: Hudson River Watertrail Association, 2003), 27.

6. training.fws.gov/library/pubs5/web_link/text/upp_hud.htm.

7. Brian Nearing, "Saving Hudson shoreline," *Times Union* (Thursday, November 15, 2007).

Athens Kayak Launch

1. J. Van Vechten Vedder, *Official History of Greene County New York, 1651–1800* (1927; reprint, Cornwallville, NY: Hope Farm Press, 1985), 21.

2. Arthur G. Adams, *The Hudson River Guidebook*, 2nd edition (New York: Fordham University Press, 1996), 247.

3. Roland Van Zandt, *Chronicles of the Hudson: Three Centuries of Travel and Adventure* (Hensonville, NY: Black Dome Press, 1992), 134.

4. www.hudsonathenslighthouse.org.

5. Robert G. Muller, *Postcard History Series: New York State Lighthouses* (Charleston, SC: Arcadia Publishing, 2005). A variety of postcards of the Hudson-Athens Lighthouse can be seen on pages 59–61.

6. www.hudsonathenslighthouse.org.

Cohotate Preserve

1. www.training.fws.gov.

2. Ibid.

3. Trail Map of the Cohotate Preserve, Greene County Environmental Education Center.

4. www.gcswcd.com/education/cohotate.html.

Dutchman's Landing

1. Historic marker.

2. Arthur G. Adams, *The Hudson River Guidebook*, 2nd edition (New York: Fordham University Press, 1996), 247.

3. Ernest Ingersoll, *Illustrated Guide to the Hudson River and Catskill Mountains* (1910; facsimile reprint, Astoria, NY: J.C. & A.L. Fawcett, 1989), 193.

4. Adams, 245.

5. www.query.nytimes.com/gst/abstract.html?res. The quote was taken from a July 30, 1912, account in *The New York Times* of Dorcas I. Snodgrass's murdered body being found on the creek.

6. Historic marker.

7. Francis P. Kimball, *The Capital Region of New York State: Crossroads of Empire*, Vol. II (New York: Lewis Historical Publishing Company, 1942), 371.

8. Adams, 246.

9. Adams, 245.

10. Shari Aber, *A Kayaker's Guide to the Hudson River Valley: The Quieter Waters, Rivers, Creeks, Lakes and Ponds* (Hensonville, NY: Black Dome Press, 2007), 172.

11. Mary Faherty-Sansaricq, "Ice Yachts on the Hudson," *Columbia County History & Heritage*, Vol. 4, no. 1 (Spring 2005), 22.

12. Ibid.

The Mohawk River

Introduction

1. Paul Schaefer, "Heartland of the Empire State: The Mohawk River Watershed," *Mohawk Valley USA*, Vol. 1, no. 2 (Sept. 1980), 35.

2. www.Zircon.union.edu/Mohawk_River/Bridge.html.

3. Arthur G. Adams, *The Hudson River Guidebook*, 2nd edition (New York: Fordham University Press, 1996), 279.

4. Nelson Greene, *The Mohawk Turnpike* (Fort Plain, NY: Nelson Greene, 1924) 31. Schaefer, 35.

5. Nelson Greene, ed., *History of the Valley of the Hudson: River of Destiny, 1609–1930*, Vol. I (Chicago: The S. J. Clarke Publishing Company, 1931), 127.

6. Philip Lord, Jr., *The Navigators: A Journal of Passage on the Inland Waterways of New York (1793)*, Bulletin 498 (Albany, NY: New York State Museum, 2003), 10. www.Zircon.union.edu/Mohawk_River/Bridge.html.

Southern Shore: Albany County

Cohoes Falls

1. James H. Stoller, *Geological Excursions: A Guide to Localities in the Region of Schenectady and the Mohawk Valley and the Vicinity of Saratoga Springs* (Schenectady, NY: Union Book Co., 1932), 31.

2. Ibid., 32.

3. Sydney Ernest Hammersley, *The History of Waterford New York* (Waterford, NY: Col. Sydney E. Hammersley, 1957), 7.

4. Historic marker at site of new Cohoes Falls Overlook Park. *Cohoes Centennial, 1870–1970* (n. p: n. d), page unnumbered.

5. Spindle City Historic Society, *Images of America: Cohoes Revisited* (Charleston, SC: Arcadia Publishing, 2005). An early-twentieth-century photograph of five people rock-hopping across the river below the falls can be seen on page 36.

6. Roland Van Zandt, *Chronicles of the Hudson: Three Centuries of Travel and Adventure* (Hensonville, NY: Black Dome Press, 1992), 58.

7 Nathaniel Bartlett Sylvester, *History of Saratoga County New York with Illustrations and Biographical Sketches of Some of Its Prominent Men and Pioneers* (Philadelphia: Everts & Ensign, 1878), 14. The author refers to *Ga-ha-oose*, meaning "the falls of the shipwrecked canoe."

8. Nelson Greene, ed., *History of the Valley of the Hudson: River of Destiny, 1609–1930*, Vol. I (Chicago: The S. J. Clarke Publishing Company, 1931), 125.

9. *Cohoes Centennial*, op cit.

10. Don Rittner, *Remembering Albany: Heritage on the Hudson* (Charleston, SC: History Press, 2009), 92.

11. www.brookfieldpower.com/.../col_robert_r_craner_veterans_park_in_cohoes_rede-774.html.

12. Ed Tremblay, Director, Community & Economic Development, City of Cohoes.

Crescent Plant

1. www.nypa.gov/facilities/hydros.htm.

2. Historic marker by Crescent Plant.

3. www.flickr.com/photos/windy_valley/sets/72157603590415509/.

4. Historic marker at new Cohoes Falls Overlook Park.

5. Wikipedia.

Freddie's Park

1. Robert M. Vogel, ed., *A Report of the Mohawk-Hudson Area Survey: A Selective Recording Survey of the Industrial Archeology of the Mohawk and Hudson River Valleys in the Vicinity of Troy, New York, June–September 1969* (Washington, DC: Smithsonian Institution Press, 1973), 183.

2. www.Zircon.union.edu/Mohawk_River/Bridge.html.

3. en.wikipedia.

4. Kiosk at Freddie's Park.

5. Francis P. Kimball, *The Capital Region of New York State: Crossroads of*

Empire, Vol. II (New York: Lewis Historical Publishing Company, 1942), 309.

Colonie Mohawk River Park

1. Francis P. Kimball, *The Capital Region of New York State: Crossroads of Empire*, Vol. II (New York: Lewis Historical Publishing Company, 1942), 309.

2. www.epodunk.com/cgi-bin/geninfo.php?locindex=546.

Northern Shore: Saratoga County

Peebles Island

1. Rich Macha, "Paddling the Urban Wilderness: The Confluence of the Mohawk and Hudson Rivers," *Adirondack Sports & Fitness* (October 2005).

2. Sydney Ernest Hammersley, *The History of Waterford New York* (Waterford, NY: Col. Sydney E. Hammersley, 1957), 9.

3. Roland Van Zandt, *Chronicles of the Hudson: Three Centuries of Travel and Adventure* (Hensonville, NY: Black Dome Press, 1992), 35.

4. Warren Broderick, Senior Archives and Records Management Specialist at NYS Archives.

5. Russell Dunn & Barbara Delaney, *Trails with Tales: History Hikes through the Capital Region, Saratoga, Berkshires, Catskills & Hudson Valley* (Hensonville, NY: Black Dome Press, 2006), 48.

6. Macha.

7. Arthur H. Masten, *The History of Cohoes, New York, from Its Earliest Settlement to the Present Time* (1877; reprint, Schenectady, NY: Eric Hugo Printing, 1969), 141.

8. www.vsicc.net.

Paradise Island

1. Nelson Greene, ed., *History of the Valley of the Hudson: River of Destiny, 1609–1930*, Vol. I (Chicago: The S. J. Clarke Publishing Company, 1931), 127.

2. Louis Rossi, *Cycling along the Canals of New York: 500 Miles of Bike Riding along the Erie, Champlain, Cayuga-Seneca, and Oswego Canals* (Montpelier, VT: Vitesse Press, 1999), 9.

3. Historic marker.

Additional Resource:

Waterford Historical Museum and Cultural Center, "The Waterford Flight: Locks of the New York State Barge Canal. Waterford, N.Y." (brochure).

Halfmoon Crescent Park

1. Historic marker.

2. www.townofhalfmoon.org/town-parks.asp.

Vandenburgh-Dunsbach Ferry

1. Historic marker.

The Old Erie Canal

1. Amelia T. O'Shea, *Canals of Albany County* (Freehold, NY: Amelia T. O'Shea, 2006), 6.

2. www.Zircon.union.edu/Mohawk_River/Bridge.html.

3. John L. Scherer, *Bits of Clifton Park History* (Clifton Park, NY: Daniel T. Cole, 2003), 44.

4. Allison Bennett, "Keepsakes from the Canal Era," *Mohawk Valley USA*, Vol. 3, no. 10 (Fall 1982), 19. The author adds that by the time of the Civil War the canal traffic consisted principally of heavy loads of lumber and grain.

Vischer Ferry Nature & Historic Preserve

1. Leland R. Palmer, "Vischer Ferry Nature and Historic Preserve," *Mohawk Valley USA*, Vol. 4, no. 2 (Summer 1983), 6.

2. Russell Dunn & Barbara Delaney, *Trails with Tales: History Hikes through the Capital Region, Saratoga, Berkshires, Catskills & Hudson Valley* (Hensonville, NY: Black Dome Press, 2006), 35.

3. William R. Washington & Patricia S. Smith, *Crossroads and Canals: The History of Clifton Park, Saratoga County, New York* (1975; reprint, Albany, NY: Fort Orange Press, 1985), 60. A photograph of Clute's Dry Dock is shown on page 61. Historic marker.

4. Claire K. Schmitt, Norton G. Miller, Warren F. Broderick, John T. Keenan & William D. Niemi, *Natural Areas of*

Rensselaer County, New York, 2nd edition (Schenectady/Troy, NY: The Rensselaer–Taconic Land Conservancy & Environmental Clearinghouse of Schenectady, 2002), 30.

5. John L. Scherer, *Bits of Clifton Park History* (Clifton Park, NY: Daniel T. Cole, 2003), 50.

Mohawk Landing

1. www.cliftonpark.org/townhall/parks-rec/pdf/bikeride.pdf. www.zwire.com/site/news.cfm.

Alplaus Creek

1. Larry Hart, *Tales of Old Schenectady*, Vol. II, *The Changing Scene* (Scotia, NY: Old Dorp Books, 1977), 53.

2. Tom Calarco, "Beyond the Pine Plains," *Schenectady Magazine*, Vol. I, no. 1 (Summer 1988), 38.

3. *Along the Bike Trail: A Guide to the Mohawk-Hudson Bikeway in Schenectady County* (Schenectady, NY: Environmental Clearinghouse of Schenectady, 1986), 27.

4. Hart, 53.

Southern Shore: Schenectady County

Railroad Station Park

1. Nelson Greene, ed., *History of the Valley of the Hudson: River of Destiny, 1609–1930*, Vol. I (Chicago: The S. J. Clarke Publishing Company, 1931), 129.

2. *Along the Bike Trail: A Guide to the Mohawk-Hudson Bikeway in Schenectady County* (Schenectady, NY: Environmental Clearinghouse of Schenectady, 1986), 7. Lloyd M. Brinkman & Members of the Niskayuna Historical Society, *Town of Niskayuna N.Y.—1809: A History of Niskayuna, New York*, Vol. I (Niskayuna, NY: n. p, 1976), 127.

3. Ibid. A painting of the train station, including a water tank, can be seen on page 128.

4. *Along the Bike Trail*, 7.

5. Ibid., 4.

6. Paul Nelson, "Session set on $3.5

M bridge plan," *Times Union* (January 15, 2008).

7. Lloyd M. Brinkman & Members of the Niskayuna Historical Society, *Town of Niskayuna N.Y. – 1809: A History of Niskayuna, New York*, Vol. I (Niskayuna, NY: n. p, 1976), 4.

8. *Along the Bike Trail*, 13.

9. William R. Washington & Patricia S. Smith, *Crossroads and Canals: The History of Clifton Park, Saratoga County, New York* (1975; reprint, Albany, NY: Fort Orange Press, 1985). A photo of the bridge before its destruction can be seen on page 112.

10. John L. Scherer, *Bits of Clifton Park History* (Clifton Park, NY: Daniel T. Cole, 2003), 53.

Lock E-7 Boat Launch

1. *Along the Bike Trail: A Guide to the Mohawk-Hudson Bikeway in Schenectady County* (Schenectady, NY: Environmental Clearinghouse of Schenectady, 1986), 14.

Kiwanis Aqueduct Park Cartop Launch

1. Russell Dunn, *Mohawk Region Waterfall Guide: From the Capital District to Cooperstown & Syracuse* (Hensonville, NY: Black Dome Press, 2007), 45.

2. Schenectady County Historical Society, *Images of America: Glenville* (Charleston, SC: Arcadia Publishing, 2005). On page 122 is a photo of the piers from the Schenectady-Saratoga Trolley Bridge.

3. William R. Washington & Patricia S. Smith, *Crossroads and Canals: The History of Clifton Park, Saratoga County, New York* (1975; reprint, Albany, NY: Fort Orange Press, 1985), 33.

4. Robert M. Vogel, ed., *A Report of the Mohawk-Hudson Area Survey: A Selective Recording Survey of the Industrial Archeology of the Mohawk and Hudson River Valleys in the Vicinity of Troy, New York, June–September 1969* (Washington, DC: Smithsonian Institution Press, 1973), 183. Several photos of the second aqueduct are shown on page 185 as well.

5. www.Zircon.union.edu/Mohawk_River/Bridge.html.

6. John L. Scherer, *Bits of Clifton Park History* (Clifton Park, NY: Daniel T. Cole, 2003), 44.

7. Vogel. On page 185 can be seen a series of photographs taken of the Upper Mohawk River Aqueduct. Despite the passage of years, these photos could just as easily have been taken yesterday.

8. *Along the Bike Trail: A Guide to the Mohawk-Hudson Bikeway in Schenectady County* (Schenectady, NY: Environmental Clearinghouse of Schenectady, 1986), 23. Larry Hart, *Schenectady: A Pictorial History*, 2nd edition (Scotia, NY: Old Dorp Books, 1990). On page 31 can be seen a photograph of Mickey Travis's Restaurant, circa 1890.

9. John L. Scherer, *Images of America: Clifton Park* (Dover, NH: Arcadia Publishing, 1996), 76. Larry Hart, *Schenectady: Changing with the Times* (Norfolk, VA: The Donning Company, 1988), 193. A nineteenth-century photograph shows how the area now occupied by the Schenectady Yacht Club once looked.

10. Susan Rosenthal, *Images of America: Schenectady* (Charleston, SC: Arcadia Publishing, 2000), 108.

11. Ibid., 108.

12. Larry Hart, *Tales of Old Schenectady*, Volume II, *The Changing Scene* (Scotia, NY: Old Dorp Books, 1977), 54. Larry Hart, *Schenectady's Golden Era (Between 1880–1930)*, third edition (Scotia, NY: Old Dorp Books, 1974), 43–44. This chapter contains additional information on Luna Park.

Gateway Landing–Rotary Park

1. *Along the Bike Trail: A Guide to the Mohawk-Hudson Bikeway in Schenectady County* (Schenectady, NY: Environmental Clearinghouse of Schenectady, 1986), 34.

2. www.contentdm.cdlc.org/cdm4/item_viewer.php?CISOROOT=/schmuse&CISOPTR=19&CISOBOX=1&REC=8.

3. Susan Rosenthal, *Images of America: Schenectady* (Charleston, SC: Arcadia Publishing, 2000), 106. A photograph shows a crowd of people skating on the river in front of Riverfront Park.

4. Philip Lord, Jr., *The Navigators: A Journal of Passage on the Inland Waterways of New York (1793)*, Bulletin 498 (Albany, NY: New York State Museum, 2003), 10. "At about one mile [from Schenectady] we met the first rapid, formed by two currents that meet at the lower point of an island where it is made apparent by the gravel which bars the river."

5. Memorial plaque.

6. Historic plaque.

7. Susan J. Staffa, *Schenectady Genesis: How a Dutch Colonial Village became an American City, ca. 1661–1800*, Vol. I (Fleischmanns, NY: Purple Mountain Press, 2004), 17.

8. Rosenthal, 9. An old map shows the Stockade section of Schenectady with the Binne Kill providing a border to the west side, Mill Creek to the south, and the Mohawk River to the north. Philip Lord, Jr., *The Navigators: A Journal of Passage on the Inland Waterways of New York (1793)*, Bulletin 498 (Albany, NY: New York State Museum, 2003), 11. The Binne Kill "ran up alongside the old stockade section of the city just before reentering the main channel."

9. Lloyd M. Brinkman & Members of the Niskayuna Historical Society, *Town of Niskayuna N.Y.—1809: A History of Niskayuna* (Niskayuna, NY: n. p., 1976), 76.

10. Rosenthal, 65.

11. Larry Hart, *Schenectady's Golden Era (Between 1880–1930)*, third edition (Scotia, NY: Old Dorp Books, 1974), 63.

12. *Glenville—Past and Present: Glenville, N.Y., Sequa-Centennial, 1820–1970* (Glenville, NY: n. p., 1970).

13. www.Zircon.union.edu/Mohawk_River/Bridge.html.

14. 75th Anniversary Committee, *Scotia 1904–1979 Album* (Scotia, NY: Village of Scotia, 1979), pages unnumbered.

15. Max Reid, *The Mohawk Valley: Its Legends and Its History, 1609–1780* (1901; Reprint, Harrison, NY: Harbor Hill Books, 1979), 53.

16. *Along the Bike Trail*, 28.

17. Staffa, 128.

Rotterdam Kiwanis Park

1. Francis P. Kimball, *The Capital Region of New York State: Crossroads of Empire*, Vol. I (New York: Lewis Historical Publishing Company, 1942), 122.

2. Myron F. Westover, ed., *Schenectady Past and Present: Historical Papers* (Strasburg, VA: Shenandoah Publishing House, 1931), 4. A picture of the Mohawk River and valley from Touareune Hill is shown.

3. Nelson Greene, *The Mohawk Turnpike* (Fort Plain, NY: Nelson Greene, 1924), 76.

4. J. Marvin Craig & John P. Papp, eds., *Rotterdam, NY: A Pictorial History* (Rotterdam, NY: Rotterdam Bicentennial Commission, undated). A photograph of the three-arch towpath bridge can be seen on page 52.

5. Gregory Rosenthal, *Electric City Pond: An Environmental History of Schenectady and the Adirondacks* (Schenectady, NY: privately published, 2008), 91. It seems likely that Viele's Creek was a narrowing of the Mohawk River along the east side of Dalys Island until the creation of the NYS Barge Canal in 1908, at which time the backing up of the river turned the passageway into a wide body of water.

6. *Along the Bike Trail: A Guide to the Mohawk-Hudson Bikeway in Schenectady County* (Schenectady, NY: Environmental Clearinghouse of Schenectady, 1986), 43.

7. Alan Darling, "The Lightning Tamer: Charles P. Steinmetz," *Mohawk Valley USA*, Vol. I, no. 3 (December 1980), pp. 10–11. Emil J. Remscheid, *Recollections of Steinmetz: A visit to the workshop of Dr. Charles Proteus Steinmetz* (Schenectady, NY: General Electric Company Research and Development Center, 1977). The story of "Lightning strike Camp Mohawk" is told in great detail on pages 23–27. Schenectady County Historical Society, *Images of America: Glenville* (Charleston, SC: Arcadia Publishing, 2005). A photograph of Camp Mohawk, taken from the river, can be seen on page 17.

8. www.spotlightnews.com.

9. Gregory Rosenthal, *Electric City Pond: An Environmental History of Schenectady and the Adirondacks* (Schenectady, NY: Gregory Rosenthal, 2008), 37.

10. Greene, 49.

11. Rosenthal, 41.

12. *Along the Bike Trail*, 37.

13. Paul Schaefer, "Heartland of the Empire State: The Mohawk River Watershed," *Mohawk Valley USA*, Vol. 1, no. 2 (Sept. 1980), 35.

Northern Shore: Schenectady County

Freemans Bridge Boat Launch

1. *Along the Bike Trail: A Guide to the Mohawk-Hudson Bikeway in Schenectady County* (Schenectady, NY: Environmental Clearinghouse of Schenectady, 1986), 30.

2. www.Zircon.union.edu/Mohawk_River/Bridge.html.

3. *Along the Bike Trail*, 32.

4. Historic marker.

Scotia Landing

1. *Along the Bike Trail: A Guide to the Mohawk-Hudson Bikeway in Schenectady County* (Schenectady, NY: Environmental Clearinghouse of Schenectady, 1986), 36.

2. Gregory Rosenthal, *Electric City Pond: An Environmental History of Schenectady and the Adirondacks* (Schenectady, NY: privately published, 2008), 148.

3. Schenectady County Historical Society, *Images of America: Glenville* (Charleston, SC: Arcadia Publishing, 2005), 79. A photograph of the pontoon bridge can be seen.

4. Ibid., 80. A photograph of the two-story structure built on stilts is shown.

5. Larry Hart, *Tales of Old Schenectady*, Volume II, *The Changing Scene* (Scotia, NY: Old Dorp Books, 1977), 107. The history of Glenotia Park, including a variety of photographs, is contained in "The Heyday of Glenotia Park" (pages 107–108) and "The Mohawk Swimming School" (pages 109–113).

6. Golden Jubilee Anniversary Committee, *Official Album* (Scotia, NY: n. p., 1954), 87.

7. 75th Anniversary Committee, *Scotia Album: 1904–1979* (Scotia, NY: Village of Scotia, 1979), pages unnumbered.

8. Larry Hart, *Schenectady: Changing with the Times* (Norfolk, VA: The Donning Company, 1988), 126. An interesting circa 1880 photo of the mansion is shown, taken from a swampy area in the river.

9. *Along the Bike Trail*, 34.

10. Susan J. Staffa, *Schenectady Genesis: How a Dutch Colonial Village became an American City, ca. 1661–1800*, Vol. I (Fleischmanns, NY: Purple Mountain Press, 2004), 33.

11. *Along the Bike Trail*, 34.

Maalwyck Park

1. www.townofglenville.org.

2. www.paulkeeslerbooks.com.

3. *Along the Bike Trail: A Guide to the Mohawk-Hudson Bikeway in Schenectady County* (Schenectady, NY: Environmental Clearinghouse of Schenectady, 1986), 42.

Lock E-9 State Canal Park

1. Schenectady County Historical Society, *Images of America: Glenville* (Charleston, SC: Arcadia Publishing, 2005), 117. An early photograph of Lock 9 can be seen.

2. Nelson Greene, *The Mohawk Turnpike* (Fort Plain, NY: Nelson Greene, 1924), 75.

3. Schenectady County Historical Society, *Images of America: Rotterdam* (Charleston, SC: Arcadia Publishing, 2004), 69.

4. Max Reid, *The Mohawk Valley: Its Legends and Its History, 1609–1780* (1901; reprint, Harrison, NY: Harbor Hill Books, 1979), 119.

5. Greene, 76.

Southern Shore: Montgomery County

Lock E-10

1. Russell Dunn, *Mohawk Region Waterfall Guide: From the Capital District to Cooperstown & Syracuse* (Hensonville, NY: Black Dome Press, 2007), 75.

2. Wikipedia.

Port Jackson Boat Launch

1. Nelson Greene, *The Mohawk Turnpike* (Fort Plain, NY: Nelson Greene, 1924), 82.

2. Historic marker on site. According to www.oldfortjohnson.org/family/html, Sir William Johnson's daughter was named Mary (Polly) and married Guy Johnson in 1763. The initial mansion was built out of wood and burned down in 1773 after being struck by lightning. Many historic papers (regrettably, including some of Sir William Johnson's) were destroyed in the fire. The house was subsequently rebuilt out of stone, which is the mansion you see today. Francis P. Kimball, *The Capital Region of New York State: Crossroads of Empire*, Vol. II (New York: Lewis Historical Publishing Company, 1942), 484.

3. www.nysm.nysed.gov/research_collections/research/history/paintedrocks/index.html. Philip Lord, Jr., *The Navigators: A Journal of Passage on the Inland Waterways of New York (1793)*, Bulletin 498 (Albany, NY: New York State Museum, 2003), 13. A full page is devoted to the Painted Rocks.

4. Greene, 79. Kimball, 102. A photograph of the plant, looking much as it does today, can be seen on page 102.

5. www.amsterdamedz.com.

6. Max Reid, *The Mohawk Valley: Its Legends and Its History, 1609–1780* (1901; reprint, Harrison, NY: Harbor Hill Books, 1979), 167.

Schoharie Crossing

1. David Veeder, *Fort Hunter—"Canal-Town, USA"* (Fort Hunter, NY: Fort Hunter Canal Society, 1968). On page 18 is an early photograph of Lock 12. A photograph of its construction is shown on page 15.

2. Allison Bennett, "Keepsakes from the Canal Era," *Mohawk Valley USA*, Vol. 3, no. 10 (Fall 1982), 16.

3. Veeder. A photo of the slack-water pool can be seen on page 6.

4. Robert M. Vogel, ed., *A Report of the Mohawk-Hudson Area Survey: A Selective Recording Survey of the Industrial Archeology of the Mohawk and Hudson River Valleys in the Vicinity of Troy, New York, June–September 1969* (Washington, DC: Smithsonian Institution Press, 1973). Extensive photos of the Schoharie Aqueduct can be seen on pages 180–181.

5. Veeder. A photograph of the enlarged 1841 Empire Lock is shown on page 13. The original lock, built in 1822, exists next to the enlarged one and can be seen on page 8.

Northern Shore: Montgomery County

Lock E-12 Dam

1 Francis P. Kimball, *The Capital Region of New York State: Crossroads of Empire*, Vol. II (New York: Lewis Historical Publishing Company, 1942), 478–479.

2. Mary Antoine de Julio, "Fort Johnson," *Mohawk Valley USA*, Vol. II, no.5 (Summer 1981); www.oldfortjohnson.org/.

Bibliography

Aber, Shari. *A Kayaker's Guide to the Hudson River Valley: The Quieter Waters, Rivers, Creeks, Lakes and Ponds.* Hensonville, NY: Black Dome Press, 2007.

Adams, Arthur G. *The Hudson River Guidebook.* 2nd edition. New York: Fordham University Press, 1996.

Along the Bike Trail: A Guide to the Mohawk-Hudson Bikeway in Schenectady County. Schenectady, NY: Environmental Clearinghouse of Schenectady, 1986.

Anderson, *Scott Edward. Walks in Nature's Empire: Exploring the Nature Conservancy's Preserves in New York State.* Woodstock, VT: The Countryman Press, 1995.

Barbagallo, Tricia, Cynthia Sauer, and John Warren. *A Historical Orientation to Albany, New York: Historic crossroad, state capital, city of neighborhoods.* Albany, NY: n. p., 1997.

Bennett, Allison. *Times Remembered: Chronicles of the Towns of Bethlehem and New Scotland.* Delmar, NY: Newsgraphic of Delmar, 1984.

———. "Keepsakes from the Canal Era." *Mohawk Valley USA.* Vol. 3, no. 10 (Fall 1982).

Brinkman, Lloyd M., and Members of the Niskayuna Historical Society. *Town of Niskayuna N.Y.—1809: A History of Niskayuna, New York.* Vol. I. Niskayuna, NY: n. p., 1976.

Bruce, Wallace. *The Hudson: Three Centuries of History, Romance and Invention. 1907.* Republished, New York: Walking News, 1982.

Brunner, Arnold W. *Studies for Albany.* Albany, NY: n. p., 1914.

Burmeister, Walter F. *Appalachian Waters 2: The Hudson River and Its tributaries.* Oakton, VA: Appalachian Books, 1974.

Calarco, Tom. "Beyond the Pine Plains." *Schenectady Magazine.* Vol. I, no. 1 (Summer 1988).

The Center for Land Use Interpretation. American Regional Landscape Series. *Up River: Man-Made Sites of Interest on the Hudson from the Battery to Troy.* New York: Blast Books, 2008.

Christensen, Don. "Hudson's South Bay: Landscape and Industry." *Columbia County History & Heritage.* Vol. 2, no. 1 (Summer 2003).

Clyne, Patricia Edwards. *Hudson Valley Trails and Tales.* Woodstock, NY: The Overlook Press, 1990.

Cohoes Centennial, 1870–1970. n. p.: n. d.

Craig, J. Marvin, and John P. Papp, eds. *Rotterdam, NY: A Pictorial History.* Rotterdam, NY: Rotterdam Bicentennial Commission, undated.

Darling, Alan. "The Lightning Tamer: Charles P. Steinmetz." *Mohawk Valley USA.* Vol. I, no. 3 (December 1980).

De Julio, Mary Antoine. "Fort Johnson." *Mohawk Valley USA.* Vol. II, no.5 (Summer 1981).

Dunn, Russell. *Hudson Valley Waterfall Guide: From Saratoga and the Capital Region to the Highlands and Palisades.* Hensonville, NY: Black Dome Press, 2005.

———. *Mohawk Region Waterfall Guide: From the Capital District to Cooperstown & Syracuse.* Hensonville, NY: Black Dome Press, 2007.

Dunn, Russell, and Barbara Delaney. *Trails with Tales: History Hikes through the Capital Region, Saratoga, Berkshires, Catskills & Hudson Valley.* Hensonville, NY: Black Dome Press, 2006.

Dunn, Shirley W. "Settlement Patterns in Rensselaerswijck: Godyns Burg, the Tobacco Experiment, and the Mills of Albert Andriessen." *de Halve Maen: Magazine of the Dutch Colonial Period in America.* Vol. LXXI, no. 2 (Summer 1998).

Dunn, Violet B., ed. *Saratoga County Heritage.* Saratoga County, NY: Saratoga County, 1974.

Faherty-Sansaricq, Mary. "A Call for the Conservation of Nutten Hook." *Columbia County History & Heritage.* Vol. 3, no. 2 (Summer 2004).

———. "Ice Yachts on the Hudson." *Columbia County History & Heritage.* Vol. 4, no. 1 (Spring 2005).

Frank, Catherine, and Margaret Holden.

A Kayaker's Guide to Lake Champlain: Exploring the New York, Vermont & Quebec Shores. Hensonville, NY: Black Dome Press, 2009.

Freitas, Marilyn. *The Glen-Sanders Story.* Schenectady, NY: The Schenectady County Historical Society, 1984.

Giddings, Edward D. *Coeymans and Past.* Coeymans, NY: Tri-Centennial Committee, 1973.

Giddy, Ian H. *The Hudson River Water Trail Guide: A River Guide for Small Boaters.* Sixth edition. New York: Hudson River Watertrail Association, 2003.

Glenville—Past and Present: Glenville, N.Y. Sequa-Centennial, 1820–1970. Glenville, NY: n. p., 1970.

Glunt, Ruth R. *Lighthouses and Legends of the Hudson.* Monroe, NY: Library Research Associates, 1990.

Goodwin, Maud Wilder. *Dutch and English on the Hudson: A Chronicle of Colonial New York.* New Haven, CT: Yale University Press, 1919.

Grant, Anne. *Memoirs of an American Lady with Sketches of Manners and Scenes in America as they existed previous to the Revolution.* 1808; reprint, New York: D. Appleton & Co., 1845.

Grasso, Thomas X. *Champlain Canal: Watervliet to Whitehall. Field Trip, Saturday, October 5, 1985.* Rochester, NY: Canal Society of New York State, 1985.

Green Island Bicentennial Commission. *Green Island Heritage and the Bicentennial.* n. p.: Green Island Bicentennial Commission, 1976.

Greene, Nelson. *The Mohawk Turnpike.* Fort Plain, NY: Nelson Greene, 1924.

———, ed. *History of the Valley of the Hudson: River of Destiny, 1609–1930.* Vol. I. Chicago: The S. J. Clarke Publishing Company, 1931.

Grondahl, Paul. *Times Union.* (December 12, 2007).

Guide to Albany, This. Albany, NY: Cyrene Temple # 18—Daughters of the Nile, 1954.

Hammersley, Sydney Ernest. *The History of Waterford New York.* Waterford, NY: Col. Sydney E. Hammersley, 1957.

Hart, Larry. *Schenectady: Changing with the Times.* Norfolk, VA: The Donning Company, 1988.

———.*Schenectady: A Pictorial History.* 2nd edition. Scotia, NY: Old Dorp Books, 1990.

———. *Schenectady's Golden Era (Between 1880–1930).* 3rd edition. Scotia, NY: Old Dorp Books, 1974.

———. *Tales of Old Schenectady.* Vol. II. The Changing Scene. Scotia, NY: Old Dorp Books, 1977.

Heald, Edward T. *Taconic Trails: By Auto and Afoot.* Albany, NY: J. B. Lyon Company, 1929.

Hine, C. G. *Albany to Tappen: The West Bank of the Hudson River.* 1906. Limited edition facsimile reprint, Astoria, NY: J.C. & A. L Fawcett, n. d.

"History of a Forgotten Family, The." *The Van Schaick Story.* n. p.: n. d.

Houghton, Raymond C. *A Revolutionary Week along the Historic Champlain Canal.* Delmar, NY: Cyber Haus, 2003.

Ingersoll, Ernest. *Handy Guide to the Hudson River and Catskill Mountains.* 1910. Reprint, Astoria, NY: J.C. & A.L. Fawcett, 1989.

Kacharian, John C. "Watervliet Arsenal." *Mohawk Valley USA.* Vol. 3, no.10 (Fall 1982).

Keesler, M. Paul. *Mohawk: Discovering the Valley of the Crystals.* n. p., NY: The Keesler Family, 2008.

Kenny, Peter M. "A New York Dutch Interior for the American Wing." *Magazine Antiques* (Jan. 2006). From Web site findarticles.com.

Kimball, Francis P. *The Capital Region of New York State: Crossroads of Empire.* Vol. I. New York: Lewis Historical Publishing Company, 1942.

———. *The Capital Region of New York State: Crossroads of Empire.* Vol. II. New York: Lewis Historical Publishing Company, 1942.

Kooij, J. A. van der. "Saga of the Half Moon of 1909." *de Halve Maen: Magazine of the Dutch Colonial Period in America.* Vol. LXVI, no. 3 (Fall 1993).

Lamb, Wallace E. *Lake Champlain and Lake George.* New York: The American Historical Company, 1940.

Lord, Philip Jr. *The Navigators: A Journal of Passage on the Inland Waterways of New York (1793)*. Bulletin 498. Albany, NY: New York State Museum, 2003.

Lossing, Benson J. *The Hudson: From the Wilderness to the Sea. 1866.* Reprint, Hensonville, NY: Black Dome Press, 2000.

Lourie, Peter. *River of Mountains: A Canoe Journey down the Hudson.* Syracuse, NY: Syracuse University Press, 1995.

Macha, Rich. "Paddling the Urban Wilderness: The Confluence of the Mohawk and Hudson Rivers." *Adirondack Sports & Fitness* (October 2005).

MacNaughton, Don. "Troy." *Mohawk Valley USA.* Vol. 2, no. 8 (Spring 1982).

Mapes, Alan. "Paddling the Hudson: Two Favorite Launches." *Adirondack Sports & Fitness* (October 2009).

Marquise, Lois Ann. "A Ford across the Mohawk: Waterford, N.Y." *Mohawk Valley USA.* Vol. 5, no.1 (Spring 1984).

Masten, Arthur H. *The History of Cohoes, New York, from Its Earliest Settlement to the Present Time. 1877.* Reprint, Schenectady, NY: Eric Hugo Printing, 1969.

McKibben, Alan, and Susan McKibben. *Cruising Guide to the Hudson River, Lake Champlain, and the St. Lawrence River: The Waterway from New York City to Montreal and Quebec City.* Burlington, VT: Lake Champlain Publishing Company, 2006.

Morrow, Ann. "A New Tour of Duty." *Metroland.* Vol. 31, no. 25 (June 19, 2008).

Muller, Robert G. *Postcard History Series: New York State Lighthouses.* Charleston, SC: Arcadia Publishing, 2005.

Nearing, Brian. "Saving Hudson Shoreline." *Times Union.* Thursday, November 15, 2007.

Nelson, Paul. "Session Set on $3.5 M Bridge Plan." *Times Union.* January 15, 2008.

Nielsen, Brian, and Becky Nielsen. *Postcard History Series: Troy in Vintage Postcards.* Charleston, SC: Arcadia Publishing, 2001.

O'Brien, Patricia J. "The House that Sander Built." *Schenectady Magazine.* Vol. I, no. 2 (Fall 1988).

O'Neil. *O'Neil's Guide Book of the Hudson River with Notes of Interest to the Summer Tourist.* 11th edition. Albany, NY: Walter S. Allen, 1892.

O'Shea, Amelia T. *Canals of Albany County.* Freehold, NY: Amelia T. O'Shea, 2006.

Palmer, Leland R. "Vischer Ferry Nature and Historic Preserve." *Mohawk Valley USA.* Vol. 4, no.2 (Summer 1983).

Papscanee Island Nature Preserve Trail Guide.

Parker, Amasa J., ed. *Landmarks of Albany County New York.* Syracuse, NY: D. Mason & Co., 1897.

Parker, Joseph A. *Looking Back: A History of Troy and Rensselaer County, 1925–1980.* Troy, NY: n. p., 1982.

Perls, Jeffrey. *Paths along the Hudson: A Guide to Walking and Biking.* Piscataway, NJ: Rutgers University Press, 1999.

Port of Albany: Gateway of the World. Albany, NY: Albany Port District Commission, 1932.

Reeve, Arthur B. "Three Hundred Years on the Hudson (1909)." In Oppel, Frank. *New York: Tales of the Empire State.* Secaucus, NJ: Castle, 1988.

Reid, Max. *The Mohawk Valley: Its Legends and Its History, 1609–1780.* 1901. Reprint, Harrison, NY: Harbor Hill Books, 1979.

Remscheid, Emil J. *Recollections of Steinmetz: A Visit to the Workshop of Dr. Charles Proteus Steinmetz.* Schenectady, NY: General Electric Company Research and Development Center, 1977.

Richman, Irvin. *Postcard History: Hudson River from New York City to Albany.* Charleston, SC: Arcadia Publishing, 2001.

Rittner, Don. *Images of America: Troy.* Charleston, SC: Arcadia Publishing, 1998.

———. *Remembering Albany: Heritage on the Hudson.* Charleston, SC: History Press, 2009.

Roseberry, C. R. *Albany: Three Centuries a County.* Albany, NY: Argus Press, 1983.

———. *Flashback: A Fresh Look at Albany's Past.* Albany, NY: Park Press, 1986.

Rosenthal, Gregory. *Electric City Pond: An Environmental History of Schenectady and the Adirondacks.* Schenectady, NY: Privately published, 2008.

Rosenthal, Susan. *Images of America: Schenectady.* Charleston, SC: Arcadia Publishing, 2000.

Rossi, Louis. *Cycling along the Canals of New York: 500 Miles of Bike Riding along the Erie, Champlain, Cayuga-Seneca, and Oswego Canals.* Montpelier, VT: Vitesse Press, 1999.

Saratogian, The. *Saratoga County New York: Our County and Its People.* Boston: The Boston History Company, 1890.

Schaefer, Paul. "Heartland of the Empire State: The Mohawk River Watershed." *Mohawk Valley USA.* Vol. 1, no. 2 (Sept. 1980).

Schenectady County Historical Society. *Images of America: Rotterdam.* Charleston, SC: Arcadia Publishing, 2004.

———. *Images of America: Glenville.* Charleston, SC: Arcadia Publishing, 2005.

Scherer, John L. *Bits of Clifton Park History.* Clifton Park, NY: Daniel T. Cole, 2003.

———. *Images of America: Clifton Park.* Dover, NH: Arcadia Publishing, 1996.

Schmitt, Claire K., and Mary S. Brennan. *Natural Areas of Albany County.* 4th edition. Niskayuna, NY: The Environmental Clearinghouse, 2004.

Schmitt, Claire K., Norton G. Miller, Warren F. Broderick, John T. Keenan, and William D. Niemi. *Natural Areas of Rensselaer County, New York.* 2nd edition. Schenectady/Troy, NY: The Rensselaer–Taconic Land Conservancy & Environmental Clearinghouse of Schenectady, 2002.

Schram, Margaret B. *Hudson's Merchants and Whalers: The Rise and Fall of a River Port.* Hensonville, NY: Black Dome Press, 2004.

Scotia Jubilee Anniversary Committee. *Official Album.* Scotia, NY: Scotia, New York, 1954.

75th Anniversary Committee. *Scotia 1904–1979 Album.* Scotia, NY: Village of Scotia, 1979.

Spindle City Historic Society. *Images of America: Cohoes Revisited.* Charleston, SC: Arcadia Publishing, 2005.

Squires, Dennis. *New York Exposed: The Whitewater State.* Vol. 2. Margaretville, NY: A White Water Outlaw Publishing, 2003.

Staffa, Susan J. *Schenectady Genesis: How a Dutch Colonial Village became an Ameri-can City, ca. 1661–1800.* Vol. I. Fleischmanns, NY: Purple Mountain Press, 2004.

Stanne, Stephen P., Roger G. Panetta, and Brian E. Forist. *The Hudson: An Illustrated Guide to the Living River.* New Brunswick, NJ: Rutgers University Press, 1996.

Stoller, James H. *Geological Excursions: A Guide to Localities in the Region of Schenectady and the Mohawk Valley and the Vicinity of Saratoga Springs.* Schenectady, NY: Union Book Co., 1932.

Sylvester, Nathaniel Bartlett. *History of Saratoga County, New York with Illustrations and Biographical Sketches of Some of Its Prominent Men and Pioneers.* Philadelphia: Everts & Ensign, 1878.

Thompson, Don, and Carol Thompson. *Seeking the Northwest Passage: The Explorations and Discoveries of Champlain and Hudson.* Fleischmanns, NY: Purple Mountain Press, 2008.

Toole, Robert M. *A Lock at Metroland: A New Guide to Its History and Heritage.* Saratoga Springs, NY: Office of R. M. Toole, 1976.

Tuers, Richard. *Lighthouses of New York: A Photographic and Historic Digest of New York State's Maritime Treasures.* Atglen, PA: Schiffer Publishing, 2007.

U.S. Army Corps of Engineers in Vermont. *Water Resources Development: New England Division.* Waltham, MA: Department of Army New England Division, Corps of Engineers, 1979.

Van Alstyne, Harriet H. K. "The Stuyvesant Lighthouse: Destruction by Ice and High Water." *Columbia County History & Heritage.* Vol. 3, no. 2 (Summer, 2004).

Vanderworker, Mrs. J. B. *Early Days in Eastern Saratoga County.* Interlaken, NY: Empire State Books, 1994.

Van Zandt, Roland. *Chronicles of the Hudson: Three Centuries of Travel and Adventure.* Hensonville, NY: Black Dome Press, 1992.

Vedder, J. Van Vechten. *Official History of Greene County New York, 1651–1800.* 1927. Reprint, Cornwallville, NY: Hope Farm Press, 1985.

Veeder, David. *Fort Hunter—"Canal-Town, USA."* Fort Hunter, NY: Fort Hunter Canal Society, 1968.

Vogel, Robert M., ed. *A Report of the Mohawk-Hudson Area Survey: A Selective Recording Survey of the Industrial Archeology of the Mohawk and Hudson River Valleys in the Vicinity of Troy, New York, June–September 1969.* Washington, DC: Smithsonian Institution Press, 1973.

Vrooman, John J. *Forts and Firesides of the Mohawk County, New York.* Johnstown, NY: Baronet Litho Co., 1951.

Ward, Richard F. "Geology of the Hudson." *North Country Life and York State Tradition.* Vol. 13, no. 2 (Spring 1959).

Washington, William R., and Patricia S. Smith. *Crossroads and Canals: The History of Clifton Park, Saratoga County, New York. 1975.* Reprint, Albany, NY: Fort Orange Press, 1985.

Washington County Planning Department for the Washington County Planning Board. *An Introduction to Historic Resources in Washington County, N.Y.* Utica, NY: 1976.

Waterford Harbor Visitor Center. "Walking Tour of the Old Champlain Canal System" (brochure).

Waterford Historical Museum and Cultural Center. "The Waterford Flight: Locks of the New York State Barge Canal. Waterford, N.Y." (brochure).

Weise, Arthur James. *City of Troy and Its Vicinity.* Troy, NY: Edward Green, 1886.

Westover, Myron F., ed. *Schenectady Past and Present: Historical Papers.* Strasburg, VA: Shenandoah Publishing House, 1931.

Wilkie, Richard W. *The Illustrated Hudson River Pilot: Being a Small-Craft Sailor's Pictorial Guide to the Tidewater Hudson, Albany to New York.* Albany, NY: Three Cities Press, 1974.

Web Sites Consulted:

www.americahistory.si.ed/collections/lighthouses

www.amsterdamedz.com

www.asm-easternny.org/docs/newsletters/2005–09

www.bizjournals.com/albany/stories/2004/07/19/daily6.html

www.books.google.com/books?isbn=1584655984

www.brookfieldpower.com/.../col_robert_r_craner_veterans_park_in_cohoes_rede-774.html

www.cliftonpark.org/townhall/parks-rec/pdf/bikeride.pdf

www.coeymans.org/history.htm

www.contentdm.cdlc.org/cdm4/item_viewer.php?CISOROOT=/schmuse&CISOPTR=19&CIS
    OBOX=1&REC=8

www.darrp.noaa.gov/northeast/hudson/habitats.html

www.dec.state.ny.us

www.dmna.state.ny.us/forts/fortsA_D/crailoFort.htm

www.ecostudies.org/images/education/chp/tides.pdf

www.en.wikipedia.org/wiki/Maiden_Lane_Bridge

www.epodunk.com/cgi-bin/geninfo.php?locindex=546

www.flickr.com/photos/windy_valley/sets/72157603590415509/

www.freepages.genealogy.rootsweb.ancestry.com/~clifflamere/History/Col/Columbiaville-
    ColCo.htm

www.gcswcd.com/education/cohotate.html

www.greenwichny.org/history/index.cfm

www.hhr.highlands.com/lhouses

www.history.rays-place.com/ny/stillwater-ny.htm

www.hudsonathenslighthouse.org
www.hudsonmohawkgateway.org/4_heritage_chron.html
www.hudsonriver.com/almanac/0497alm.htm
www.hudsonvalleyruins.org/yasinsac/columbia/empire.html
www.kinderhooklanding.com/history.html
www.lakehouse.com
www.mstruct.neric.org/schuyler
www.newyorkstatehistory.org/
www.nypa.gov/facilities/hydros.htm
www.nysm.nysed.gov/research_collections/research/history/paintedrocks/index.html
www.nysm.nysed.gov/services/KnoxTrailkthistory.html
www.nysparks.state.ny.us/sites/info.asp?siteID=7
www.nysthruway.gov/environmental/recycling.html
www.nyswaterfronts.com
www.oldfortjohnson.org/
www.oldfortjohnson.org/family/html
www.orionline.org/pages/ogn/vieworg.cfm?action=one&ogn_org_ID=619&viewby=name
www.paulkeeslerbooks.com
www.powermag.com
www.query.nytimes.com
www.query.nytimes.com/gst/abstract.html?res...
www.reel-time.com/forum/showthread.php?p=77038
www.rensselaercounty.org/Environment.htm
www.rootsweb.ancestry.com/~nygreen2/era_of_romance_boats_on_the_hudson.htm
www.schenectadyhistory.org
www.spotlightnews.com
www.townofglenville.org
www.townofhalfmoon.org/townparks.asp
www.training.fws.gov
www.training.fws.gov/library/pubs5/web_link/text/upp_hud.htm
www.ulster.net/~hmm/halfmoon/manual.htm
www.usgennet.org. From the writings of Captain Franklin Ellis' From Stuyvesant
    Landing: Stuyvesant, Columbia County, N.Y.
www.ussslater.org/history.html
www.vanschaickmansion.org
www.villageofcoxsackie.com
www.villageofschuylerville.org/Areas-of-.../Schuyler-House.asp
www.vsicc.net
www.Zircon.union.edu/Mohawk_River/Bridge.html
www.zwire.com/site/news.cfm

About the Author

Russell Dunn is the author of a five-part series of guidebooks on the waterfalls of eastern New York State and western Massachusetts: *Adirondack Waterfall Guide: New York's Cool Cascades* (Black Dome Press, 2003); *Catskill Region Waterfall Guide: Cool Cascades of the Catskills & Shawangunks* (Black Dome Press, 2004); *Hudson Valley Waterfall Guide: From Saratoga and the Capital Region to the Highlands and Palisades* (Black Dome Press, 2005); *Mohawk Region Waterfall Guide: From the Capital District to Cooperstown and Syracuse* (Black Dome Press, 2007); and *Berkshire Region Waterfall Guide: Cool Cascades of the Berkshires & Taconics* (Black Dome Press, 2008).

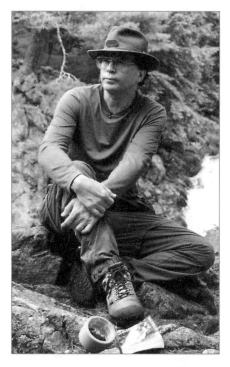

Dunn is also author of *Adventures Around the Great Sacandaga Lake* (Nicholas K. Burns Publishing, 2002), and coauthor with his wife, Barbara Delaney, of *Trails with Tales: History Hikes through the Capital Region, Saratoga, Berkshires, Catskills and Hudson Valley* (Black Dome Press, 2006) and *Adirondack Trails with Tales: History Hikes through the Adirondack Park and the Lake George, Lake Champlain & Mohawk Valley Regions* (2009).

Dunn has had numerous articles published in regional magazines and newspapers including *Adirondack Life, Adirondac Magazine, Hudson Valley, Catskill Mountain Region Guide, Glens Falls Chronicle, Kaatskill Life, Northeastern Caver, Voice of the Valley, Sacandaga Times, Edinburg Newsletter, Adirondack Explorer, Adirondack Sports & Fitness, Shawangunk Mountain Guide,* and the *Conservationist*.

Russell Dunn is a New York State-licensed hiking guide. Together with his wife Barbara Delaney, also a NYS-licensed guide, he leads hikes to waterfalls in the Adirondacks, Catskills, and Hudson Valley, as well as to other areas of exceptional beauty and historical uniqueness, always with the emphasis being placed on history.

Dunn is a popularizer of waterfalls and has given numerous lecture and slideshow presentations to regional historical societies, libraries, museums, civic groups, organizations, and hiking clubs.

He can be reached at rdunnwaterfalls@yahoo.com.

Index